Microsoft®

OFFICE ACCESS 2003

Complete Course

by Pasewark and Pasewark*, Cable

William R. Pasewark, Sr., Ph.D.
Professor Emeritus, Business Education, Texas Tech
University

Scott G. Pasewark, B.S.
Occupational Education, Computer Technologist

William R. Pasewark, Jr., Ph.D., CPA
Professor, Accounting, Texas Tech University

Carolyn Denny Pasewark, M.Ed.
National Computer Consultant, reading and Math
Certified Elementary Teacher, K-12 Certified Counselor

Jan Pasewark Stogner, MBA
Financial Planner

Beth Pasewark Wadsworth, B.A.
Graphic Designer

*Pasewark and Pasewark is a trademark of the
Pasewark LTD.

Sandra Cable, Ph. D.
Texas A&M University

THOMSON
COURSE TECHNOLOGY

Australia • Canada • Mexico • Singapore • Spain • United Kingdom • United States

THOMSON

COURSE TECHNOLOGY

Microsoft® Office Access 2003 Complete Course
by Pasewark and Pasewark*, Cable

Authors

William R. Pasewark, Sr., Ph.D.
Professor Emeritus, Texas Tech University

William R. Pasewark, Jr., Ph.D., CPA
Professor of Accounting, Texas Tech University

Scott G. Pasewark, B.S.
Occupational Education, Computer Technologist

Jan Pasewark Stogner, MBA
Financial Planner

Beth Pasewark Wadsworth, B.A.
Graphic Designer

Carolyn Pasewark Denny, M.Ed.
National Computer Consultant, Reading and Math Certified Elementary Teacher, Certified Counselor, K-12

Sandra Cable, Ph. D.
Texas A&M University

Publishers

Cheryl Costantini
Executive Director

Kim Ryttel
Senior Marketing Manager

Alexandra Arnold
Senior Editor

Robert Gaggin
Product Manager

Meagan Putney
Associate Marketing Manager

Justine Brennan
Editorial Assistant

GEX Publishing Services
Production Services

CEP Inc.
Developmental Editor
Production Editor

ISBN 0-619-18355-1

Experience Office for the Future!

This series offers a flexible, accessible program for a wide range of students. All of the books are written at a basic reading level and provide a variety of instructional hours to best meet your course needs.

Users Love This Series Because It:
- Teaches students with a variety of abilities and previous computer experience
- Contains numerous step-by-step exercises, review exercises, and case projects to enhance students' learning experiences
- Includes strong end-of-lesson material, including Commands, Skills, Concepts Review, and On-the-Job simulations
- Incorporates a Capstone Simulation at the end of the book that provides students with the opportunity to apply the skills they've learned, either individually or in a team setting

NEW! for Microsoft Office 2003 Introductory and Advanced Courses:
- Instructor notes rate the level of difficulty for activities and projects (Introductory)
- New Careers marginal learning boxes encourage students to explore future careers (Introductory)
- Time Savers provide Office tips, tricks, and shortcuts for completing tasks (Advanced and Complete)
- Integration Tips offer explanations on how features in a lesson can be useful when integrating applications in the Office 2003 suite (Advanced and Complete)
- Grading Rubrics, Annotated Solutions, and a Spanish Glossary on the Instructor Resources CD
- Durable, hardcover and hardcover, spiral-bound editions available

NEW! Microsoft Office 2003 Introductory Course by Pasewark and Pasewark
75+ hours of instruction for beginning features on Word, Excel, PowerPoint, and Access.

0-619-18339-X	Textbook, hardcover
0-619-18387-X	Textbook, hardcover, spiral-bound
0-619-18340-3	Textbook, softcover
0-619-18342-X	Activities Workbook
0-619-18341-1	Annotated Instructor Edition (AIE)
0-619-18343-8	Instructor Resources (IR) CD, includes testing software
0-619-18344-6	Review Pack (Data CD)

NEW! Microsoft Office 2003 Advanced Course by Cable, CEP, Inc., Morrison
75+ hours of instruction for intermediate through advanced features on Word, Excel, PowerPoint, and Access.

0-619-18345-4	Textbook, hardcover
0-619-18388-8	Textbook, hardcover, spiral-bound
0-619-18346-2	Textbook, softcover
0-619-18348-9	Activities Workbook
0-619-18347-0	Annotated Instructor Edition (AIE)
0-619-18349-7	Instructor Resources (IR) CD, includes testing software
0-619-18350-0	Review Pack (Data CD)

NEW! Microsoft Office Word 2003 by Pasewark and Pasewark, Morrison

0-619-18352-7	Complete, hardcover, Expert Microsoft Office Specialist Certification, 75+ hours
0-619-18351-9	Introductory, softcover, spiral-bound, Specialist Microsoft Office Specialist Certification, 35+ hours

NEW! Microsoft Office Excel 2003 by Pasewark and Pasewark, Cable

0-619-18354-3	Complete, hardcover, Expert Microsoft Office Specialist Certification, 75+ hours
0-619-18353-5	Introductory, softcover spiral-bound, Specialist Microsoft Office Specialist Certification, 35+ hours

NEW! Microsoft Office PowerPoint 2003 by Pasewark and Pasewark, CEP, Inc.

0-619-18358-6	Complete, hardcover, Specialist Microsoft Office Specialist Certification, 75+ hours
0-619-18357-8	Introductory, softcover, spiral-bound, Specialist Microsoft Office Specialist Certification, 35+ hours

NEW! Microsoft Office Access 2003 by Pasewark and Pasewark, Cable

0-619-18355-1	Complete, hardcover, Specialist Microsoft Office Specialist Certification, 75+ hours
0-619-18356-X	Introductory, softcover, spiral-bound, Specialist Microsoft Office Specialist Certification, 35+ hours

Join Us On the Internet **http:www.course.com**

TABLE OF CONTENTS

INTRODUCTORY MICROSOFT ACCESS UNIT

ADVANCED MICROSOFT ACCESS UNIT

Overview of This Book

What makes a good computer instructional text? Sound pedagogy and the most current, complete materials. That is what you will find in *Microsoft® Office Access 2003: Complete*. Not only will you find an inviting layout, but also many features to enhance learning.

Objectives— Objectives are listed at the beginning of each lesson, along with a suggested time for completion of the lesson. This allows you to look ahead to what you will be learning and to pace your work.

SCANS—(Secretary's Commission on Achieving Necessary Skills)—The U.S. Department of Labor has identified the school-to-careers competencies. The eight workplace competencies and foundation skills are identified in exercises where they apply. More information on SCANS can be found on the *Instructor Resources* CD.

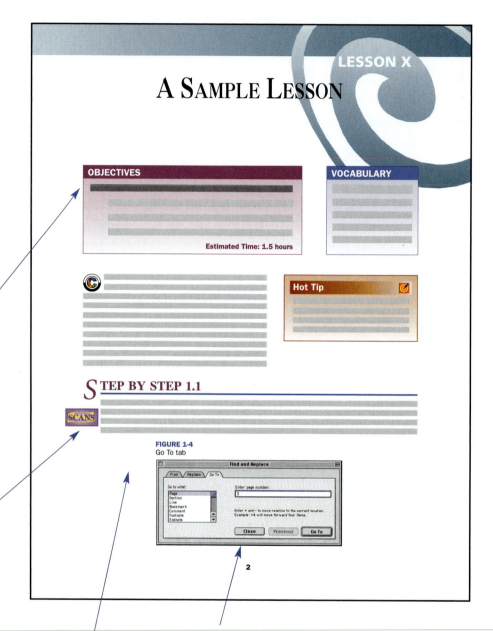

Learning Boxes— These boxes expand and enrich learning with additional information or activities: Hot Tips, Did You Know?, Computer Concepts, Internet, Extra Challenge, Teamwork, and Careers.

Enhanced Screen Shots—Screen shots come to life on each page with color and depth.

Overview of This Book

Summaries—At the end of each lesson, prepare you to complete the end-of-lesson activities.

Vocabulary/Review Questions—Review material at the end of each lesson and each unit enables you to prepare for assessment of the content presented.

Lesson Projects—End-of-lesson hands-on application of what has been learned in the lesson allows you to actually apply the techniques covered.

Critical Thinking Activities—Each lesson gives you an opportunity to apply creative analysis and use the Help system to solve problems.

Command Summary—At the end of each unit, a command summary is provided for quick reference.

End-of-Unit Projects—End-of-unit hands-on application of concepts learned in the unit provides opportunity for a comprehensive review.

Unit Simulation—A realistic simulation runs throughout the text at the end of each unit, reinforcing the material covered in the unit.

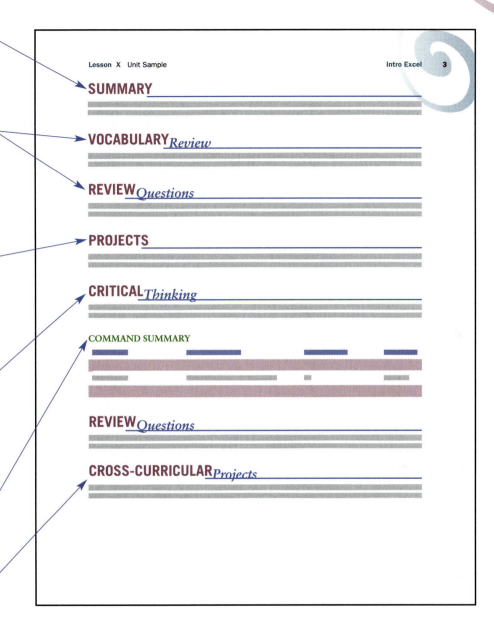

Lesson X Unit Sample

Intro Excel **3**

SUMMARY

VOCABULARY *Review*

REVIEW *Questions*

PROJECTS

CRITICAL *Thinking*

COMMAND SUMMARY

REVIEW *Questions*

CROSS-CURRICULAR *Projects*

Capstone Simulation—There is a comprehensive simulation at the end of the text, to be completed after all the lessons have been covered, to give you an opportunity to apply all of the skills you have learned and see them come together in one application.

Appendices—Appendices cover Windows Basics, Computer Concepts, Concepts for Microsoft Office Programs, The Microsoft Office Specialist Program, and Keyboarding Touch System Improvement. The Models for

Formatted Documents, E-Mail Writing Guide, Letter Writing Guide, Proofreader's Marks, Speech Recognition Basics lesson, and Spanish Glossary are located on the *Instructor Resources* CD.

PREFACE

Why This Is an Ideal Book for Everyone

Because computers are such an important subject for all learners, instructors need a well-designed, educationally sound textbook that is supported by strong ancillary instructional materials. *Microsoft® Office Access 2003: Complete Course* is just such a book.

The textbook includes features that make learning easy and enjoyable—yet challenging—for learners. It is also designed with many features that make teaching easy and enjoyable for you.

This book is ideal for computer courses with learners who have varying abilities and previous computer experiences. It includes a wide range of learning experiences from activities with one or two commands to simulations and projects that challenge and sharpen learners' problem-solving skills.

The lessons in this course contain the following features designed to promote learning:

- Objectives that specify goals students should achieve by the end of each lesson.
- Concept text that explores in detail each new feature.
- Screen captures that help to illustrate the concept text.
- Step-by-Step exercises that allow students to practice the features just introduced.
- Summaries that review the concepts in the lesson.
- Review Questions that test students on the concepts covered in the lesson.
- Projects that provide an opportunity for students to apply concepts they have learned in the lesson.
- Critical Thinking Activities that encourage students to use knowledge gained in the lesson or from the application's Help system to solve specific problems.

Each unit also contains a Unit Review with the following features:

- A Command Summary that reviews menu commands and toolbar shortcuts introduced in the unit.
- Review Questions covering material from all lessons in the unit.
- Projects that give students a chance to apply many of the skills learned in the unit.

TEACHING AND LEARNING RESOURCES FOR THIS BOOK

Instructor Resources CD

The *Instructor Resources CD* contains a wealth of instructional material you can use to prepare for teaching Office 2003. The CD stores the following information:

- Both the data and solution files for this course.

- ExamView® tests for each lesson. ExamView is a powerful testing software package that allows instructors to create and administer printed, computer (LAN-based), and Internet exams. ExamView includes hundreds of questions that correspond to the topics covered in this text, enabling learners to generate detailed study guides that include page references for further review. The computer-based and Internet testing components allow learners to take exams at their computers, and also save the instructor time by grading each exam automatically.

- Instructor's Manual that includes lecture notes for each lesson, answers to the lesson and unit review questions, and references to the solutions for Step-by-Step exercises, end-of-lesson activities, and Unit Review projects.

- Instructor lesson plans that can help to guide students through the lesson text and exercises.

- Copies of the figures that appear in the student text, which can be used to prepare transparencies.

- Grids that show skills required for Microsoft Office Specialist certification, SCANS workplace competencies and skills, and activities that apply to cross-curricular topics.

- Suggested schedules for teaching the lessons in this course.

- Additional instructional information about individual learning strategies, portfolios and career planning, and a sample Internet contract.

- Answers to the Activities Workbook exercises.

- PowerPoint presentations showing Office 2003 features for each unit.

- Speech Recognition Basics lesson

- Spanish Glossary

- Models for Formatted Documents, such as a business letter, resume, research paper, etc.

- E-Mail Writing Guide and Letter Writing Guide

- Proofreader's Marks

Annotated Instructor Edition

The Annotated Instructor Edition helps you to prepare for and to teach Office 2003.

Activities Workbook

An *Activities Workbook* is available to supply additional paper-and-pencil exercises and hands-on computer applications for each unit of this book.

SCANS

The Secretary's Commission on Achieving Necessary Skills (SCANS) from the U.S. Department of Labor was asked to examine the demands of the workplace and whether new learners are capable of meeting those demands. Specifically, the Commission was directed to advise the Secretary of Labor on the level of skills required to enter employment.

SCANS workplace competencies and foundation skills have been integrated into Microsoft® Office 2003: Introductory Course. The workplace competencies are identified as 1) ability to use resources, 2) interpersonal skills, 3) ability to work with information, 4) understanding of systems, and 5) knowledge and understanding of technology. The foundation skills are identified as 1) basic communication skills, 2) thinking skills, and 3) personal qualities.

Exercises in which learners must use a number of these SCANS competencies and foundation skills are marked in the text with the SCANS icon.

The Microsoft Office Specialist Program

What Does This Logo Mean?

It means this courseware has been approved by the Microsoft® Office Specialist Program to be among the finest available for learning Microsoft Office 2003, Microsoft Office Word 2003, Microsoft Office Excel 2003, Microsoft Office PowerPoint® 2003, and Microsoft Office Access 2003. It also means that upon completion of this courseware, you may be prepared to become a Microsoft Office Specialist.

What is a Microsoft Office Specialist?

A Microsoft Office Specialist is an individual who has certified his or her skills in one or more of the Microsoft Office desktop applications of Microsoft Office Word, Microsoft Office Excel, Microsoft Office PowerPoint®, Microsoft Office Outlook®, or Microsoft Access. The Microsoft Office Specialist Program typically offers certification exams at the "Specialist" and "Expert" skill levels.* The Microsoft Office Specialist Program is the only Microsoft approved program in the world for certifying proficiency in Microsoft Office desktop applications. This certification can be a valuable asset in any job search or career advancement.

More Information

To learn more about becoming a Microsoft Office Specialist, visit *www.microsoft.com/ learning/mcp/officespecialist*. To purchase a Microsoft Office Specialist certification exam, visit *www.DesktopIQ.com.*

*The availability of Microsoft Office Specialist certification exams varies by application, application version, and language.

Assessment Instruments

SAM 2003 Assessment & Training

SAM 2003 helps you energize your class exams and training assignments by allowing students to learn and test important computer skills in an active, hands-on environment.

With SAM 2003 Assessment, you create powerful interactive exams on critical applications such as Word, Outlook, PowerPoint, Windows, the Internet, and much more. The exams simulate the application environment, allowing your students to demonstrate their knowledge and think through the skill by performing real-world tasks.

- Build hands-on exams that allow the student to work in the simulated application environment

- Add more muscle to your lesson plan with SAM 2003 Training. Using highly interactive text, graphics, and sound, SAM 2003 Training gives your students the flexibility to learn computer applications by choosing the training method that fits them the best.

- Create customized training units that employ various approaches to teach computer skills

- Designed to be used with the Microsoft Office 2003 series, SAM 2003 Assessment & Training includes built-in page references so students can create study guides that match the Microsoft Office 2003 textbooks you use in class. Powerful administrative options allow you to schedule exams and assignments, secure your tests, and run reports with almost limitless flexibility.

- Deliver exams and training units that best fit the way you teach

- Choose from more than one dozen reports to track testing and learning progress

ExamView®

ExamView is a powerful objective-based test generator that enables you to create paper, LAN, or Web-based tests from test banks designed specifically for your Course Technology text. Utilize the ultra-efficient QuickTest Wizard to create tests in less than five minutes by taking advantage of Course Technology's question banks, or customize your own exams from scratch.

MESSAGE FROM THE AUTHORS

Acknowledgments

The authors gratefully thank Rhonda Davis for coordinating the preparation of manuscript and for using her business experiences to write several segments of Office 2003.

All of our books are a coordinated effort by the authors and scores of professionals working with the publisher. The authors appreciate the dedicated work of all these publishing personnel and particularly those with whom we have had direct contact:

- Course Technology: Robert Gaggin, Cheryl Costantini, and Meagan Putney

- Custom Editorial Productions, Inc.: Rose Marie Kuebbing and Jean Findley

- Many professional Course Technology sales representatives make educationally sound presentations to instructors about our books. We appreciate their valuable work as "bridges" between the authors and instructors.

About the Authors

Pasewark LTD is a family-owned business. We use Microsoft® Office in our business, career, personal, and family lives. Writing this book, therefore, was a natural project for six members of our family who are identified on the title page of this book.

The authors have written more than 100 books about computers, accounting, and office technology.

Pasewark LTD authors are members of several professional associations that help authors write better books.

The authors have been recognized with numerous awards for classroom teaching. Effective classroom teaching is a major ingredient for writing effective textbooks.

Our Mission Statement

The authors have more than 90 years of combined experience authoring award-winning textbooks. During that time, they developed their mission statement:

To help our students live better lives.

When students learn how computers can help them in their personal, school, career, and family activities, they can live better lives — now and in the future.

Our Commitment

In writing this series, the authors have dedicated themselves to creating a comprehensive and appealing instructional package to make teaching and learning an interesting, challenging, and rewarding experience.

With these instructional materials, instructors can create realistic learning experience so learners can successfully master concepts, knowledge, and skills that will help them live better lives—now and in the future.

Award-Winning Books by the Pasewarks

The predecessors to this book, *Microsoft® Office 2000: Introductory* and *Microsoft Office XP: Introductory*, by the Pasewarks, won the Text and Academic Authors Association *Texty Award* for the best el-hi computer book for the years 2000 and 2002.

In 1994, the Pasewarks also won a *Texty* for their Microsoft Works computer book. Their book, *The Office: Procedures and Technology*, won the first William McGuffey Award for Textbook Excellence and Longevity. The Pasewarks' book *Microsoft® Works 2000 BASICS* won the Texty Award for the best computer book for the year 2001.

GETTING STARTED

Start-Up Checklist

HARDWARE

Minimum Configuration

✓ PC with Pentium 233 MHz or higher processor. Pentium III recommended.

✓ RAM requirements:

   ✓ Windows XP - 128 MB of RAM

   ✓ Windows 2000 Professional – 128 MB of RAM

✓ Hard disk with 400 MB free for typical installation

✓ CD-ROM drive

✓ Super VGA monitor with video adapter. (800 × 600) or higher-resolution.

✓ Microsoft Mouse, IntelliMouse, or compatible pointing device

✓ For e-mail, Microsoft Mail, Internet SMTP/POP3, or other MAPI-compliant messaging software

✓ Printer

GUIDE FOR USING THIS BOOK

Please read this Guide before starting work. The time you spend now will save you much more time later and will make your learning faster, easier, and more pleasant.

Terminology

This text uses the term keying to mean entering text into a computer using the keyboard. Keying is the same as "keyboarding" or "typing."

Text means words, numbers, and symbols that are printed.

Conventions

The different type styles used in this book have special meanings. They will save you time because you will soon automatically recognize from the type style the nature of the text you are reading and what you will do.

WHAT YOU WILL DO	TYPE STYLE	EXAMPLE
Text you will key	**Bold**	Key **Don't litter** rapidly.
Individual keys you will press	**Bold**	Press **Enter** to insert a blank line.

WHAT YOU WILL SEE	TYPE STYLE	EXAMPLE
Filenames in book	**Bold upper and lowercase**	Open **IW Step2-1** from the data files.
Glossary terms in book	***Bold and italics***	The ***menu bar*** contains menu titles.
Words on screen	*Italics*	Highlight the word *pencil* on the screen.
Menus and commands	**Bold**	Open the **File** menu and choose **Open**.
Options/features with long names	*Italics*	Select **Normal** from the *Style for following paragraph* text box.
Names of sections/boxes	*Italics*	Click **Monthly Style** in the *Print Style* box.

Review Pack CD

All data files necessary for the Step-by-Step exercises, end-of-lesson Projects, end-of-unit Projects and Jobs, and Capstone Simulation exercises in this book are located on the *Review Pack* CD. Data files for the *Activities Workbook* are also stored on the *Review Pack* CD.

Data files are named according to the first exercise in which they are used and the unit of this textbook in which they are used. A data file for a Step-by-Step exercise in the Introductory Microsoft Word unit would have a filename such as **IW Step1-1**. This particular filename identifies a data file used in the first Step-by-Step exercise in Lesson 1. Other data files have the following formats:

- End-of-lesson projects: **IW Project1-1**
- End-of-unit projects: **IW Project2**
- Simulation jobs: **IW Job3**

INTRODUCTION

Unit

Lesson 1   1.5 hrs
Microsoft® Office 2003 Basics and the Internet

🕐 **Estimated Time for Unit: 1.5 hours**

MICROSOFT® OFFICE 2003 BASICS AND THE INTERNET

OBJECTIVES

Upon completion of this lesson, you should be able to:

- Explain the concept of an integrated software package.

- Start an Office application from Windows.

- Explain an Office application's opening screen and how to use the application's menus and toolbars.

- Open an existing Office document.

- Save and close an Office document.

- Know the shortcuts for opening recently used documents.

- Use the Office Help system, including the Office Assistant.

- Quit an Office application.

- Access the Internet and use a Web browser.

Estimated Time: 1.5 hours

VOCABULARY

Close

Default

Drop-down menu

Home page

Icon

Integrated software package

Internet

Internet Explorer

Intranet

Link

Menu

Open

Save

Task pane

Toolbar

Uniform Resource Locators (URLs)

World Wide Web

Web browser

Introduction to Microsoft Office 2003

Office 2003 is an integrated software package. An *integrated software package* is a program that combines several computer applications into one program. Office consists of a word processor application, a spreadsheet application, a database application, a presentation application, a schedule/organization application, and a desktop publishing application.

> **Internet**
>
> For more information on Microsoft Word and other Microsoft products, visit Microsoft's Web site at *http://www.microsoft.com*.

The word processor application (Word) enables you to create documents such as letters and reports. The spreadsheet application (Excel) lets you work with numbers to prepare items such as budgets or to determine loan payments. The database application (Access) organizes information such as addresses or inventory items. The presentation application (PowerPoint) can be used to create slides, outlines, speaker's notes, and audience handouts. The schedule/organization application (Outlook) increases your efficiency by keeping track of e-mail, appointments, tasks, contacts, events, and to-do lists. The desktop publishing application (Publisher) helps you design professional-looking documents.

Because Office is an integrated program, the applications can be used together. For example, numbers from a spreadsheet can be included in a letter created in the word processor or in a presentation.

Starting an Office Application

To open an Office application, click the Start button, point to All Programs, point to Microsoft Office, and then click the name of the application you want to open.

Hot Tip

You can use the Windows Quick Launch bar to quickly open an Office program, file, or folder.

Computer Concepts

You can open a new file from within an application by opening the **File** menu and choosing **New**. You can also click the **New** button in the standard toolbar to create a new file. In the Word program, the button is titled, **New Blank Document**.

STEP-BY-STEP 1.1

1. Click the **Start** button to open the Start menu.

2. Point to **All Programs**, point to **Microsoft Office**, and then click **Microsoft Office PowerPoint 2003.** PowerPoint starts and a blank presentation appears, as shown in Figure 1-1.

FIGURE 1-1
A blank presentation in the PowerPoint program

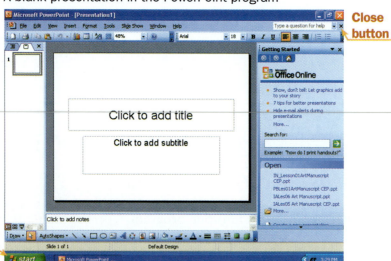

3. Click the **Close** button on the right side of the menu bar to close the blank presentation. The PowerPoint program will remain open.

STEP-BY-STEP 1.1 Continued

4. Click the **Start** button again.

5. Point to **All Programs**, point to **Microsoft Office**, and then click **Microsoft Office Word 2003**. Word starts and a blank document appears, as shown in Figure 1-2. Leave Word and PowerPoint open for use in the following Step-by-Steps.

FIGURE 1-2
Word opening screen

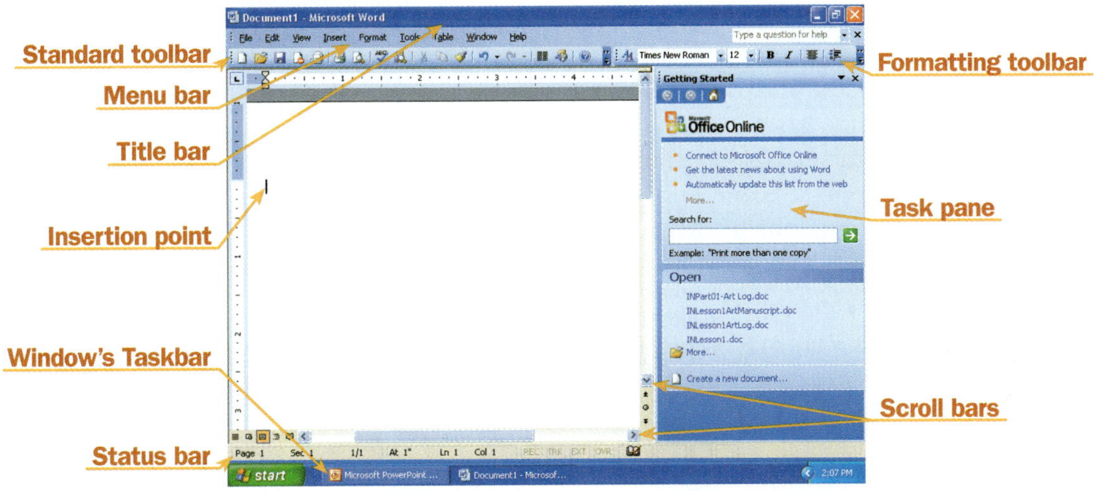

Understanding the Opening Screen

Most of the features you will use to complete tasks in an Office application can be found within the opening screen of each application. Look carefully at the parts of the opening screen for the Word program labeled in Figure 1-2. These basic parts of the screen are similar in all of the Office programs and are discussed below in Table 1-1.

TABLE 1-1
Understanding the opening screen

ITEM	FUNCTION
Title bar	Displays the name of the Office program and the current file.
Menu bar	Contains the menu titles from which you can choose a variety of commands. All features of an application can be accessed from within the menus.
Standard toolbar	Contains buttons you can use to perform common tasks.
Formatting toolbar	Contains buttons for changing formatting, such as alignment and type styles.
Insertion point	Shows where text will appear when you begin keying.
Scroll bars	Allow you to move quickly to other areas of an Office application.
Status bar	Tells you the status of what is shown on the screen.
Taskbar	Shows the Start button, the Quick Launch toolbar, and all open programs.
Task pane	Opens automatically when you start an Office application. Contains commonly used commands that pertain to each application.

The *task pane* is a separate window on the right-hand side of the opening screen, as shown in Figure 1-1 and Figure 1-2. It opens automatically when you start an Office application and contains commonly used commands that can help you work more efficiently. To close the task pane, simply click the Close button in the upper right corner of the task pane. To view the task pane, open the View menu and choose Task Pane.

Using Menus and Toolbars

A *menu* in an Office application is like a menu in a restaurant. You look at the menus to see what the program has to offer. Each title in the menu bar represents a separate *drop-down menu*. By choosing a command from a drop-down menu, you give the program instructions about what you want to do.

When you first use a program, each menu displays only basic commands. To see an expanded menu with all the commands, click the arrows at the bottom of the menu. As you work, the program adjusts the menus to display the commands used most frequently, adding a command when you use it and dropping a command when it hasn't been used recently. Figure 1-3 compares the short and expanded versions of the Edit menu.

FIGURE 1-3
Short menu vs. expanded menu

Arrows

Toolbars provide another quick way to choose commands. The toolbars use *icons*, or small pictures, to remind you of each button's function. Toolbars can also contain drop-down menus. Unless you specify otherwise, only the Standard and Formatting toolbars are displayed, but many more are available. To see a list of the toolbars you can use, right-click anywhere on a toolbar; or you can open the View menu and select Toolbars.

> ### Computer Concepts
> If you do not know the function of a toolbar button, move the mouse pointer to the button, but do not click. The name of the function will appear below the button.

As with the menus, toolbars initially display buttons only for basic commands. To see additional buttons, click Toolbar Options (the button at the far right on each toolbar) on the toolbar and choose from the list that appears, as shown in Figure 1-4. When you use a button from the list, it is added to the toolbar. If you haven't used a button recently, it is returned to the Toolbar Options list.

FIGURE 1-4
Toolbar Options list

Opening, Saving, and Closing Office Documents

In all Office applications, you *open*, *save*, and *close* files in the same way. Opening a file means loading a file from a disk onto your screen. Saving a file stores it on a disk. Closing a file removes it from the screen.

Opening an Existing Document

To open an existing document, you can choose Open in an application's File menu, select the Open button from the Standard toolbar, or choose the option to open an existing document from the task pane. In all Office applications, you would choose the More option in the Open section of the task pane. No matter which option is selected, the Open dialog box appears (see Figure 1-5).

FIGURE 1-5
Open dialog box

Look in box

Folders and resources located on the computer

My Places bar - shortcuts to common places for storing data

Files of type box

Open button

Look in: My Computer

3½ Floppy (A:)
Local Disk (C:)
Removable Disk (D:)
CD Drive (E:)
Shared Documents
RD's Documents
PLTD's Documents

My Recent Documents
Desktop
My Documents
My Computer
My Network Places

File name:
Files of type: All Files (*.*)

Open
Cancel

The Open dialog box enables you to open a file from any available disk or folder. The *Look in* box, near the top of the dialog box, is where you locate the disk drive that contains the file you want to open. Below that is a list that shows you the folders or resources that are on the disk. Double-click a folder to see what files and folders are contained within. To see all the files or office documents in the folder instead of just those created with a particular application, choose All Files from the *Files of type* drop-down list box located near the bottom of the dialog box. The My Places bar on the left side of the dialog box provides a shortcut for accessing some of the common places to store documents.

When you have located and selected the file you want to open, click the Open button. If you click the down arrow next to the Open button, a menu is displayed, as shown in Figure 1-6. Among other choices, you can choose to open a copy of the document or open the document in your browser if it is saved in Web page format.

FIGURE 1-6
Open menu

S TEP-BY-STEP 1.2

1. With Word on the screen, choose **More** in the Open section of the task pane. The Open dialog box appears, as shown in Figure 1-5. (If the task pane is not displayed, open the **View** menu and choose **Task Pane**.)

2. Click the down arrow to the right of the *Look in* box to display the available disk drives.

3. Click the drive that contains your data files and locate the **Employees** folder, as shown in Figure 1-7.

FIGURE 1-7
Employees folder

4. Double-click the **Employees** folder. The folders within the Employees folder appear (see Figure 1-8).

FIGURE 1-8
Contents of the Employees folder

5. Double-click the **Perez** folder. The names of all the files in the Perez folder display. (If necessary, click the down arrow at the right of the *Files of type* box and select **All Files** to display all the files.)

6. Click **Schedule Memo** to select it and then click **Open** to open the file. Leave the file open for the next Step-by-Step.

You can see how folders help organize and identify documents. The Perez folder also contains a spreadsheet with the work schedule for the first two weeks in April. In the next Step-by-Step, you will start Excel, the Office spreadsheet application, and open the spreadsheet that goes with the memo.

STEP-BY-STEP 1.3

1. Open another Office document by clicking the **Start** button.

2. Point to **All Programs**, point to **Microsoft Office**, and then click **Microsoft Office Excel 2003.** Excel starts and a blank spreadsheet appears.

3. Open the **File** menu and choose **Open**. The Open dialog box appears.

4. Click the down arrow at the right of the *Look in* box. If necessary, click the drive that contains your data files and locate the Employees folder.

5. Double-click the **Employees** folder; then double-click the **Perez** folder.

6. Double-click **April Schedule** to open the file. The April Schedule spreadsheet appears on the screen, as shown in Figure 1-9. Leave the file open for the next Step-by-Step.

FIGURE 1-9
April Schedule file

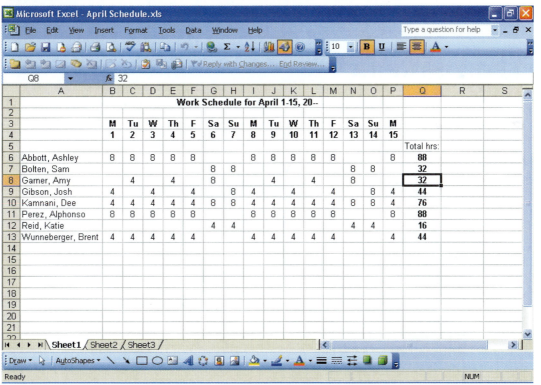

Saving a File

Saving is done two ways. The Save command saves a file on a disk using the current name. The Save As command saves a file on a disk using a new name. The Save As command can also be used to save a file to a new location.

FILENAMES

Unlike in programs designed for the early versions of Windows and DOS, filenames are not limited to eight characters. With Windows, a filename may contain up to 255 characters and may include spaces. However, you will rarely need this many characters to name a file. Name a file with a descriptive name that will remind you of what the file contains, such as Cover Letter or Quarter 1 Sales. The filename can include most characters found on the keyboard, with the exception of those shown in Table 1-2.

TABLE 1-2
Characters that cannot be used in filenames

CHARACTER	NAME	CHARACTER	NAME
*	asterisk	<	less than sign
\	backslash	;	semicolon
[ ]	brackets	/	slash
:	colon	"	quotation mark
=	equal sign	?	question mark
>	greater than sign	|	vertical bar

STEP-BY-STEP 1.4

1. *April Schedule* should be on the screen from the last Step-by-Step. Open the **File** menu and choose **Save As**. The Save As dialog box appears, as shown in Figure 1-10.

FIGURE 1-10
Save As dialog box

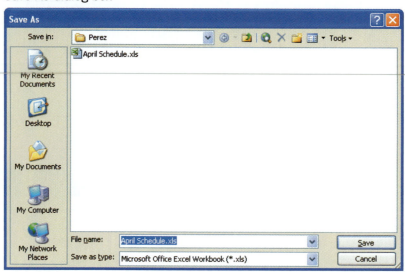

STEP-BY-STEP 1.4 Continued

2. In the *File name* box, key **April Work Sched**, followed by your initials.

3. Click the down arrow to the right of the *Save in* box and choose the **Employees** folder.

4. Double-click the **Garner** folder.

5. Click **Save** to save the file with the new name in the Garner folder. Leave the document open for the next Step-by-Step.

Closing an Office Document

You can close an Office document either by opening the File menu and choosing Close or by clicking the Close button on the right side of the menu bar. If you close a file, the application will still be open and ready for you to open or create another file.

> **Hot Tip**
>
> All of the programs in Office 2003 allow you to open new documents while you are working in other documents. You can even work in documents created in another Office program, such as Excel, while working in Word. To move back and forth between documents just click the taskbar button for the document you want to display.

STEP-BY-STEP 1.5

1. Open the **File** menu and choose **Close**. *April Work Sched* closes.

2. Click the **Microsoft Word** button on the taskbar to make it active. *Schedule Memo* should be displayed.

3. Click the **Close** button in the right corner of the menu bar to close *Schedule Memo*.

4. Leave Word open for the next Step-by-Step.

Shortcuts for Loading Recently Used Files

Office offers you two shortcuts for opening recently used files. The first shortcut is to choose My Recent Documents from the Start menu. A menu will open listing the fifteen most recently used documents, similar to that shown in Figure 1-11. To open one of the recently used files, click the file you wish to open.

FIGURE 1-11
Most recently used files

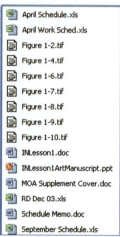

The second and third shortcuts can be found on each Office application's File menu and task pane. The bottom part of the File menu and the Open section of the task pane show the filenames of the four most recently opened documents, with the most recently opened first, as shown in Figure 1-12. When a new file is opened, each filename moves down to make room for the new most recently opened file. To open one of the files, you simply choose it as if it were a menu selection. If the document you are looking for is not on the File menu, use Open to locate and select the file.

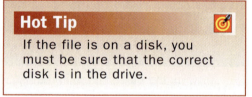

Hot Tip

If the file is on a disk, you must be sure that the correct disk is in the drive.

FIGURE 1-12
Most recently used files on the File menu and task pane

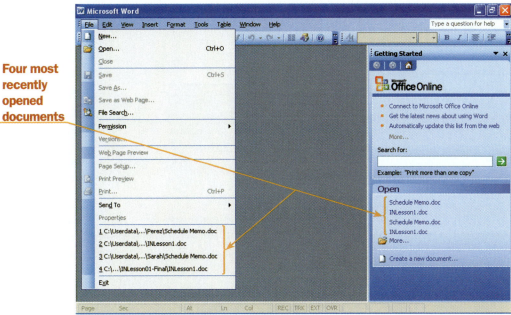

Office Help

This lesson has covered only a few of the many features of Office applications. For additional information, use the Office Help system as a quick reference when you are unsure about a function. To get specific help about topics relating to the application you are using, access help from the Help menu on the application's menu bar. Or, key a question in the *Type a question for help* box on the menu bar. Then, from the Help task pane, shown in Figure 1-13, you can choose to see a Table of Contents displaying general topics and subtopics or search the Help system using a keyword. You can also access the Microsoft Office Online Help system to find more information on various topics.

FIGURE 1-13
Word Help task pane

Many topics in the Help program are linked. A *link* is represented by colored, underlined text. By clicking a link, the user "jumps" to a linked document that contains additional information about that topic.

STEP-BY-STEP 1.6

1. Display the Word Help task pane, shown in Figure 1-13, by opening the **Help** menu and choosing **Microsoft Office Word Help**.

2. Click the **Table of Contents** link to display a list of topics. If you have Internet access, this information is downloaded from the Microsoft Online Help system. If you do not have Internet access, the information is accessed from the Offline Table of Contents.

3. Click the topic, **Working with Text**, click **Copy and Paste**, and then click **Move or copy text and graphics**. A list of topics displays in a separate window.

4. Click the **Move or copy a single item** topic in the Microsoft Office Word Help window.

5. Read the contents of the Help window and leave it open for the next Step-by-Step.

When you want to search for help on a particular topic, use the *Search for* box and key in a word. Windows will search alphabetically through the list of help topics to try to find an appropriate match. Click a topic to see it explained in the Help window, as shown in Figure 1-14.

FIGURE 1-14
Help topic explained in the Help window

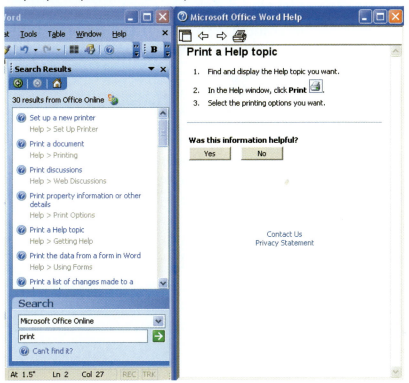

STEP-BY-STEP 1.7

1. Double-click the green back arrow at the top of the Word Help task pane to display the *Search for* box. (*Note:* You may need to drag the Microsoft Office Word Help window out of the way to see the task pane.)

2. Click in the *Search for* box to place the insertion point within it, key **print**, and click the green *Start searching* arrow.

3. Search through the list of results until you find **Print a Help topic**. Click it to display information in the Microsoft Office Word Help window, as shown in Figure 1-14.

4. Read the information, then print the information by following the instructions you read.

5. Close the Help program by clicking the **Close** button in the Help window as well as in the task pane.

Office Assistant

The Office Assistant is a feature found in all the Office programs that offers a variety of ways to get help. The Assistant, shown in Figure 1-15, is an animated character that offers tips, solutions, instructions, and examples to help you work more efficiently. The default Office Assistant character is a paper clip, named Clippit. A *default* setting is the one used unless another option is chosen.

FIGURE 1-15
Default Office Assistant

The Office Assistant monitors the work you are doing and anticipates when you might need help. It appears on the screen with tips on how to save time or use the program's features more effectively. For example, if you start writing a letter in Word, the Assistant pops up to ask if you want help, as shown in Figure 1-16.

FIGURE 1-16
Office Assistant automatically volunteering assistance

If you have a specific question, you can use the Office Assistant to search for help. To display the Office Assistant if it is not on the screen, choose Show the Office Assistant from the Help menu. Key your question and click Search. The Assistant suggests a list of help topics in response.

STEP-BY-STEP 1.8

1. If necessary, open the **Help** menu and choose **Show the Office Assistant**. The Office Assistant appears, as shown in Figure 1-15. Click the **Office Assistant** to display the text box.

2. Key **How do I use the Office Assistant?** in the text box.

3. Click **Search**. A list of help topics is displayed in the Search Results task pane.

STEP-BY-STEP 1.8 Continued

4. Choose one of the topics listed and click it to display information in the Microsoft Office Help window.

5. Read and print the information.

6. Click the **Close** boxes in the Help window and the task pane to remove the Help window from the screen.

7. Click the **New Blank Document** button in the standard toolbar to open a new Word document.

8. Key **Dear Zack,** and press **Enter**. A message from the Office Assistant appears, asking if you want help writing your letter, as shown in Figure 1-16. (*Note:* If the message does not appear, you may not have keyed the comma after Zack. Add the comma and press Enter again. The message should display.)

9. Click **Just type the letter without help**.

10. Close the Word document without saving. Leave Word open for the next Step-by-Step.

Quitting an Office Application

The Exit command on the File menu provides the option to quit Word or any other Office application. You can also click the Close button on the right side of the title bar. Exiting an Office application takes you to another open application or back to the Windows desktop.

STEP-BY-STEP 1.9

1. Open the **File** menu. Notice the files listed toward the bottom of the menu. These are the four most recently used files mentioned previously in this lesson.

2. Choose **Exit**. Word closes and Excel is displayed on the screen.

3. Click the **Close** button in the right corner of the title bar. Excel closes and the desktop appears on the screen. The taskbar shows an application is still open.

4. Click the **PowerPoint** button on the taskbar to display it on the screen. Exit PowerPoint. The desktop appears on the screen again.

Accessing the Internet

The *Internet* is a vast network of computers linked to one another. The Internet allows people around the world to share information and ideas through Web pages, newsgroups, mailing lists, chat rooms, e-mail, and electronic files.

Connecting to the Internet requires special hardware and software and an Internet Service Provider. Before you can use the Internet, your computer needs to be connected, and you should know how to access the Internet.

The *World Wide Web* is a system of computers that share information by means of hypertext links on "pages." The Internet is its carrier. To identify hypertext documents, the Web uses addresses called *Uniform Resource Locators (URLs)*. Here are some examples of URLs:

http://www.senate.gov

http://www.microsoft.com

http://www.course.com

The Web toolbar, shown in Figure 1-17, is available in all Office programs. It contains buttons for opening and searching documents. You can use the Web toolbar to access documents on the Internet, on an *Intranet* (a company's private Web), or on your computer. To display the Web toolbar in an application, choose View, Toolbars, Web.

FIGURE 1-17
Web toolbar

The Back button takes you to the previous page and the Forward button takes you to the next page. Click the Stop button to stop loading the current page. The Refresh button reloads the current page. Click the Start Page button to load your *home page*, the first page that appears when you start your browser. The Search the Web button opens a page in which you can type keywords and search the Web. The Favorites button shows a list to which you can add your favorite sites so that you can return to them easily. From the Go button's menu, you can choose to go to different sites or key in an address using the Open Hyperlink command. Click Show Only Web Toolbar when you want to hide all the toolbars except the Web toolbar. When you know the specific address you want to jump to, key it in the Address box.

To view hypertext documents on the Web, you need special software. A *Web browser* is software used to display Web pages on your computer monitor. Microsoft's *Internet Explorer* is a browser for navigating the Web that is packaged with the Office software. When you click the Start Page button or the Search the Web button, or key an URL in the Address box of the Web toolbar, Office automatically launches your Web browser. Depending on your type of Internet connection, you may have to connect to your Internet Service Provider first. Figure 1-18 shows a Web page using Word as a browser.

Computer Concepts

There are two basic types of Internet connections, dial-up and direct. Dial-up access uses a modem and a telephone line to communicate between your computer and the Internet. Most individual users have dial-up access. Direct access uses a special high-speed connection, such as a DSL cable, between your computer and the Internet. This access is faster but more expensive than dial-up access. Most businesses and institutions, and some individuals, have direct access.

Hot Tip

Toolbars display buttons for basic commands only. To see additional buttons, click **Toolbar Options** on the toolbar and choose from the list that appears. When you use a button from the list, it is added to the toolbar. If you haven't used a button recently, it is added to the Toolbar Options list.

FIGURE 1-18
Web browser

STEP-BY-STEP 1.10

1. Connect to your Internet Service Provider if you are not connected already.

2. Open **Word**. Open the **View** menu, choose **Toolbars**, and then choose **Web** from the submenu if the Web toolbar isn't displayed already.

3. Click the **Start Page** button on the Web toolbar. The Start Page begins loading, as shown in Figure 1-18. Wait a few moments for the page to load. (Your start page may be different from the one shown.)

4. Close Internet Explorer by clicking its **Close** button, and return to Microsoft Word.

5. Click the **Search the Web** button. The Internet Explorer program opens and displays the MSN Search screen.

Hot Tip

You can display the Web toolbar in any Office application and use it to access the World Wide Web.

Hot Tip

Since this page is updated every day, your page may not look exactly like the one shown even if you enter the same URL.

STEP-BY-STEP 1.10 Continued

6. Key **pets** in the *Search* box.

7. Click **Search** and a list of pet-related Web sites appears.

8. Click on one of the Web sites to display more information on pets.

9. Click the **Back** button to return to the previous page. Click another Web site to display.

10. Click the **Home** button to return to the Start Page for Internet Explorer.

11. Close Internet Explorer. Close Word. If a message appears asking you if you want to save changes, click **No**.

12. If necessary, disconnect from your Internet Service Provider.

SUMMARY

In this lesson, you learned:

■ Microsoft Office 2003 is an integrated software package that consists of a word processor application, a spreadsheet application, a database application, a presentation application, a schedule/organizer application, and a desktop publishing application. The documents of an integrated software package can be used together.

■ Office applications can be started by clicking the Start button, pointing to All Programs, pointing to Microsoft Office, and then clicking the name of the application.

■ Most Office tasks can be completed from the opening screen of each application. The basic parts of the opening screen are similar in all of the Office programs except Outlook. The task pane is a separate window on the right-hand side of the opening screen. The task pane contains commonly used commands that can help you work more efficiently.

 Careers

Find out about careers in business by going to www.careers-in-business.com.

■ Each title in the menu bar represents a separate drop-down menu. When you first use a program, each menu displays only basic commands. As you work, the program adjusts the menus to display the commands used most frequently, adding a command when you choose it and dropping a command when it hasn't been used recently.

■ Toolbars provide another quick way to choose commands. The toolbars use icons, or small pictures, to remind you of each button's function. Toolbars can also contain drop-down menus.

■ You can open an existing document from the File menu or from the task pane. You can also click the Open button on the Standard toolbar. The Open dialog box will be displayed, enabling you to open a file from any available disk or directory.

■ No matter which Office application you are using, files are opened, saved, and closed the same way. Filenames may contain up to 255 characters and may include spaces.

■ Recently used files can be opened quickly by choosing the filename from the bottom of the File menu or from the task pane. You can also click the Start button and select My Recent Documents to list the fifteen most recently used files. To exit an Office application, open the File menu and choose Exit or click the Close button on the title bar.

■ The Office Help program provides additional information about the many features of the Office applications. You can access the Help program from the menu bar and use the Table of Contents or the *Search* box to get information. You can also access the Microsoft Office Online Help system to find more information on various topics.

■ The Office Assistant is a help feature found in all Office applications. It offers tips, advice, and hints on how to work more effectively. You can also use it to search for help on any given topic.

VOCABULARY*Review*

Define the following terms:

Close	Internet Explorer	Task pane
Default	Intranet	Toolbar
Drop-down menu	Link	Uniform Resource Locators
Home page	Menu	(URLs)
Icon	Open	World Wide Web
Integrated software package	Save	Web browser
Internet		

REVIEW *Questions*

WRITTEN QUESTIONS

Write a brief answer to the following questions.

1. List four of the applications that are included in Office 2003.

2. How do you start an Office application?

3. What is the difference between the Save and Save As commands?

4. If the Web toolbar is not on the screen, how do you display it?

5. What is the location and the function of the title bar, menu bar, status bar and taskbar?

TRUE/FALSE

Circle T if the statement is true or F if the statement is false.

T F 1. In all Office applications, you open, save, and close files in the same way.

T F 2. A filename may include up to 356 characters and may include spaces.

T F 3. The Office Assistant is available in all Office programs.

T F 4. The Web uses addresses called URLs to identify hypertext links.

T F 5. As you work in Office, the menus are adjusted to display the commands used most frequently.

PROJECTS

PROJECT 1-1

You need to save a copy of April's work schedule into each of the employee's folders.

1. Open Word and a blank document appears.

2. Open Excel. Use the **File** menu to locate the **Employees** folder in the data files. Open the **April Schedule** file from the **Perez** folder.

3. Use the **Save As** command to save the file as **April Work Sched,** followed by your initials, in the Abbott folder.

4. Repeat the process to save the file in the **Bolten, Gibson, Kamnani, Reid,** and **Wunneberger** folders.

5. Close April Work Sched and exit Excel. The blank Word document should be displayed.

6. Use the task pane to open the **Schedule Memo** Word file from the **Perez** folder.

7. Save the file with the same name in the **Garner** folder.

8. Close **Schedule Memo.** Close the Word document without saving and exit Word.

PROJECT 1-2

1. Open Word and access the Help system.

2. Search on the word **tip.**

3. Choose from the list of topics to find out how to show the tip of the day when Word starts.

4. Print the information displayed in the Microsoft Office Help window.

5. Search on the question **What should I do if the Office Assistant is distracting?**

6. Choose from the list of topics to find out how to troubleshoot Help.

7. In the Microsoft Office Help window, choose the option to find out what to do if the Office Assistant is distracting.

8. Print the information displayed in the Microsoft Office Help window.

9. Close the Help system and exit Word.

 Careers

For help in choosing a career or college major, go to *www.careerkey.org*. You can take a test that measures your skills, abilities, talents, values, interest, and personality. Based upon your answers, a list of promising careers and jobs is identified.

PROJECT 1-3

1. If necessary, connect to your Internet Service Provider.

2. Open your Web browser.

3. Search for information on the Internet about Microsoft products.

4. Search for information about another topic in which you are interested.

5. Return to your home page.

6. Close your Web browser and disconnect from the Internet, if necessary.

CRITICAL *Thinking*

 ### ACTIVITY 1-1

Describe how you would use each of the Office applications in your personal life. Imagine that you are a business owner and describe how each of the Office applications would help you increase productivity.

 ### ACTIVITY 1-2

Use the Office Help system to find out how to change the Office Assistant from a paper clip to another animated character. Write down the steps and then change your Office Assistant to another character.

 ### ACTIVITY 1-3

Open your Web browser. Compare the toolbar of your browser with the Web toolbar shown in Figure 1-17. Use the Help system if necessary and describe the function of any buttons that are different. Then describe the steps you would take to print a Web page.

 ### ACTIVITY 1-4

You work for a small advertising agency whose employees depend heavily on reliable and speedy access to the Internet to do their jobs. Recently, some of the employees have complained about sluggish downloads and problems connecting to the Internet. You have decided to evaluate your current Internet service provider and research other ISPs in the area.

Search the Internet for information on at least three ISPs. Use the table below as a guide for gathering information that would be helpful in your evaluation. Which ISP would you recommend? Why?

INTERNET SERVICE PROVIDER	SETUP COSTS/ EQUIPMENT REQUIREMENTS	COST PER MONTH	SPEED	CUSTOMER SERVICE	SYSTEM MAINTENANCE DOWNTIME

INTRODUCTORY MICROSOFT ACCESS

Unit

🕐 **Estimated Time for Unit: 9 hours**

ACCESS BASICS

VOCABULARY

Database management system

Datasheet view

Design view

Entry

Field

Field name

Primary key

Record

Database Basics

Access is a program known as a *database management system*. A computerized database management system allows you to store, retrieve, analyze, and print information. You do not, however, need a computer to have a database management system. A set of file folders can be a database management system. Any system for managing data is a database management system. There are distinct advantages, however, to using a computerized database management system.

A computerized database management system (DBMS) is much faster, more flexible, and more accurate than using file folders. A computerized DBMS is also more efficient and cost-effective. A program such as Access can store thousands of pieces of data in a computer or on a disk. The data can be quickly searched and sorted to save time otherwise spent digging through file folders. For example, a computerized DBMS could find all the people with a certain zip code faster and more accurately than you could by searching through a large list or through folders.

Starting Access

To start Access, click the Start button on the taskbar. Select All Programs, select Microsoft Office, and then click Microsoft Office Access 2003 to load Access. After a few moments, the Access startup screen appears, as shown in Figure 1-1. This screen gives you the option of opening an existing database or creating a new one. After selecting *Create a new file*, you can also choose to create a new database from an existing one or use a template to simplify the process of creating a database.

FIGURE 1-1
Access startup screen

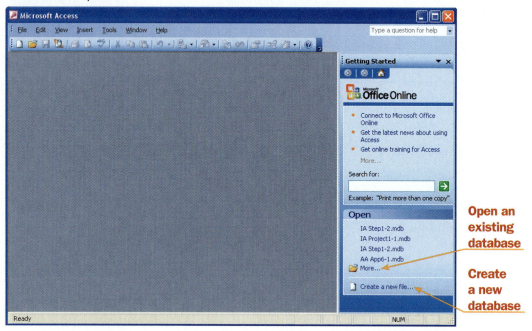

Open an existing database

Create a new database

STEP-BY-STEP 1.1

1. With Windows running, click **Start** on the taskbar.

2. Point to **All Programs**, and then **Microsoft Office**. Click **Microsoft Office Access 2003**.

3. Access opens and the Access startup screen appears, as shown in Figure 1-1. Leave this screen open for the next Step-by-Step.

Opening a Database

You can open an existing database from the File menu or from the Getting Started task pane displayed on the right side of the screen. To open a database from the Getting Started task pane, click the *More. . .* option from the *Open* section and choose a database from the Open dialog box. To create a new database, click the *Create a new file* option below the *Open* section. If you choose *Blank database*, you must manually create the database. If you choose *From existing file*, you can create the new file from an existing one. To be guided through the creation of the database using a template, either key a template keyword in the *Search online for* box or choose *On my computer* from the *Templates* section. You will learn more about creating databases later in this lesson.

When you open an existing database, the Database window appears, like that shown in Figure 1-2. The Objects bar on the left side of the window lists the types of database objects. The database objects window lists the various functions for creating the selected object as well as any objects that already exist. In Figure 1-2, for example, three functions for creating a table and one table named *service club members* are listed. You will learn about database objects later in this lesson.

FIGURE 1-2
Database window

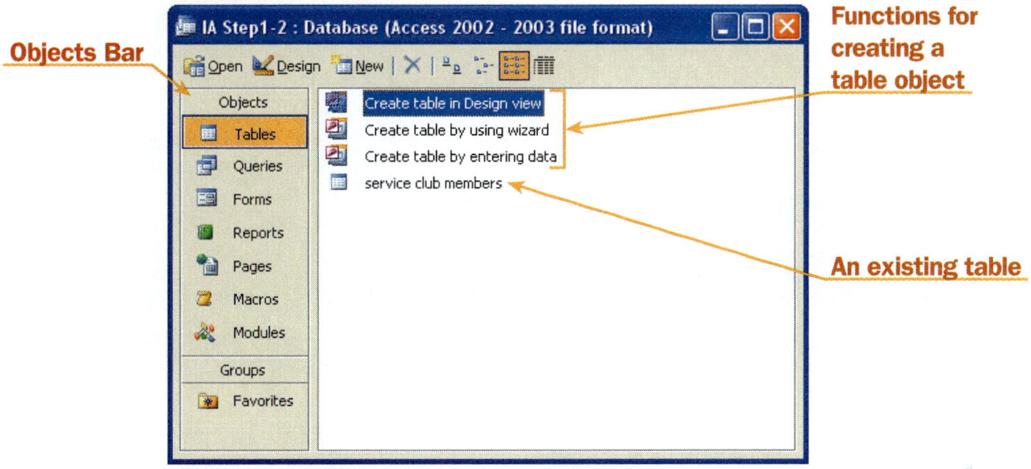

S TEP-BY-STEP 1.2

1. Click the **More . . .** option in the *Open* section of the *Getting Started* task pane. The Open dialog box displays. If the **More . . .** option is not displayed, choose **Open . . .** instead.

2. Open the file **IA Step1-2** from the data files. The Database window appears, as previously shown in Figure 1-2. Leave the database open for the next Step-by-Step.

The Access Screen

Like other Office 2003 applications, the Access screen has a title bar, menu bar, and toolbar. At the bottom of the screen is the status bar. If necessary, click the down arrow in the Objects bar to view the other objects. Figure 1-3 shows the Access screen with the *IA Step1-2* database open.

FIGURE 1-3
Access screen

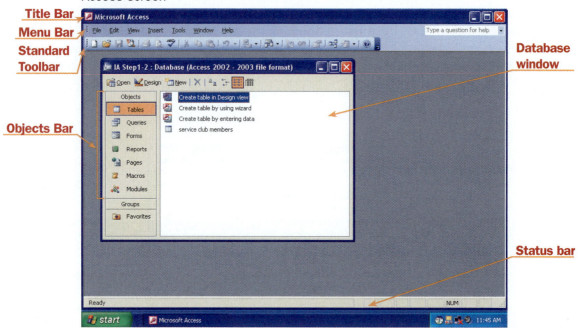

As you use Access, various windows and dialog boxes will appear on the screen. Unlike Word and Excel, Access does not have a standard document view. In Access the screen changes based on how you interact with the database.

Database Objects

When a database is saved, the file that is saved contains a collection of objects. These objects work together to store data, retrieve data, display data, print reports, and automate operations. The Objects bar in the Database window displays a button for each type of object. If necessary, click the down arrow on the bar to view the additional objects.

Table 1-1 briefly explains the purpose of each type of object.

TABLE 1-1
Database objects

OBJECT	DESCRIPTION
Table	Tables store data in a format similar to that of a worksheet. All database information is stored in tables.
Query	Queries search for and retrieve data from tables based on given criteria. A query is a question you ask the database.
Form	Forms allow you to display data in a custom format. You might, for example, create a form that matches a paper form.
Report	Reports also display data in a custom format. Reports, however, are especially suited for printing and summarizing data. You can even perform calculations in a report.
Page	Data access pages let you design other database objects so that they can be published to the Web.
Macro	Macros automate database operations by allowing you to issue a single command that performs a series of operations.
Module	Modules are like macros but allow much more complex programming of database operations. Creating a module requires the use of a programming language.

S TEP-BY-STEP 1.3

1. Make sure **Tables** is selected on the Objects bar. Highlight the **service club members** table in the database objects window, and click the **Open** button. The table appears, as shown in Figure 1-4.

2. Open the **File** menu and choose **Close** to close the table. The database objects window is visible again.

3. Click **Queries** on the Objects bar. There is one query object named *Lubbock*. This query locates members who live in Lubbock.

4. Click **Forms** on the Objects bar. There is one form object named *service members form*.

5. Open the **File** menu and choose **Close** to close the database. Leave Access open for the next Step-by-Step.

FIGURE 1-4
Database table

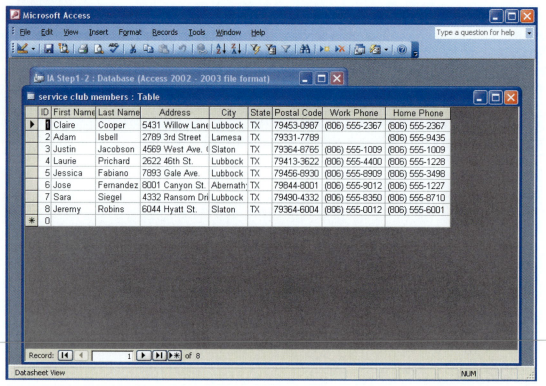

Database Terminology

Four terms are essential to know when working with databases. These terms relate to the way data is organized in a table. A *record* is a complete set of data. In the *service club members* table, each member is stored as a record. In a table, a record appears as a row, as shown in Figure 1-5.

Each record is made up of *fields*. For example, the first name of each member is placed in a special field that is created to accept first names. In a table, fields appear as columns. In order to identify the fields, each field has a *field name*. The data entered into a field is called an *entry*. In the *service club members* database, for example, the first record has the name *Claire* as an entry in the First Name field.

FIGURE 1-5
Records and fields

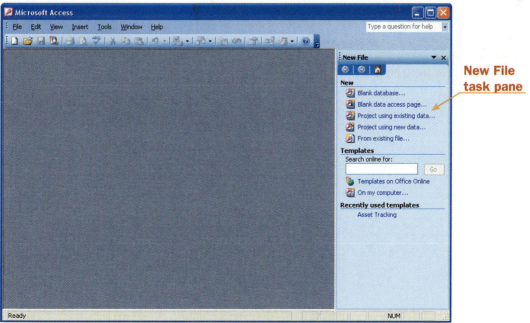

Creating a Database

The first step in creating a database is to create the file that will hold the database objects. To do this, you open the File menu and choose New. The Access startup screen appears, as shown in Figure 1-6. In the New File task pane on the right side of the screen, choose *Blank Database* and the File New Database dialog box appears. This is where you will name the file and store it with your other data files. Choose *Create*, and the Database window appears, as shown in Figure 1-7. It will not contain any objects yet, because none have been created.

FIGURE 1-6
Access startup screen

FIGURE 1-7
Database window

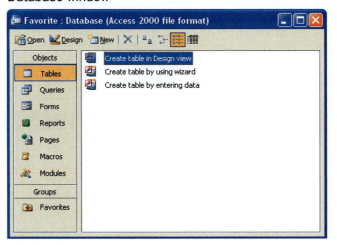

 ## STEP-BY-STEP 1.4

1. Open the **File** menu and choose **New**. The Access startup screen appears, as shown in Figure 1-6.

2. In the New File task pane on the right side of the screen, choose **Blank database** and the File New Database dialog box appears.

3. Save the database as **Favorite**, followed by your initials, and then click **Create**. Your Database window should look like that shown in Figure 1-7.

4. Double-click **Create table by entering data**. A new table appears in Datasheet view, as shown in Figure 1-8.

5. Open the **File** menu and choose **Close** to go back to the Database window. Leave the window open for the next Step-by-Step.

> ### Extra Challenge
>
> Create a new database using a database wizard. In the New File task pane, click **On my computer** and then the **Databases** tab. Select one of the database formats already designed for you and follow the screens to add your own information.

FIGURE 1-8
New table in Datasheet view

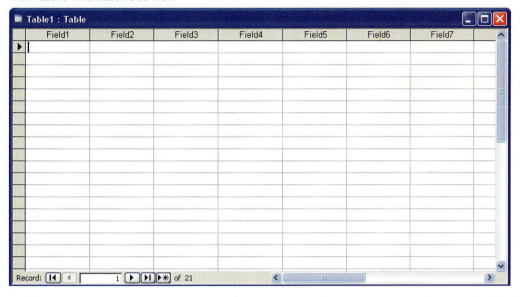

Creating Tables

Because all other database objects rely on the existence of a database table, creating a table is the next step after creating a database. In many database management systems, data is stored using more than one table. To create a table, click *Tables* on the Objects bar. Click the New button and the New Table dialog box appears, as shown in Figure 1-9.

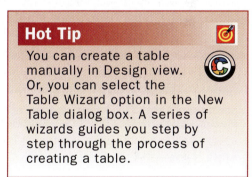

Hot Tip

You can create a table manually in Design view. Or, you can select the Table Wizard option in the New Table dialog box. A series of wizards guides you step by step through the process of creating a table.

FIGURE 1-9
New Table dialog box

The New Table dialog box lists several ways to create a table. The most common way is to create the table in *Design view*. This is the view where you will design new tables and modify the design of existing tables. You create a table in Design view by double-clicking *Create table in Design view* in the Database window.

STEP-BY-STEP 1.5

1. Click **Tables** on the Objects bar, if necessary, and then click **New**. The New Table dialog box appears, as shown in Figure 1-9.

2. Choose the **Design View** option and click **OK**. The *Design view* window opens. Leave the window on the screen for the next Step-by-Step.

Designing a Table

Now you are ready to design your table. You create the table's fields in the Design view window. As you can see in the window on your screen, each field in a table is divided into three sections: *Field Name*, *Data Type*, and *Description*. You will insert data in each of these three sections to create a table.

Field Names

First you have to decide what data you need to store. You should divide the data into categories to create fields. For example, suppose you want to create a database of your family members' birthdays. Some fields to include would be the person's name, address, and birth date. An example of a record would be: Halie Jones (name), 3410 Vicksburg Ave., Dallas, TX 75224 (address), and 10/28/89 (birth date).

Key the names of these fields in the Field Name column of the Table design window. It is helpful if you create meaningful field names that identify the types of data stored.

Data Type

After keying the field name, press the Tab key to move to the Data Type column. Then determine the type of data to be stored in each field and choose an appropriate data type. The data type tells Access what kind of information can be stored in the field. Table 1-2 briefly describes the basic data types.

> **Did You Know?**
>
> You can set a default value for a field that usually contains the same value. For example, if most of the people in a database of names and addresses live in Texas, you can enter TX as the default value of the State field. The State field will automatically contain TX, unless you change it.

TABLE 1-2
Data types

DATA TYPE	DESCRIPTION
Text	The Text data type allows letters and numbers (alphanumeric data). A text field can hold up to 255 characters. Data such as names and addresses are stored in fields of this type.
Memo	The Memo data type also allows alphanumeric data. A memo field, however, can hold thousands of characters. Memo fields are used for data that does not follow a particular format. For example, you might use a Memo field to store notes about a record.
Number	The Number data type holds numeric data. There are variations of the Number type, each capable of storing a different range of values.
Date/Time	The Date/Time data type holds dates and times.
Currency	The Currency data type is specially formatted for dealing with currency.
AutoNumber	The AutoNumber data type is automatically incremented by Access for each new record added. Counters are used to give each record in a database a unique identification.
Yes/No	The Yes/No data type holds logical values. A Yes/No field can hold the values Yes/No, True/False, or On/Off.
OLE Object	The OLE Object data type is used for some of the more advanced features. It allows you to store graphics, sound, and even objects such as spreadsheets in a field.
Hyperlink	The Hyperlink data type is used to store a hyperlink as a UNC path or URL.
Lookup Wizard	The Lookup Wizard creates a field that allows you to choose a value from another table or from a list of values.

Choosing the correct data type is important. For example, you might think a telephone number or zip code should be stored in a field with a Number data type. However, you should only use Number data types when you intend to do calculations with the data. You won't be adding or subtracting zip codes. Numbers that will not be used in calculations are best stored as Text.

For a table of favorite restaurants, the name of the restaurant and its address would be stored in fields of Text type, which is the default data type. The typical meal cost is ideal for the Currency type. The date you last ate at the restaurant would be Date type, and a Yes/No data type could specify whether reservations are required. Use the Lookup Wizard to create a Lookup field that allows you to choose from a list the type of food the restaurant specializes in.

To choose a data type, click the arrow that appears in the Data Type column when the insertion point is in that column or when you key the first letter of the word. This button is called a drop-down arrow. A menu appears allowing you to choose a data type.

Description

The last step in designing a table is to key a description for each field. The description explains the data in the field. For example, a field for the *Restaurants* database named Last Visit could have a description such as *Date I last ate at the Restaurant*. The description clarifies the field name. It does not appear in a table, but does display in the status bar when you select the field.

STEP-BY-STEP 1.6

1. Key **Name** in the first row of the Field Name column.

2. Press **Tab** (or **Enter**). The data type will default to Text, which is appropriate for the name of the restaurant.

3. Press **Tab** to move to the Description column.

4. Key **Name of restaurant** and press **Enter** to move to the next row.

5. Key the other fields and descriptions shown in Figure 1-10. All of the fields are Text data type.

FIGURE 1-10
Defining fields in a table

6. Click in the **Data Type** box for the Specialty field. A down arrow will appear.

7. Click the arrow and choose **Lookup Wizard** from the drop-down menu that appears. The Lookup Wizard screen displays.

8. Choose **I will type in the values that I want** and click **Next**. A second Lookup Wizard screen displays.

STEP-BY-STEP 1.6 Continued

9. Leave the *Number of columns* at 1 and key the Lookup values as shown in Figure 1-11, using the Tab key to move down through the list. Click **Finish** when finished.

FIGURE 1-11
Lookup Wizard screen

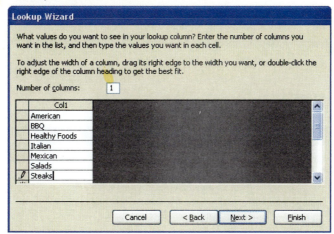

10. In the first blank row, key **Last Visit** in the Field Name column and press **Tab**.

11. Click the arrow in the **Data Type** field and choose **Date/Time** from the drop-down menu that appears.

12. Press **Tab**.

13. Key **Date I last ate at the restaurant** in the Description column. Press **Tab**.

14. Key **Reservations** in the Field Name column, choose **Yes/No** as the data type, and key **Are reservations required?** in the Description column. Leave the Design view window on the screen for the next Step-by-Step.

Naming and Saving a Table

After designing a table, you must give it a name and save the design. To save a table, open the File menu and choose Save. The Save As dialog box appears, as shown in Figure 1-12. Key a name for the table and click OK. A message appears asking you if you want to create a *primary key*, which is a special field that assigns a unique identifier to each record. You can have Access create the primary key for you, in which case each record is automatically assigned a unique number. Or you can designate an existing field to be a primary key. For example, in a table containing the names and addresses of customers, you might create a field that contains a customer identification number. You could set this as the primary key, as it will be a unique number for each customer.

FIGURE 1-12
Save As dialog box

STEP-BY-STEP 1.7

1. Open the **File** menu and choose **Save**. The Save As dialog box appears, as shown in Figure 1-12.

2. Key **Restaurants** in the *Table Name* box and click **OK**.

3. A message box appears asking if you want to create a primary key. Click **No**.

4. Open the **File** menu and choose **Close** to close the Design view window and return to the Database window. Note that your *Restaurants* table now appears as an object, as shown in Figure 1-13. Leave the Database window open for the next Step-by-Step.

FIGURE 1-13
Database window showing Restaurants table as an object

Modifying Tables

To modify the design of a table, you must be in Design view. Go to Design view by highlighting the name of the table in the Database window and clicking the Design button. In Design view, you can make changes to the names of fields, data formats, and descriptions.

You can add fields to the end of the list, or you can insert a new row for a field between existing fields. To insert a new row, place the insertion point in the row below where you want the new row to appear. Then, open the Insert menu and choose Rows. You can delete a field by placing the insertion point in the row you want to delete and choosing Delete Rows on the Edit menu. You can also insert and delete rows by clicking the Insert Rows or Delete Rows button on the Standard toolbar.

It is important to make sure you don't delete the wrong data in Design view; but if you do, you can click the Undo button on the toolbar. The Undo button reverses your last command.

You can delete an entire table by highlighting the table in the Database window and choosing Delete on the Edit menu.

When you finish changing fields, open the File menu and choose Save or click the Save button on the toolbar.

> **Did You Know?**
>
> A primary key field is a unique identifier for a record. To set a field as a primary key, open the table in Design view and click the row selector for the desired field. Click the **Primary Key** button on the toolbar.

S TEP-BY-STEP 1.8

1. Highlight the **Restaurants** table in the Database window if it's not selected already.

2. Click the **Design** button. The table appears in Design view.

3. Click in the first blank row's Field Name column to place the insertion point there. You may need to scroll down.

4. Key **Meal Cost** in the Field Name column. Press **Tab**.

5. Choose **Currency** as the data type. Press **Tab**.

6. Key **Typical meal cost** as the description.

7. Place the insertion point in the **Last Visit** field name.

8. Click the **Insert Rows** button on the toolbar. A blank row is inserted above the Last Visit field.

9. In the blank row, key **Favorite Dish** as the field name, choose **Text** as the data type, and key **My favorite meal** as the description.

10. Place the insertion point in the **Reservations** field name.

11. Click the **Delete Rows** button on the toolbar. The Reservations field is deleted.

12. Click the **Undo** button on the toolbar. The Reservations field reappears.

13. Click the **Save** button on the toolbar to save the design changes. Remain in this screen for the next Step-by-Step.

Navigating and Entering Records in Datasheet View

 Once a table is created and designed, you can enter records directly into the table using *Datasheet view*. In Datasheet view, the table appears in a form similar to a spreadsheet, as you saw earlier in the lesson. As with a spreadsheet, the intersection of a row and a column is called a cell. To get to Datasheet view, select the table in the Database window and click the Open button, or click the View button on the toolbar while in Design view. You can switch back to Design view by clicking the View button again.

View, Datasheet   View, Design

The techniques used to enter records in the table are familiar to you. Press Enter or Tab to move to the next field as you enter the data. Access will consider the data types as you enter data. For example, you must enter a valid date in a Date/Time field and you must enter a number in a Number field. If you don't, an error message appears.

After entering records in a table in Datasheet view, you do not need to save the changes. Access saves them for you automatically. Remember to always save changes to the table design in Design view.

You can use the mouse to move the insertion point to a particular cell in the table. You can also use the keys in Table 1-3 to navigate through a table.

> **Did You Know?**
>
> You can switch to the Datasheet or Design view using options on the View menu.

TABLE 1-3
Navigating in Datasheet view

KEY	DESCRIPTION
Enter, Tab, or right arrow	Moves to the following field.
Left arrow or Shift+Tab	Moves to the previous field.
End	Moves to the last field in the current record.
Home	Moves to the first field in the current record.
Up arrow	Moves up one record and stays in the same field.
Down arrow	Moves down one record and stays in the same field.
Page Up	Moves up one screen.
Page Down	Moves down one screen.

STEP-BY-STEP 1.9

1. Click the **View** button on the toolbar to switch to Datasheet view. The *Restaurants* table looks like that shown in Figure 1-14. Notice how the View button now displays a different icon to indicate that clicking it will switch you back to Design view.

STEP-BY-STEP 1.9 Continued

FIGURE 1-14
Datasheet view

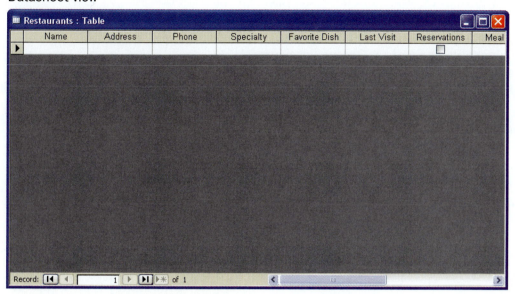

2. Key **Rosa's** in the Name field. Press **Tab**.

3. Key **8722 University Ave.** in the Address field. Press **Tab**.

4. Key **555-6798** in the Phone field. Press **Tab**.

5. Click the down arrow in the Specialty field and choose **Mexican** from the lookup list. Press **Tab**.

6. Key **Chicken Fajitas** in the Favorite Dish field. Press **Tab**.

7. Key today's date (XX/XX/20XX) in the Last Visit field. Press **Tab**. (If you do not key the year, it will be added automatically.)

8. The Reservations field has a blank check box in it. Click the check box or press the spacebar to place a check in the box. Press **Tab**.

9. Key **5.99** as the typical meal cost. Press **Tab**. Leave the database table open for the next Step-by-Step.

Extra Challenge

Create a database of your own favorite local restaurants. Use the fields from this *Restaurants* exercise, and any others that may apply.

Printing a Table

You can print a database table in Datasheet view. Open the File menu and choose the Print command to display the Print dialog box. As shown in Figure 1-15, you can choose to print all the records, only those selected, or for long tables you can specify the pages to print. Click Setup and the Page Setup dialog box appears, as shown in Figure 1-16. Here you can change the margins. To change the orientation, click Properties in the Print dialog box.

You can also click the Print button on the toolbar to print the database table. However, the Print dialog box will not appear for updates to the page setup.

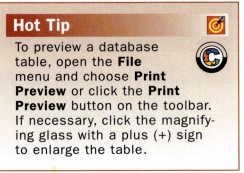

Hot Tip

To preview a database table, open the **File** menu and choose **Print Preview** or click the **Print Preview** button on the toolbar. If necessary, click the magnifying glass with a plus (+) sign to enlarge the table.

FIGURE 1-15
Print dialog box

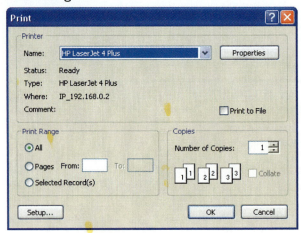

FIGURE 1-16
Page Setup dialog box

STEP-BY-STEP 1.10

1. Open the **File** menu and choose **Print**. The Print dialog box appears, as shown in Figure 1-15.

2. Click **Setup**. The Page Setup dialog box appears, as shown in Figure 1-16.

3. For the margins, key **.5** in the Left box and **.5** in the Right box.

4. Click **OK**.

5. In the Print dialog box, click **Properties**. The Properties dialog box appears.

6. Click on the *Layout* tab, if necessary. (If the Layout tab is not displayed, click the tab which displays the Orientation options.)

7. In the Orientation options, click **Landscape**.

8. Click **OK**.

9. In the Print dialog box, click **All** from the *Print Range* options, if it isn't already selected. Click **OK**.

10. Close the table. The record has been saved in the table automatically.

Exiting Access

As in other Office 2003 programs, you exit Access by opening the File menu and choosing Exit. Exiting Access takes you back to the Windows desktop. Remember to remove any floppy disks, and properly shut down Windows before turning off the computer.

STEP-BY-STEP 1.11

1. Open the **File** menu and choose **Close**. The database closes.

2. Open the **File** menu and choose **Exit**. The Windows desktop appears (assuming no other programs are open and maximized).

SUMMARY

In this lesson, you learned:

■ Access is a program known as a database management system. A computerized database management system allows you to store, retrieve, analyze, and print information. Start Access from the All Programs menu.

■ You can open an existing database from the File menu or from the Getting Started task pane displayed on the right side of the screen. The Access screen has a title bar, menu bar, and toolbar. Access, however, does not have a standard document view.

■ A database is a collection of objects. The objects work together to store data, retrieve data, display data, print reports, and automate operations. The object types are tables, queries, forms, reports, macros, and modules.

■ A record is a complete set of data. Each record is made up of fields. Each field is identified by a field name. The actual data entered into a field is called an entry.

■ Creating a database creates a file that will hold database objects. To store data, a table must first be created. In Design view, you can create fields and assign data types and descriptions to the fields. After a table has been created and designed, you can enter records in Datasheet view.

■ As in other Office 2003 applications, you exit Access by choosing the Exit command from the File menu.

VOCABULARY *Review*

Define the following terms:

Database management system	Design view	Field name
Datasheet view	Entry	Primary key
	Field	Record

REVIEW *Questions*

TRUE/FALSE

Circle T if the statement is true or F if the statement is false.

T   F   **1.** A computerized DBMS is more efficient than paper filing.

T   F   **2.** Opening a database automatically displays the data in the table.

T   F   **3.** Access has a standard document view that remains on the screen as long as a database is open.

T   F   **4.** A database file is a collection of database objects.

T   F   **5.** Fields are identified by field names.

WRITTEN QUESTIONS

Write a brief answer to the following questions.

1. Which window appears after you open a database?

2. List three types of database objects.

3. Which database object allows you to search for and retrieve data?

4. What is the term for the data entered in a field?

5. Which view is used to design tables?

PROJECTS

 PROJECT 1-1

1. Start Access.

2. Open the **IA Project1-1** database.

3. Open the **Restaurants** table in Datasheet view.

4. Insert the records shown in Figure 1-17.

5. Print the table in landscape orientation.

6. Close the table and database.

Name + Project N

FIGURE 1-17

Name	Address	Phone	Specialty	Favorite Dish	Last Visit	Reservations	Meal Cost
Health Hut	3440 Slide Rd.	555-6096	Healthy Foods	Fruit Delight	6/30/2006	☐	$5.59
Stella's	7822 Broadway	555-8922	Italian	Lasagna	7/6/2006	☑	$9.99
Tony's BBQ	2310 82nd St.	555-3143	BBQ	Baby Back Ribs	5/1/2006	☑	$10.99
Westside Café	5660 Salem	555-6621	American	Daybreak Muffins	7/12/2006	☐	$4.59
Salads and Stuff	8910 Main St.	555-3440	Salads	Chicken Caesar Salad	4/29/2006	☐	$5.99
Saltlick Steakhouse	2100 Hwy. 281	555-6700	Steaks	Rib Eye	3/10/2006	☑	$13.99
Alamo Diner	451 San Jacinto	555-9833	American	Cheeseburger	8/4/2006	☐	$5.59

PROJECT 1-2

1. Open the **IA Project1-2** database.

2. Create a new table named **Stores** using the field names, data types, and descriptions shown in Figure 1-18.

FIGURE 1-18

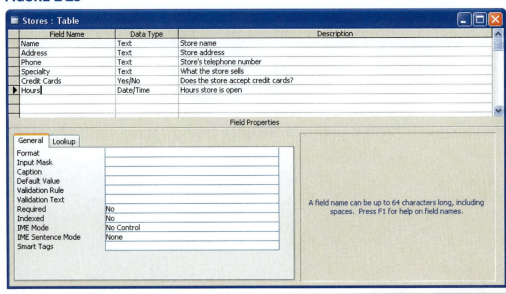

3. Save the table as **Stores** and close it. No primary key is necessary.

4. Open the table in Datasheet view and enter the record shown in Figure 1-19.

FIGURE 1-19

Name	Address	Phone	Specialty	Credit Cards	Hours
Electronics Plus	6443 Elgin St.	555-2330	Electronics	☑	10am to 6pm
				☐	

5. After keying the Hours field entry, a message appears telling you the value you entered is not valid for the field. Click **OK** and delete the data in the Hours field.

6. Close Datasheet view and open the table in Design view.

7. Change the data type for the Hours field to **Text**.

8. Insert a new row above the Hours field and key a new field named **Checks** with the **Yes/No** data type, and **Does the store accept personal checks?** as the description.

9. Save the changes and switch to Datasheet view.

10. Click the check box (for yes) in the Checks field.

11. Key **10am to 6pm** in the Hours field.

12. Enter the records shown in Figure 1-20.

FIGURE 1-20

Name	Address	Phone	Specialty	Credit Cards	Checks	Hours
Music Master	2700 Canton	555-9820	Music - CDs	☑	☐	11am to 9pm
Rag Doll	2136 Quaker	555-4560	Ladies clothes	☑	☑	10am to 5pm
Vision Computers	6720 Data Drive	555-2300	Computers	☑	☑	10am to 8pm
Athletics Express	8904 Richmond	555-7811	Shoes	☑	☑	11am to 8pm
College Clothiers	3340 University	555-3570	Clothes	☐	☑	12pm to 6pm

name + project number

13. Change the left and right margins to .5 inches and print the table.

14. Close the table and database.

PROJECT 1-3

1. Open the **IA Project1-3** database.

2. Open the **Stores** table in Design view.

3. Delete the **Checks** field.

4. Change the data type for the Credit Cards field to **Text**.

5. Save the changes and switch to Datasheet view.

6. Change the left and right margins to .75" and print the table.

7. Close the table and database.

name + project number

under Lesson 2

PROJECT 1-4

SCANS

1. Create a new database named **Music**.

2. With the Music database open, create a new table named **The 80's** using the field names, data types, and descriptions shown in Figure 1-21.

FIGURE 1-21

Field Name	Data Type	Description
Name	Text	Musical artist's name
Title	Text	Title of CD
Year	Number	Year title was released

3. Save the table as **The 80's**. No primary key is necessary.

4. Switch to Datasheet view and enter the records shown in Figure 1-22.

FIGURE 1-22

Name	Title	Year
Dire Straits	Money for Nothing	1988
Mariah Carey	Music Box	1989
Van Morrison	Moondance	1981
Kenny G.	Silhouette	1987
Natalie Merchant	Blind Man's Zoo	1989
Billy Joel	Glass Houses	1980

5. Print the table.

6. Open **The 80's** table in Design view.

7. Change the data type for the Year field to **Text**.

8. Save the change.

9. Switch to Datasheet view and add the records as shown in Figure 1-23.

FIGURE 1-23

Name	Title	Year
Pretenders	The Isle Of View	1986
Jackson Browne	Looking East	1985
Genesis	Three Sides Live	1988

10. Print the table.

11. Close the table and database.

two print outs

name + project

CRITICAL *Thinking*

 ## ACTIVITY 1-1

 Select a type of collection or a personal interest and create a database to organize it. Give the database a name that accurately reflects the data.

Create and design a table for your data using the Table Wizard. Carefully consider the fields your database will need.

To start the Table Wizard, double-click **Create table by using wizard** in the Database window and follow the screens to create your table. In the first screen, choose the **Personal** category and one of the Sample tables. In the Sample Fields column, select the fields for your new table. When finished with the first screen, click the **Next** button. In the second screen, enter the name of your table and choose **No, I'll set the primary key**. When finished with the second screen, click **Finish**. The table will appear in Datasheet view. Enter at least two records in the table. Change the margins if necessary and print the table. Close the table and exit Access.

 ## ACTIVITY 1-2

When creating a database with many of the same types of fields, it is helpful to know how to copy the definition of a field. Use the Help feature and search for the steps to copy a field's definition within a table. Write down these basic steps.

MANIPULATING DATA

VOCABULARY

Field properties

Field selectors

Record pointer

Record selectors

Editing Records

To make editing records easier, Access provides navigation buttons on your screen. The navigation buttons are used to move around the datasheet. These buttons may not be necessary when working with databases as small as those you used in the previous lesson. As databases get larger, however, the navigation buttons become very useful. Figure 2-1 shows the locations of the navigation buttons.

FIGURE 2-1
Navigation buttons

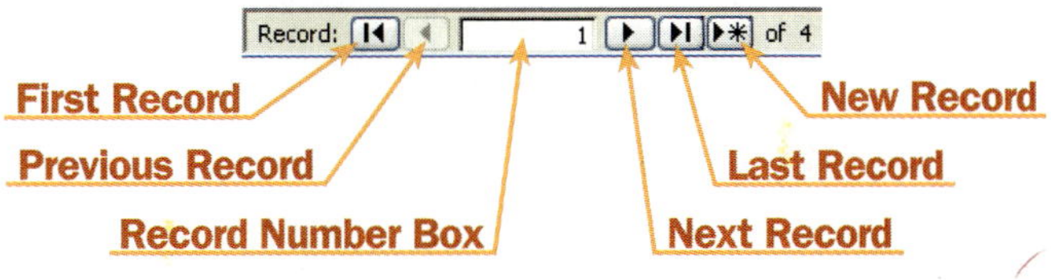

Record: [◄◄] [◄] [1] [►] [►►] [►*] of 4

First Record
Previous Record
Record Number Box
New Record
Last Record
Next Record

The First Record button is used to move quickly to the top of the table and the Last Record button is used to move to the bottom of the table. There are also buttons used to move to the next or previous record. To move to a specific record number, click the Record Number box and key the number of the record into the field. Press Tab to move to the specified record. To add a new record, click the New Record button.

An arrow to the left of the record indicates the current record. The computer keeps track of the current record using a *record pointer*. When you move among records in Datasheet view, you are actually moving the record pointer.

If you use the Tab key to move to a cell, Access highlights the contents of the cell. As in a spreadsheet, you can replace the contents of the cell by keying data while the existing data is highlighted. If you click a cell with the mouse, the insertion point appears in the cell, allowing you to edit the contents.

Undoing Changes to a Cell

There are three ways to undo changes to a cell. If you make a mistake keying data in a cell, you can open the Edit menu and choose Undo Typing or click the Undo Typing button on the toolbar. This reverses your last action. If you have already entered the data in a cell and moved to the next cell (or any cell), open the Edit menu and choose Undo Current Field/Record or click the Undo Current Field/Record button on the toolbar. You can also press the Esc key to restore the contents of the entire record.

STEP-BY-STEP 2.1

1. Start Microsoft Access and open **IA Step2-1** from the data files.

2. Open the **Calls** table in Datasheet view. The purpose of this table is to keep a log of telephone calls.

3. Click the **Last Record** button at the bottom of the table to move the record pointer to the last record.

4. Click the **First Record** button to move the record pointer to the first record.

5. Click the **Next Record** button to move the record pointer to the next record.

6. In the second record, the time is shown as 11:00 AM when it should be 10:30 AM. Press **Tab** until the Call Time field is highlighted.

7. Key **10:30** in the Call Time field and press **Tab**. (The field is formatted for AM.)

8. Move the mouse pointer to the Subject field in the third record. Click to place the pointer at the beginning of the field (where the pointer becomes a thick plus sign). The entire field will be highlighted.

9. Key **Computers** and press **Tab**.

10. Press **Esc**. The word *Computers* changes back to *Hardware*.

11. The entry in the Notes field of the third record is highlighted. Press **Delete**. The entry is deleted.

12. Click the **Undo** button on the toolbar. The Notes field entry reappears. Leave the table on the screen for the next Step-by-Step.

Selecting Records and Fields

You can quickly select records and fields by clicking the record or field selectors. *Field selectors* are at the top of a table and contain the field name. Figure 2-2 shows the Name field selected. *Record selectors* are located to the left of a record's first field. Clicking in the upper-left corner of the datasheet selects all records in the database.

You can select more than one field by clicking the field selector in one field, holding down the Shift key, and clicking the field selector in another field. The two fields, and all the fields in between, will be selected. You can use the same method to select multiple records. You can also select multiple fields or records by clicking and dragging across the field or record selectors.

FIGURE 2-2
Record and field selectors

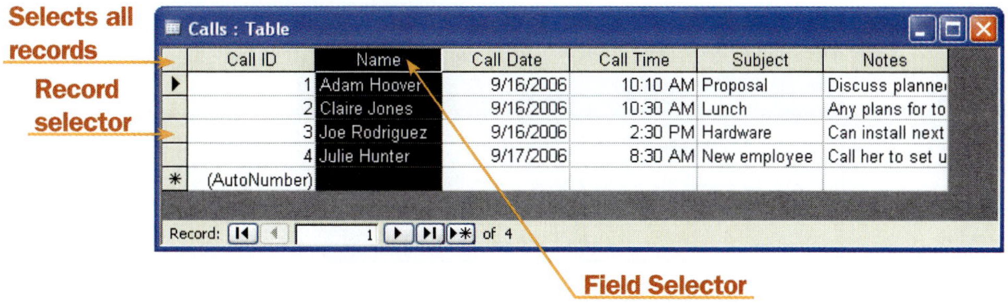

Selects all records

Record selector

Field Selector

STEP-BY-STEP 2.2

1. Click the **Name** field selector to select the entire column.

2. Click the **Subject** field selector to select the entire column.

3. Select the **Name** field again.

4. Hold down the **Shift** key and click the **Call Time** field selector. The Name, Call Date, and Call Time fields are selected, as shown in Figure 2-3.

5. Click the record selector of the **Claire Jones** record. The entire record is selected.

6. Select the **Julie Hunter** record. Leave the table on the screen for the next Step-by-Step.

FIGURE 2-3
Selecting multiple columns

Deleting Records

 To delete an entire record, select the record and open the Edit menu and choose Delete Record or press the Delete key. You can also click the Delete Record button on the toolbar. A message box appears, as shown in Figure 2-4, warning you that you are about to delete a record. Click Yes to permanently delete the record or No to cancel the deletion. After you've deleted a record using the Delete Record command, you cannot use the Undo command or Esc key to restore it.

You cannot delete fields in Datasheet view the same way you delete records. As you learned in Lesson 1, you can delete fields in Design view only.

FIGURE 2-4
Message warning that you are about to delete a record

S TEP-BY STEP 2.3

1. Click the **Previous Record** button to move to the Joe Rodriguez record.

2. Click the **Delete Record** button on the toolbar. A message appears, as shown in Figure 2-4, warning you that you are about to delete the record.

3. Click **Yes**. The record is deleted. Notice that the numbers in the Call ID field do not renumber when a record is deleted. The reason is that the number in the Call ID field is automatically assigned when the record is created and does not change. Leave the table on the screen for the next Step-by-Step.

Cutting, Copying, and Pasting Data

 The Cut, Copy, and Paste commands in Access work the same way as in other Office applications. You can use the commands to copy and move data within a table or between tables. To cut or copy an entire record, select the record and choose Cut or Copy on the Edit menu or click the Cut or Copy buttons on the toolbar.

Using Cut, Copy, and Paste can sometimes be tricky. You must be aware that data pasted in a table will overwrite the existing data. If you want to cut or copy an entire record and paste it into a table as a new record, open the Edit menu and choose Paste Append. You can also highlight the blank record at the bottom of a table, open the Edit menu and choose Paste, or click the Paste button on the toolbar. When you select a record and choose the Cut command, you will get the same message as when you use the Delete command. The difference is that with the Cut command, you can restore the record to the end of the table by using the Paste Append command.

STEP-BY-STEP 2.4

1. Select the **Adam Hoover** record.

2. Click the **Copy** button on the toolbar.

3. Click the **New Record** button. The new record appears at the bottom of the database. Click the **Paste** button on the toolbar to insert the information copied from Record 1.

4. Change the date and time of Record 4 to **September 17 at 5:00 PM**.

5. In the Notes field, delete the existing text and key **Proposal ready on Monday morning**.

6. Select the **Claire Jones** record.

7. Click the **Cut** button on the toolbar. The message saying that you are about to delete a record appears.

8. Click **Yes**.

9. Select the empty record at the end of the table.

10. Open the **Edit** menu and choose **Paste Append**. The Claire Jones record appears as shown in Figure 2-5. Leave the table on the screen for the next Step-by-Step.

> **Did You Know?**
>
> If you delete data or objects from a database, the database can become fragmented and use disk space inefficiently. Compacting rearranges how the database is stored on disk and optimizes the performance of the database. Access combines compacting and repairing into one process. Specify the database you want to compact and repair, open the **Tools** menu and choose **Database Utilities**, and then select **Compact and Repair Database**.

FIGURE 2-5
Using the Cut and Paste buttons to add a record

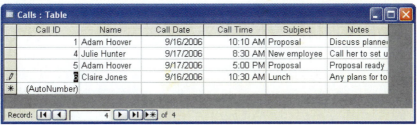

Changing Datasheet Layout

 You can make many changes to the datasheet layout, including changing row height and column width, rearranging columns, and freezing columns.

Changing Row Height

You can adjust the row height in a datasheet, but the adjustment affects all the rows. To change the height, position the pointer on the lower border of a row selector, and it will turn into a double arrow, as shown in Figure 2-6. Using the double arrow, click and drag the row border up or down to adjust the row height.

FIGURE 2-6
Adjusting the row height

You can also specify an exact row height. Open the Format menu and choose Row Height and the Row Height dialog box appears, as shown in Figure 2-7. Key a height in points (like font sizes) for the row.

FIGURE 2-7
Row Height dialog box

S TEP-BY-STEP 2.5

1. Position the mouse pointer on the lower border of the record selector for **Claire Jones**. You will know you have the pointer correctly positioned when it changes to a double arrow.

2. Drag the row border down slightly to increase the height of the row. When you release the mouse button, all rows are affected by the change.

3. Select the **Julie Hunter** record.

4. Open the **Format** menu and choose **Row Height**. The Row Height dialog box, shown in Figure 2-7, appears.

5. Key **30** in the Row Height box and click **OK**. The row height increases to a height that allows the data in the Subject and Notes field to be read more easily. Leave the table on the screen for the next Step-by-Step.

> **Hot Tip** 🎯
>
> Instead of opening the **Format** menu and choosing **Row Height**, you can right-click the record selector and select **Row Height** on the shortcut menu that appears.

Changing Column Width

 Often, the column widths provided by default are too wide or too narrow for the data in the table. Adjusting column width is similar to adjusting row height. To adjust the column width, place the mouse pointer in the field selector on the border of the column. The pointer changes to a double arrow. Click and drag to the width you want. Unlike rows, which must all have the same height, each field can have a different width.

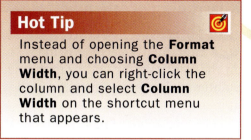

Hot Tip

Instead of opening the **Format** menu and choosing **Column Width**, you can right-click the column and select **Column Width** on the shortcut menu that appears.

When you open the Format menu and choose Column Width, the Column Width dialog box appears, as shown in Figure 2-8. You can key a specific width or click the Best Fit button. The Best Fit button automatically selects the best width for the data in the column. Another way to choose the "best fit" is to place the mouse pointer on the field border and double-click when it turns into a double arrow.

FIGURE 2-8
Column Width dialog box

STEP-BY-STEP 2.6

1. Position the pointer on the right border of the **Notes** field selector.

2. Drag to make the column wide enough to allow all the information to fit in the field.

3. Select the **Call ID** field.

4. Open the **Format** menu and choose **Column Width**. The Column Width dialog box appears, as shown in Figure 2-8.

5. Click **Best Fit**. The column narrows.

6. Use the Best Fit option to adjust the width of the **Call Date** field.

7. Select the **Call Time** field.

8. Open the **Format** menu and choose **Column Width**. The Column Width dialog box appears.

9. Key **16** into the Column Width box and click **OK**.

10. Change the width of the **Subject** field to **25**.

11. Print the table in landscape orientation. Leave the table on the screen for the next Step-by-Step.

Rearranging Columns

In Datasheet view, Access allows you to rearrange fields by dragging them to a new location. First, select the field you want to move. Then, click and hold down the mouse button on the field selector and drag the field to the new location. A vertical bar follows your mouse pointer to show you where the field will be inserted. Release the mouse button to insert the field in its new location.

STEP-BY-STEP 2.7

1. Select the **Call Date** field.

2. Click and drag the **Call Date** field to the left until the vertical bar appears between the Call ID and Name fields. Release the mouse button. The Call Date column appears between the Call ID and Name columns, as shown in Figure 2-9. Leave the table on your screen for the next Step-by-Step.

FIGURE 2-9
Rearranging fields

Call ID	Call Date	Name	Call Time	Subject	Notes
1	9/16/2006	Adam Hoover	10:10 AM	Proposal	Discuss planned budget
4	9/17/2006	Julie Hunter	8:30 AM	New employee	Call her to set up 3 interviews
5	9/17/2006	Adam Hoover	5:00 PM	Proposal	Proposal ready on Monday morning
6	9/16/2006	Claire Jones	10:30 AM	Lunch	Any plans for today?
*	(AutoNumber)				

Record: |◄ ◄ 1 ► ►| ►* of 4

Freezing Columns

If a table has many columns, it may be helpful to freeze one or more columns, allowing them to remain on the screen while you scroll to columns that are not currently visible.

To freeze columns, select the column or columns you want to freeze, and then open the Format menu and choose Freeze Columns. To unfreeze columns, open the Format menu and choose Unfreeze All Columns.

STEP-BY-STEP 2.8

1. Select the **Call ID** field.

2. While holding down the **Shift** key, click the **Name** field. The Call ID, Call Date, and Name fields are all highlighted.

3. Open the **Format** menu and choose **Freeze Columns**.

STEP-BY-STEP 2.8 Continued

4. Click the horizontal scroll arrow at the bottom right of the table window to scroll to the Notes field. Notice that the frozen fields remain on the screen. (Note: If you do not have a horizontal scroll arrow, your screen is large enough to include all of the columns. Continue to Step 5.)

5. Open the **Format** menu and choose **Unfreeze All Columns**.

6. Open the **File** menu and choose **Close**. You will be asked if you want to save changes to the layout of the table.

7. Click **Yes**. The Database window is visible on the screen. Leave the database open for the next Step-by-Step.

Changing Field Properties

When you defined fields for a table in Lesson 1, you specified only the field name, data type, and description. Now that you have created and used fields in a variety of situations, it is time to learn about field properties. *Field properties* allow you to further customize a field beyond merely choosing a data type.

You can view and change field properties in a table or form's Design view. Figure 2-10 shows the field properties available for a Text data type; you will learn about the most common ones. The field properties available will vary depending on the field's selected data type.

FIGURE 2-10
Field properties in Design view

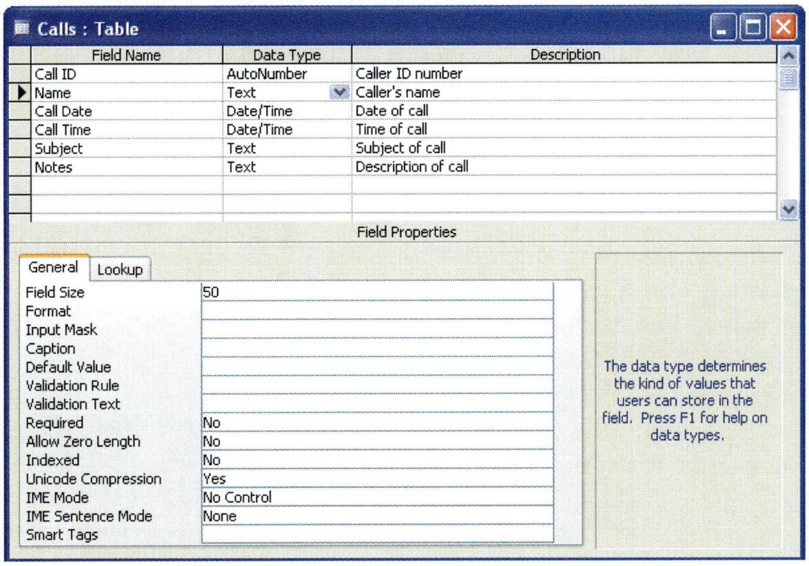

Field Size

One of the most common field properties is Field Size. In fields of Text type, the Field Size is merely the number of characters allowed in the field. You can specify that the field allow up to 255 characters. The default size is 50.

In fields of Number type, the Field Size allows you to specify the internal data type that Access will use to store the number. The available options are Byte, Integer, Long Integer, Single, Double, Replication ID, and Decimal. If you have computer programming experience, the available field sizes may be familiar to you. If the options mean nothing to you, don't worry. There

is an easy way to select the appropriate field size. If your field is to store whole numbers only, use the Long Integer field size. If your field will store fractional numbers with decimal places, choose the Double field size.

Format

Use the Format field property to specify how you want Access to display numbers, dates, times, and text. For example, the default format for dates is *10/28/2006*. Using the Format property, you can change the format to *28-Oct-06* or *Tuesday, October 28, 2006*. You can also include the time with the date such as *10/28/2006 11:54:30 AM*.

Input Mask

An input mask allows you to control the data pattern or format allowed in the field. You can also specify characters that will be put into the field automatically. For example, you can specify that a phone number be formatted with area code in parentheses, and the rest of the number split by a hyphen. When you key records, you won't have to key the parentheses or the hyphen; Access will insert them for you automatically. You can use the Input Mask Wizard to set the field's pattern or format.

Caption

The text you provide in the caption field property will be used *instead* of field names in forms, tables in Datasheet view, reports, and queries. For example, if the field name is *EmailName*, you could enter *E-mail address* in the caption field property. When you create a form that includes the field, the more descriptive name will appear as the field name.

Default Value

Another useful field property is Default Value. Use this field property when you have a field that usually contains the same value. For example, if most of the people in a database of names and addresses live in California, you can enter CA as the Default Value of the State field. The State field will automatically contain CA, unless you change it to another state.

Required

The Required field property specifies whether you must enter a value in the field. For example, in an employee database, you might specify that each field requires a telephone number. If you try to enter a record without including a telephone number, Access will alert you that you must enter one.

Decimal Places

Number and Currency fields have a field property called Decimal Places. This property usually adjusts automatically depending on the data in the field. You can specify a number of decimal places here to override the automatic setting.

STEP-BY-STEP 2.9

1. Open the **Calls** table in Design view.

2. Select the **Name** field.

3. Under the *Field Properties* section beside Field Size, double-click **50** to highlight it. Key **40**.

4. In the *Caption* box, key **Caller's Name**.

5. Click in the **Required** field property box. A down arrow will appear at the right end of the box.

6. Click the down arrow and choose **Yes** from the menu.

7. Select the **Call Date** field.

8. Click in the **Format** field property box. A down arrow appears.

9. Click the down arrow. A menu of date and time formats appears.

10. Choose **Medium Date**.

11. Click in the **Input Mask** field property box. Three periods appear on the right side of the box.

12. Click the three periods. The Input Mask Wizard screen appears with a list of date and time formats. (If a message box opens asking if you would like to install the Input Mask Wizard, click **Yes**. If another message box opens stating that the table must be saved, click **Yes**. A message may appear stating that some data may be lost because you changed the setting for a field size to a shorter size. Click **Yes** to continue. Another message may appear asking if you want the existing data tested with the new rules. Click **Yes**.)

13. Choose **Medium Date** on the Input Mask Wizard screen. (You may need to scroll down to choose Medium Date.) Click **Next**.

14. A second Input Mask Wizard screen appears asking if you want to change the input mask. Click **Finish**.

15. Choose **Yes** in the Required field property.

16. Select the **Notes** field.

17. Change the Field Size to **100**.

STEP-BY-STEP 2.9 Continued

18. Save the table design. A message may appear stating that some data may be lost because you changed the setting for a field size to a shorter size. Click **Yes** to continue. Another message may appear asking if you want the existing data tested with the new rules. Click **Yes**.

19. Switch to Datasheet view to see the format changes to the Call Date field. Click in the **Call Date** field in the blank record at the bottom of the table to see the input mask you added. The Name field now contains the caption you entered. The other changes aren't visible.

20. Adjust the row height, if necessary, so you can see all the record data in each field. Print the table in landscape orientation.

21. Save and close the table and then close the database by clicking the **Close** button in the Database window.

SUMMARY

In this lesson, you learned:

■ The navigation buttons are used to move around the datasheet. They allow you to move to the first record, the last record, the previous record, or the next record. You can also use a navigation button to add a new record.

■ There are three ways to undo changes to cells. If you make mistakes while keying data in a cell, you can click the Undo button. If you have already entered data and moved to the next cell, press Esc. To reverse all the changes to the previous record, open the Edit menu and choose Undo Saved Record.

■ To delete a record, use the Delete Record command. Entire records and fields can be selected by clicking the record and field selectors. Cut, Copy, and Paste are available in Datasheet view to move and copy data. The Paste Append command pastes a record at the end of the database.

■ You can make many changes to a datasheet. You can change the row height and column width. You can also rearrange and freeze columns.

■ Field properties allow you to further customize a field beyond merely choosing a data type. Some of the more common field properties are Field Size, Input Mask, Caption, Default Value, Format, Required, and Decimal Places.

VOCABULARY *Review*

Define the following terms:

Field properties	Record pointer	Record selectors
Field selectors		

REVIEW *Questions*

TRUE/FALSE

Circle T if the statement is true or F if the statement is false.

T   F   **1.** If you click a cell with the mouse, the insertion point appears in the cell.

T   F   **2.** Holding down the Alt key allows you to select more than one field.

T   F   **3.** In Access, you can use the Cut, Copy, and Paste commands.

T   F   **4.** Changing the height of one row changes the height of all datasheet rows.

T   F   **5.** You can delete records and fields in Datasheet view.

WRITTEN QUESTIONS

Write a brief answer to the following questions.

1. What is the record pointer?

2. How do you delete a record in Datasheet view?

3. What does the Paste Append command do?

4. Why would you want to freeze columns in Datasheet view?

5. In what view do you change field properties?

PROJECTS

PROJECT 2-1

1. Open the **IA Project2-1** database from the data files.

2. Open the **Employee Information** table in Datasheet view.

3. Go to record 7 and change the address to **4582 104th St.**

4. Go to record 11 and change the birth date to **12/14/1961.**

5. Go to record 14 and change the first name to **Alex.**

6. Go to record 1 and change the last name to **Abraham.**

7. Undo your last change.

8. Delete record 5.

9. Change the width of the Address field to **20** and the Zip Code field to **13.**

10. Change all other field widths using **Best Fit.**

11. Change the row height to 15.

12. Change the left and right margins to **.5 inches** and print the table in landscape orientation.

13. Close the table. Click **Yes** if prompted to save changes to the layout of the table. Close the database.

PROJECT 2-2

1. Open the **IA Project2-2** database.

2. Open the **Employee Information** table in Datasheet view.

3. Copy record **4** and paste it at the bottom of the table.

4. In the pasted record, change the First Name to **Mike**, the SS Number to **343-26-9432**, the Title to **Account Executive**, the Birthdate to **9/28/61**, and the Salary to **2950.**

5. Move the **Birthdate** field to between the Zip Code and Department fields.

6. Freeze the **Employee Number, Last Name,** and **First Name** fields.

7. Scroll to the right until the **Birthdate** field is beside the **First Name** field.

8. Change the birthdate of Hillary Davis to **10/28/68.**

9. Unfreeze the columns.

10. Change the left and right margins to **.5 inches** and print the table in landscape orientation.

11. Close the table. Click **Yes** if prompted to save changes to the layout of the table. Close the database.

name & project no.

PROJECT 2-3

1. Open the **IA Project2-3** database.

2. Open the **Employee Information** table in Design view.

3. Format the **Salary** field for Currency.

4. Select **Medium Date** from the Format field properties for the **Birthdate** field .

5. Select **Medium Date** from the Input Mask formats for the **Birthdate** field. If a message appears stating that the table must be saved, click **Yes**.

6. Key **Employee Number** as the Caption field property for the **Emp Number** field.

7. Make the **Zip Code** field **Required**.

8. Change the field size of the **Zip Code** field to **10**.

9. Save the table design. A message may appear asking if you want to continue. Click **Yes**. Another message may appear asking if you want the existing data tested with the new rules. Click **Yes**.

10. Switch to Datasheet view and insert the following records at the end of the table.

   16 Wells Wendy 404-76-5234 2610 21st St 79832-2610 15-Feb-72 Sales Executive Assistant **$2,150.00**

   17 Abbott Donna 372-98-2036 1824 Saratoga 79833-1900 12-Jan-59 Human Resources Manager **$2,880.00**

11. Widen the **Salary** column and any other fields to show all data and column titles.

12. Change the left and right margins to **.3 inches** and print the table in landscape orientation.

13. Close the table. Click **Yes** if prompted to save changes to the layout of the table. Close the database.

name & project no

Careers

For information on careers, access the Occupational Outlook Handbook at *www.bls.gov/oco*. Web sites and addresses change constantly. If you can't find the information at this site, try another.

CRITICAL *Thinking*

SCANS ACTIVITY 2-1

Open the database you created for the Critical Thinking Activity in Lesson 1. Add two new records using the New Record button. Select a field and make a change to the data. Delete an entire record. Copy one record and paste it into the table as a new record. If necessary, increase the column width and row height to see all the data. Rearrange the columns. Print and close the table.

SCANS ACTIVITY 2-2

You can use the Office Clipboard to collect and paste multiple items from the various Office programs. The Office Clipboard automatically copies multiple items when you do any of the following:

1. Copy or cut two different items in succession in the same program.

2. Copy one item, paste the item, and then copy another item in the same program.

3. Copy one item twice in succession.

   Using the Help system, find the steps to collect and paste multiple items. Briefly write the steps in numbered order.

CREATING AND MODIFYING FORMS

Creating Forms

Datasheet view is useful for many of the ways you work with a database table. Often, however, you may want a more convenient way to enter and view records. For example, the form shown in Figure 3-1 places all of the important fields from the Calls table into a convenient and attractive layout.

Forms can be created in Design view by placing fields on a blank form, arranging and sizing fields, and adding graphics. The Form Wizard makes the process easier by asking you detailed questions about the fields, layout, and format and then creates a form based on your answers. Creating a form in Design view gives you more flexibility, but the Form Wizard can create the form you need quickly and efficiently. You can also use the AutoForm feature, which automatically creates a form that displays all the fields and records of the database table.

FIGURE 3-1
Forms can make entering and editing data easier

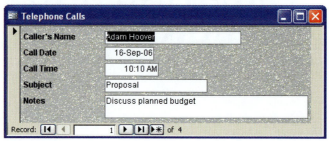

Using the Form Wizard

To create a form, click the Forms button on the Objects bar. Click the New button and the New Form dialog box appears, as shown in Figure 3-2. The New Form dialog box gives you several options for creating a form. In the next Step-by-Step, you will use the Form Wizard option. The New Form dialog box also asks you to specify the table or query to use as a basis for the form. In more complex databases, you may have to choose among several tables or queries.

FIGURE 3-2
New Form dialog box

You can also create a form using the Form Wizard by double-clicking *Create form by using wizard* in the Database window.

S TEP-BY-STEP 3.1

1. Open the **IA Step 3-1** database from the data files. Click the **Forms** button on the Objects bar.

2. Click **New**. The New Form dialog box appears, as shown in Figure 3-2.

3. Choose the **Form Wizard** option and the **Calls** table from the drop-down list.

4. Click **OK**. The Form Wizard dialog box appears, as shown in Figure 3-3. Leave the Form Wizard dialog box on the screen for the next Step-by-Step.

FIGURE 3-3
Form Wizard dialog box

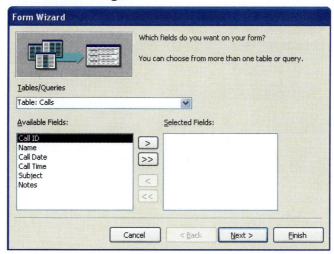

The next step is to choose the fields you want to appear on the form. To add a field to the form, click the field name in the *Available Fields* list and click the > button. To add all of the fields at once, click the >> button. If you plan to include almost all of the fields, click >> to include them all, then use the < button to remove the ones you do not want.

STEP-BY-STEP 3.2

1. Click **>>**. All of the field names appear in the *Selected Fields* list.

2. Select the **Call ID** field in the *Selected Fields* list.

3. Click **<**. The **Call ID** field is moved back to the *Available Fields* list.

4. Click the **Next** button. The Form Wizard dialog box changes to ask you to select a layout for the form, as shown in Figure 3-4.

STEP-BY-STEP 3.2 Continued

FIGURE 3-4
Selecting a layout for a form

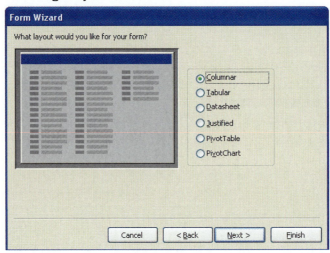

5. Leave the dialog box open for the next Step-by-Step.

You have a choice of six different layouts for the form: Columnar, Tabular, Datasheet, Justified, PivotTable, and PivotChart. The Columnar layout is the most common type. The form in Figure 3-1 is an example of a Columnar layout. As data is entered, the insertion point moves down the fields.

The Tabular layout creates forms that look similar to a table in Datasheet view. The Tabular layout gives you the ability to make a more attractive Datasheet view. Figure 3-5 is an example of a form created using a tabular layout.

FIGURE 3-5
Tabular form layout

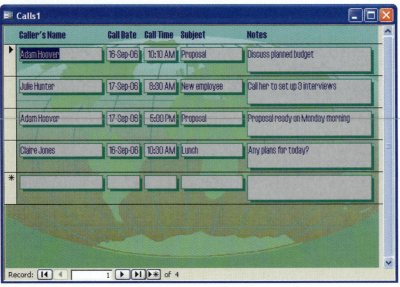

STEP-BY-STEP 3.3

1. If not already selected, click the **Columnar** option.

2. Click **Next.** This dialog box asks you to choose a style, as shown in Figure 3-6.

FIGURE 3-6
Choosing a style for a form

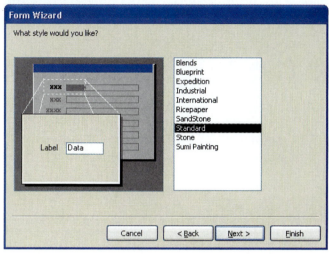

3. Leave the dialog box open for the next Step-by-Step.

The style you select has no effect on the function of the form. Choosing a style allows you to personalize your form or give it flair. There are several styles from which to choose.

After you choose a style, you will be asked to name the form. The name you provide will appear in the Form section of the Database window. You are also given the option to begin using the form once it is created or to modify the form after the Form Wizard is complete.

STEP-BY-STEP 3.4

1. If not already selected, choose the **Standard** style from the list. The preview box shows you what this form style looks like. It should look similar to Figure 3-6.

2. Click the other styles to see what they look like.

STEP-BY-STEP 3.4 Continued

3. Choose the **SandStone** style and click **Next**. The final Form Wizard dialog box appears, as shown in Figure 3-7.

FIGURE 3-7
Naming the form

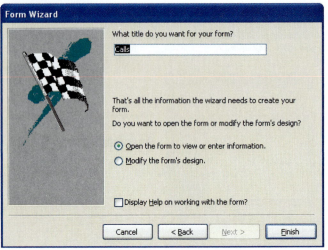

4. Key **Telephone Calls** into the title box.

5. Click the **Open the form to view or enter information** button if it's not chosen already.

6. Click **Finish**. Access creates the form, which should look like that shown in Figure 3-8.

FIGURE 3-8
A custom form

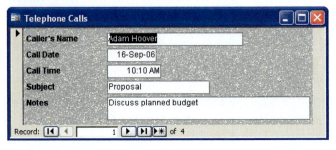

7. Open the **File** menu and choose **Close** to close the form. Leave the database open for the next Step-by-Step.

Using the AutoForm Feature

The AutoForm feature automatically creates a form that displays all the fields and records of the database table. This is the quickest way to create a simple form because no detailed questions are asked about the fields, layout, or format.

To create a form using AutoForm, click the Forms button on the Objects Bar. Click the New button and the New Form dialog box appears, as shown in Figure 3-9. Choose one of the five AutoForm options listed that describe the name of the layout you want for the form. Specify the table or query to use as a basis for the form. The form is automatically created and displayed in the selected layout.

FIGURE 3-9
New Form dialog box

S TEP-BY-STEP 3.5

1. If not already selected, click **Forms** on the Objects bar.

2. Click **New**. The New Form dialog box appears, as shown in Figure 3-9.

3. Choose the **AutoForm: Columnar** option and the **Calls** table from the drop-down list.

4. Click **OK**. AutoForm creates the form with the columnar layout, as shown in Figure 3-10.

FIGURE 3-10
Form created with the AutoForm feature

5. Open the **File** menu and choose **Close**. A message will appear asking if you want to save changes to the form.

6. Click **Yes**. The Save As dialog box appears.

7. Key **Calls AutoForm** into the **Form Name** box.

8. Click **OK**. Leave the database open for the next Step-by-Step.

Using Forms

Using a form is basically the same as using Datasheet view. The same keys move the insertion point among the fields. You see the same set of navigation buttons at the bottom of the form, as shown in Figure 3-11. As with Datasheet view, you can move to a specific record by clicking in the Record Number box and entering the number of the record you want to see.

FIGURE 3-11
Navigation controls at the bottom of the form

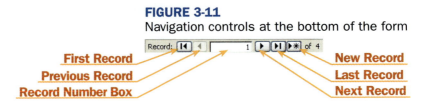

First Record
Previous Record
Record Number Box

New Record
Last Record
Next Record

Table 3-1 summarizes the ways to move around when a form is displayed, including keyboard shortcuts.

TABLE 3-1
Navigating a form

TO MOVE TO THE...	BUTTON	KEYBOARD SHORTCUT
First record	First Record button	Ctrl+Home
Last record	Last Record button	Ctrl+End
Next record	Next Record button	Page Down
Previous record	Previous Record button	Page Up

To add a new record, click the Next Record button until the blank record at the end of the database appears, or click the New Record button. Key the new record. To edit an existing record, display the record and make changes in the fields of the form.

After entering or editing records in a form, you do not need to save the changes. Access saves them for you automatically. Remember to always save changes to the form design in Design view.

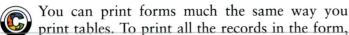

You can print forms much the same way you print tables. To print all the records in the form, open the File menu and choose Print. The Print dialog box appears. In the Print dialog box, choose All from the Print Range options if you want to print all the records. Access will fit as many forms on each page as possible. To print only one record, display the record on the screen. Open the File menu and choose Print. Click the Selected Record(s) option from the Print Range options.

> ### Hot Tip
> You can preview a form the same way you preview a table in datasheet view. To preview a form, open the **File** menu and choose **Print Preview** or click the **Print Preview** button on the toolbar. If necessary, click the magnifying glass with a plus (+) sign to enlarge the form.

STEP-BY-STEP 3.6

1. Open the **Telephone Calls** form.

2. Click the **New Record** button. A blank record appears in the form.

3. Enter the following information in the form:

   Caller's Name: **Excel Travel Agency**

   Call Date: **18-Sep-06**

   Call Time: **10:21 AM**

   Subject **Seattle trip**

   Notes **Flight 412 Departs 7:40 AM/Arrives 1:30 PM**

4. Click in the record number box. Delete the **5**, key **4**, and press **Enter**.

5. Highlight the word **today** in the Notes field.

6. Key **Friday**.

7. Display record **5**, then open the **File** menu and choose **Print**. The Print dialog box appears.

8. Click the **Selected Record(s)** option from the **Print Range** options, and click **OK**. (The printed form may cut off the data in some of the fields.)

9. Open the **File** menu and choose **Close** to close the form. Leave the database open for the next Step-by-Step.

Modifying Forms

 Any form, whether created manually or with a Form Wizard, can be modified. You make changes to a form in Design view, which shows the structure of the form. To access Design view, select the form in the Database window, and then click the Design button. The form appears in Design view, as shown in Figure 3-12.

FIGURE 3-12
Design view

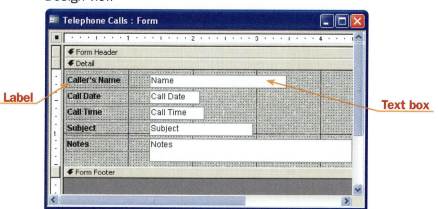

The form is divided into three sections: Form Header, Detail, and Form Footer. The *Form Header* section displays information that remains the same for every record, such as the title for a form. A Form Header appears at the top of the screen in Form view and at the top of the first page of the forms when printed. The *Detail* section displays records. You can display one record on the screen or as many as possible. A *Form Footer* section displays information that remains the same for every record, such as instructions for using the form. A form footer appears at the bottom of the screen in Form view or after the last Detail section on the last page of the forms when printed.

The Toolbox, shown in Figure 3-13, which appears when you switch to Design view, has controls that you can use to modify and enhance the sections and objects on a form. The Label and Text Box tools are labeled in Figure 3-13 because they are used frequently. To determine the other controls available, you can hold your mouse over each of the icons on the Toolbox to view the ScreenTip. There are three types of controls: bound, unbound, and calculated. A *bound control* is connected to a field in a table and is used to display, enter, and update data. An *unbound control* is not connected to a field and is used to display information, lines, rectangles, and pictures. The Label control, which is an unbound control, allows you to add text as a title or instructions to a form. Look again at Figure 3-12. Notice that the field name is contained in a Label control, and the field entry is contained in the Text Box control. A Text Box control is tied to, or bound to, a field in the underlying table, whereas the Label control is not.

FIGURE 3-13
Toolbox

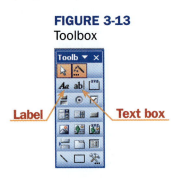

Label   Text box

In Design view, you can change the font, size, style, and other attributes of labels and text box data. Simply select the control, and use the buttons on the Formatting toolbar. Or, you can double-click a control to open its Properties dialog box and modify the attributes and other properties listed on the various tabs.

S TEP-BY-STEP 3.7

1. If not already selected, click **Forms** on the Objects bar. Choose the **Telephone Calls** form, and click the **Design** button. The form appears in Design view, as shown in Figure 3-12. If necessary, position the pointer on the bottom edge of the form until a double arrow appears. Click and drag down to enlarge the form past the Form Footer section, as shown in Figure 3-12.

2. If necessary, display the Toolbox by clicking the **Toolbox** button. Click the **Line** button in the Toolbox.

3. Position the pointer in the *Detail* section between the Caller's Name label and the data field and click to place a line as shown in Figure 3-14.

STEP-BY-STEP 3.7 Continued

FIGURE 3-14
Inserting a line

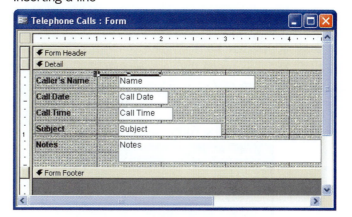

4. Position the pointer at the right end of the line until a double arrow appears. Click and drag the right end of the line to the bottom of the form until it is vertical between the field labels and data fields as shown in Figure 3-15.

FIGURE 3-15
Repositioning the line object

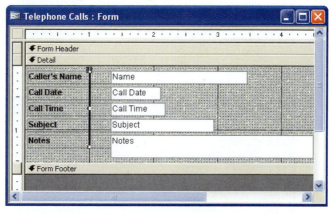

5. In the *Detail* section, double-click on the **Caller's Name** label. The Label properties window opens, as shown in Figure 3-16. If necessary, select the **All** tab.

FIGURE 3-16
The Label screen

STEP-BY-STEP 3.7 Continued

6. Change the caption to **Name** and close the Properties window.

7. Double-click on the **Call Date** label and change the caption to **Date**. Double-click on the **Call Time** label and change the caption to **Time**.

8. Position the pointer on the line between the *Form Header* section and *Detail* section until a double arrow appears as shown in Figure 3-17.

FIGURE 3-17
Resizing the Form Header

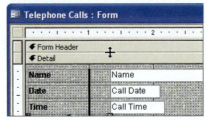

9. Click and drag the line down about a half-inch to increase the height of the *Form Header* section.

10. Click the **Label** button in the Toolbox.

11. Position the pointer in the *Form Header* section and click and drag to draw a text box as shown in Figure 3-18.

FIGURE 3-18
Inserting a text box

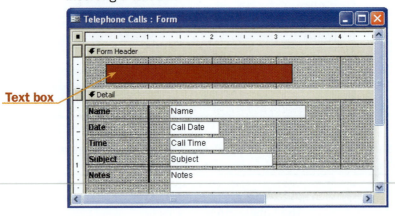

12. Key **TELEPHONE CALLS** at the insertion point that appears in the text box.

13. Click outside the text box to view the title. Double-click on the text box to display the Label properties dialog box.

14. Scroll through the list of properties until you locate the Font Name and Font Size properties. Click in the **Font Name** text box, click the down arrow, and select **Arial Black**. Click in the **Font Size** box, click the down arrow, and change the size to **12**. Close the dialog box.

STEP-BY-STEP 3.7 Continued

15. Position the pointer on the line at the bottom of the *Detail* section until a double arrow appears as shown in Figure 3-19. You may need to scroll down to view the bottom of the Detail section.

FIGURE 3-19
Resizing the Detail section

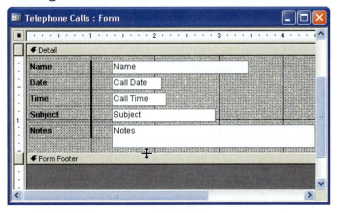

16. Click and drag down about a quarter-inch to increase the height of the *Detail* section.

17. Click the **Check Box** button in the Toolbox.

18. Position the pointer in the *Detail* section and click to place a check box as shown in Figure 3-20. Your text box to the right of the check mark will contain a different number from the one showing in the figure.

FIGURE 3-20
Detail section with check box

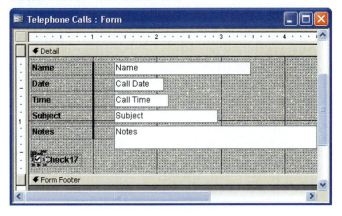

19. Double-click the text box to the right of the check mark. The Label properties dialog box appears.

20. Change the caption to **Return Call** and close the dialog box.

21. Click on the right border of the text box and drag to see the entire caption.

22. Position the pointer on the line at the bottom of the *Form Footer* section until a double arrow appears. You may need to scroll down to view the *Form Footer* section.

STEP-BY-STEP 3.7 Continued

23. Click and drag the line down about a half-inch to increase the height of the *Form Footer* section.

24. Click the **Label** button in the Toolbox.

25. Position the pointer in the *Form Footer* section below the Return Call check box. Click and drag to draw a text box about 3 inches wide.

26. At the insertion point in the text box, key **If possible, include the Caller's phone number in the Notes box.**

27. Open the **File** menu and choose **Close**. A message appears asking if you want to save changes. Click **Yes**. You are returned to the Database window.

28. With the name of the form highlighted, click **Open**. The modified form appears on the screen.

29. If necessary, click the **Next Record** button at the bottom of the form to see all of the records. Go back to **Record 1**, open the **File** menu and select **Print**, make sure the **Selected Record(s)** option is selected, and click **OK**. Close the form and the database.

> **Hot Tip**
>
> To delete a line or other object on a form, make sure you are in Design view, click on the line or object to select it, and press the **Delete** key or open the **Edit** menu and choose **Delete**.

Working with Calculated Controls

A *calculated control* on a form uses an expression to generate the data value for a field. For example, on an Orders form you might use the expression Unit Cost multiplied by Units Ordered or =*Unit Cost*Units Ordered*, to determine the value in the Total Cost field.

To create a calculated control on a form, open the Properties dialog box for the text box that will contain the calculation. The Properties dialog box will look like that shown in Figure 3-21. In the Control Source text box, key the expression for calculating the field value. You can also key a name for the calculated field in the Name text box, and determine the numerical format in the Format text box. When the form is opened, the value for the calculated field is calculated for each record.

FIGURE 3-21
Text Box properties dialog box

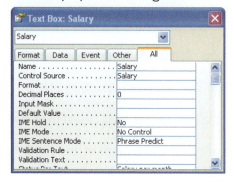

STEP-BY-STEP 3.8

1. Open the **IA Step3-8** database from the data files.

2. Click **Forms** on the Objects bar. Choose the **Employee Bonus** form and click the **Design** button. The form appears in Design view, as shown in Figure 3-22.

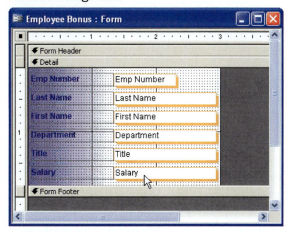

FIGURE 3-22
Form in Design view

3. Position the pointer on the **Salary** text box as shown in Figure 3-22. Double-click to display the Text Box: Salary properties dialog box, as shown in Figure 3-21. If not already selected, choose the **All** tab.

4. Key **Bonus** into the *Name* box.

5. Key **=[Salary]*.10** into the *Control Source* box. The bonus field will be 10% of the employee's salary.

6. Click in the **Format** text box, click the down arrow, and choose **Currency**.

7. Close the Properties dialog box. Double-click on the **Salary** label box, which is to the left of the text box. The Label properties dialog box displays, as shown in Figure 3-23.

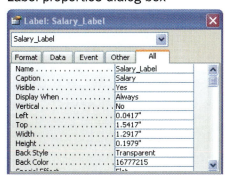

FIGURE 3-23
Label properties dialog box

STEP-BY-STEP 3.8 Continued

8. Change the **Caption** field to **Bonus** and close the dialog box. Switch to **Form** view by clicking the **View** button (on the Formatting toolbar).

9. If necessary, click the **Next Record** button at the bottom of the form to see all the records. Print the form for **Record 2**. Close the form, save your changes, and leave the database open for the next Step-by-Step.

Working with Hyperlinks

As you learned in Lesson 1, you can define a field in a database table as a hyperlink data type. This type of field actually stores the path to another database object, specified file, or address of a Web site.

You can also insert a hyperlink in a form (or report or page objects in a database) that links you to another object in the database, another file, or a Web site. For example, you might have a form in a company database that you use to enter information regarding employees, such as their addresses, start dates, department, responsibilities, and so forth. You also maintain an Excel spreadsheet that tracks employees' salaries, bonuses, benefits, and so forth. You could insert a hyperlink in the database form that, when clicked, immediately links you to the spreadsheet. The hyperlink provides you with an easy way to gain quick access to more information.

To insert a hyperlink, you must be in the form's Design view. Make sure the pointer is in the section of the form in which you want the hyperlink to appear, and then click the Insert Hyperlink button. In the Insert Hyperlink dialog box, select the file or Web page you want to link to, and then click OK.

Compacting and Repairing a Database

If you delete data or objects from a database, the database can become fragmented and use disk space inefficiently. Compacting rearranges how the database is stored on disk and optimizes the performance of the database. Access combines compacting and repairing into one process.

STEP-BY-STEP 3.9

1. Be sure no one else has the IA Step3-8 database open before continuing.

2. Open the **Tools** menu and choose **Database Utilities**.

3. Click **Compact and Repair Database**.

4. When finished, close the table and database.

> **Hot Tip**
>
> Follow the steps in Step-by-Step 3.9 to compact and repair a database that is not open. Dialog boxes will display asking you to specify the database to compact and the new file name for the compacted database. If you use the same name, the original file will be replaced with the new compacted file.

SUMMARY

In this lesson, you learned:

■ Forms can be created in Design view by placing fields on a blank form, arranging and sizing fields, and adding graphics. The Form Wizard makes the process of creating a form easier by asking you detailed questions about the fields, layout, and format and then creates a form based on your answers. You can also use the AutoForm feature that automatically creates a form displaying all of the fields and records of the database table.

■ Any form, whether created manually or with a Form Wizard, can be modified. You make changes to a form using Design view, which shows the structure of the form.

■ The form in Design view is divided into three sections: form header, detail, and form footer. The Form Header section displays information that remains the same for every record, such as the title for a form. A form header appears at the top of the screen in Form view and at the top of the first page of records when printed. The Detail section displays records. You can display one record on the screen or as many as possible. A Form Footer section displays information that remains the same for every record, such as instructions for using the form. A form footer appears at the bottom of the screen in Form view or after the last Detail section on the last page of records when printed.

■ The Toolbox has controls that you can use to modify and enhance the sections within a form. There are three types of controls: bound, unbound, and calculated. A bound control is connected to a field in a table and is used to display, enter, and update data. An unbound control is not connected to a field. A calculated control on a form uses an expression to calculate the data value for a field.

■ If you delete data or objects from a database, the database can become fragmented and use disk space inefficiently. Compacting the database rearranges how the database is stored on disk and optimizes the performance of the database.

VOCABULARY *Review*

Define the following terms:

Bound control	Detail	Form footer
Calculated control	Form header	Unbound control

REVIEW *Questions*

TRUE/FALSE

Circle T if the statement is true or F if the statement is false.

T   F   1. The style you select for a form has an effect on the function of the form.

T   F   2. The Toolbox has tools that you can use to modify forms.

T   F   3. You make modifications to a form in Datasheet view.

T   F   4. If you delete data or objects from a database, the database can become fragmented and use disk space inefficiently.

T   F   5. The AutoForm feature is the quickest way to create a simple form as no detailed questions are asked about the fields, layout, and format.

WRITTEN QUESTIONS

Write a brief answer to the following questions.

1. What are the six different layouts for a form?

2. How do you move to a specific record using a form?

3. What will happen if you use the same name for a newly compacted database?

4. What view is similar to a Tabular layout for a database?

5. In what view do you change the properties for a control?

PROJECTS

 PROJECT 3-1

1. Open the **IA Project3-1** database from the data files. Create a new form with the Form Wizard using the **Employee Information** table.

2. Add the **First Name, Last Name, Department, Title,** and **Birthdate** fields.

3. Use the **Columnar layout** and the **Standard** style.

4. Title the form **Employee Birthdays** and open the form.

5. Go to **Record 3**, Trent Broach, and change the title to **Director of Sales**. *& Birthday*

6. Go to **Record 16**, Donna Abbott, and change the birth date to **10-Jan-59.**

7. Print **Record 16.** *3*   *Selected Records*

8. Close the form and leave the database open for the next project.

 PROJECT 3-2

1. Open the **Employee Bonus** form in Design view.

2. Increase the size of the **Form Header** section about 1/2 inch.

3. Using the Label control, add a text box. In the text box, key **EMPLOYEE BONUS.** *& many Betty Garlieb*

4. Change the Font Name to **Arial Black** and the Font Size to **12.**

5. Increase the size of the **Detail** section about 1/4 inch.

6. Below the Bonus label, add a check box titled **Eligible for Stock Plan** (use the Check Box control). If necessary, increase the size of the text box to see all of the title.

7. Increase the size of the **Form Footer** section about 1/2 inch.

8. Using the Label control, add a text box. In the text box, key **Employees are eligible for Stock Plan after one year of employment.**

9. When finished, save the changes and switch to **Form** view.

10. Display and print **Record 11** (Be sure the Selected Record(s) option is selected in the Print dialog box.)

11. Close the form and leave the database open for the next project.

 PROJECT 3-3

1. Create a new form for the **Employee Information** table.

2. Use the **AutoForm: Columnar** option to create the form.

3. After the form is created, scroll through the records until you find the information on **Mark Mendoza.**

4. Print the information on **Mark Mendoza.** (Be sure the Selected Record(s) option is selected in the Print dialog box.)

5. Save the form as **Employee Data.**

6. Close the form.

7. Compact and repair the database. Close the database.

CRITICAL *Thinking*

 ACTIVITY 3-1

 Open the database you created for the Critical Thinking Activity 1-1 in Lesson 1. Use the Form Wizard to create a Tabular form that includes the fields of your database table. Choose an attractive style for the form. Add a record to the table using the new form. Print the record and close the form. Close the database.

 ACTIVITY 3-2

Using the Help feature, look up the definition of a subform and how it works. Write down a short definition and provide an example of a form and subform relationship used in a business setting. Be sure to mention the name of the field used to link the form and subform.

FINDING AND ORDERING DATA

OBJECTIVES

Upon completion of this lesson, you should be able to:

- Find data in a database.
- Query a database.
- Use filters.
- Sort a database.
- Index a database.
- Establish relationships in a database.
- Create a query from related tables.

Estimated Time: 1.5 hours

VOCABULARY

And operator

Ascending sort

Descending sort

Filter

Indexing

Multitable query

One-to-many relationship

Or operator

Primary key

Query

Referential integrity

Relationship

Search criteria

Subdatasheet

Using Find

The Find command is the easiest way to quickly locate data in a database. The Find command allows you to search the database for specified information. There are several options that allow you flexibility in performing the search. These options appear in the Find and Replace dialog box, shown in Figure 4-1.

FIGURE 4-1
Find and Replace dialog box

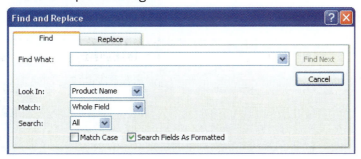

You can access the Find and Replace dialog box by opening the Edit menu and choosing Find or by clicking the Find button on the toolbar. The Find command is available only when a datasheet or form is displayed.

To search for the data in a particular field, place your insertion point in the field you want to search and click the Find button. The Find and Replace dialog box opens with the Look In box containing the field name to search. Key the data for which you are searching into the Find What box.

The Match text box has a drop-down list that lets you choose what part of the field to search. If you want to match exactly the entire contents of a field, choose Whole Field. More commonly, however, you will not want to enter the field's entire contents. For example, if you are searching a database of books for titles relating to history, you might want to search for titles with the word *history* anywhere in the title. In that case, you would choose Any Part of Field from the list. You can also specify that the search look only at the first part of the field by choosing the Start of Field option. For example, if you need to search a table of names for people whose last name begins with *Mc*, the Start of Field option would be convenient.

Click the drop-down arrow for the Search text box to display a list in which you can specify whether you want to search up from the current record position, down from the current record position, or the entire table. The Match Case check box gives you the option of a case-sensitive search. Click the Search Fields as Formatted check box to search a field that has been formatted with a data pattern, such as an Input Mask.

> ### Hot Tip
>
> Use the Find command when searching for one record at a time. Use the Filter tool when searching for multiple records. You will learn about filters later in this lesson.

Click Find Next to display the next record that matches the criteria you've specified. When the entire database has been searched, a message appears stating that the search item was not found.

S TEP-BY-STEP 4.1

1. Open **IA Step4-1** from the data files. This database includes a table of products. The products represent the inventory of a small office supply store.

2. Open the **Products** table in Datasheet view.

3. Place the insertion point in the **ProductName** field of the first record.

4. Click the **Find** button. The Find and Replace dialog box appears.

5. Key **Fax Machine** into the *Find What* box.

6. Be sure the **ProductName** field appears in the *Look In* box.

7. Click the down arrow to the right of the *Match* box and choose **Any Part of Field** from the list.

8. Be sure **All** appears in the *Search* box. The Match Case and Search Fields As Formatted options should not be selected.

STEP-BY-STEP 4.1 Continued

9. Click the **Find Next** button. ProductID 32 is selected, as shown in Figure 4-2.

10. Click **Find Next** again. A message appears telling you that the search item was not found. There is only one fax machine in the product line. Click **OK**.

11. Click **Cancel** to close the Find and Replace dialog box.

12. Close the table and leave the database open for the next Step-by-Step.

FIGURE 4-2
Finding data

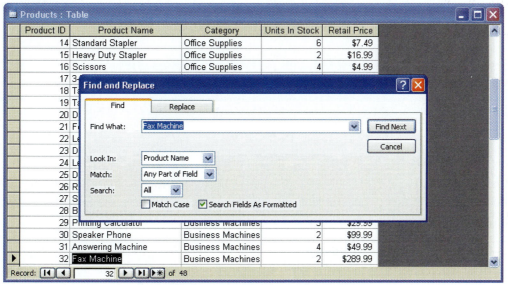

Using Queries

The Find command is an easy way of finding data. Often, however, you will need to locate data based on more complex criteria. For example, you may need to search for products with a value greater than $10. You cannot do that with the Find command. A special operation, called a *query*, will let you combine criteria to perform complex searches. For example, a query can locate products with a value greater than $10, of which fewer than three are in stock.

Queries allow you to "ask" the database almost anything about your data. In addition, you can create queries to display only the fields relevant to the search. For example, if you are querying a database of customers to locate those with a total purchased amount of $10,000 or more, you might want to display only the customers' names and total purchased amounts, rather than all the data in the table.

Creating a Query in Design View

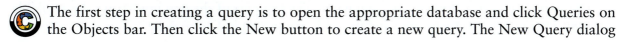 The first step in creating a query is to open the appropriate database and click Queries on the Objects bar. Then click the New button to create a new query. The New Query dialog

box appears, as shown in Figure 4-3. The New Query dialog box gives you the option to create a query manually or to use one of several Query Wizards. To create a query manually, use the Design View option in the New Query dialog box.

FIGURE 4-3
New Query dialog box

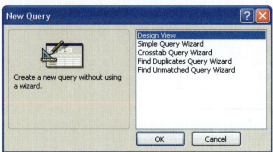

S TEP-BY-STEP 4.2

1. Click **Queries** on the Objects bar.

2. Click the **New** button. The New Query dialog box appears, as shown in Figure 4-3.

3. Choose **Design View**, if it is not already selected, and click **OK**. The Show Table dialog box appears from which you select a table to query, as shown in Figure 4-4. Leave the Show Table dialog box on the screen for the next Step-by-Step.

FIGURE 4-4
Show Table dialog box

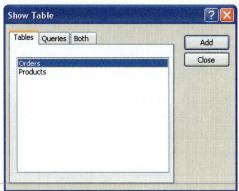

Because databases often include more than one table, you can choose the table you want to use in the Show Table dialog box. The Add button adds the fields from the highlighted table to your new query. After choosing a table and adding fields, click Close to close the Show Table dialog box. The fields you added now appear in a dialog box in the top pane of the query's design window, as shown in Figure 4-5.

The query window is divided into two parts. The top part of the window shows the available tables and fields (the Products table and its fields are shown in Figure 4-5).

FIGURE 4-5
Query window

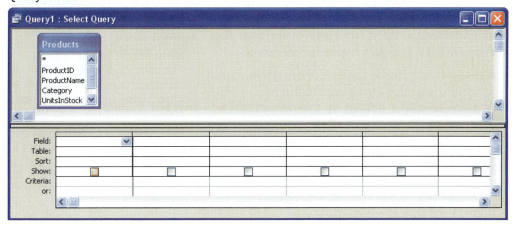

The bottom part of the window contains a grid that allows you to specify the information needed to create a query. To create a query, you must supply three pieces of information: the fields you want to search, what you are searching for (called the *search criteria*), and what fields you want to display with the results. The Field row is where you select a field to be part of the query. Click the down arrow to display the available fields. To include more than one field in a query, click in the next column of the Field row and choose another field.

The Sort row allows you to sort the results of the query. The Show check box determines whether the field is to be displayed in the query results. Normally, this will be checked. Occasionally, however, you may want to search by a field that does not need to appear in the query results.

For the fields you want to search, enter search conditions in the Criteria row. For example, if you want to find only records that contain the words Office Supplies in the Category field, you would key "Office Supplies" into the Criteria row of the Category field. When keying text into the Criteria row, always enclose it with quotation marks.

You can refine a search by using operators. For example, you might want to find all employees in a database table who make more than $30,000 a year, or you might want to search an inventory table for products of which there are less than five in stock. You can use the relational operators listed in Table 4-1 to conduct these types of searches.

TABLE 4-1
Relational operators

OPERATOR	DESCRIPTION
>	Greater than
<	Less than
=	Equal to
>=	Greater than or equal to
<=	Less than or equal to
<>	Not equal

You can also use the *And* or the *Or* operators. If you want to find records that meet more than one criteria, such as employees who make more than $30,000 a year *and* who have been with the company for less than two years, you would use the ***And operator***. Simply enter the criteria in the same Criteria row for the fields you want to search.

If you want to find records that meet one criteria or another, you would use the ***Or operator***. Enter the criteria in different rows for the fields you want to search.

After choosing the fields and entering search criteria, you should save the query by opening the File menu and choosing Save and then keying in a name for the query. To run a query, click the Run button in the query's Design view. Or, you can run a query directly from the Database window. Select the query, and then click the Open button.

Hot Tip

To modify a query, open it in Design view. You can change the fields to be searched, the search criteria, and the fields to be displayed in the query results.

S TEP-BY-STEP 4.3

1. Select the **Products** table in the Show Table dialog box and click **Add**. The fields of the *Products* table appear in the query window. Click **Close** to close the Show Table dialog box.

2. In the query grid, click the down arrow in the **Field** row of the first column and choose **ProductName**, as shown in Figure 4-6.

FIGURE 4-6
Selecting fields to query

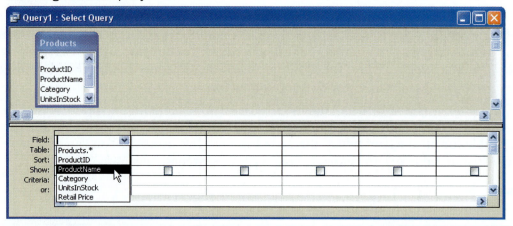

3. Click in the **Field** row of the second column, click the down arrow, and choose **ProductID** from the menu.

4. Click in the **Sort** row of the **ProductID** column, click the down arrow, and choose **Ascending** from the menu. This tells Access to sort the selected records in ascending order by ProductID.

5. Click in the **Field** row of the third column, click the down arrow, and choose **UnitsInStock** from the menu.

Hot Tip

You can display the down arrow menu in one step by clicking on the right side of the cell that you are accessing.

STEP-BY-STEP 4.3 Continued

6. In the **Criteria** row of the **UnitsInStock** column, key **<3**. This tells Access to display any records with fewer than 3 items in stock.

7. In the fourth column, choose the **Retail Price** field.

8. In the **Field** row of the fifth column, key **[Retail Price]*.90**.

9. Click in the **Table** row, click the down arrow, and choose **Products**.

10. Click in the **Field** row again and highlight **Expr1**. Replace *Expr1* by keying **Discount Price**. (Microsoft Access enters the default field name Expr1. Unless replaced by a more appropriate name this is the column heading you will see in Datasheet view.)

11. With the cursor in the Discount Price field box, right-click and choose **Properties** on the shortcut menu. The Field Properties dialog box will display.

12. Click in the **Format** box on the General tab, click the down arrow, and scroll down to click **Currency**. Close the dialog box.

13. Open the **File** menu and choose **Save**. You are prompted for a name for the query.

14. Key in **Reorder Query** and click **OK**.

15. Open the **File** menu and choose **Close**.

16. To run the query, highlight **Reorder Query** in the Database window and click **Open**. The results of the query appear, as shown in Figure 4-7.

Did You Know?

You can save a table, form, or query as a data access page, which allows you to view the database using the Web. To save an object as a data access page, open the **File** menu and choose **Save As**. The Save As dialog box appears. Key in the name of the data access page and choose **Data Access Page** as the type. Click **OK**.

FIGURE 4-7
Running a query

Product Name	Product ID	Units In Stock	Retail Price	Discount Price
Heavy Duty Stapler	15	2	$16.99	$15.29
Letter Sorter	24	2	$7.99	$7.19
Speaker Phone	30	2	$99.99	$89.99
Fax Machine	32	2	$289.99	$260.99
Cash Register	33	0	$269.99	$242.99
Photocopier	34	1	$699.00	$629.10
Typewriter	35	2	$129.99	$116.99
Computer Desk	39	2	$299.00	$269.10
Oak Office Desk	40	1	$399.00	$359.10
Bookshelf	41	2	$99.99	$89.99
Guest Chair	43	2	$159.00	$143.10

17. Open the **File** menu and choose **Print** to print the table with the query applied. Click **OK**.

18. Open the **File** menu and choose **Close** to close the results of the query. Leave the database open for the next Step-by-Step.

Using the Simple Query Wizard

You can also create a query using the Simple Query Wizard. The Simple Query Wizard will ask you questions and then create a query based upon your answers. When creating a query using the Wizard, you do not have as many options to choose from as when you create a query in Design view. For instance you can choose the fields to display, however you cannot sort, group, or specify search criteria. To access the Simple Query Wizard, choose Queries on the Objects bar and then click New. In the New Query dialog box, choose Simple Query Wizard. Click OK and follow the screens to create the query.

STEP-BY-STEP 4.4

1. Click **Queries** on the Objects bar.

2. Click the **New** button. The New Query dialog box appears.

3. Choose **Simple Query Wizard** and click **OK**. The Simple Query Wizard dialog box appears, as shown in Figure 4-8.

4. Click the down arrow in the **Tables/Queries** box and choose **Table: Products**. The fields from the Products table will appear in the Available Fields list.

5. In the Available Fields list, choose **ProductID** and click **>**. The field name will appear in the Selected Fields list.

6. Do the same for the **ProductName** and **Category** fields.

7. Click **Next**. The Simple Query Wizard dialog box changes to ask if you would like a detail or summary query. Choose **Detail** if not already selected.

8. Click **Next**. The Simple Query Wizard dialog box changes to ask you for a title, as shown in Figure 4-9.

FIGURE 4-8
Simple Query Wizard dialog box

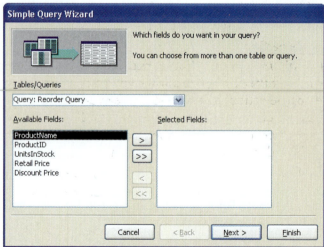

STEP-BY-STEP 4.4 Continued

FIGURE 4-9
Keying a title for the query

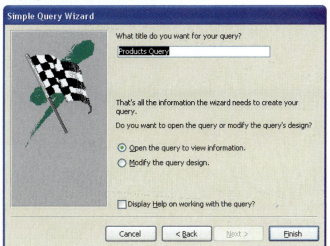

9. If not already there, key **Products Query**. Be sure the option to open the query to view the information is selected.

10. Click **Finish**. The results of the query appear.

11. Open the **File** menu and choose **Print** to print the results of the query. Click **OK**.

12. Open the **File** menu and choose **Close** to close the results of the query. Leave the database open for the next Step-by-Step.

Filters

Queries are very powerful and flexible tools. In many cases, however, less power is adequate. *Filters* provide a way to display selected records in a database more easily than using queries. Think of a filter as a simpler form of a query. A filter "filters out" the records that do not match the specified criteria. When you use a filter, all of the fields are displayed, and the filter cannot be saved for use again later.

There are four types of filters: Filter by Form, Filter by Selection, Filter Excluding Selection, and Advanced Filter/Sort. The Filter by Form allows you to select records by keying the criteria into a form. To use Filter by Selection (the fastest and easiest option), you highlight a value or part of a value in a field as the criteria for the selection. The Filter Excluding Selection excludes the value you highlight as the criteria for the selection. To duplicate a query or create a more complicated selection use the Advanced Filter/Sort option.

To create a filter, a table must be open. Open the Records menu and select Filter and then select one of the filter types from the submenu. If you select the Advanced Filter/Sort option, a

Filter window like the one in Figure 4-10 appears. Notice that the Filter window is very similar to the query window. (Since there is only one table in this database, it's automatically added to the top part of the window.) Also notice that there is no *Show* row in the grid—all fields are displayed when you use a filter. In the grid, you select only those fields for which you want to enter criteria. When you have included all of the field specifications, open the Filter menu and choose Apply Filter/Sort or click the Apply Filter button on the toolbar.

FIGURE 4-10
Design view for an advanced filter

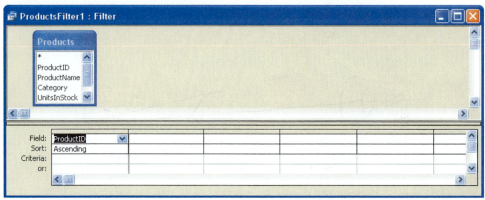

If you select Filter by Form, only the field names in the datasheet are displayed. When you click in a field, the filter arrow appears, as shown in Figure 4-11. Click the arrow and choose a data value from the list of all data values entered in the field. When finished, apply the filter. To create a Filter by Selection you must first highlight the criteria in the table. Click Filter by Selection on the submenu and the filtered records display.

FIGURE 4-11
Filter by Form

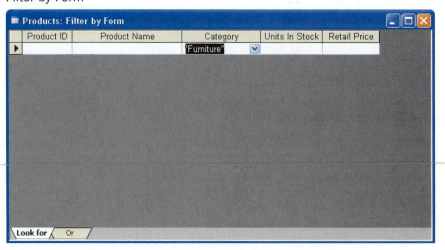

S TEP-BY-STEP 4.5

1. In the Database window, click **Tables** on the Objects bar.

2. Open the **Products** table in Datasheet view.

STEP-BY-STEP 4.5 Continued

3. Open the **Records** menu and choose **Filter**, then select **Advanced Filter/Sort** on the submenu. The Filter window appears, as shown in Figure 4-10.

4. Click the down arrow in the **Field** row of the first column and choose **Category** from the menu.

5. Key **"Furniture"** into the **Criteria** field of the first column. Include the quotation marks.

6. Click the **Apply Filter** button on the toolbar. The filter is applied, and only the products in the Furniture category are displayed, as shown in Figure 4-12.

FIGURE 4-12
A filter displaying the Furniture category

Product ID	Product Name	Category	Units In Stock	Retail Price
39	Computer Desk	Furniture	2	$299.00
40	Oak Office Desk	Furniture	1	$399.00
41	Bookshelf	Furniture	2	$99.99
42	Executive Chair	Furniture	3	$259.99
43	Guest Chair	Furniture	2	$159.00
44	Desk Chair	Furniture	3	$129.99
45	4-Drawer Filing Cabinet	Furniture	4	$139.99
46	2-Drawer Filing Cabinet	Furniture	3	$79.99
47	Folding Table (8')	Furniture	4	$76.00
48	Oak Credenza	Furniture	4	$199.00

7. Print the table with the filter applied.

8. Click the **Remove Filter** button to remove the filter and display all records.

9. Open the **Records** menu and choose **Filter**, then select **Filter by Form** on the submenu. A form appears, as shown in Figure 4-11.

10. Click the down arrow in the **Category** field. (Furniture was the criteria in the previous filter.)

11. Choose **Desk Accessories** from the list of options.

12. Click the **Apply Filter** button on the toolbar. The filter is applied, and only the products in the Desk Accessories category are displayed, as shown in Figure 4-13.

FIGURE 4-13
A filter displaying the Desk Accessories category

Product ID	Product Name	Category	Units In Stock	Retail Price
22	Letter Tray	Desk Accessories	4	$2.99
23	Desk Accessory Set	Desk Accessories	3	$21.99
24	Letter Sorter	Desk Accessories	2	$7.99
25	Drawer Tray	Desk Accessories	5	$3.49
26	Rotary Card File	Desk Accessories	3	$25.99

13. Print the table with the filter applied.

14. Click the **Remove Filter** button.

STEP-BY-STEP 4.5 Continued

15. To create a Filter by Selection, highlight **Calculator** in the **ProductName** field for ProductID number **27**.

16. Open the **Records** menu and choose **Filter**, then select **Filter by Selection** on the submenu. The filter is applied, and only the calculator products are displayed, as shown in Figure 4-14.

FIGURE 4-14
A filter displaying the calculator products

Product ID	Product Name	Category	Units In Stock	Retail Price
29	Printing Calculator	Business Machines	3	$29.99
28	Basic Calculator	Business Machines	7	$6.99
27	Scientific Calculator	Business Machines	3	$19.98

17. Print the table with the filter applied.

18. Click the **Remove Filter** button. Leave the table on the screen for the next Step-by-Step.

Sorting

 Sorting is an important part of working with a database. Often you will need records to appear in a specific order. For example, you may normally want a mailing list sorted by last name. But when preparing to mail literature to the entire mailing list, you may need the records to appear in zip code order. Access provides buttons on the toolbar to quickly sort the records of a table.

To sort a table, open the table and place the insertion point in the field by which you want to sort. Then click either the Sort Ascending or Sort Descending button. An *ascending sort* arranges records from A to Z or smallest to largest. A *descending sort* arranges records from Z to A or largest to smallest.

S TEP-BY-STEP 4.6

1. The **Products** table should be open in Datasheet view. Suppose you want to sort the records from least in stock to most in stock. Place the insertion point in the first record of the **UnitsInStock** field.

2. Click the **Sort Ascending** button. The records appear in order by UnitsInStock.

3. Suppose you want to sort the records from most expensive to least expensive. Place the insertion point in the first record of the **Retail Price** field.

4. Click the **Sort Descending** button. The products are sorted from most to least expensive.

5. Print the table and leave it open for the next Step-by-Step.

Sorting using the Sort Ascending and Sort Descending buttons is quick and easy. However, you will sometimes need to sort by more than one field. For example, suppose you want to sort the Products table by Category, but within each category you want the items to appear from most to least expensive. To perform this kind of sort, you must create a filter.

To use a filter to sort, create a filter as you normally do, but select an ascending or descending sort for the desired field or fields by clicking the down arrow in the Sort row. If the filter window has information left over from a previous sort or filter, you may need to click the cells with existing data and press the Backspace key to clear them.

S TEP-BY-STEP 4.7

1. Open the **Records** menu and choose **Filter**, and then choose **Advanced Filter/Sort** on the submenu.

2. Choose the **Category** and **Retail Price** fields as shown in Figure 4-15. Click the down arrow in the *Sort* row and choose **Ascending** for the Category field, and **Descending** for the Retail Price field. You may need to clear some existing data from the filter window.

3. Click the **Apply Filter** button.

4. Scroll through the datasheet to see that the records have been sorted according to the specifications in the filter.

5. Print the table with the filter applied. Leave the table and filter window open for the next Step-by-Step.

FIGURE 4-15
Sorting by more than one field

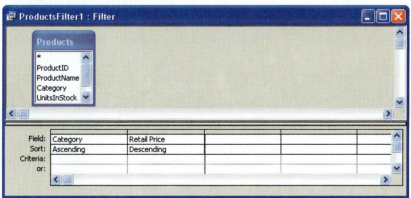

To filter and sort at the same time, add the information for both to the same filter window. Open the Records menu and choose Filter and then select Advanced/Filter Sort. In the filter window select the field to which you want to apply a filter and the field to be sorted. Click the Apply Filter button on the toolbar.

S TEP-BY-STEP 4.8

1. Open the **Records** menu and choose **Filter**, and then choose **Advanced Filter/Sort** on the submenu.

2. Suppose you want to display only the products with a retail price greater than $150. Key **>150** in the **Criteria** row of the **Retail Price** column. Leave the Category column as is.

STEP-BY-STEP 4.8 Continued

3. Click the **Apply Filter** button. Only eight of the records meet the filter criteria and they are sorted by retail price within the categories, as shown in Figure 4-16.

4. Print the table with the filter applied.

5. Click the **Remove Filter** button to remove the filter. All of the records appear again.

6. Close the table. If prompted to save the design of the table, click **No**. Leave the database open for the next Step-by-Step.

FIGURE 4-16
Filtering and sorting records

Product ID	Product Name	Category	Units In Stock	Retail Price
34	Photocopier	Business Machines	1	$699.00
32	Fax Machine	Business Machines	2	$289.99
33	Cash Register	Business Machines	0	$269.99
40	Oak Office Desk	Furniture	1	$399.00
39	Computer Desk	Furniture	2	$299.00
42	Executive Chair	Furniture	3	$259.99
48	Oak Credenza	Furniture	4	$199.00
43	Guest Chair	Furniture	2	$159.00

Indexing

Indexing is an important part of database management systems. In small databases, indexes do not provide much benefit. Large databases, however, rely on indexing to quickly locate data. In an Access database, you can specify that certain fields be indexed. Access can find data in an indexed field faster than it can find data in a field that is not indexed.

For each field in Design view, you can specify whether you want the field to be indexed. To index a field, go to Design view and choose Yes for Indexed in the Field Properties section.

If indexing improves speed, why not index all of the fields? The reason is that each indexed field causes more work and uses more disk space. Before indexing a database, you should be sure that the benefit of indexing a field outweighs the negatives caused by indexing. As a general rule, index fields only in large databases, and index only those fields that are regularly used to locate records.

Setting a Primary Key

When you save a newly created table in a database, a message appears asking if you want to create a *primary key*. This is a special field that assigns a unique identifier to each record. You can have Access create the primary key for you, in which case each record is automatically assigned a unique number. Or, you can set the primary key to an existing field within the table. The existing field should contain a unique value such as an ID number or part number. Primary keys must be set before creating table relationships, which are covered in the next section.

To designate a field as the primary key, open the table in Design view. Choose the field you want to set as the primary key by clicking the row selector. Click the Primary Key button on the toolbar. A primary key icon will now appear next to the primary key field.

S TEP-BY-STEP 4.9

1. In the **IA Step4-1** database, open the **Products** table in **Design** view.

2. Click the **row selector** for the **ProductID** field.

3. Click the **Primary Key** button on the toolbar. A key icon appears next to the **ProductID** field, as shown in Figure 4-17. Click the row selector for the field below to view the icon more clearly.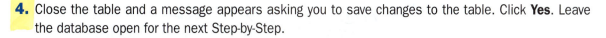

4. Close the table and a message appears asking you to save changes to the table. Click **Yes**. Leave the database open for the next Step-by-Step.

FIGURE 4-17
Setting the primary key

Relationships

By defining *relationships* between the different tables within a database, you can create queries, forms, and reports to display information from several tables at once. You can create a relationship between tables that contain a common field. For example, you might have a table that contains the name, telephone number, and other data on real estate agents. A second table might contain information including the name of the listing agent or properties for sale. You could set up a relationship between the two tables by joining the fields containing the agents' names. Then, you could create forms, queries, and reports that include fields from both tables.

The common fields must be of the same data type, although they can have different field names. In most relationships, the common field is also the primary key in at least one of the tables. It is referred to as the foreign key in the other table(s).

To ensure valid relationships between tables and prevent invalid data from being entered, Access utilizes *referential integrity* rules. These also help ensure that related data is not accidentally deleted or changed. To enforce referential integrity between tables, choose the Enforce Referential Integrity option when creating the relationship. If you break one of the rules with the related tables, Access displays a message and doesn't allow the change.

A *one-to-many relationship*, as illustrated in Figure 4-18, is the most common type of relationship. In a one-to-many relationship, a record in Table A can have matching records in Table B, but a record in Table B has only one matching record in Table A. In Figure 4-18, the ProductID field is the primary key in the Products table and the foreign key in the Orders table.

FIGURE 4-18
One-to-many relationship

You define a relationship by opening the Tools menu and clicking Relationships or by clicking the Relationships button on the toolbar. Add the tables you want to relate to the Relationships window. Next, drag the key field from one table to the key field in the other table.

STEP-BY-STEP 4.10

1. The **IA Step4-1** Database window should still be open. Open the **Tools** menu and choose **Relationships** or click the **Relationships** button on the toolbar. If the Show Table dialog box does not appear, as shown in Figure 4-19, open the **Relationships** menu and choose **Show Table**.

FIGURE 4-19
Show Table dialog box

2. Choose the **Products** table and click **Add**. Repeat this step for the **Orders** table.

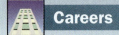 **Careers**

List three careers that would require using a database. For each career, describe the database and its contents.

STEP-BY-STEP 4.10 Continued

3. When finished, click **Close**. The Relationships window should appear as shown in Figure 4-20.

FIGURE 4-20
Relationships window

4. Click the **ProductID** field in the **Products** table. Drag and drop it on the **Product ID** field in the **Orders** table. (*Remember:* The common fields don't have to have the same field name; they just need to be of the same data type.) The Edit Relationships dialog box will appear as shown in Figure 4-21.

FIGURE 4-21
Edit Relationships dialog box

5. Check to be sure the ProductID field appears for both the Products and Orders tables. Click the **Enforce Referential Integrity** check box.

6. Click **Create**. The Relationships window appears as shown in Figure 4-22.

FIGURE 4-22
Table relationships

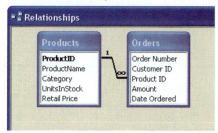

7. Close the Relationships window and a message appears asking if you want to save changes to the layout of Relationships. Click **Yes** to save the changes. Leave the database open for the next Step-by-Step.

To print a database relationship, open the Tools menu and choose Relationships to display the Relationships window. Open the File menu and choose Print Relationships and a report listing the table relationships will display. Open the File menu and choose Print or save the report for future reference.

STEP-BY-STEP 4.11

1. With the **IA Step4-1** Database window open, open the **Tools** menu and choose **Relationships**. The Relationships window appears (see Figure 4-22).

2. Open the **File** menu and choose **Print Relationships**. A report listing the table relationships will display as shown in Figure 4-23.

FIGURE 4-23
Table relationships report

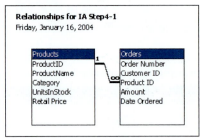

3. Open the **File** menu and choose **Print** and the Print dialog box appears. Click **OK** to print the report.

4. Close the Report window. A message displays asking if you want to save changes to the design of the report. Click **No**.

5. Close the Relationships window. Leave the database open for the next Step-by-Step.

Viewing Related Records

To view the related records between two tables you can add a *subdatasheet*. To insert a subdatasheet, open the table with the primary key in Datasheet view, and then open the Insert menu and choose Subdatasheet. In the Insert Subdatasheet window, choose the related table and click OK. The table with the primary key will reappear. Click the expand indicator icon (+) to the left of each row to display a subdatasheet of related records.

STEP-BY-STEP 4.12

1. Open the **Products** table in Datasheet view.

2. Open the **Insert** menu and choose **Subdatasheet**. The Insert Subdatasheet dialog box will appear as shown in Figure 4-24.

STEP-BY-STEP 4.12 Continued

FIGURE 4-24
Insert Subdatasheet dialog box

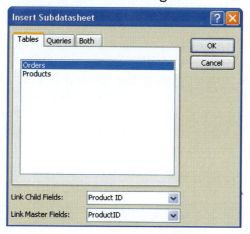

3. Choose the **Orders** table and click **OK**. The Products table will reappear.

4. Place the insertion point in the first record of the **ProductID** field and click the **Sort Ascending** button.

5. Click the expand indicator button (+) to the left of ProductID number **3** to display a subdatasheet of related records as shown in Figure 4-25.

FIGURE 4-25
Subdatasheet of related records

Product ID	Product Name	Category	Units In Stock	Retail Price
1	Stick-It Notes (8 pack)	Office Supplies	112	$6.59
2	Copy paper	Office Supplies	36	$5.99
3	Colored copy paper	Office Supplies	8	$5.99

Order Number	Customer ID	Amount	Date Ordered
10002	C112	3	9/1/2006
10003	R102	4	9/1/2006
*		0	

Product ID	Product Name	Category	Units In Stock	Retail Price
4	Legal copy paper	Office Supplies	7	$7.99
5	Legal Pads (4 pack)	Office Supplies	21	$2.49
6	Quadrille Pads (2 pack)	Office Supplies	9	$1.79
7	Clipboard	Office Supplies	3	$1.29
8	Envelopes (9" x 12") (100 cc	Office Supplies	6	$6.49
9	Envelopes #10 (500 count)	Office Supplies	11	$11.99
10	Envelopes #6.75	Office Supplies	5	$7.99
11	3-ring binders (1")	Office Supplies	18	$1.49
12	3-ring binders (2")	Office Supplies	9	$2.99
13	File folders (1/3 cut) (100 co	Office Supplies	14	$6.49
14	Standard Stapler	Office Supplies	6	$7.49
15	Heavy Duty Stapler	Office Supplies	2	$16.99

Record: 1 of 48

6. Click the indicator button (-) again to close the subdatasheet. Close the **Products** table. A message displays asking if you want to save the changes to the Products table. Click **Yes** to save. Leave the database open for the next Step-by-Step.

Creating a Multitable Query

After defining relationships in a database, you can create a *multitable query* to display the shared information from the related tables at once. For example, you might want to view customer information with the orders placed by the customers. To do this you would need data from both the Customers and Orders tables.

Except for a few additional steps, you will create a multitable query using the same procedure you've used to create queries. After opening the appropriate database, choose Queries on the Objects bar, and then click the New button to create a new query. The New Query dialog box appears. Choose the Design View option to create a query manually. In the Show Table dialog box, choose to add the related tables to the query. The fields in the related tables will appear in small boxes in the top part of the Select Query window, as shown in Figure 4-26.

FIGURE 4-26
Query window

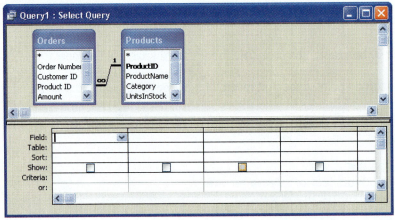

In the lower pane of the query window, specify the information needed from both tables to create the query. After choosing the fields and entering the search criteria, save the query.

STEP-BY-STEP 4.13

1. Click **Queries** on the Objects bar. Click the **New** button. The New Query dialog box appears.

2. Choose **Design View**, if it is not already selected, and click **OK**. The Show Table dialog box appears to allow you to choose the related tables for the query.

3. Select the **Orders** table, if necessary, and then click **Add**. The fields of the Orders table appear in the query window.

4. Select **Products** in the Show Table dialog box and click **Add**. The fields of the Products table appear in the query window.

5. Close the **Show Table** dialog box. The query window should look like Figure 4-26.

STEP-BY-STEP 4.13 Continued

6. Click the down arrow in the **Field** row of the first column and choose **Orders.Order Number**, as shown in Figure 4-27.

FIGURE 4-27
Select fields to display in the query results

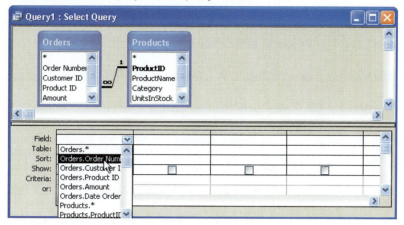

7. In the **Sort** row of the **Order Number** column, click the down arrow, and choose **Ascending** from the menu.

8. Click the down arrow in the **Field** row of the second column and choose **Orders.Product ID**.

9. In the third column, choose **Products.ProductName**.

10. In the fourth column, choose **Orders.Amount**.

11. In the fifth column, choose **Products.Retail Price**.

12. Open the **File** menu and choose **Save**, and enter **Invoice Query - Detail** as the name for the query. Click **OK**.

13. Click the **Run** button. The results of the query appear, as shown in Figure 4-28.

FIGURE 4-28
Results of a multitable query

Order Number	Product ID	Product Name	Amount	Retail Price
10000	10	Envelopes #6.75	2	$7.99
10001	31	Answering Machine	1	$49.99
10001	24	Letter Sorter	1	$7.99
10002	46	2-Drawer Filing Cabinet	1	$79.99
10002	11	3-ring binders (1")	10	$1.49
10002	3	Colored copy paper	3	$5.99
10003	25	Drawer Tray	2	$3.49
10003	17	3-hole punch	1	$9.99
10003	3	Colored copy paper	4	$5.99
10004	20	Date Stamp	2	$6.49
10004	32	Fax Machine	1	$289.99
10005	4	Legal copy paper	3	$7.99
10005	26	Rotary Card File	1	$25.99
10006	1	Stick-It Notes (8 pack)	10	$6.59

Record: 1 of 24

STEP-BY-STEP 4.13 Continued

14. Open the **File** menu and choose **Print** to print the table with the query applied. Click **OK**.

15. Open the **File** menu and choose **Close** to close the query.

16. Click **Queries** on the Objects bar. Click the **New** button. The New Query dialog box appears.

17. Choose **Design View**, if it is not already selected, and click **OK**. The Show Table dialog box appears. Add the **Orders** table and **Products** table. Close the Show Table dialog box.

18. Open the **View** menu and choose **Totals**. A Total row is added to the query grid.

19. Click the down arrow in the **Field** row of the first column and choose **Orders.Order Number**.

20. If necessary, in the **Total** row of the **Order Number** column, click the down arrow, and choose **Group By** from the menu.

21. In the Field row of the second column, key **Total Amount: [Amount]*[Retail Price]**.

22. In the **Total** row of the second column, click the down arrow, and choose **Sum** from the menu.

23. Save the query as **Invoice Query – Total**.

24. Run the query. The results of the query appear, as shown in Figure 4-29.

FIGURE 4-29
Results of a multitable query using an aggregate function (SUM)

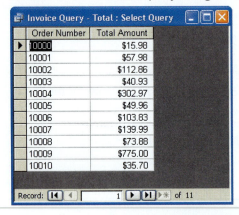

25. Print and close the query. Close the database.

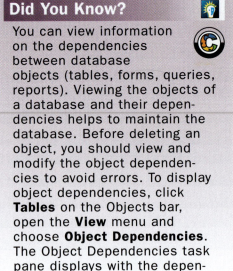

Did You Know?

You can view information on the dependencies between database objects (tables, forms, queries, reports). Viewing the objects of a database and their dependencies helps to maintain the database. Before deleting an object, you should view and modify the object dependencies to avoid errors. To display object dependencies, click **Tables** on the Objects bar, open the **View** menu and choose **Object Dependencies**. The Object Dependencies task pane displays with the dependent objects.

SUMMARY

In this lesson, you learned:

■ The Find command is the easiest way to locate data in the database. The Find command searches the database for specified information.

■ Queries allow more complex searches. A query allows you to search records using multiple and complex criteria and allows you to display selected fields. You can save a query and apply it again later.

■ A filter is similar to a query; however, it displays all fields and cannot be saved. A filter can be used to sort records, or records can be sorted directly in a table without the use of a filter. Using a filter to sort records allows you to sort by more than one criterion.

■ Sorting is an important part of working with a database since often you will need records to appear in a specific order.

■ Indexing is an important part of database management systems. Indexing allows records to be located quickly, especially in large databases.

■ A primary key is a special field that assigns a unique identifier to each record. Primary keys must be set before creating table relationships.

■ By defining relationships between the different tables within a database, you can create queries, forms, and reports to display information from several tables at once. Matching data in key fields sets up a relationship. To ensure valid relationships between tables and prevent invalid data from being entered, Access utilizes referential integrity rules.

■ A multitable query displays the shared information from related tables in a database.

VOCABULARY *Review*

Define the following terms:

And operator	Multitable query	Referential integrity
Ascending sort	One-to-many relationship	Relationship
Descending sort	Or operator	Search criteria
Filter	Primary key	Subdatasheet
Indexing	Query	

REVIEW *Questions*

TRUE/FALSE

Circle the T if the statement is true or F if the statement is false

T   F   **1.** The Find command can search for data in all fields.

T   F   **2.** The Find Next button in the Find dialog box finds the next record that matches the criteria you've specified.

T   F   **3.** A query automatically displays all fields in the table.

T   F   **4.** Filters cannot be saved for later use.

T   F   **5.** An ascending sort arranges records from Z to A.

WRITTEN QUESTIONS

Write a brief answer to the following questions.

1. What is the easiest way to quickly locate data in a database?

2. What three pieces of information must you supply when creating a query?

3. What menu is used to access the command that creates a filter?

4. What button is used to sort records from largest to smallest?

5. What view allows you to index a field?

PROJECTS

 **PROJECT 4-1**

1. Open the **IA Project4-1** database file from the data files.

2. Open the **Houses** table in Datasheet view.

3. Use the **Find** command to locate the first house with wood exterior.

4. Use the **Find** command to locate any remaining houses with wood exterior.

5. Close the table.

6. Create a query that displays houses with two bedrooms. Have the query display only the **Address**, **Bedrooms**, and **Price** fields. Save the query as **2 Bedrooms**. + name

7. Run the query and print the results. Close the query. Leave the database open for the next project. + print

 PROJECT 4-2

1. Open the **Houses** table in the **IA Project4-1** database in Datasheet view.

2. Sort the table so that the houses are displayed from most expensive to least expensive.

3. Change the column width to **Best Fit** for all the columns.

4. Print the results of the sort in landscape orientation.

5. Create a filter to display only the houses listed with **Brad Gray** as the agent. You do not have to sort the records.

6. Print the results of the filter in landscape orientation.

7. Remove the filter to show all the records in the table. Leave the database open for the next project.

PROJECT 4-3

1. With the **Houses** table in the **IA Project4-1** database open, create a filter that displays three-bedroom houses only, sorted from least to most expensive.

2. Print the results of the filter in landscape orientation.

3. Remove the filter to show all records in the table.

4. Create a filter that displays only houses with two-car garages and brick exterior.

5. Print the results of the filter in landscape orientation.

6. Remove the filter to show all records in the table. Leave the database open for the next project.

PROJECT 4-4

1. With the **Houses** table in the **IA Project4-1** database open, use the **Find** command to locate the houses that were listed during December.

2. Create a query that displays the houses listed with **Nina Bertinelli** or **John Schultz** as the agent. Have the query display only the **Address, List Date, Price,** and **Agent** fields and sort the **Price** field from most to least expensive. Save the query as **Bertinelli/Schultz**.

3. Run the query and print the results. Close the query. *print* *+ name*

4. Open the **Houses** table and create a filter that sorts the houses from most to least bathrooms and the price from least to most expensive. *1.5 left + Right margins*

5. Print the results of the filter in landscape orientation.

6. Remove the filter to show all records in the table.

7. Close the table and the database.

CRITICAL *Thinking*

SCANS ACTIVITY 4-1

You are a Realtor with three new clients who are ready to buy homes. List on paper each client's requirements in a home. For example, Buyer #1 might want a three-bedroom house with a brick exterior and the maximum price is $90,000.

Using the **IA Project4-1** database and the **Houses** table, create a filter or query to locate the information for each client and print the results.

SCANS ACTIVITY 4-2

Referential integrity is a set of rules that Access uses to check for valid relationships between tables. It also ensures that related data is not accidentally deleted or changed. Using the Help system, determine the conditions that must be met before you can enforce referential integrity. Write a brief essay that explains the importance of referential integrity in a relational database and why users of the database objects would benefit from it.

SCANS ACTIVITY 4-3

Open the **IA Activity4-3** database. Create a duplicates query using the **Customers** table to find which customers are located in the same city. To create the query, in the **New Query** dialog box, choose **Find Duplicates Query Wizard**, and follow the directions in the Wizard dialog boxes. Select the **City** field as the field that might contain duplicate information. Select the **Customer ID** and **Customer Name** fields to show in addition to the duplicate fields. Name the query **Customers in the same city** and print the results.

ACTIVITY 4-4

Open the **IA Activity4-3** database. Create an unmatched query using the **Customers** and **Orders** tables to find which customers do not have orders. To create the query, in the **New Query** dialog box, choose **Find Unmatched Query Wizard**, and follow the directions in the Wizard dialog boxes. Select the **Customer ID** field as the matching field in each table. Select the **Customer ID, Customer Name,** and **Salesperson** as the fields to see in the query results. Name the query **Customers without orders** and print the results.

 ACTIVITY 4-5

Open the **IA Activity4-3** database. Create a crosstab query using the **Ordered Products** query. To create the query, in the **New Query** dialog box, choose **Crosstab Query Wizard**, and follow the directions in the Wizard dialog boxes. Select the **ProductName** field as the row heading. Select the **Customer ID** field as the column heading. Select the **Retail Price** field and the **Sum** function as the number to be calculated for each row and column intersection. Remove the check mark to not include row sums. Name the query **Ordered Products – Crosstab**. Change the orientation to Landscape and print the results.

REPORTS AND MACROS

OBJECTIVES

Upon completion of this lesson, you should be able to:

- Create a report using a Report Wizard.
- Modify a report.
- Create and run a macro.

Estimated Time: 1.5 hours

VOCABULARY

Database report

Grouping

Macro

Reports

Databases can become large as records are added. Printing the database from Datasheet view may not always be the most desirable way to put the data on paper. Creating a ***database report*** allows you to organize, summarize, and print all or a portion of the data in a database. You can even use reports to print form letters and mailing labels. Figure 5-1 shows two examples of database reports. Database reports are compiled by creating a report object.

FIGURE 5-1
Database reports

Employees by Department

Department	Last Name	First Name	Salary
Advertising			
	Abernathy	Mark	$2,375.00
	Barton	Brad	$2,590.00
	Denton	Scott	$2,600.00
	Doss	Derek	$2,200.00
Marketing			
	Martinez	Christine	$1,780.00
	Powell	Lynne	$2,970.00
	Powers	Sarah	$1,500.00
Personnel			
	Davis	Lee	$2,680.00
Public Relations			
	Smith	Shawna	$2,950.00
Sales			
	Best	Trent	$2,800.00
	Broach	Margie	$2,450.00
	Collins	Greg	$2,750.00
	Collins	Dave	$2,620.00
	Davis	Hillary	$2,620.00
	Sims	Jennifer	$1,550.00
	West	Debbie	$3,100.00

Page 1 of 1

Products by Units in Stock — Tiffany Matthews

UnitsInStock	Product Name	Product ID	Category	Retail Price
0	Cash Register	33	Business Machines	$229.00
1	Oak Office Desk	40	Furniture	$399.00
	Photocopier	34	Business Machines	$599.00
2	Bookshelf	41	Furniture	$89.99
	Computer Desk	39	Furniture	$299.00
	Fax Machine	32	Business Machines	$249.99
	Guest Chair	43	Furniture	$199.00
	Heavy Duty Stapler	15	Office Supplies	$19.99
	Letter Sorter	24	Desk Accessories	$7.99
	Speaker Phone	30	Business Machines	$99.99
	Typewriter	35	Business Machines	$149.99
3	2-Drawer Filing Cabinet	46	Furniture	$89.99
	Clipboard	7	Office Supplies	$0.99
	Desk Accessory Set	23	Desk Accessories	$17.99
	Desk Chair	44	Furniture	$189.99
	Executive Chair	42	Furniture	$259.99
	Printing Calculator	29	Business Machines	$29.99
	Rotary Card File	26	Desk Accessories	$24.99
	Scientific Calculator	27	Business Machines	$19.98
	Surge Protector	37	Computer Supplies	$19.99
4	4-Drawer Filing Cabinet	45	Furniture	$149.99
	Answering Machine	31	Business Machines	$49.99
	Disk Storage Box	38	Computer Supplies	$6.99
	Folding Table (8')	47	Furniture	$44.99
	Letter Tray	22	Desk Accessories	$2.99
	Scissors	16	Office Supplies	$2.99
	Tape Dispenser	19	Office Supplies	$5.99
5	Drawer Tray	25	Desk Accessories	$2.99
	Envelopes #6.75	10	Office Supplies	$7.99
6	Envelopes (9" x 12") (10	8	Office Supplies	$5.99
	Standard Stapler	14	Office Supplies	$7.99
7	3-hole punch	17	Office Supplies	$9.99
	Basic Calculator	28	Business Machines	$3.99
	Date Stamp	20	Office Supplies	$1.99
	Fax paper	4	Office Supplies	$5.49
8	Colored paper assortme	3	Office Supplies	$4.99
9	3-ring binders (2")	12	Office Supplies	$2.99
	3.5" HD Diskettes (Box o	36	Computer Supplies	$8.99

Page 1 of 2

Printing a database from Datasheet view is a form of a report. Printing from Datasheet view, however, offers you much less flexibility than creating a report and printing it. In this lesson, you will learn how to create report objects.

Creating a Report

 The report database object lets you create reports that include selected fields, groups of records, and even calculations. As with other Access objects, you can create a report object manually or use the Report Wizard. In this lesson, you will create a report using the Report Wizard.

To create a report, click Reports on the Objects bar, and click the New button. The New Report dialog box appears, as shown in Figure 5-2.

FIGURE 5-2
New Report dialog box

In the New Report dialog box, choose the method to create the report. To use a Report Wizard, choose Report Wizard from the list. Click the down arrow to select the table or query Access will use to create a report. Choose a table if you want to include the entire table in the report. Choose a query to include only certain data in the report. In many cases, you will want to create a query before creating a report.

S TEP-BY-STEP 5.1

1. Open **IA Step5-1** from the data files.

2. Click the **Reports** button on the Objects bar.

3. Click **New**. The New Report dialog box appears, as shown in Figure 5-2.

4. Choose **Report Wizard** from the list.

5. Click the down arrow and choose the table **Products** from the drop-down list. Click **OK**. The Report Wizard dialog box appears, as shown in Figure 5-3. Leave the Report Wizard dialog box on the screen for the next Step-by-Step.

FIGURE 5-9
Layout options

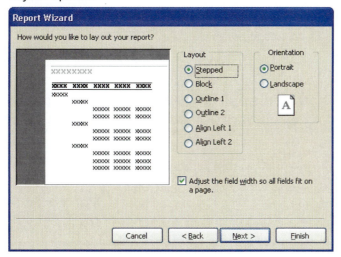

The next dialog box, shown in Figure 5-10, allows you to choose a style for the report. The style options are designed to give you some control over the report's appearance. The style you choose tells the reader of the report something about the data being presented. Some reports may call for a formal style, while others may benefit from a more casual style. When you choose a style, a sample is shown in the preview box.

FIGURE 5-10
Style options

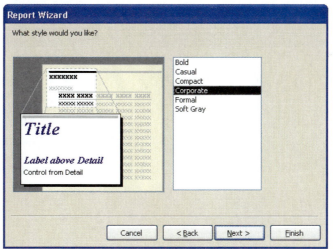

S TEP-BY-STEP 5.5

1. Choose the **Outline 2** layout. The sample layout is shown in the preview box. Click the other options to look at the other layouts. When you have seen all of the available options, choose **Stepped** as the layout.

STEP-BY-STEP 5.5 Continued

2. Choose **Portrait** as the page orientation, if it is not already selected. Make sure the **Adjust the field width so all fields fit on a page** box is checked.

3. Click **Next**.

4. Choose the **Casual** style. The sample style is shown in the preview box. Click on the other options to look at the other styles. When you have seen all of the available options, choose **Corporate** as the style.

5. Click **Next**. The final Report Wizard dialog box appears. Leave the Report Wizard on the screen for the next Step-by-Step.

Naming the Report

The final step is naming the report, as shown in Figure 5-11. Use a name that gives an indication of the report's output. A report name can be up to 64 characters including letters, numbers, spaces, and some special characters. For example, if a report from a database of customers prints only the customers with companies in your city, you might name the report Local Customers.

> **Did You Know?**
>
> You can create a chart in either a form's or a report's Design view. Open the Insert menu and choose Chart. On the form or report, click where you want the chart to appear. Follow the steps in the Chart Wizard to create the chart based on the tables and the fields you select.

FIGURE 5-11
Naming the report

In addition to naming the report, this dialog box presents you with options for what you want displayed when the Report Wizard completes its work. Most of the time you will want to preview the report you have created, so preview is the default option. After Access creates the report, it is shown on your screen in Preview mode. You may instead choose to make modifications to the report. You will get a brief look at how modifications are made later in this lesson.

After creating a report, you do not need to save it. Access saves it for you automatically with the title you entered into the Report Wizard. You will, however, need to save any modifications made later to the design of the report.

S TEP-BY-STEP 5.6

1. Key **Category Report** as the title of the report.

2. Make sure the option to preview the report is selected and click **Finish**. The report appears in a window, as shown in Figure 5-12.

FIGURE 5-12
Previewing a report

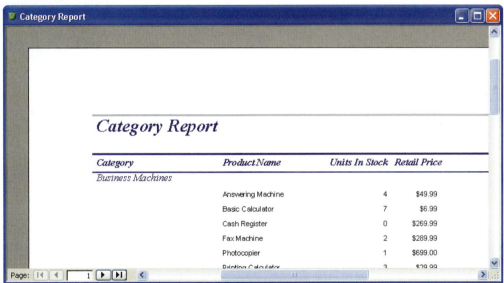

3. Scroll through the report to see the various categories.

4. Click the **Print** button to print the report.

5. Open the **File** menu and choose **Close**. The report will be saved automatically. Leave the Database window open for the next Step-by-Step.

Modifying a Report

Any report, whether created manually or with the Report Wizard, can be modified. Make changes to a report using Design view, which shows the structure of

---

Did You Know?

To add a graphic to a report, open it in Design view, and click the **Image** button in the Toolbox. Click where you want to place the graphic in the report and the Insert Picture dialog box displays. Select the file where the picture is located. When finished, click **OK**. Access creates an image control that will display the graphic.

a report. To open a report in Design view, select the report in the Database window, and then click the Design button. Figure 5-13 shows a report in Design view.

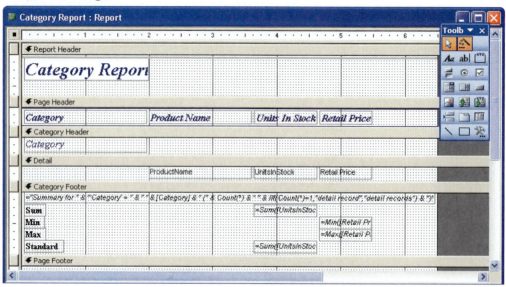

Like a form, the report is divided into sections, each identified by a band. Each section controls a part of the report and can be modified. Table 5-1 summarizes the purpose of each of the sections in the report.

TABLE 5-1
Report sections

SECTION	DESCRIPTION
Report Header	Contents appear at the top of the first page of the report.
Page Header	Contents appear at the top of each page of the report.
Category Header	Contents appear at the top of each group. Because your report is grouped by Category, the band is called Category Header.
Detail	Specifies the fields that will appear in the detail of the report.
Category Footer	Contents appear at the end of each group. The summary options appear in this band.
Page Footer	Contents appear at the end of each page of the report.
Report Footer	Contents appear at the end of the report.

Like a form, the sections in a report contain controls that represent each object on the report. These objects include field names, field entries, a title for the report, or even a graphical object, such as a piece of clip art. You can modify the format, size, and location of the controls in Design view to enhance the appearance of the data on the report.

In Design view, you can change the font, size, style, and other attributes of labels and text box data. Simply select the control, and use the buttons on the Formatting toolbar. Or you can double-click a control to open its Properties dialog box, and then change attributes and other properties.

Did You Know?

In Design view and Print Preview mode, you can change the margins and page orientation for a report. Open the **File** menu and choose **Page Setup**. The Page Setup dialog box displays. Click the **Margins** tab and key the new margins. Click the **Page** tab and select either **Portrait** or **Landscape** orientation. When finished, click **OK**.

The Toolbox, shown in Figure 5-14, has tools that you can use to modify reports. The Label tool, for example, allows you to add text. (The buttons in the Toolbox may appear in two columns instead of the three shown in Figure 5-14.)

FIGURE 5-14
Toolbox

S TEP-BY-STEP 5.7

1. If not already selected, click **Reports** on the Objects bar. Choose the **Category Report** and click the **Design** button. The report appears in Design view, as shown in Figure 5-13.

2. Click the **Label** button in the Toolbox. (If the Toolbox is not displayed, *right*-click on the report and choose **Toolbox** on the shortcut menu.)

3. In the **Report Header**, position the pointer to the right of the *Category Report* text, and click and drag to draw a text box as shown in Figure 5-15.

STEP-BY-STEP 5.7 Continued

FIGURE 5-15
Inserting text

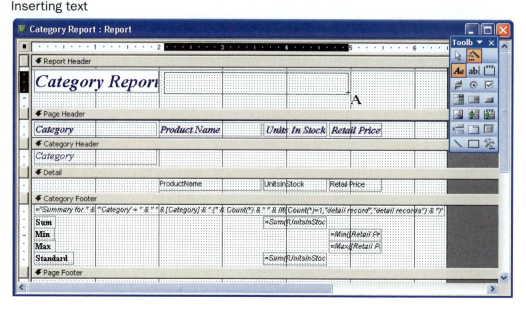

4. Key your name at the insertion point that appears in the text box. Click outside the text box to view the text.

5. Double-click the text box to display its properties dialog box, as shown in Figure 5-16. If not already selected, click the **All** tab. (*Note:* The label number that appears in your properties dialog box depends on the number of label controls you have added.)

FIGURE 5-16
Label properties dialog box

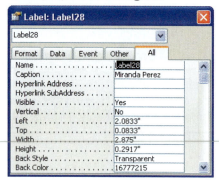

6. Scroll down through the list of properties until you locate the **Font Name** and **Font Size** properties. Click in the *Font Name* text box, click the down arrow, and select **Mistral** (or a comparable font). Then click in the *Font Size* text box, click the down arrow, and choose **14**. Close the properties dialog box.

7. Scroll down to the *Report Footer* section. Position the pointer on the **Grand Total** label box as shown in Figure 5-17, and double-click to open its properties dialog box. If not already selected, click the **All** tab.

STEP-BY-STEP 5.7 Continued

FIGURE 5-17
Modifying the Grand Total label

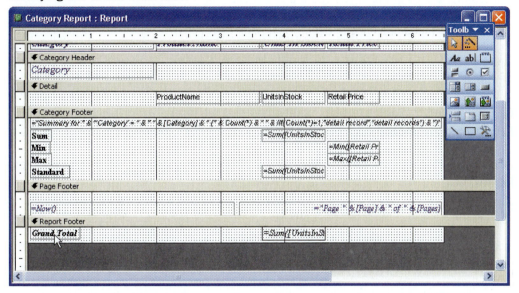

8. Change the **Caption** to **Total Units in Stock**. Change the **Font Size** to **12**. Close the dialog box.

9. With the **Total Units in Stock** label still highlighted, increase the label size by dragging the handle on the right border to the right until you see the entire caption.

10. In the *Detail* section, double-click the **Retail Price** box to open its properties dialog box, as shown in Figure 5-18. If not already selected, choose the **All** tab.

FIGURE 5-18
Text Box properties dialog box

11. Click in the **Name** text box and key **Discount Price**. Then close the dialog box.

12. In the *Page Header* section, double-click the **Retail Price** label box to open its properties dialog box.

13. Change the Caption to **Discount Price** and close the dialog box.

STEP-BY-STEP 5.7 Continued

14. With the **Discount Price** label still highlighted, increase the label size by dragging the handle on the right border to the right until you see the entire caption.

15. Open the **File** menu and choose **Save**.

16. In the *Detail* section, double-click the **Retail Price** text box to open its properties dialog box. Click the **All** tab, if necessary.

17. Click in the **Control Source** text box, delete the existing text, and key **=[Retail Price]*.90**. Click in the **Format** property text box, click the down arrow, and select **Currency**. Then, close the dialog box.

18. In the *Category Footer* section, double-click the **Min ([Discount Price])** box to open its properties dialog box. Click the **All** tab, if necessary.

19. Click in the **Control Source** text box, and change the word *Discount* to **Retail**. Close the dialog box.

20. In the *Category Footer* section, double-click the **Max ([Discount Price])** box to open its properties dialog box. Click the **All** tab, if necessary.

21. Click in the **Control Source** text box, and change the word *Discount* to **Retail**. Close the dialog box.

22. Click the **View** button to switch to **Print Preview**. If a message appears asking if you want to save changes, click **Yes**.

23. If necessary, scroll to the right to see your name on the report. Open the **File** menu and choose **Print**. In the Print dialog box, click **Pages** from the *Print Range* options. Specify that you want to print only page 1 by keying **1** in the *From* box and **1** in the *To* box. Click **OK**.

24. Close the report. Click **Yes** if you are asked if you want to save the report. Leave the database open for the next Step-by-Step.

> **Hot Tip**
>
> To delete a text box, click on the text box and press the **Delete** key or open the **Edit** menu and choose **Delete**. To move a text box, click inside the box and drag. To resize a text box, click on the edge of the text box and drag.

Macros

One of the nice features of database management systems such as Access is the ability to automate tasks that are performed often. This is done by creating an object called a *macro*. A macro is a collection of one or more actions that Access can perform on a database. You can think of a macro as a computer program you create to automate some task you perform with the database.

Creating macros can be challenging, and there are many details to learn before you can become an expert. In this book you will get a taste of how macros work by creating a macro and running it.

Creating a Macro

To create a macro, click Macros on the Objects bar, and click the New button. The Macro window appears, allowing you to specify the actions to be performed by the macro. Figure 5-19 shows a macro in Design view with an example of actions that a macro can perform. The macro will perform the actions specified in the Action list.

FIGURE 5-19
Macro in Design view

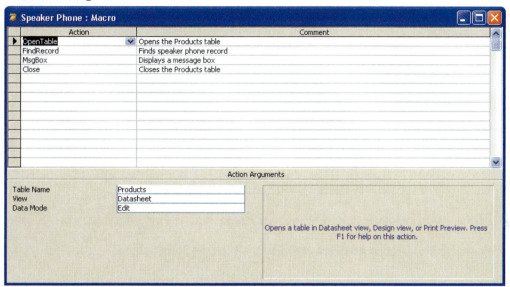

STEP-BY-STEP 5.8

1. Click **Macros** on the Objects bar.

2. Click **New**. A blank macro window appears. Leave the window open for the next Step-by-Step.

Adding Actions to a Macro

You can choose an action by clicking the down arrow in the Action column cells. There are many available actions, some of which perform advanced operations. You can key an explanation of the action into the Comment column. The lower portion of the Macro window shows the action arguments for the chosen action. Action arguments contain detailed information that Access needs in order to perform the specified action. For example, if you choose the OpenTable action in the Action column, you would specify which table to open, such as the Products table, in the *Action Arguments* section.

Different actions require different detailed information in the *Action Arguments* section, as you will see in the next Step-by-Step. You will create a macro that will open the Products table, find the first speaker phone in the table, present a message box and beep, and close the table.

STEP-BY-STEP 5.9

1. Click the down arrow in the **Action** column of the first blank row to display the list of available actions.

2. Scroll down and choose **OpenTable** from the menu.

3. In the *Comment* section, key **Opens the Products table**.

4. In the *Action Arguments* section, place the insertion point in the **Table Name** box. A down arrow appears. Notice that the box to the right of the Action Arguments contains an explanation of the data to be specified.

5. Click the down arrow and choose **Products**.

6. Leave the remaining Action Arguments at the default settings.

7. Place the insertion point in the second row of the **Action** column. Click the drop-down list arrow.

8. Scroll down and choose **FindRecord** from the list.

9. In the *Comment* section, key **Finds speaker phone record**.

10. In the *Action Arguments* section, key **Speaker Phone** into the **Find What** box.

11. In the *Match* box, choose **Any Part of Field** from the drop-down list.

12. Leave the next two action arguments at the default setting. In the *Search As Formatted* box, choose **Yes** from the drop-down list.

13. In the *Only Current Field* box, choose **No** to search all the fields in each record.

14. In the *Find First* box, choose **Yes**, if it's not chosen already. Your screen should look similar to Figure 5-20.

FIGURE 5-20
Specifying Action Arguments

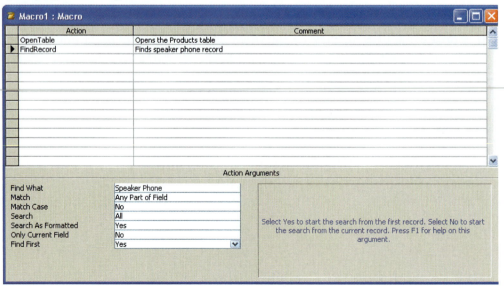

STEP-BY-STEP 5.9 Continued

15. Place the insertion point in the third row of the **Action** column, scroll down, and choose **MsgBox** from the list.

16. Key **Displays a message box** into the *Comment* section.

17. In the *Action Arguments* section, key **Record Found** into the *Message* box.

18. Choose **Yes** in the *Beep* box, if it is not already chosen.

19. Choose **Information** in the *Type* box.

20. Key **Results:** into the *Title* box.

21. Place the insertion point in the fourth row of the *Action* column and choose **Close** from the list.

22. Key **Closes the Products table** into the *Comment* section.

23. In the *Action Arguments* section, choose **Table** in the *Object Type* box.

24. Choose **Products** in the *Object Name* box. Leave the window open for the next Step-by-Step.

Saving and Running a Macro

After creating a macro, you will need to name and save it. This process is similar to the way you named and saved other database objects. Open the File menu, choose Save As, and key a name. To close the macro, open the File menu and choose Close. When you want to run a macro, highlight it in the Database window and click Run.

STEP-BY-STEP 5.10

1. Open the **File** menu and choose **Save As**. The Save As dialog box appears.

2. In the first box, key **Speaker Phone**, as shown in Figure 5-21. Click **OK**.

FIGURE 5-21
Save As dialog box

STEP-BY-STEP 5.10 Continued

3. Open the **File** menu and choose **Close** to close the macro window. You are returned to the Database window.

4. Select **Macros** on the Objects bar, if necessary. Highlight the **Speaker Phone** macro, if it is not already highlighted. Click the **Run** button. The Products table opens, the computer beeps, and the message box generated by the macro appears, as shown in Figure 5-22.

FIGURE 5-22
Macro message box

5. Click **OK** to close the message box. The table closes because of the Close action in the macro.

6. Open the **Speaker Phone** macro in Design view.

7. Highlight the row with the **MsgBox** action. Open the **Edit** menu and choose **Delete**.

<table>
<tr><td>

Extra Challenge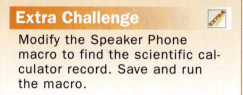

Modify the Speaker Phone macro to find the scientific calculator record. Save and run the macro.

</td></tr>
</table>

8. Open the **Insert** menu and choose **Rows** to insert a row.

9. Click the down arrow in the **Action** column of the inserted row. Scroll down to choose the **PrintOut** action.

10. Key **Prints speaker phone record** into the *Comment* section.

11. In the *Action Arguments* section, choose **Selection** from the **Print Range** drop-down list.

12. Open the **File** menu and choose **Save** to save the design changes.

13. Close the macro window.

14. Highlight the **Speaker Phone** macro, if it is not already highlighted. Click the **Run** button.

15. The Products table opens, the Speaker Phone record prints, and the table closes. Close the database.

<table>
<tr><td>

Did You Know?

You can also run a macro by double-clicking on it in the Database window.

</td></tr>
</table>

SUMMARY

In this lesson, you learned:

■ Database reports allow you to organize, summarize, and print all or a portion of the data in a database. Database reports are compiled by creating a report object.

■ The easiest way to create a report object is to use the Report Wizard. When using the Report Wizard, first choose the table on which you want to base the report and the fields of that table you want to include in the report. You can also choose to group the records and sort them.

■ The Report Wizard also allows you to choose a style for your report. The style can give a report a casual or formal look.

■ Reports are modified using Design view. Each report is divided into sections. Each section controls a different part of the report and can be modified.

■ Macros automate tasks you perform often. The Macro window allows you to create a macro object.

VOCABULARY *Review*

Define the following terms:

| Database report | Grouping | Macro |

REVIEW *Questions*

TRUE/FALSE

Circle T if the statement is true or F if the statement is false.

T   F   **1.** Database reports are prepared by creating a report object.

T   F   **2.** The Report Wizard always includes all fields in a report.

T   F   **3.** Like file names, report names can contain only eight characters.

T   F   **4.** Action arguments contain detailed information about an action.

T   F   **5.** To run a macro, highlight it in the Database window and click Run.

WRITTEN QUESTIONS

Write a brief answer to the following questions.

1. What are the two ways to create a report?

2. How does sorting affect a group?

3. List three possible sections in a report.

4. How do you use the Label tool to add text to a report?

5. When creating a macro, what action displays a message box?

PROJECTS

 PROJECT 5-1

1. Open **IA Project5-1** from the data files.

2. Use the Report Wizard to create a report using all the fields in the **Products** table. Group the report by **UnitsInStock** and sort it by **ProductName**.

3. Choose the **Block** layout, **Portrait** orientation, and **Compact** style.

4. Title the report **Products by Units in Stock**. Select the option to preview the report.

5. Close the report after previewing.

6. Modify the report in Design view. Use the label tool to insert your name in the Report header. Save the changes.

7. Print the report.

8. Close the report and the database.

 PROJECT 5-2

1. Open **IA Project5-2** from the data files.

2. Use the Report Wizard to create a report. Use the **Employee Information** table and choose the **Last Name, First Name, Department,** and **Salary** fields.

3. Group the records by **Department** and sort by **Last Name**.

4. Choose the **Stepped** layout, **Portrait** orientation, and **Corporate** style.

5. Title the report **Employees by Department**. Select the option to preview the report.

6. Save the report.

7. Print and close the report. Leave the database open for the next project.

PROJECT 5-3

1. With the **IA Project5-2** database open, create a new macro that will open the **Employee Birthdays** form in Form view and find the **Shapiro** record. For the **FindRecord Action Arguments**, select **Any Part of Field** in the *Match* box, **No** in the *Match Case* box, **All** in the *Search* box, **Yes** in the *Search As Formatted* box, **No** in the *Only Current Field* box, and **Yes** in the *Find First* box. Then, have the macro print the Shapiro record only (*Print Range = Selection*), and close the Employee Birthdays form.

2. Save the macro as **Print Form Record** and close it.

3. Run the macro. Leave the database open for the next project.

PROJECT 5-4

1. Create a new macro in the **IA Project5-2** database that will open the **Managers** query in Datasheet view and find the **Marketing** record. (For the **FindRecord Action Arguments,** select **Any Part of Field** in the *Match* box, **No** in the *Match Case* box, **All** in the *Search* box, **Yes** in the *Search As Formatted* box, **No** in the *Only Current Field* box, and **Yes** in the *Find First* box. Then, have the macro print the Marketing record (Selection) only, and close the **Managers** query.

2. Save the macro as **Print Marketing Manager** and close it.

3. Run the macro. Close the database.

CRITICAL *Thinking*

ACTIVITY 5-1

Using the **IA Activity5-1** database file in the data files and the **Houses** table, create a report listing all of the information in the table by agent. Save the report as **Houses by Agent** and print the results. Also, create a macro that will open the **2 Bedrooms** query, find all of the two-bedroom houses, print the results (*Print Range = All*), and close the query. Save the macro as **2 Bedroom Houses for Sale**. Run the macro and close the database.

ACTIVITY 5-2

Using the Help feature, look up the definition of a *subreport*. In your own words, write a brief essay that defines a subreport and provide an example of when you might use a subreport. For your example, assume you have a database containing tables on customers and product sales.

ACTIVITY 5-3

Using the **IA Activity5-1** database file create a PivotChart view of the **Houses** table to show the total amount of listings by agent. Open the **Houses** table and change the view to **PivotChart**. From the Chart Field List, drag and drop the **Agent** field to the *Drop Category Fields Here* box located at the bottom of the chart. Next, drag and drop the **Price** field to the *Drop Data Fields Here* box located at the top of the chart. The chart should show the total amount of listings by agent. Print the chart. Close the table and save changes. Close the database.

INTEGRATING ACCESS

VOCABULARY

Data access page

Data source

Form letter

Main document

Merge fields

Importing and Exporting Data

Because Office is an integrated suite of programs, you can easily import and export data between applications. You can export an Access table to an Excel worksheet, or you can merge records in a table with a Word document. In this lesson, you'll learn how to share data between Access and other applications.

Word to Access

Suppose you have been given a list of names and addresses in a Word file. The names need to be entered into a database. You can easily paste or import the information into an Access table, where you can then edit and sort it, and create forms, queries, reports, and pages from it. If the text from Word is set up as a table or is separated by tabs, Access will automatically create the fields and enter the data as records. If the text is in a single block, all of the text will be pasted into the currently highlighted field.

Access to Word

You can also export table records from an Access database into a Word document. The data is formatted with tabs when it enters the Word document. This feature could be used to create a table in Word, based on data from Access. Merging database records with a Word document to create a form letter is another method for integrating Access and Word, and is discussed later in this lesson.

Access to Excel

There are times when you might want to export Access data into an Excel worksheet. Excel provides powerful calculation and data analysis features that can easily be applied to database records that are exported to an Excel workbook file. Each record in the table appears as a row in the worksheet, and each field is converted to a column.

Excel to Access

You can also import data from an Excel worksheet into an Access database table. A worksheet is set up as columns and rows, much like a database table. The cells cut or copied from the worksheet will appear in the database beginning with the highlighted entry.

You could also use the Import Spreadsheet Wizard to insert Excel data into an Access table. Open the database file, open the File menu and select the Get External Data, and then select Import on the submenu. An Import dialog box opens, where you can select the file you want to import. The Wizard then guides you through the process of placing the spreadsheet data in a table.

 ## S TEP-BY-STEP 6.1

1. Open the **IA Step6-1** database from the data files.

2. Open the **File** menu and choose **Get External Data**, and then select **Import** on the submenu. The Import dialog box appears, similar to that shown in Figure 6-1. From the *Look in* drop-down list, select the folder containing the data files for this course.

Careers

Databases are helpful in the sales business. Salespersons can create a database to store detailed information on each of their customers. They can then create queries and filters to search the customer database for specific information. They can also use the customer database to easily create reports, form letters, and mailing labels.

STEP-BY-STEP 6.1 Continued

FIGURE 6-1
Import dialog box

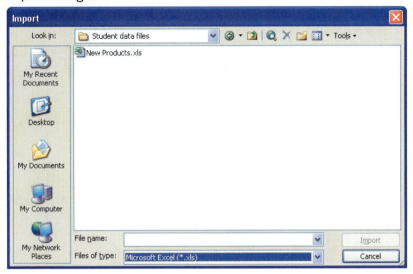

3. Click the down arrow in the *Files of type* box and choose **Microsoft Excel** from the list.

4. Select the **New Products** Excel workbook from the data files.

5. Click **Import**. The Import Spreadsheet Wizard opens, as shown in Figure 6-2. Notice the data from the New Products worksheet appears in the grid.

FIGURE 6-2
Import Spreadsheet Wizard dialog box

6. Click **Next** and a second Wizard dialog box opens, asking if the first row of the spreadsheet contains the column headings.

7. Click **Next** since the first row does contain the column headings and the option is already selected. A third Wizard dialog box appears asking where you would like to store your data.

STEP-BY-STEP 6.1 Continued

8. If not already selected, choose the **In a New Table** option. Click **Next** and a fourth Wizard dialog box appears as shown in Figure 6-3.

FIGURE 6-3
Import Spreadsheet Wizard lets you tailor Excel data

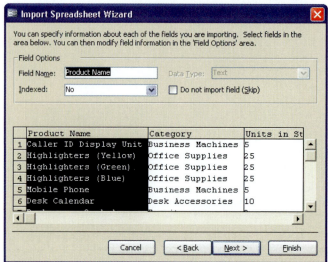

9. Scroll to the right in the grid to view all the field columns in the table. Then click **Next**. This Wizard dialog box asks you to let Access add a primary key to the table.

10. Choose **No primary key** and click **Next**.

11. Key **New Products** into the *Import to Table* box. Click **Finish**.

12. A message appears stating that the Wizard is finished importing the file. Click **OK**.

13. The New Products table should be listed in the Database window. Open the table in Datasheet view. Print the table.

14. Close the table and the database.

Hot Tip

Backing up files on your computer should be a regular practice. To back up a database, open the **File** menu and choose **Back Up Database**. The Save Backup As dialog box displays. Click the down arrow in the *Save in* box and select another location for the backup, such as a CD, DVD, zip disk, etc. The name of the database, along with the current date, is in the *File name* box. If this name for the backup file is okay, click **Save**. If not, key another name and click **Save**. A back up of the database is then created. To restore the database, simply copy the backup database file to the appropriate folder or disk. You can also use Windows Explorer or other backup software to copy a database file to a backup medium.

Form Letters

Another way to integrate Access and Word is through form letters. A *form letter* is a word processor document that uses information inserted from a database in specified areas to personalize a document.

For example, you might send a letter to all of the members of a professional organization using a form letter. In each letter, the information is the same but the names of the recipients will be different. One letter may begin "Dear Mr. Hartsfield" and another "Dear Ms. Perez."

Creating a Form Letter

To create form letters, export information from a data source, such as an Access database, to a document in Word, called the main document. The *main document* contains the information that will stay the same in each form letter. The *data source* contains the recipient information, such as names and addresses, which will vary in each form letter. You can insert the field names, or *merge fields*, in the main document where you want to print the recipient information from the data source. The merge fields you place in the Word document are enclosed in angle brackets (<< Field Name >>). When the main document and the data source are merged, the merge fields in the main document are replaced with the individual recipient information from the data source to create personalized form letters.

Word provides a Mail Merge task pane that makes it easy to create a form letter. To access the Mail Merge task pane, as shown in Figure 6-4, open the Tools menu in Word and choose the Letters and Mailings command. Select Mail Merge from the submenu and the Mail Merge task pane appears on the right side of the screen, as shown in Figure 6-4. You will complete six steps in the Mail Merge task pane to create a form letter. To specify the main document, click Letters in Step 1 and then select the starting document in Step 2. To specify a data source, click *Use an existing list* in Step 3, and click Browse. When the Select Data Source dialog box appears, choose the file you want to use as the data source. To insert the merge fields in Step 4, position the insertion point in the main document and choose the merge field or item, such as an Address Block, to be inserted. Insert all of the merge fields until your main document is complete. In Step 5, you can preview the letters and edit the recipients to be included in the merge. To edit the recipients, click *Edit recipient list* and the Mail Merge Recipients dialog box will appear, as shown in Figure 6-5. You can then choose which recipients you want to merge, and print. When ready, complete the merge and print the letters.

FIGURE 6-4
Mail Merge task pane

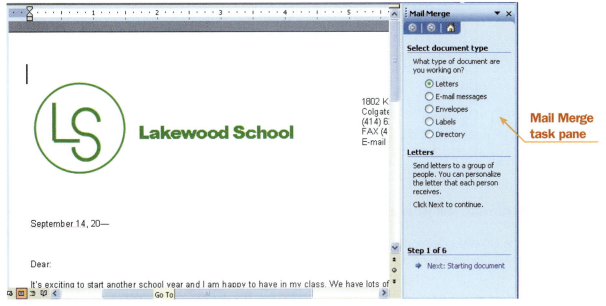

S TEP-BY-STEP 6.2

1. Open **Word** and the **Lakewood letter** document from the data files.

2. Save the file as **Fourth Grade letter**, followed by your initials.

3. Open the **Tools** menu and choose **Letters and Mailings**, and then select **Mail Merge** on the submenu. The Mail Merge task pane appears on the right side of the screen, as shown in Figure 6-4.

4. If not already selected, choose **Letters** in the *Select document type* section of the task pane.

5. Click **Next: Starting document** at the bottom of the task pane. The second Mail Merge task pane appears.

6. If not already selected, choose **Use the current document** in the *Select starting document* section.

7. Click **Next: Select recipients** at the bottom of the task pane. The third Mail Merge task pane appears.

8. If not already selected, choose **Use an existing list** in the *Select recipients* section.

9. Click **Browse** in the *Use an existing list* section. The Select Data Source dialog box appears.

10. Click the down arrow in the **Look in** box to find and select the **Lakewood parents** database in the data files. Click **Open**. The Mail Merge Recipients dialog box appears with the data from the Fourth Grade table, as shown in Figure 6-5. Click **OK**.

FIGURE 6-5
Mail Merge Recipients dialog box

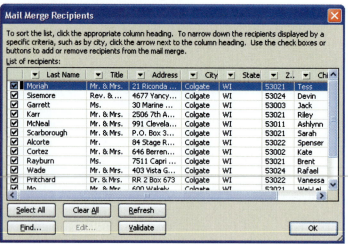

11. Click **Next: Write your letter** at the bottom of the task pane.

12. Within the *Lakewood letter* document (on the left side of the screen), place the insertion point on the second line after the date.

STEP-BY-STEP 6.2 Continued

13. Click **Address block** in the *Write your letter* section of the task pane. The Insert Address Block dialog box appears, as shown in Figure 6-6. (The Address Block is a predefined layout of an address that automatically links the data source with the merge fields.)

FIGURE 6-6
Insert Address Block dialog box

14. Click **OK** and the Address Block merge field is inserted.

15. Within the letter, place the insertion point between *Dear* and the colon (:). Add a blank space.

16. Click **More items** in the task pane. The Insert Merge Field dialog box appears, as shown in Figure 6-7.

FIGURE 6-7
Insert Merge Field dialog box

STEP-BY-STEP 6.2 Continued

17. If not already selected, choose **Title** from the list of fields and click **Insert**. The Title is inserted as a merge field. Click **Close** to close the dialog box.

18. Insert the **Last Name** and **Child's Name** fields, as shown in Figure 6-8, using the same method. (Be sure to add spaces where necessary.)

FIGURE 6-8
Insert Merge fields

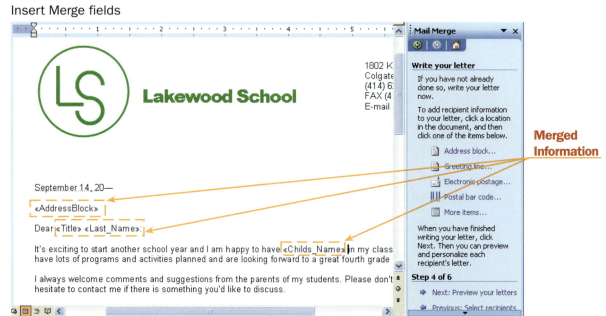

19. When finished, click **Next: Preview your letters** at the bottom of the task pane. The data from the Lakewood parents database is inserted into the merge fields to create the form letters.

20. Click the scroll buttons in the *Preview your letters* section of the task pane to see the other form letters.

21. Save the file. Leave Word open for the next Step-by-Step.

Editing the Recipient List and Printing Form Letters

After the form letters have been created, they are ready to print. If you don't want to print every letter, you can click *Edit recipient list* in the *Make changes* section of the task pane. The Mail Merge Recipients dialog box will reappear, and you can choose which recipients you want to merge and print.

STEP-BY-STEP 6.3

1. The **Fourth Grade Letter** document should be open on your screen. Save it as **Fourth Grade Letter 2**, followed by your initials.

2. Click **Edit recipient list** in the *Make changes* section of the task pane. The Mail Merge Recipients dialog box appears, as shown in Figure 6-5.

3. Click the **Clear All** button to remove the check marks.

4. You want to print only the letters to the parents of *Devin Sisemore* and *Kate Cortez*. Click the check boxes to select their information, as shown in Figure 6-9. Click **OK.**

FIGURE 6-9
Mail Merge Recipients dialog box

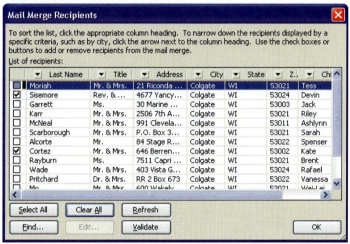

5. Click the scroll buttons in the task pane to see the two form letters.

6. Click **Next: Complete the merge** at the bottom of the task pane. The last Mail Merge task pane appears.

7. Click **Print** in the *Merge* section of the task pane. The Merge to Printer dialog box appears, as shown in Figure 6-10.

FIGURE 6-10
Merge to Printer dialog box

8. If not already selected, choose **All**. Click **OK** and the Print dialog box appears.

9. Click **OK**. Save and close the file.

Mailing Labels

Creating mailing labels is very similar to creating form letters. The main difference is that mailing labels place information from more than one record on the same page. This is because mailing labels usually come in sheets that have as many as 30 labels per page.

To create mailing labels, you will use the Mail Merge task pane again. This time, choose Labels as the starting document. Specify a main document and a data source. You can then choose the label options you want. Next, insert merge fields that contain the address information, and print your mailing labels.

STEP-BY-STEP 6.4

1. Open a new Word document.

2. Save the file as **Fourth Grade labels**, followed by your initials.

3. Open the **Tools** menu and choose **Letters and Mailings**, and then select **Mail Merge** on the submenu. The Mail Merge task pane appears on the right side of the screen.

4. Choose **Labels** in the *Select document type* section of the task pane.

5. Click **Next: Starting document** at the bottom of the task pane. The second Mail Merge task pane appears.

6. Choose **Label options** in the *Change document layout* section of the task pane. The Label Options dialog box appears, as shown in Figure 6-11.

FIGURE 6-11
Label Options dialog box

7. In the Printer information section, be sure the correct type of printer (either **Laser and ink jet** or **Dot matrix**) is chosen, and then select the Tray option that you wish to use with your printer. (Typically, if you are printing out only one sheet of mailing labels you would manually feed that sheet into the printer.)

STEP-BY-STEP 6.4 Continued

8. For our example, the *Label products* box should have **Avery standard** chosen. In the *Product number* box, scroll down to highlight **5160 – Address**. (Many different companies' products are available from which to choose.)

9. Click **OK**. A page of blank labels appears on the screen.

10. Click **Next: Select recipients** at the bottom of the task pane. The third Mail Merge task pane appears.

11. If not already selected, choose **Use an existing list** in the *Select recipients* section.

12. Click **Browse** in the *Use an existing list* section. The Select Data Source dialog box appears.

13. Click the down arrow in the **Look in** box and find the **Lakewood parents** database in the data files. Click **Open**. The Mail Merge Recipients dialog box appears with the data from the Fourth Grade table. Click **OK**.

14. Click **Next: Arrange your labels** at the bottom of the task pane.

15. Be sure the insertion point appears within the first label. (If you cannot see the individual labels, open the **View** menu and choose **Show Gridlines**.)

16. Click **Address block** in the *Arrange your labels* section of the task pane. The Insert Address Block dialog box appears.

17. Click **OK** and the Address Block merge field is inserted.

18. Scroll down to the bottom of the task pane. Click **Update all labels** in the *Replicate labels* section of the task pane. The layout of the first label is copied to the other labels on the page, as shown in Figure 6-12.

FIGURE 6-12
Inserted merge fields

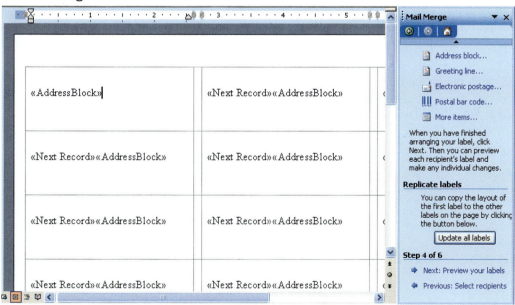

STEP-BY-STEP 6.4 Continued

19. Click **Next: Preview your labels** at the bottom of the task pane. The data from the Lakewood parents database is inserted into the merge fields to create the mailing labels.

20. Click the scroll buttons within the document to view the other labels.

21. When finished, click **Next: Complete the merge** at the bottom of the task pane. The last Mail Merge task pane appears.

22. Click **Print** in the *Merge* section of the task pane. The Merge to Printer dialog box appears.

23. If it is not already selected, choose **All**. Click **OK** and the Print dialog box appears.

24. Click **OK**. Save and close the file. Close Word.

Data Access Pages

A *data access page* is an object created in a database that lets you publish other objects, such as tables, forms, and reports, to the Web. You can then view the database using the Web.

Creating a Data Access Page

 As with other Access objects, you can create a data access page manually or use the Page Wizard. The Page Wizard will ask you detailed questions about the fields, format and layout, and then create a page based on your answers. In this lesson, you will create a data access page using the Page Wizard.

> **Hot Tip**
>
> Most of the same features of forms and reports, such as grouping and sorting, are also used in the design of a data access page.

STEP-BY-STEP 6.5

1. Open Access and the **IA Step6-5** database from the data files.

2. Click **Pages** on the Objects bar.

3. Click **New**. The New Data Access Page dialog box appears, as shown in Figure 6-13.

STEP-BY-STEP 6.5 Continued

FIGURE 6-13
New Data Access Page dialog box

4. Choose **Page Wizard** from the list.

5. Click the down arrow and choose the **Products** table from the drop-down list. Click **OK**. The Page Wizard dialog box appears, as shown in Figure 6-14.

FIGURE 6-14
Page Wizard dialog box

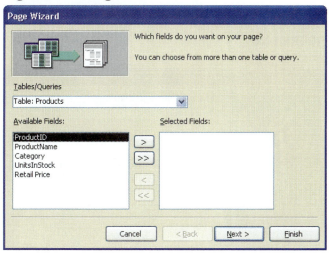

6. Click **>>** to move all of the *Available Fields* to the *Selected Fields* box.

7. Click **Next**. The Page Wizard now gives you the option to group the data.

8. Click **Next**. For this data access page, you will not group the data. The Page Wizard asks you which fields you want to sort by, as shown in Figure 6-15.

STEP-BY-STEP 6.5 Continued

FIGURE 6-15
Sorting a data access page

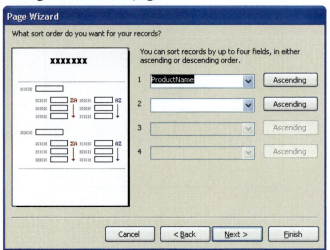

9. Click the down arrow next to the number 1 box and choose **ProductName** as the first sort field. For this data access page, you will have an ascending sort by one field only.

10. Click **Next**. The final Page Wizard dialog box appears, as shown in Figure 6-16.

FIGURE 6-16
Naming the data access page

STEP-BY-STEP 6.5 Continued

11. Key **Products Page** as the title of the page.

12. Choose the option to **Open the page** and click **Finish**.

13. The data access page appears, as shown in Figure 6-17.

FIGURE 6-17
The Products Page data access page

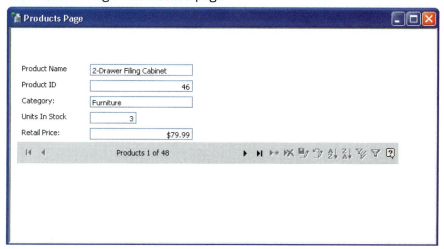

14. Click the **Next** button to scroll through the data until you find the Disk Storage Box in the Product Name box.

15. Open the **File** menu and choose **Print**. The Print dialog box appears.

16. Click **Print**. The product information for the Disk Storage Box will print.

17. Open the **File** menu and choose **Close**. A message will appear asking if you want to save changes to the data access page. Click **Yes**.

18. The Save As Data Access Page dialog box appears, as shown in Figure 6-18.

> ### Did You Know?
>
> To display a data access page as it will appear to users on the Web, open the **File** menu and choose **Web Page Preview**. This will start Internet Explorer and display the page. Note that users using other Web browsers may see the pages differently. You should test your page in several browsers.

STEP-BY-STEP 6.5 Continued

FIGURE 6-18
Save As Data Access Page dialog box

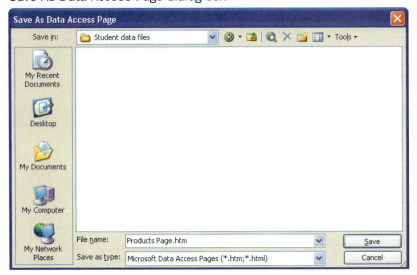

19. Click the down arrow in the *Save in* box to find the location in which to save the file.

20. If necessary, key **Products Page** in the *File name* box and click **Save**. A message will appear warning you that the page might not be able to connect to data through the network. Click **OK**.

21. The Products Page is now listed as a Pages object in the Database window. Close the database.

SUMMARY

In this lesson, you learned:

- Because Microsoft Office is an integrated suite of programs, you can easily import and export data between applications. No matter which applications you are using, the data is automatically formatted so that it can be used in the destination file.

- A form letter is a word processor document that uses information from a database in specified areas to personalize a document. To create form letters, you insert merge fields in the main document that are replaced with information from the data source.

- Creating mailing labels is very similar to creating form letters. The Mail Merge task pane makes it easy to create form letters or mailing labels.

- A data access page is an object created in a database that lets you publish other objects, such as tables, forms, and reports, to the Web. You can then view the database using the Web.

VOCABULARY *Review*

> **Define the following terms:**
>
> Data access page   Form letter   Merge fields
> Data source   Main document

REVIEW *Questions*

TRUE/FALSE

Circle T if the statement is true or F if the statement is false.

T F **1.** A merge field is a field name in the main document where you want to print the information from the data source.

T F **2.** When moving and copying data within the Office suite of programs, the data is automatically formatted so it can be used in the destination file.

T F **3.** The data source contains the information that stays the same in each form letter.

T F **4.** A data access page is an object that allows you to view a database using the Web.

T F **5.** You can use the Mail Merge task pane to create mailing labels.

WRITTEN QUESTIONS

Write a brief answer to the following questions.

1. What option do you click to choose the records you want to merge and print in a form letter?

2. Creating mailing labels involves integrating which two Office applications?

3. What is the Main Document in a form letter?

4. After opening a new Word document, what option do you choose on the Tools menu to create mailing labels?

5. What is a form letter?

PROJECTS

PROJECT 6-1

1. Open **Word** and the **InfoTech letter** document from the data files.

2. Save the file as **Employee Dinner letter**, followed by your initials.

3. Using the Mail Merge task pane, create a form letter by merging the **Employee Dinner letter** document with data from the **Employee Information** table in the **IA Project6-1** database.

4. Insert the merge fields as shown in Figure 6-19.

5. Preview the letters.

6. Save the file and leave it open for the next project.

FIGURE 6-19

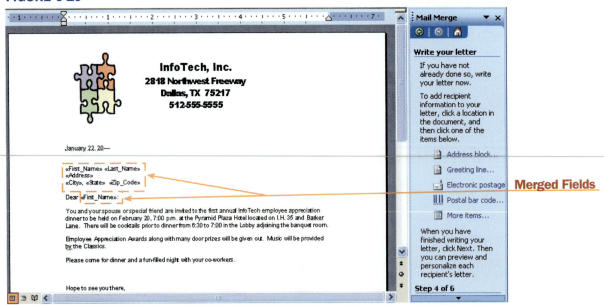

 **PROJECT 6-2**

1. The Employee Dinner letter should be open on your screen. Save it as **Employee Dinner letter 2**, followed by your initials.

2. In the Mail Merge task pane, click **Edit recipient list** and select only the employees in the Public Relations department.

3. When finished, preview the form letters.

4. Merge and print the form letters.

5. Save and close the file.

 **PROJECT 6-3**

1. Open a new Word document.

2. Save the file as **Employee Dinner labels**, followed by your initials.

3. Use the Mail Merge task pane to create mailing labels. Merge the **Employee Information** table from the **IA Project6-1** database.

4. In the Label Options dialog box, be sure **Laser and ink jet** is chosen as the Printer information. Select the Tray option that you wish to use with your printer. Choose **Avery standard** as the Label product. Highlight **5160 – Address** as the Product number.

5. Insert the **Address block** merge field within the first label. Be sure to copy the layout of the first label to the other labels on the page, as shown in Figure 6-20.

6. When finished, merge and print the labels.

7. Save and close the file.

FIGURE 6-20

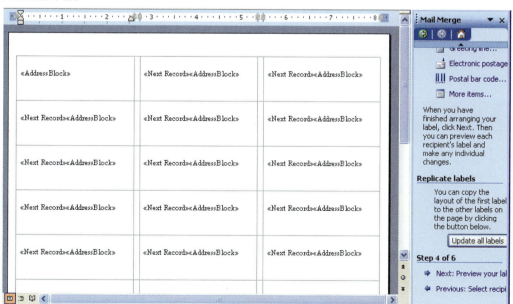

PROJECT 6-4

1. Open **Access** and the **IA Project6-4** database from the data files.

2. Using the **Page Wizard,** create a data access page for the **Employee Information** table.

3. Select all of the available fields. Do not group the data. Sort by the **Last Name** field in ascending order.

4. Key **Employee Page** as the title of the page and choose to **Open the page**.

5. Scroll through the data until you find the employee information on **Alex Pharr**.

6. Print the information.

7. Save the new data access page as **Employee Page,** followed by your initials. (Click **OK** if a message appears warning you that the page might not be able to connect to data through the network.)

8. Close the database.

CRITICAL *Thinking*

  ACTIVITY 6-1

Teachers need to send consent forms to each student's parents at the beginning of the year. This allows the students to participate in field trips or special activities away from the school. Create a consent form letter by merging the **Consent letter** with data from the **Third grade** table in the **Washington parents** database. The letter and database are stored in the data files. Save the new document as **Third Consent letter**. Merge and print letters for only the students with last names of **Davis, Hope, Shihab,** and **Ellis**. Save the new document as **Third Consent letter 2**.

 ACTIVITY 6-2

Using the Help feature, look up the steps for adding a hyperlink to a form or report in a database. Write down the basic steps. Give an example of why you might add a hyperlink to an Inventory, Customer, or Vendor database.

INTRODUCTORY
MICROSOFT ACCESS

COMMAND SUMMARY

FEATURE	MENU COMMAND	TOOLBAR BUTTON	LESSON
Close	File, Close	☒	1
Close a Table	File, Close	☒	1
Column Width	Format, Column Width		2
Compact and Repair a Database	Tools, Database Utilities, Compact and Repair Database		3
Copy Record	Edit, Copy	📋	2
Cut Record	Edit, Cut	✂	2
Database (Create)	File, New	▢	1
Delete Record	Edit, Delete Record	▶✕	2
Delete Row	Edit, Delete Rows	▤	1
Design View	Highlight Name of Object, Design	◪	1
Exit Access	File, Exit		1
Field Properties	Highlight Name of Table, Design	◪	2
File, Create	File, New	▢	1
Filter, Apply	Filter, Apply Filter/Sort	▽	4
Filter, Create	Records, Filter		4
Filter, Remove	Filter, Remove Filter/Sort	▽	4
Find Data	Edit, Find	🔍	4
First Record		◁◁	2
Form, Create	Forms, New		3
Form, Modify	Highlight Name of Form, Design	◪	3
Freeze Column	Format, Freeze Columns		2
Index Field	Highlight Name of Table, Design	◪	4
Insert Hyperlink	Highlight Name of Object, Design, Insert, Hyperlink	🌐	3
Insert Row	Insert, Rows	▤	1
Last Record		▷▷	2
Macro, Create	Macro, New		5

FEATURE	MENU COMMAND	TOOLBAR BUTTON	LESSON
Mailing Labels, Create	Tools, Letters and Mailings, Mail Merge		6
Mail Merge Wizard	Tools, Letters and Mailings, Mail Merge		6
New Record			2
Next Record			2
Open Existing Database	File, Open		1
Paste Record	Edit, Paste		2
Previous Record			2
Primary Key, Create	Highlight Name of Table, Design, Highlight Name of field		4
Print	File, Print		1
Query, Create	Queries, New		4
Relationships, Define	Tools, Relationships		4
Relationships, Print	File, Print Relationships		4
Report, Create	Reports, New		5
Report, Modify	Highlight Name of Report, Design		5
Row Height	Format, Row Height		2
Save	File, Save		1
Sort Ascending	Records, Sort, Sort Ascending		4
Sort Descending	Records, Sort, Sort Descending		4
Start Access	Start, All Programs, Microsoft Office, Microsoft Office Access 2003		1
Subdatasheet, Insert	Insert, Subdatasheet		4
Table, Create	Tables, New		1
Table, Modify	Highlight Name of Table, Design		1
Toolbox, Display	View, Toolbox		3
Undo Changes in Cell	Edit, Undo Typing		2
Undo Changes in Previous Cell	Edit, Undo Current Field/ Record or Esc key		2
Unfreeze All Columns	Format, Unfreeze All Columns		2
View, Datasheet			1
View, Design			1

REVIEW *Questions*

TRUE/FALSE

Circle T if the statement is true or F if the statement is false.

T   F   **1.**   A record appears as a column in Datasheet view.

T   F   **2.**   The navigation buttons are used to move around the datasheet.

T   F   **3.**   Queries allow the most complex searches.

T   F   **4.**   Sections are shown in Modify Report view.

T   F   **5.**   In the Label Options dialog box, you choose the data source you will be using for the mailing labels.

WRITTEN QUESTIONS

Write a brief answer to the following questions.

1.   What data type is used to store dollar amounts?

2.   What option makes Access choose the width of a column?

3.   What button displays the results of a filter?

4.   What is a macro?

5.   In what document are merge fields inserted?

PROJECTS

PROJECT 1

1. Open the **IA Project1** database from the data files.

2. Open the **Stores** table in Datasheet view.

3. Move the **Hours** column between the **Specialty** and **Credit Cards** fields.

4. Move record **4** to the bottom of the table.

5. Close the table. Click **Yes** if prompted to save changes to the table.

6. Open the **Stores** table in Design view.

7. Insert a field between the **Hours** and **Credit Cards** fields. Name the field **Last Visit** with the **Date/Time** data type and **Date of last visit** in the description field.

8. Choose **Medium Date** for the format of the **Last Visit** field.

9. Change the field size of the **Specialty** field to **25**.

10. Make the **Name** field **Required**.

11. Save the table design. A message may appear asking if you want to continue. Click **Yes**. Another message may appear asking if you want to test the changes. Click **Yes**.

12. Switch to Datasheet view and print the table in landscape orientation.

13. Close the table and the database.

PROJECT 2

1. Open **IA Project2** from the data files.

2. Create a new form with the Form Wizard using the **Stores** table.

3. Add the **Name, Specialty, Hours,** and **Credit Cards** fields.

4. Use the **Tabular** layout and the **Standard** style.

5. Title the form **Store Form.**

6. Using the **Store Form,** add the following record:

Name	Specialty	Hours	Credit Cards
Sports Authority	Sporting Goods	9am to 9pm	Yes

7. Print all the records in the form.

8. Close the form and the database.

PROJECT 3

1. Open **IA Project3** from the data files.

2. Open the **Employee Information** table in Datasheet view.

3. Sort the table so that the employees' salaries are listed from lowest to highest.

4. Change the left and right margins to .5" and print the results of the sort in landscape orientation.

5. Create a query that displays the employees with a title of manager. Have the query display only the **Last Name**, **First Name**, **Department**, **Title**, and **Salary** fields. Save the query as **Managers**.

6. Run the query and print the results. Close the query. If prompted, save the changes and then close the database.

PROJECT 4

1. Open **IA Project4** from the data files.

2. Open the **Employee Information** table, and use the Find command to locate the employees with a title of Account Executive.

3. Create a Filter By Selection to display only the employees in the **Sales** department.

4. Change the left and right margins to .5" and print the results of the filter in landscape orientation.

5. Show all the records in the table.

6. Close the table and the database.

PROJECT 5

1. Open **IA Project5** from the data files.

2. Use the Report Wizard to create a report. Use the **Products** table and choose the **ProductName**, **Category**, and **RetailPrice** fields.

3. Group the report by **Category** and sort by **RetailPrice** in descending order. (Click the **Ascending** button to change the sort to Descending.)

4. Choose **Stepped** layout, **Portrait** orientation, and **Bold** style.

5. Title the report **Products by Retail Price**. Select the option to preview the report.

6. Print the report.

7. Close the report and the database.

PROJECT 6

1. Open the **IA Project6** database from the data files.

2. Create a macro to open the **Products** table in Datasheet view, print all the pages, and close the table.

3. Save the macro as **Print Products Table**.

4. Run the macro.

5. Close the database.

SIMULATION

You work at the Java Internet Café, which has been open a short time. The café serves coffee, other beverages, and pastries, and offers Internet access. Seven computers are set up on tables along the north side of the store. Customers can come in, have a cup of coffee, a Danish, and explore the World Wide Web.

All membership fees for March were due on March 1. A few members have not paid their monthly dues. Your manager asks you to write a letter to the members as a reminder.

SCANS JOB 1

1. Open **Word** and the **Payment Late Letter** from the data files.

2. Save the document as **Payment Late Merge Letter**, followed by your initials.

3. Open **Excel** and the **Computer Prices** workbook from the data files.

4. In the spreadsheet, copy the range **A1** through **B11**, and paste it between the first and second paragraphs of the **Payment Late Merge Letter**. Make sure there is one blank line before and after the spreadsheet data.

5. Close **Computer Prices** without saving, and exit Excel.

6. Open **Access**, open the **Java members** database from the data files, and then open the **Membership** table.

7. Scott Payton just paid his membership fee. Key **$10.00** into the March Paid field of his record.

8. Add the following new member to the end of the database:

   Ms. Halie Shook, 1290 Wood Crest Apt. 224, Boulder, CO 80302, March Paid = $10

9. Close the table and save changes. Close the database and Access. The *Payment Late Merge Letter* document should be displayed.

10. Use the Mail Merge task pane to create form letters by merging the **Payment Late Merge Letter** document with the **Membership** table in the **Java members** database. Leave a blank line after the date, and then insert a merge field for *Name* on the next line, a merge field for *Address* on the next line, and a merge field for *City*, *State*, and *Zip* on the next line below the address.

11. When finished, preview the letters.

12. In the Mail Merge task pane, click **Edit recipient list** and select only the members with **0** in the **March Paid** field. (There should be three form letters.)

13. Merge and print the three form letters.

14. Save and close **Payment Late Merge Letter**. Leave Word open for the next job.

SCANS **JOB 2**

You need to create mailing labels for the form letters you printed yesterday.

1. Open a new Word document.

2. Save the file as **Java labels**.

3. Use the Mail Merge task pane to create mailing labels.

4. In the Label Options dialog box, be sure **Laser and ink jet** is chosen as the *Printer Information*. Select the *Tray* option that you wish to use with your printer. Choose **Avery standard** as the *Label Product*. Highlight **5160 – Address** as the *Product number*.

5. Merge the **Membership** table from the **Java Members** database.

6. Insert the merge fields **Name**, **Address**, and **City_State_Zip** within the first label. Be sure to copy the layout of the first label to the other labels on the page.

7. When finished, merge and print the labels.

8. Save and close **Java labels**. Exit **Word**.

ADVANCED MICROSOFT® ACCESS

Unit

 Estimated Time for Unit: 13 hours

MODIFYING TABLE DESIGN

VOCABULARY

Customize

Input mask

Lookup field

Properties

Validation rule

Introduction

Microsoft Access is a powerful database application that lets you store, organize, and manipulate vast amounts of data. You should already be familiar with the primary objects that comprise a database: tables, forms, and reports. In these advanced lessons, you'll learn more about each of these objects, plus other features that help you manage and control your database records.

In this lesson, you will learn more about the various data types you can apply when defining fields in a table. You will also explore the properties associated with particular fields. This lesson discusses the use of input masks in setting up data types for fields. You will also learn about applying validation rules to data and how to create a lookup field.

Selecting and Customizing an Input Mask

An input mask is a pattern for certain types of data entered in a field. For example, if you need to enter phone numbers in the format (XXX) XXX-XXXX, it might get tiresome typing both the parentheses and the dash. Instead, you can apply Access's Phone Number input mask and then all you need to type is the numbers. The input mask inserts the parentheses and hyphen in the correct positions. You may also *customize* an input mask.

To create an input mask, you must be in the table's Design view. Select the field for which you want to create the input mask and then click in the Input Mask text box in the Field Properties pane. The Build button (an ellipsis) appears at the end of the text box, as shown in Figure 7-1.

FIGURE 7-1
Build button for Input Mask

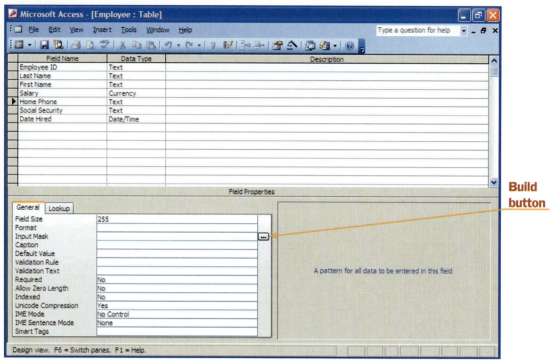

When you click the Build button, a message box displays requesting that you save the table before continuing. Click Yes to save the table. Access will then start the Input Mask Wizard, as shown in Figure 7-2. There are several common input mask formats from which you can choose.

FIGURE 7-2
Input Mask Wizard

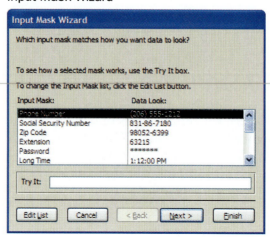

STEP-BY-STEP 7.1 Continued

16. Click **Finish** to apply your mask. Click the **Save** button on the Standard toolbar. Your screen should look like Figure 7-7.

FIGURE 7-7
Social Security Number input mask

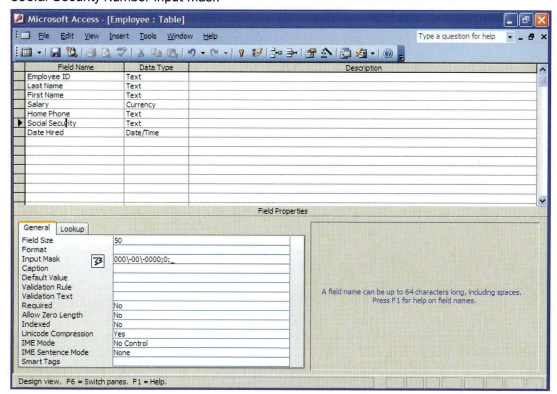

17. Let's customize an input mask. Click in the **Social Security** field.

18. Click in the **Input Mask** property box. Replace the hyphens with underscores as shown in Figure 7-8.

Select an input mask and then click in the Try It box to see an example of how your data will look. Clicking the Edit List button provides one method for editing or creating a custom input mask. Once you select the mask you need, click the Next button to go to the next step in the Input Mask Wizard, as shown in Figure 7-3.

FIGURE 7-3
Applying an Input Mask

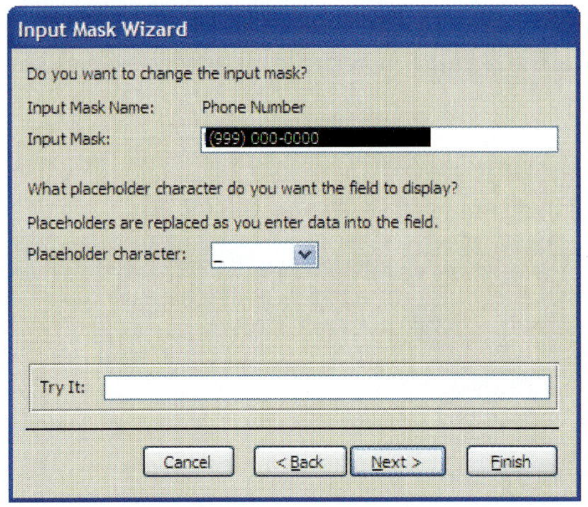

This step of the wizard asks you if you need to make changes to this mask. You may also select the placeholder for your number. The default placeholder is the underscore. The placeholder simply identifies in the table that there is an input mask assigned to the field. The placeholder is replaced by the data you enter in the field. Click the Next button and the Input Mask Wizard dialog box shown in Figure 7-4 appears.

FIGURE 7-4
Storing data in the Input Mask Wizard

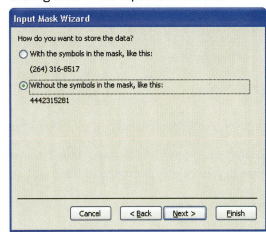

In this step of the wizard, you will decide how to store the data. For example, you may want a date field stored in the format mm-dd-yy. Just select this format and Access will store newly entered dates with this format. Most often, data will be stored with the symbols. Click the Next button and the final Input Mask Wizard dialog box appears, as shown in Figure 7-5. Clicking the Finish button will create your mask. You may create an input mask when you first define a field in a table or after the field is defined and data entered in the field.

> ### Hot Tip
>
> When you apply an input mask to an existing field that already contains data, Access may ask you to check the existing data with the new rules.

FIGURE 7-5
Final Input Mask Wizard dialog box

STEP-BY-STEP 7.1

1. Open the **AA Step7-1** database from the data files.

2. Open the **Employee** table in **Design View**.

3. Select the **Home Phone** field name.

4. In the General tab of the *Field Properties* pane, click in the **Input Mask** text box.

5. Click the **Build** button to start the Input Mask Wizard. *Note:* If this is the first time you are using the Input Mask Wizard, you may be prompted to install it.

6. Select the **Phone Number** input mask, if necessary. Click in the **Try It** box to view the pattern. Click **Next**.

7. You will not change the input mask. Click **Next**.

8. Select the **With the symbols in the mask, like this** option. Click **Next**.

STEP-BY-STEP 7.1 Continued

9. Click **Finish** to apply your input mask. Your screen should look similar to Figure 7-6. (When you sav or move to another field, Access may add additional punctuation to the mask.) Click the **Save** butto

FIGURE 7-6
Phone Number input mask

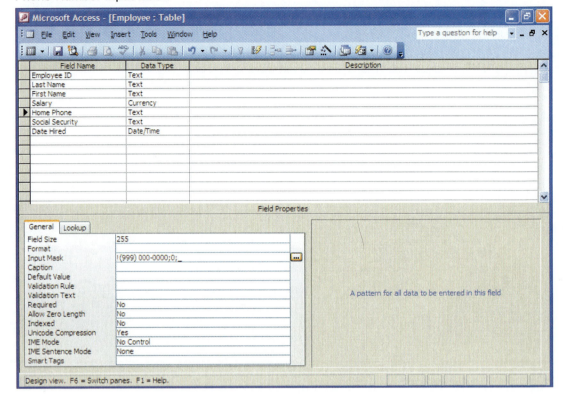

10. Let's create another input mask. Switch to Design View. Select the **Social Security** field name.

11. In the *Field Properties* pane, click in the **Input Mask** text box.

12. Click the **Build** button to start the Input Mask Wizard.

13. Click the **Social Security Number** input mask. Click in the **Try It** box to view the pattern, the click **Next**.

14. You will not change the input mask. Click **Next**.

15. Select the **With the symbols in the mask, like this** option. Click **Next**.

STEP-BY-STEP 7.1 Continued

FIGURE 7-8
Customized input mask

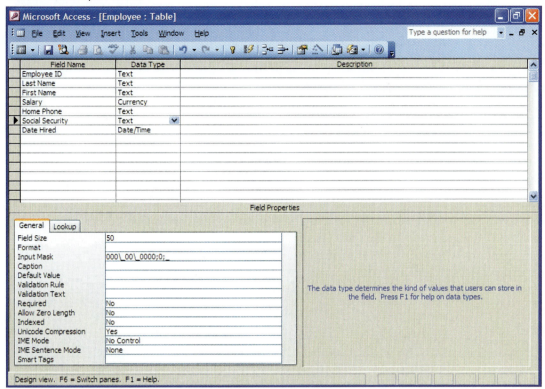

19. Click the **Save** button and then switch to the **Datasheet View**. Note that the Input Mask is not applied to existing records. Remain in the Employee table (Datasheet View) for the next Step-by-Step.

Entering Data into Input Mask Fields

After you have applied an input mask to a field, the format will be applied automatically as you enter new records. In this next Step-by-Step, you will enter data into fields and Access will reformat the data according to the input mask.

STEP-BY-STEP 7.2

1. Go to the **Home Phone** field of record **5** and select the value currently entered.

2. Type 8175557373. When you start to type, underscores appear. This indicates that a mask has been applied to the field.

3. Press **Tab** to go to the **Social Security** field.

4. Type **000000005**. Notice how the input mask inserts the underscores as previously defined in the customized input mask.

STEP-BY-STEP 7.2 Continued

5. Click in a different record to save the changes.

6. Adjust the column widths in the table as you feel appropriate. Then print the table in landscape orientation. Close the table but leave the database open for the next Step-by-Step.

Setting Validation Rules

You can enhance the efficiency of data entry by setting validation rules. *Validation rules* are properties applied to a field that either require certain values to be entered or prevent them from being entered in a field. For example, validation rules can require that data entered in a salary field not exceed a certain dollar amount, such as $50,000. This feature can help prevent data entry errors and increase accuracy and conformity.

When you set a validation rule on a field, you are given the option to create a message that explains the validation rule to the data entry person. The validation text is displayed in a message box that appears when data entered into the cell does not meet the validation rule. Using the above example, if a dollar amount greater than $50,000 is entered in the salary field, the validation message might be "Salary amounts cannot exceed $50,000."

STEP-BY-STEP 7.3

1. Click **Tables** on the *Objects* bar, if necessary, and double-click **Create table in Design view**.

2. Define two fields for the table: The first field should be named **Product Description** and should be the **Text** data type. The second field should be named **Product Price** and should be the **Currency** data type.

3. Click the **Save** button, enter **Product Sales** as the table name, and click **OK**.

4. Select **No** if asked to create a primary key field.

5. Select the **Product Price** field name.

6. In the *Field Properties* pane, click in the **Validation Rule** box and enter **<50**. This will restrict any product price that is equal to or more than $50 from being entered.

7. Click in the **Validation Text** box and enter **All product prices are less than $50**. See Figure 7-9.

STEP-BY-STEP 7.3 Continued

FIGURE 7-9
Validation Rule and Validation Text

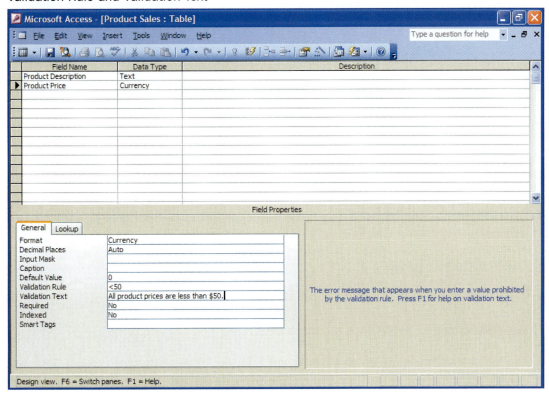

8. Click the **Save** button and then switch to Datasheet view.

9. Enter the following records:

Product Description	Product Price
Dog Carrier - Small	$27.50
Dog Carrier - Large	$500.00

10. When you press **Enter**, you should see a message box that displays the validation text as shown in Figure 7-10. Click **OK.** (Your message boxes may appear in a different format depending upon your use of the Office Assistant.)

> **Speech Recognition**
>
> If you have speech recognition capabilities, enable the Voice Command mode and say the appropriate steps to select Create table in Design view.

FIGURE 7-10
Message box

11. Enter **$47.50** for the Product Price and press **Enter**. Notice that Access accepts this amount as it is less than $50. Leave this table open for the next Step-by-Step.

Setting Required Properties

 For some fields, you may want to apply the Required *property*, which means that a field cannot be left blank when records are entered. For example, you might set up a table so that a customer's phone number must be entered in the phone number field. Access will not move to another record until data is entered in this field.

STEP-BY-STEP 7.4

1. Switch to Design View for the **Product Sales** table.

2. Select the **Product Description** field and then click in the **Required** property text box.

3. Click the down arrow that appears at the end of the *Required* text box and click **Yes**.

4. Click the **Save** button. Access displays a message box that asks if you want to test the existing field information with the new required property selection. Click **Yes**.

5. Switch to Datasheet View.

6. Go to the first empty **Product Price** field

7. Key **$43.00** for the Product Price and press **Enter**.

8. You will see a warning box as shown in Figure 7-11 that explains that the Product Description field cannot contain a Null value. Click **OK** to close the warning box.

FIGURE 7-11
Warning box

9. Click in the **Product Description** field for the record you are adding and enter **Cat Carrier - Medium**.

10. Close the table. Leave the database open for the next Step-by-Step.

> **Speech Recognition**
>
> If you have speech recognition capabilities, enable the Voice Command mode and say the appropriate steps to close the table.

Creating Lookup Fields

You can define a lookup field in a table as a field that actually "looks up" and pulls data from a field in another table or query in the database. Looking up data from existing tables can help prevent data entry errors. You can create a lookup field by using the Lookup Wizard. Or you can click the Lookup tab in the *Field Properties* pane and specify the table or query containing the data you want to look up as shown in Figure 7-12.

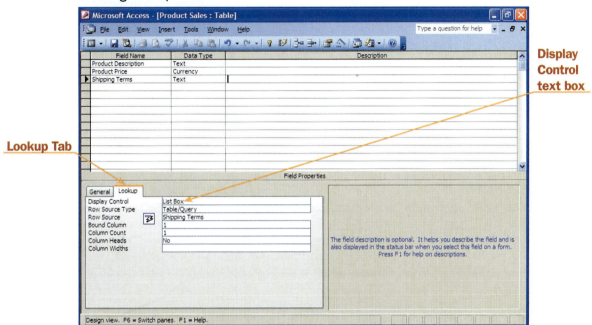

In the following Step-by-Step, you will create a table that has only one field. This field will contain several shipping payment terms. After this table is created, you will open an existing table and "look up" data in the new table in order to insert values in the existing table.

STEP-BY-STEP 7.5

1. Create a new table in Design view.

2. Define a field named **Shipping Terms** of **Text** data type.

3. Click the **Save** button, enter **Shipping Terms** as the table name, and click **OK**.

4. Select **No** if asked to create a primary key field.

5. Click the **View** button to switch to Datasheet View.

STEP-BY-STEP 7.5 Continued

6. Enter the following shipping terms as new records:

Record 1	Net 10th
Record 2	COD
Record 3	Cash Only
Record 4	1% in 10 Days

7. Save and close the **Shipping Terms** table.

8. Open the **Product Sales** table in Design View.

9. Define a new field named **Shipping Terms** with the **Text** data type.

10. With the **Shipping Terms** field selected, click the **Lookup** tab in the *Field Properties* pane.

11. Click in the *Display Control* box.

12. Click the down arrow at the end of the *Display Control* box and click **List Box**.

13. Click in the *Row Source* box. Note that Table/Query displays in the *Row Source Type* box.

14. Click the down arrow at the end of the *Row Source* text box and click **Shipping Terms**.

15. Click the **Save** button and switch to Datasheet View.

16. Add a new record: enter **Cat Carrier - Small** in the Product Description field and **$23.50** in the Product Price field.

STEP-BY-STEP 7.5 Continued

17. In the Shipping Terms field, click the down arrow. Your screen should look similar to Figure 7-13. Choose **1% in 10 Days**.

FIGURE 7-13
Lookup field

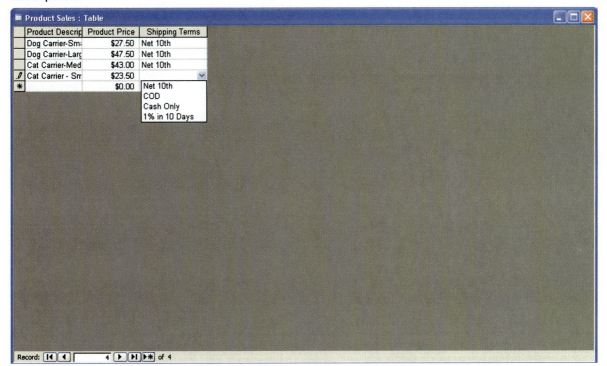

18. Enter **Net 10th** as the shipping term for the existing records.

19. Adjust the column widths in the table, if necessary. Click the **Save** button. Then print the table and close the database.

<table>
<tr><td>**Speech Recognition** </td></tr>
<tr><td>If you have speech recognition capabilities, enable the Voice Command mode and say the appropriate steps to print and close the table.</td></tr>
</table>

Time Saver

Access has several time saving shortcuts for entering data. For example, Ctrl + ' (apostrophe) copies the value from the same field in the previous record, Ctrl + ; (semicolon) enters the current date into the field and Ctrl + : (colon) enters the current time.

<table>
<tr><td>**Integration Tip** </td></tr>
<tr><td>You can copy data from an Excel spreadsheet or a table in Word and paste it into a table in Access. You will first need to select the location in Access where the data will be pasted.</td></tr>
</table>

STEP-BY-STEP 7.6

1. Open the **Time Savers** database from the data files.

2. Open the **Book Sales** table.

3. Key the following records.

ORDER ID	ORDER DATE	PART NUMBER	CUSTOMER ID	QUANTITY SOLD	PRICE
11	Press CRTL+; (semicolon)	231T2005	20932	50	40.95
12	Press Ctrl+' (apostrophe)	Press Ctrl+' (apostrophe)	Press Ctrl+' (apostrophe)	55	39.95

4. Close the table and close the database.

SUMMARY

In this lesson, you learned:

■ Input masks are used to save data entry time and improve accuracy of the data entered. You may also create custom input masks.

■ After the input mask is created, data entered into the field will display the new format. In most instances, an input mask created on an existing field will apply the formatting changes to values already entered in the field.

■ Validation rules can help prevent data entry errors by indicating when incorrect data is entered.

■ When you apply the required property to a field, Access requires that a value be entered in the field before it lets you complete the record entry. Access will not allow another field to be selected until the field with required properties has data entered.

■ A lookup field lets you pull or "look up" data from another table or query in the same database.

VOCABULARY *Review*

Define the following terms:

Customize	Lookup field	Validation rule
Input mask	Properties	

REVIEW *Questions*

WRITTEN QUESTIONS

Write a brief answer to the following questions.

1. List three input masks that are provided in the Input Mask Wizard.

2. To which data types can you add an input mask?

3. What does the Input Mask Wizard do?

4. When you assign an input mask to a field that already contains data, what happens to that data?

5. Why would you want to assign an input mask to a field?

6. Explain the difference between a validation rule and validation text.

7. Explain the purpose of the Required field property.

8. What is the benefit of creating a Lookup field?

9. Explain the steps for creating a Lookup field.

10. Explain the steps for setting a Required property field to Yes.

PROJECTS

PROJECT 7-1

1. Open the database **AA Project7-1** from the data files.

2. Open the **Employees** table in Design View.

3. Enter an input mask for the **Social Security** field.

4. Make this field a *Required* field.

5. Print the table in landscape orientation.

6. Save the table, if necessary, and close the database.

Betty project no SSno

PROJECT 7-2

1. Open the database **AA Project7-2** from the data files.

2. Open the **Employees** table in Design View.

3. Make the **Employee ID** field a *Required* field and create an input mask for the *Phone Number* field.

4. Print the table.

5. Save the table, if necessary, and close the database.

Landscape

Betty project no employee ID

CRITICAL *Thinking*

ACTIVITY 7-1

You are the office manager for the Sadie Products Corporation. After viewing the company's existing database, **AA Activity7-1,** you realize that a new table needs to be created for recording sales information.

1. Define the following fields in the table:
    Customer ID
    Employee ID
    Product ID
    Quantity Sold

2. Save the table as **January Sales.**

3. For the **Employee ID** field, apply the lookup property so that you can pull data from the **Employee** table, using the **List Box** display control. Save your edits.

4. For the **Product ID** field, apply the lookup property so that you can pull data from the Products table, using the **List Box** display control. Save your edits.

5. Change **Customer ID** to a *Required* property field. Save your edits and change to the Datasheet View, click in the Lookup fields, and then click the down arrows to display the lists.

6. Save and close the table. Close the database.

ACTIVITY 7-2

Use the Access Help system to find information on Data Validation and Record Validation. Write a brief explanation of these features.

RELATIONSHIPS IN TABLES AND QUERIES

VOCABULARY

Junction Table

One-to-many relationship

One-to-one relationship

Primary key

Primary table

Referential integrity

Relationship

Introduction

In this lesson, you will learn how to create relationships between tables. When tables are related, or joined, you have the ability to create forms, queries, and reports that display fields and records from each table in the relationship. You'll also discover how to create several types of relationships, such as one-to-many, one-to-one, and many-to-many.

Understanding Table Relationships

Relating tables gives you the flexibility of putting data from two or more tables together, without reentering the information. This feature saves you time and increases your productivity. After relating tables, you're able to create queries, forms, and reports using data from the tables in the relationship.

Most databases contain more than one table. In addition, chances are one or more of the tables contain identical data in at least one field. For example, a business might have a table containing customer names, *customer ID number*, and addresses. Let's say they also have a table that includes *customer ID number*, and order information. If two or more tables have a common field, such as the *customer ID number* field in this example, you can link these fields to create a relationship between the tables.

Hot Tip

Remember, if a table has a primary key field, each record must have unique (nonmatching) information in this field.

There are several types of relationships that may be created in Access: a one-to-many relationship, a one-to-one relationship, and a many-to-many relationship. A *one-to-many relationship* exists when you relate a table whose common field is a *primary key* field to a table whose common field is not a primary key field. As you may remember, a *primary key* is a field that contains a value that uniquely identifies the record. Each value in this field must be unique. A *foreign key* is a field that refers to the related field in a related table; however, it is not a primary key field.

> ### Hot Tip
> Related fields are not required to have the same field name. However, related fields must be of the same data type, such as text or date.

Table 8-1 illustrates a one-to-many relationship. The Salesperson Number field in the Salesperson table is a primary key field. This field is a primary key field because you will want only one Salesperson identification number assigned to each salesperson. In the Invoice table, the Salesperson Number is not a primary key field because each salesperson will likely make many sales and you would need to enter the Saleperson Number for each sale.

TABLE 8-1
One-to-many relationship

SALESPERSON TABLE FIELDS	INVOICE TABLE FIELDS
Salesperson Number	Invoice Number
First Name	Product Sold
Last Name	Salesperson Number
	Total Invoice
	Date Invoiced

Enforcing Referential Integrity

Referential integrity simply refers to letting Access check data as it's entered into related tables, to be certain that the data matches. For example, if you have tables with related fields as shown in Table 8-1, Access would check the Salesperson Number as it's entered into the Invoice Table to be sure that the Salesperson Number exists in the Salesperson table. If it does not, the person entering data receives an error message indicating that Referential integrity has been violated. This message prompts the user to double-check the number being entered.

When defining a relationship between selected tables, you will first need to open the Relationships windows and add the desired tables as shown in Figure 8-1. Then you simply drag a field from the primary table (primary key field will display in bold) to the common field in the related table. In this example, you would drag and drop the Employee ID field in the primary table to the Employee ID field in the related table.

FIGURE 8-1
Relationships window with tables displayed

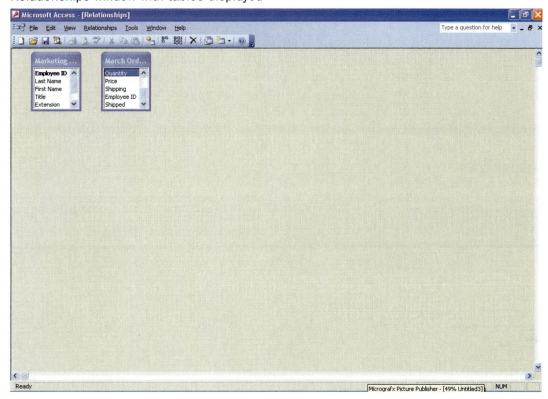

Once you release the mouse button, the Edit Relationships dialog box appears, as shown in Figure 8-2.

FIGURE 8-2
Edit Relationships dialog box

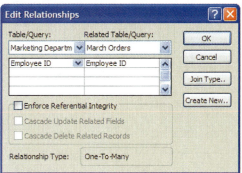

The Edit Relationships dialog box displays options for enforcing referential integrity. Referential integrity is enforced between tables in the same database.

If you choose to enforce referential integrity, two options in the dialog box become available. The first option, *Cascade Update Related Fields*, allows updates to occur between the primary table and the related table(s) in the joined fields. For example, to change a salesperson's ID number, you would first change the number in the primary table. Then, records in the related table(s) would automatically update their salesperson ID field to reflect this change.

The second option, *Cascade Delete Related Records*, lets you delete a record in the primary table, such as a salesperson. After this record is deleted, related records in other tables, such as invoices with the deleted salesperson, are removed.

Notice the symbols on the relationship line in the one-to-many relationship connecting the two tables in Figure 8-3. The 1 indicates the primary table and the infinity symbol (∞) indicates the related table. These symbols refer to the type of relationship that is created. In this example, the 1 refers to the one time that Employee ID number can appear in the Employee ID field in the Marketing Department table. However, because each employee can have many sales in March, the Employee ID can appear more than once in the March Orders table; thus, the infinity symbol.

FIGURE 8-3
Relationship established

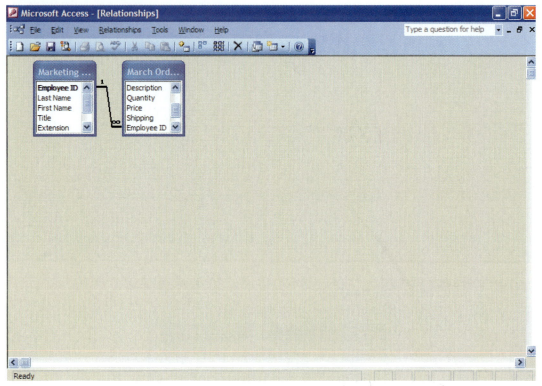

S TEP-BY-STEP 8.1

1. Open the database **AA Step8-1** from the data files.

2. Click the **Relationships** button on the toolbar. Then select **Show Table** on the **Relationships** menu. The Show Table dialog box appears, as shown on Figure 8-4.

3. Select **Marketing Department** and then click **Add**. The Marketing Department table is added to the Relationships window.

FIGURE 8-4
Show Table dialog box

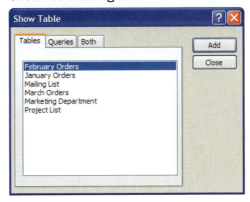

4. Select the **March Orders** table and click **Add**.

5. Click the **Close** button to close the Show Table dialog box.

6. If necessary, scroll the **March Orders** table to display the **Employee ID** field.

7. Select the **Employee ID** field in the **Marketing Department** table (from the bold type, you can tell that this is the primary key) and drag and drop it on top of the **Employee ID** field in the **March Orders** table.

8. In the Edit Relationships dialog box, click the check box beside **Enforce Referential Integrity**.

STEP-BY-STEP 8.1 Continued

9. Click **Create**. Your Relationships window should look like that shown in Figure 8-5.

FIGURE 8-5
Relationships window

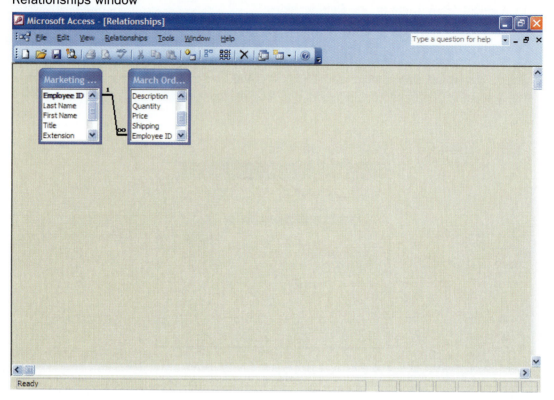

10. Close the **Relationships** window.

11. Click **Yes** to save the layout changes.

12. Open the **March Orders** table.

13. Click the **New Record** button. Enter the following information:

Field Name	Information
Order No.	3050
Order Date	3/15/03
Code	DB-BB
Description	Beginning Databases
Quantity	155
Price	$19.00
Shipping	$2.00
Employee ID	S555
Shipped	No

STEP-BY-STEP 8.1 Continued

14. Press **Enter**. A message box appears as shown in Figure 8-6. Access cannot add the record to the table because the primary Marketing Department table does not contain Employee ID **S555**.

15. Click **OK** to close the message box.

16. You now realize that the correct Employee ID number is N205. Change the **Employee ID** number to **N205** and press **Enter** twice. Note that a message box does not appear.

> **Hot Tip**
>
> You can press Ctrl + ; (semicolon) to enter the current date. Or, you can press Ctrl + ' (apostrophe) to duplicate information into the selected cell from the cell above it.

FIGURE 8-6
Message box

17. Close the **March Orders** table and open the **Marketing Department** table.

18. Click the **New Record** button and add the following record.

Field Name	Information
Employee ID	S555
Last Name	Walters
First Name	William
Title	Marketing Rep
Extension	229
Date Hired	3/15/03
Salary	$62,000

> **Hot Tip**
>
> You can edit or delete relationships by *right*-clicking the relationship line between tables and choosing either the Edit or Delete options on the shortcut menu.

19. Close the **Marketing Department** table. Now that the personnel record for this employee is entered in the Marketing Department table, you may enter customer orders sold by this salesperson in the March Orders table.

20. Open the **March Orders** table.

21. Click the **New Record** button, and enter the following information:

Field Name	Information
Order No.	3051
Order Date	3/15/03
Code	DB-BD
Description	Beginning Publishing
Quantity	193

STEP-BY-STEP 8.1 Continued

Price		$15.95
Shipping		$3.00
Employee ID		S555
Shipped		No

22. Adjust column widths in the table, if necessary. Print the table in landscape orientation and then close it.

23. Close the database.

Adding Tables to a Relationship

You may have several tables in a relationship. For example, in the previous exercise, you created a relationship between the Marketing Department table and the March Orders table. Access makes it easy to add other tables to a relationship. Simply add the table(s) to the Relationships window and relate the primary and common fields. For example, you might want to relate the January Orders and February Orders tables to the Marketing Department table.

> **Hot Tip**
>
> If you close the table and reopen it, the records will be sorted according to the primary key field. In this Step-by-Step, records are sorted by Employee ID.

STEP-BY-STEP 8.2

1. Open the database **AA Step8-2** from the data files.

2. Click the **Relationships** button. The current table relationship is displayed in the Relationships window.

3. Click the **Show Table** button.

4. Select the **February Orders** table, click **Add**, and then select the **January Orders** table and click **Add**.

5. Click **Close** to close the Show Table dialog box.

6. From the **Marketing Department** table, drag the **Employee ID** field to the **Employee ID** field in the **February Orders** table (you may have to scroll the table first to see the field). In the Edit Relationships dialog box, click the **Enforce Referential Integrity** check box and click **Create**. Repeat this procedure for the **January Orders** table. Your screen should look similar to Figure 8-7. (You may want to move the boxes around in order to clearly view the join lines.)

STEP-BY-STEP 8.2 Continued

FIGURE 8-7
Multiple table relationship

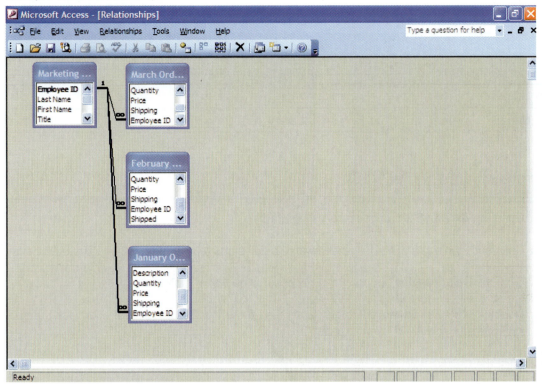

7. Click the **Save** button to save the relationships. Close the Relationships window.

8. Close the database.

Establishing One-to-One Relationships

In a *one-to-one relationship*, each record in Table A can have only one matching record in Table B and each record in Table B can have only one matching record in Table A. The common fields in these tables are both primary key fields.

> **Computer Concepts**
>
> You can resize and move the table windows in the Relationships window just as you can any other window. To resize, move your mouse pointer over the edge of the table window you want to resize until you get the double arrow pointer and then drag in the direction you want to resize. To move, drag on the title bar of the table.

Table 8-2 illustrates a one-to-one relationship. Notice that in the Salesperson table, the Salesperson Number is a primary key field. In the Salary table, the Salesperson Number is also a primary key field for obvious reasons, since you wouldn't want to send one salesperson two checks.

TABLE 8-2
One-to-many relationship

SALESPERSON TABLE FIELDS	SALARY TABLE FIELDS
Salesperson Number ←——————→	Salesperson Number
First Name	Title
Last Name	Salary

S TEP-BY-STEP 8.3

1. Open the **AA Step8-3** database from the data files.

2. Open each table to familiarize yourself with the fields and records. Close the tables after viewing them.

3. Click the **Relationships** button and, if necessary, the **Show Table** button.

4. Double-click the **Employee** table and the **Benefits Package** table to add them to the Relationships window.

5. Click the **Close** button to close the Show Table dialog box.

6. Join the **Employee ID** field in the **Employee** table to the **Employee ID** field in the **Benefits Package** table.

7. In the Edit Relationships dialog box, notice that the relationship is shown at the bottom as *One-To-One*, as shown in Figure 8-8.

8. Click the **Enforce Referential Integrity** check box and click **Create** to create the relationship. Your screen should look similar to Figure 8-9.

9. Click the **Save** button to save the relationship.

STEP-BY-STEP 8.3 Continued

10. Close the Relationships window, then close the database.

FIGURE 8-8
Edit Relationships dialog box

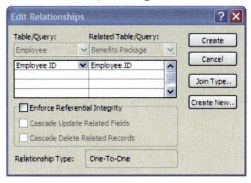

FIGURE 8-9
One-to-one relationship

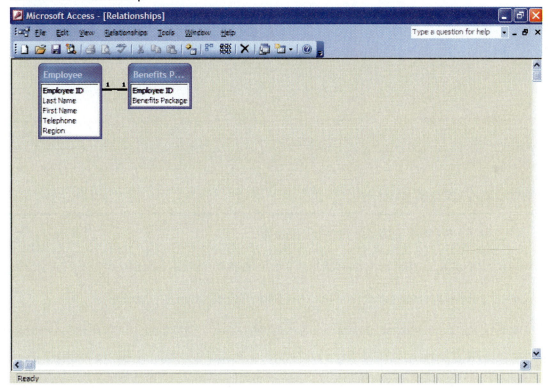

Establishing Many-to-Many Relationships

To create a many-to-many relationship, you'll need at least three tables. Two of the tables will have a one-to-many relationship. The third table, called a *junction table*, will contain two primary key fields. Each primary key field in the third table should relate to a primary key field in the other two tables.

A many-to-many relationship is shown in Figure 8-10. In this example, customers are only allowed a one-time discount purchase. And one salesperson is assigned to each customer, as these orders are typically very large.

FIGURE 8-10
Many-to-many relationship

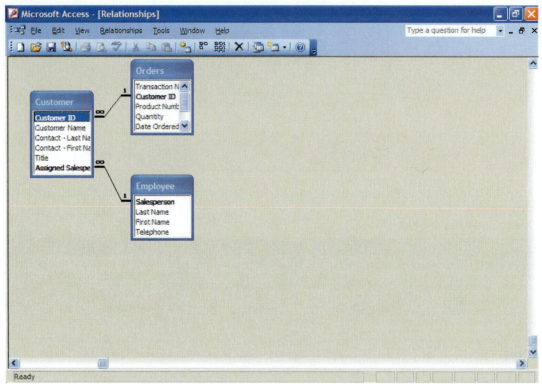

S TEP-BY-STEP 8.4

1. Open the **AA Step8-4** database from the data files.

2. Open each table to familiarize yourself with the fields and records. Close the tables after viewing them.

3. Click the **Relationships** button and then the **Show Table** button, if necessary.

4. Double-click the **Customer**, **Orders**, and **Employee** tables to add them to the Relationships window.

5. Click the **Close** button to close the Show Table dialog box. Access may identify a many-to-many relationship for you after adding the tables. Delete these join lines so that you may create this relationship yourself. To delete a join line, simply click on the line, press the Delete key, and select Yes.

6. Join the **Customer ID** fields in the **Customer** and **Orders** tables. Click the **Enforce Referential Integrity** check box and click **Create** to create the relationship.

7. Join the **Assigned Salesperson** field in the Customer table with the **Salesperson** field in the **Employee** table. **Enforce Referential Integrity** and click **Create** to create the relationship.

STEP-BY-STEP 8.4 Continued

8. Click the **Save** button to save the relationship.

9. Close the Relationships window, and then close the database file.

Time Saver

To quickly delete records when you hands are already on the keyboard, you can simply select the record and press Ctrl + - (minus sign).

STEP-BY-STEP 8.5

1. Open the **Time Saver** database from the data files and open the **Book Sales** table.

2. Select the **Record 2**.

3. Press **Ctrl + –** (minus sign).

4. Press **Enter** to confirm the deletion.

5. Close the table and then close the database file.

SUMMARY

In this lesson, you learned:

- Creating a relationship between tables allows you to use information from both tables. In order to create a relationship, the tables must contain a common field of data.

- A one-to-many relationship exists when you relate one table with a primary key field to another table whose common field is *not* a primary key field. Information in the primary key table's field will appear only once in the table, whereas information in the common field in the related table can appear many times.

- Referential integrity refers to having Access check new data as it is entered into related fields. This feature assists with the accuracy and consistency of data entered.

- A one-to-one relationship exists when the common field is a primary key field in both tables.

- A many-to-many relationship can exist among three or more tables.

VOCABULARY *Review*

Define the following terms:

Junction table	Primary key	Referential integrity
One-to-many relationship	Primary table	Relationship
One-to-one relationship		

REVIEW *Questions*

WRITTEN QUESTIONS

Write a brief answer to the following questions.

1. Why would you want to link tables together in a database?

2. In creating relationships, what is a primary table?

3. Explain referential integrity.

4. What is a one-to-many relationship?

5. Define a one-to-one relationship.

MATCHING

Match the correct term in the right column to its description in the left column.

---- 1. Requires unique data to be
entered into every record.

---- 2. A field that may be related to
a primary key field.

---- 3. Checks data entry in a related table against
data in the primary key table to be
certain data exists in both tables.

---- 4. In this type of relationship, a table with a
primary key field is related to a non-primary
key field in another table.

---- 5. In this type of relationship, the common
field in related tables is the primary
key field in the tables.

A. Referential Integrity

B. One-to-many relationship

C. One-to-one relationship

D. Primary key field

E. Common field

PROJECTS

 PROJECT 8-1

1. Open the database **AA Project8-1** from the data files.

2. Create a one-to-many relationship between the Products and Transactions tables by linking a primary and common field. (*Hint*: Remember, the field names may not necessarily be the same.)

3. Enforce referential integrity. Save and close the relationship.

4. Close the database.

 PROJECT 8-2

1. Open the database **AA Project8-2** from the data files.

2. Create a one-to-many relationship for Marketing Department table and the April, May, and June Orders tables.

3. Enforce referential integrity.

4. Save the relationship.

5. Close the database file.

CRITICAL *Thinking*

ACTIVITY 8-1

You have created a database that contains a number of tables. One of these tables is named Customers and another table is named Purchases. There is a Customer Number field in the Customers table that identifies each customer with an individual number. The Purchases table has a Customer Number field as well. You want to create a relationship between the two tables. Write a brief essay that explains which relationship you would choose for these tables and why. If necessary, use Access's Help system to assist with your decision.

ACTIVITY 8-2

Using the Help feature in Access, find the steps for editing a relationship within a database.

ADVANCED FORM FEATURES

Introduction

A database *form* is a tool used primarily for data entry. You've already discovered how to create a basic form and modify its design. In this lesson, you will learn more about customizing and designing forms. You will also learn how to work with subforms.

Creating a Subform

You may remember that forms are created from database tables or queries. Any of the fields in a table or a query may be used to build your form. You may create any number of forms using the same table, a query, or related tables. A *subform* is simply a form that is inserted within another form, called the main form. Subforms are very useful when you want to show records within the subform that are related to a specific record in the main form.

For example, let's say you have a table containing data on each of your customers. The fields in this table might include the customer's name, address, phone number, and *customer identification number*. You have another table in the database that tracks orders. The fields in this table might include the product ordered, transaction amount, customer name, and the *customer identification number*. Because there is a common field between these two tables (customer identification number), Access will allow you to view information from both tables at one time in a form that contains a subform. Your main form would include fields from the customers table and the subform would include information from the orders table. The main form and subform are displayed together on your screen. A subform may also be thought of as a form within a form. An example of a main form with an inserted subform is shown in Figure 9-1.

FIGURE 9-1
Form with subform

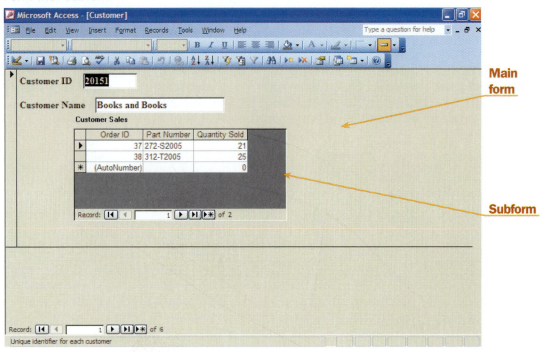

To add a subform to a main form, you will first need to open the main form in Design View. Click the Subform/Subreport button in the Toolbox. Then click within the area of the main form where you want the subform to appear. Typically, you'll want the subform to appear in the Detail section of the form. The Subform/Subreport Wizard will begin and take you step-by-step through the process of creating a subform.

S TEP-BY-STEP 9.1

1. Open the **AA Step9-1** database from the data files.

2. Click **Forms** on the *Objects* bar and then double-click the **Customer Information** form to open it.

3. View the information in the form and then switch to Design View. If necessary, display the Toolbox toolbar by clicking the Toolbox button. The Control Wizards button will also need to be turned on. If necessary, click the Control Wizards button.

4. Enlarge the *Detail* section so that it's about 3" high. To enlarge the Detail section, place your mouse pointer over the top of the Form Footer bar until a double-headed arrow appears. Drag the Form Footer bar down.

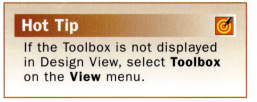

Hot Tip

If the Toolbox is not displayed in Design View, select **Toolbox** on the **View** menu.

STEP-BY-STEP 9.1 Continued

5. Click the **Subform/Subreport** button in the Toolbox. Then position the crosshair at the intersection of the 1" marks on the horizontal and vertical rulers and click. The SubForm Wizard displays, as shown in Figure 9-2.

FIGURE 9-2
SubForm Wizard

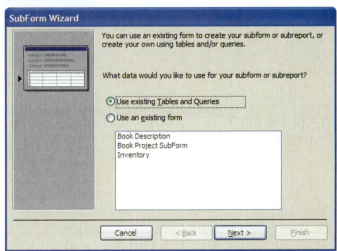

6. Make sure that the *Use existing Tables and Queries* option is selected and then click **Next**. The SubForm Wizard asks you which fields you want to include on the subform.

7. Click the down arrow of the *Tables/Queries* box and choose the **Table: Book Sales** table.

8. Double-click the **Order ID**, **Part Number**, and **Quantity Sold** fields to place them in the *Selected Fields* box. See Figure 9-3.

Hot Tip

If the SubForm Wizard does not start after clicking the Subform/Subreport button, make sure the **Control Wizards** button is selected in the Toolbox and then try step 5 again.

FIGURE 9-3
SubForm Wizard

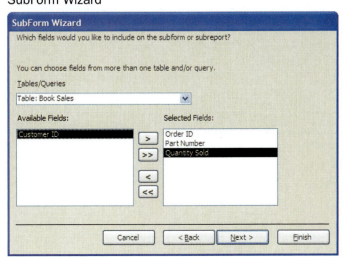

STEP-BY-STEP 9.1 Continued

9. Click **Next**. The SubForm Wizard lets you define the fields that link the main form to the subform. See Figure 9-4.

FIGURE 9-4
SubForm Wizard

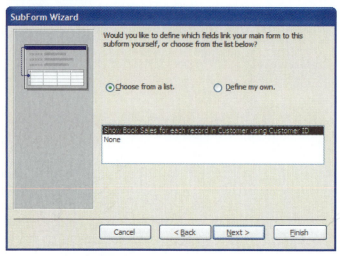

10. The *Choose from a list* option should be selected. From the list, select **Show Book Sales for each record in Customer using Customer ID**, if necessary.

11. Click **Next**. The final SubForm Wizard dialog box displays. Figure 9-5 shows the dialog box with a default name entered for the subform. You may accept this name or enter another subform name.

FIGURE 9-5
Subform Wizard

STEP-BY-STEP 9.1 Continued

12. Enter **Customer Sales** for the subform name and click **Finish**. The main form/subform should look similar to that shown in Figure 9-6. You may need to adjust the size of the subform to view the records. To resize a subform, simply drag one of its sizing handles.

FIGURE 9-6
Main form/subform

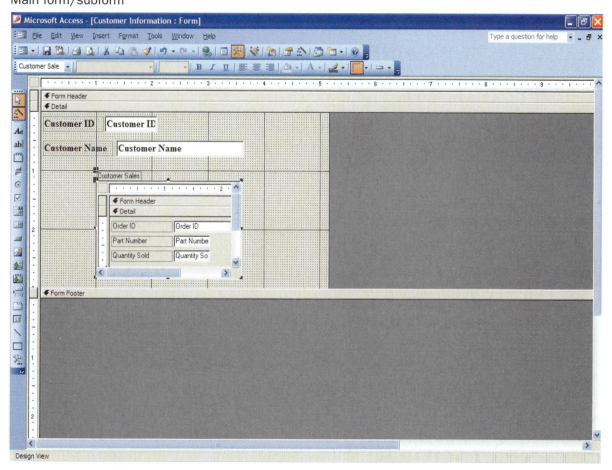

13. Switch to Form View. Notice that some of the column widths in the subform may not be wide enough to accommodate the field names. Adjust the widths as necessary by double-clicking the border between the field names (or the right side of the field border you wish to adjust). If necessary, switch back to Design View to make additional adjustments to the subform as needed. When completed, switch back to Form View.

14. Click the **Save** button. Scroll through the records in the main form and notice how the subform records change accordingly.

15. Print the form for record 1. Leave the Customer Information form open for the next Step-by-Step.

Adding or Deleting Records in a Subform

You can add, edit, or delete a record in the main form or the subform. In other words, Access lets you make additions, changes, or deletions to records in a main form or a subform just as you would in any other form.

STEP-BY-STEP 9.2

1. In the main form, go to the record for **Official Gardening Center**.

2. You will now enter a new record in the subform. Click in the *Part Number* field for a new record and enter **272-S2005**.

Hot Tip

The Order ID field is an AutoNumber field, so Access will assign the number automatically for you.

3. Enter **75** for the **Quantity Sold**.

4. Go to the **Projects Store** record in the main form and delete order number **39** from the subform. You will want to click on the record selector in front of this record. Press the **Delete** key and click **Yes** to confirm that you want to make the deletion.

5. Open the **Book Sales** table and confirm that order number 39 is now deleted and that there is a new order number 50. Close the Book Sales table.

6. Print the **Official Gardening Center** record and its associated subform. Leave the Customer Information form open for the next Step-by-Step.

Modifying a Subform

You can control the basic appearance and operation of a form or a subform by changing its properties. For example, there are scroll bars and record navigation buttons that appear in both the main form and the subform. You might decide to change the appearance of the subform by selecting a Special Effect. Or you can also choose to alter many other property options, such as scroll bars, navigation buttons, or record selectors. In addition, you may add a picture to the form background.

Integration Tip

To take a picture of an Access report that's currently displayed on your computer screen and put it into a Word document or PowerPoint presentation. Simply press PrintScreen (PrtSc) and paste it into another document.

STEP-BY-STEP 9.3

1. Switch to Design View. Place your mouse pointer over the top left sizing handle of the **Customer Sales** subform, right–click, and select **Properties** from the shortcut menu. The Subform/Subreport: Customer Sales properties dialog box should appear.

2. If necessary, select the **All** tab. Scroll in the Subform/Subreport: Customer Sales properties dialog box until you see the *Special Effect* option. Click in the **Special Effect** option box and then click the down arrow. Choose **Shadowed**. The properties dialog box should appear similar to Figure 9-7.

FIGURE 9-7
Form properties dialog box

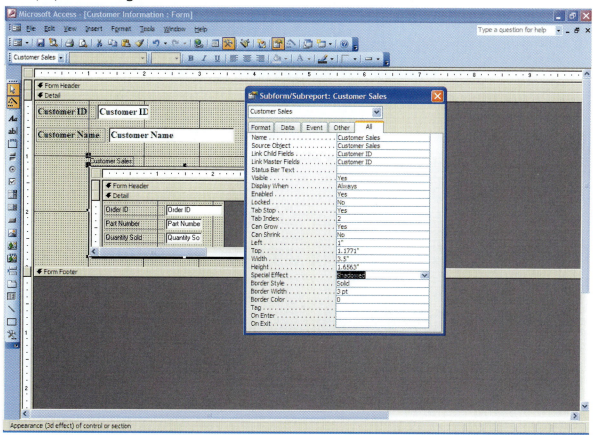

3. Close the Properties dialog box.

STEP-BY-STEP 9.3 Continued

4. Save the form and switch to Form View. Your screen should appear similar to Figure 9-8.

FIGURE 9-8
Form with shadowed subform

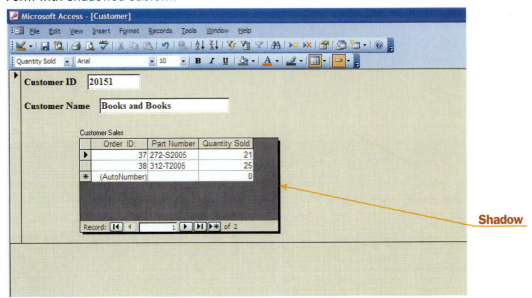

5. Close the form, then close the database.

Creating and Modifying a Form in Design View

As you probably know, you can create a form using the Form Wizard; however, you may also design it from scratch in Design View. Forms are developed primarily to streamline data entry. That's why Access provides you with a number of tools and options for designing forms that are user-friendly. You can rearrange the order of fields, change field names, add and delete fields, and insert graphics and pictures in order to customize the appearance of the form and maximize data entry time and effort.

STEP-BY-STEP 9.4

1. Open the **AA Step9-4** database from the data files.

2. Click **Forms** on the *Objects* bar.

3. Double-click **Create form in Design view**.

STEP-BY-STEP 9.4 Continued

4. Place your mouse pointer in a blank area outside the *Detail* section of the form but within the Form window, and *right*-click. Choose **Properties** on the shortcut menu. The Form properties dialog box should now be displayed.

> **Hot Tip**
>
> You can also click in the gray form area and then click the Properties button.

5. In the Form properties dialog box, select the **All** tab if necessary. Click in the *Record Source* text box, click the down arrow, and select **Qry–Book Titles**. You will use this query to create your form. The field list for this query should now display floating on your screen.

6. Close the Properties box.

7. Click the **Part Number** field and drag it to the intersection of the 1" marks on the horizontal and vertical rulers. Then, click and drag the **Book Title** field and position it beneath the Part Number field. Finally, click and drag the **Quantity Sold** and position it below the Book Title field and then close the Qry-Book Titles field list box.

8. Now, let's customize the form's header section. Open the **View** menu and then select **Form Header/Footer**. You should now see these sections in Design view.

9. Click the **Label** button in the Toolbox and then click in the *Form Header* section.

> **Did You Know?**
> You can also view a forms header and footer by right-clicking the *Detail* bar and selecting **Form Header/Footer** from the shortcut menu.

10. Key **Recent Sales** and press **Enter**. You should see selection handles around this box. If not, click on the label box to select it.

11. Click the **Bold** button on the Formatting toolbar. Then, click the down arrow on the **Font Size** button and choose **16**. To automatically increase the size of the label box, double-click on the middle right selection handle. (You may need to move the label up first.)

12. Click on the background of the **Form Header** section (dotted area), click the **Fill/Back Color** button arrow (on the Formatting toolbar) and select a teal color. Now, select the background of the *Detail* section, click the **Fill/Back Color** button arrow and select a teal color. Add a teal color to the *Form Footer* section as well.

13. Try using the alignment feature. Select the **labels** and **text boxes** in the *Detail* section. (You may use the mouse to draw a box around these items. To draw a box around these items, simply place your mouse pointer at a corner area outside the labels and text boxes and drag around every adjacent box you wish to select. You may also click on one of the boxes, hold down the **Shift** key, and then click on the remaining boxes in the Detail section.) Choose the **Format** menu, choose **Align**, and then click on **Right**. Notice how the boxes changed positions.

14. To insert a graphic, click the **Unbound Object Frame** button in the Toolbox and draw a box in the upper left corner of the *Detail* section that's about 1 inch tall and 2 inches wide. The Microsoft Office Access dialog box should open.

STEP-BY-STEP 9.4 Continued

15. Click **Microsoft Clip Gallery** in the *Object Type* list box and click **OK**.

16. Choose any available clip art picture and click the **Insert clip** option.

17. To modify the graphic so it fits in the box you drew, *right*-click on the clip art and choose **Properties** from the shortcut menu.

18. With the **All** tab selected, click in the *Size Mode* text box, click the down arrow, and choose **Zoom** or **Stretch** depending on the desired look. Close the Properties dialog box and view the results. Switch to Form View. Your screen may appear similar to Figure 9-9 depending on your clip art selection.

> ### Hot Tip
> If the Microsoft Clip Gallery is not a selection in the *Object Type* list box, select **Paintbrush Picture** and draw a picture to place in the form.

> ### Speech Recognition
> If your computer has speech recognition capabilties, enable Voice Command and say the appropriate steps to save the form.

FIGURE 9-9
Form created in Design view

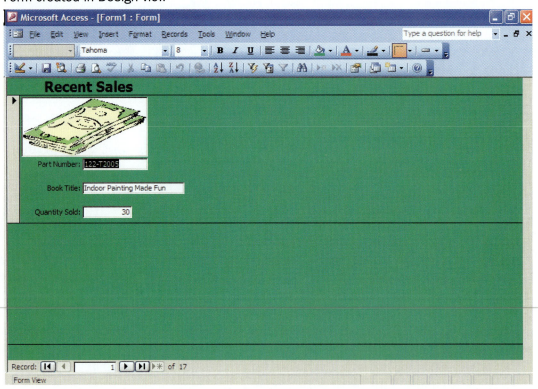

STEP-BY-STEP 9.4 Continued

19. Save the form as **Sales**. Print the form for the first record.

20. Close the **Sales** form and then close the database.

Speech Recognition

If your computer has Speech capabilties, enable the Voice Command Mode and say the appropriate steps to close the form and then close the database file.

Time Saver

Access lets you quickly move between records using keystrokes.

S TEP-BY-STEP 9.5

1. Open the **Time Saver** database from the data files and open the **Book Sales** table.

2. Press **F5** to place your insertion point in the *Record Number* box.

3. Key **9** and press **Enter**.

4. Close the table and then close the database file.

SUMMARY

In this lesson, you learned:

- A subform is simply a form within a form. This feature allows you to view, add, or make changes to information in more than one form at one time.

- After you create a subform, you can easily add or edit records within the subform as you would any form.

- You can create a form from scratch in Design View. Access provides you with great flexability in designing and modifying a form so that data entry time and effort are truly maximized.

- You can change properties of a form or a subform. For example, you may want the subform to appear in a shadowed special effect.

VOCABULARY *Review*

Define the following terms:	
Form	Subform

REVIEW *Questions*

WRITTEN QUESTIONS

Write a brief answer to the following questions.

1. What is a subform?

2. Why would you want to use a subform?

3. How can you change the column width in a subform?

4. How can you add a new record to a subform?

5. How do you open the Properties dialog box for the entire form?

6. List three form properties that you can change with regard to navigation.

7. Describe the differences between a main form and subform.

8. Can a record be added to a main form even though it contains a subform? If so, why is this possible?

9. If all of the field names do not appear in your subform, what can you do to make them display?

10. How does Access recognize that there is a common field between a main form and a subform?

PROJECTS

 PROJECT 9-1

1. Open the database **AA Project9-1** from the data files.

2. Create a one-to-many relationship between the **Marketing Department** table and the **January Orders** table using the **Employee ID** field as the common field and enforce referential integrity.

3. Create a form using the Form Wizard for the **Marketing Department** table. Include the **Employee ID, Last Name,** and **First Name** fields on the form. Choose the **Columnar** layout and select a style of your choice. Name the form **Marketing Department Sales**.

4. Create a subform in the Marketing Department Sales form using the **January Orders** table. Include the **Order No, Order Date, Description, Quantity,** and **Price** fields in the subform. Accept the default name of **January Orders subform** for the subform.

5. Modify the subform to display an etched effect.

6. Resize the form as necessary and make any other changes to the design of the forms that you think will make them more attractive and professional.

7. Print the form for record **4** in landscape orientation. Then close the form and the database.

CRITICAL *Thinking*

ACTIVITY 9-1

You have just taken over as the database administrator for the Last Resort Sales Company. You view the existing database file, named **AA Activity9-1** in the data files. You decide to create a main form/subform, using the **Employees** table for the main form and the **Personnel Information** table for the subform. Create the main form in Design View. The form should display the employee's ID, last name, first name, and telephone number fields. Note: Telephone number is located in the Personnel table.

ACTIVITY 9-2

As the personnel director for the New Cruise Line Company, you want to create a form that will display each employee's ID number, first name, and last name. You also want this form to display salary information that is contained in another table. Use Access's Help system to find more information on creating subforms. Write a brief essay that explains how you would proceed in setting up the main form and subform for the New Cruise Line Company.

ANALYZING DATA

Introduction

Databases are designed primarily to store and organize data. Queries provide analytical capabilities that make using databases extremely powerful. A *query* is simply a method that Access uses to locate records that contain specific information. Queries are often thought of as questions. For example, when you create a query, you enter precise information (*criteria*) so that you can find the records that have this information in them. What you're really doing is asking Access the question, "Can you locate any records from the selected tables that contain this information?"

Queries may be used in a variety of ways. For example, you can display records that meet specific criteria. Or, you might need to view or change certain records that the query has found.

There are several types of queries available in Access. In this lesson, you'll learn how to use queries to locate, calculate, and analyze records.

Basic Queries

Queries simply ask questions. For example, you may use a query to locate records for sales personnel that work in the north region. After creating the query, you save the query. Because you are saving the query, or "the question", it can be used over and over again. If new sales personnel are hired to work in the north region, Access will look at the selected tables and re-ask the question each time the query is run. Therefore, all records from the table that meet this criteria will be displayed. In the following exercise, you will create a basic query to get a feel for how the process works.

STEP-BY-STEP 10.1

1. Open the **AA Step10-1** database from the data files.

2. Click **Queries** on the Objects bar and then double-click **Create query in Design view**.

3. Double-click the **Employee** table to add this table to the query. Click **Close** to close the Show Table dialog box. Your screen should appear similar to Figure 10-1.

FIGURE 10-1
Query window

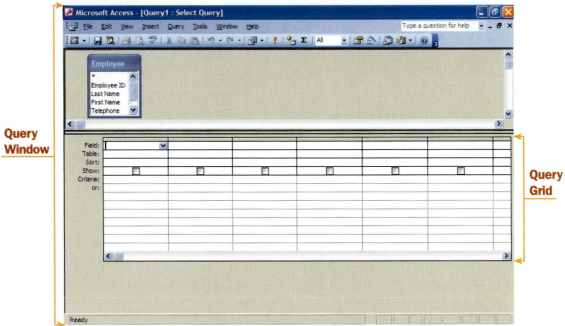

4. Double-click the **Employee ID** field. Placing this field in the query grid means that Access will display it in the results. Double-click the **Last Name** field and the **Region** field to place them in the query grid. You may need to scroll down in the Employee Field list to see the Region Field. Your query will look like Figure 10-2.

STEP-BY-STEP 10.1 Continued

FIGURE 10-2

Query window with selected fields

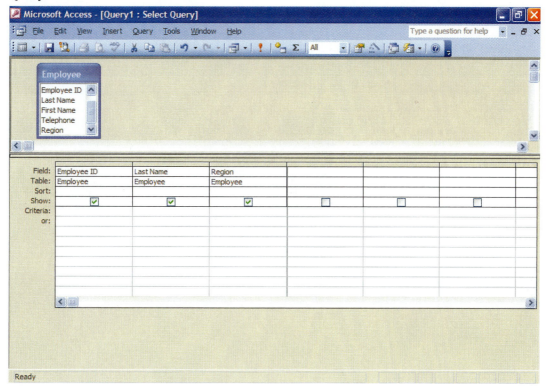

STEP-BY-STEP 10.1 Continued

5. Click the **View** button to look at the results. Notice how the selected fields are displayed in the results as shown in Figure 10-3.

FIGURE 10-3
Query results

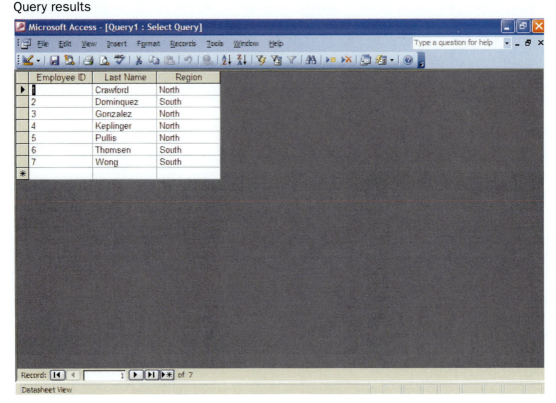

6. Click the **View** button to switch back to the Design window.

7. Click in the *Criteria* cell under *Region* in the query grid, key **North**, and then press **Enter**. When you press Enter, quotation marks are added to north. Access adds the quotation marks automatically to indicate that you're looking for text. By adding this criteria, Access will display only records for employees that work in the North region. Your screen should appear similar to Figure 10-4.

STEP-BY-STEP 10.1 Continued

FIGURE 10-4
Query window with criteria entered

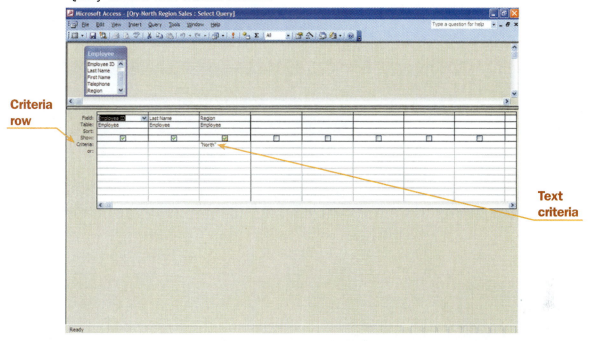

Criteria row

Text criteria

STEP-BY-STEP 10.1 Continued

8. Click the **View** button to look at the results. Notice how the selected fields are displayed in the results as shown in Figure 10-5.

FIGURE 10-5
Query results

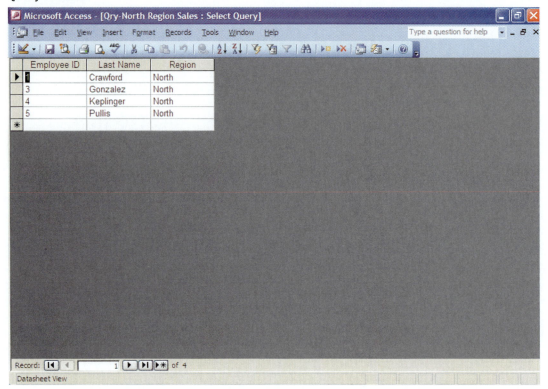

9. Click the **View** button to switch to the Design window.

10. Click the **Save** button and enter **Qry-North Region Sales** for the query name. It is good practice to add Qry in front of a query name because some list boxes do not display whether a list name refers to a table or a query. Click **OK**.

11. Close the query. Leave the database open for the next Step-by-Step.

Hot Tip

Remember, when you save a query, you are saving the query question. In the above exercise, you wanted to find each sales-person who worked in the north region, which resulted in four records. If two new north sales personnel were added to the Employee table tomorrow, the next time you double-click on the query name to open it, you would see these four sales people plus the two new north sales people in the query results.

Building Summary Queries

You can summarize values in a field by creating a summary query. For example, if you wanted to know total sales for sales records in a table, you would create a query with the desired fields and then click on the Sum function located in the query grid. Access already has several functions ready to use. A list of some of Access's predefined functions is shown in Table 10-1.

TABLE 10-1
Commonly used functions

FUNCTION	HOW IT IS USED
Sum	Totals the values in a field
Avg	Calculates the average value of field data
Min	Finds the lowest value in a field
Max	Finds the highest value in a field
Count	Counts the number of items in a field
StDev	Calculates the statistical standard deviation of values in the field
Var	Calculates the statistical variance of values in the field
First	Locates the first value within the field
Last	Locates the last value within the field
Expression	Lets you enter an expression in a Criteria cell for the field

In some instances, you'll want to group records for the summary results. For example, you might want to know the total number of sales accomplished by each salesperson. You would first group the records by the salesperson and then sum the sales for each salesperson.

To group records, you will need to display the Total row in the query grid. To display the Total row, simply click the Totals button. Then click the arrow to display the *Group By* option and the predefined functions.

STEP-BY-STEP 10.2

1. Click **Queries** on the *Objects* bar, if necessary, and then double-click **Create query in Design view**.

2. Double-click the **Employee** table and then double-click the **TRANSACTIONS** table adding them both to the query. Click **Close** to close the Show Table dialog box.

3. Double-click the **Employee ID** field in the **Employee** table to place it in the query grid. Double-click the **Quantity** field in the **TRANSACTIONS** table.

STEP-BY-STEP 10.2 Continued

4. Click the **Totals** button. A *Total* row now appears in the query grid as displayed in Figure 10-6. Notice that the *Group By* option appears in the *Total* boxes for both fields.

FIGURE 10-6
Total row displayed in query grid

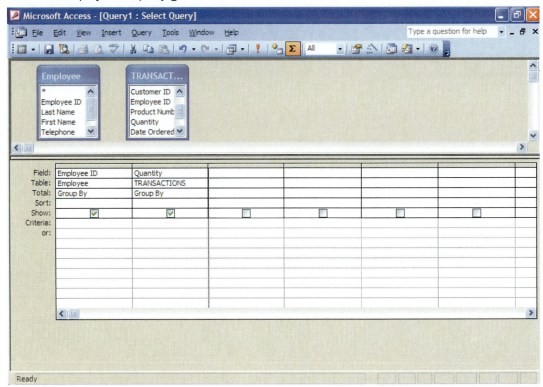

5. You want the query to summarize quantity of transactions for each person in the sales department, so leave *Group By* in the *Employee ID* column. First, you need to create a relationship between the tables in the query. To do this join simply place your mouse pointer over the **Employee ID** field in the Employee table and click and drag it to the **Employee ID** field in the Transactions table. You should now see a relationship line between the tables.

6. Click in the *Total* row of the *Quantity* column. Then, click the **Total** down arrow and click **Sum**. The Sum function will total the orders for each salesperson. Your screen should look similar to Figure 10-7.

STEP-BY-STEP 10.2 Continued

FIGURE 10-7
Query exercise window

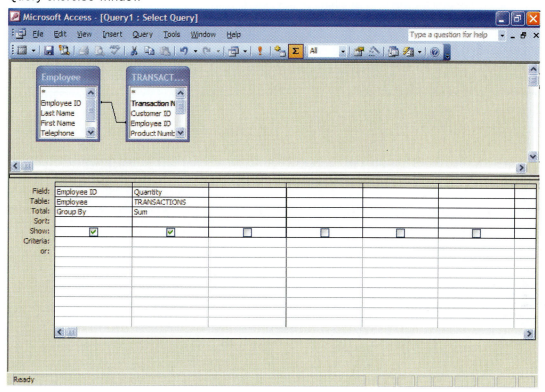

STEP-BY-STEP 10.2 Continued

7. Click the **View** button to look at the results. Note that the column heading, *SumOfQuantity*, is automatically created for the field as displayed in Figure 10-8.

FIGURE 10-8
Query results window

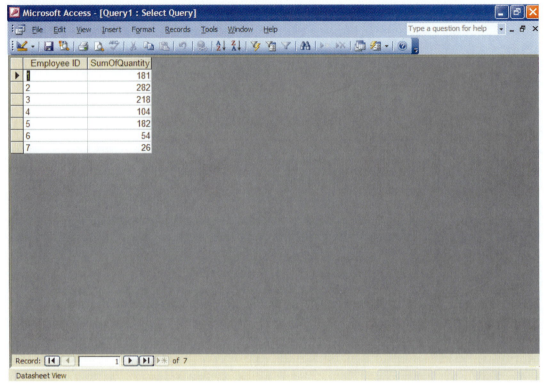

8. Save the query as **Qry-Sales Totals**. Click **OK**.

9. Close the query. Now, double-click on the query name to reopen the query.

10. Print the query results and then close the query.

11. You will now create a Count query to count the number of transactions for each employee. Double-click **Create query in Design view**.

12. Double-click the **Employee** table and then double-click the **TRANSACTIONS** table adding them both to the query. Click **Close** to close the Show Table dialog box.

13. Double-click the **Employee ID** field in the Employee table to place it in the query grid. Double-click the **Transaction Number** field in the TRANSACTIONS table.

14. Click the **Totals** button.

15. You want the query to count the quantity of transactions for each person, so leave *Group By* in the *Employee ID* column. If necessary, create a relationship between the tables in the query.

STEP-BY-STEP 10.2 Continued

16. Click the **Total** down arrow for the *Transaction Number* column and then click **Count**. This applies the Count function to count the number of transactions.

17. Click the **View** button to look at the results. Note that the column heading, *CountOfTransaction Number*, is automatically created for the field.

18. Close the query without saving the changes. You can view query results without saving changes if you do not want to keep the query for future reference. Close the database file.

Creating an AND Query

You may also query a table or form for records that meet more than one set of criteria. For example, you might want to find records in an inventory database that have a cost of \$.99 and a selling price of \$1.99. This feature is referred to as an AND query. To create an AND query, enter the search criteria for the appropriate fields in the same Criteria row. Let's see how this feature works.

STEP-BY-STEP 10.3

1. Open the **AA Step10-3** database from the data files.

2. Click **Tables** on the *Objects* bar, if necessary, and open the **TRANSACTIONS** table. View the records to familiarize yourself with them. Then close the table.

3. Click **Queries** on the *Objects* bar. Then double-click **Create query in Design view**.

4. Double-click the **TRANSACTIONS** table in the Show Table dialog box. Then close the Show Table dialog box.

> **Speech Recognition**
>
> If your computer has speech recognition capabilites, enable the Voice Command mode and say the appropriate steps to open the database file.

5. Double-click the **Transaction Number**, **Customer ID**, **Employee ID**, and **Quantity** fields to add them to the design grid.

6. Click the **Criteria** cell of the *Customer ID* field and key in **5**. (This represents customer number 5.)

> **Hot Tip**
>
> Notice that the number 5 in the Customer ID criteria cell does not have quotation marks, but the number 1 in the Employee ID criteria cell does have quotation marks. Because quotation marks indicate text, the Employee ID field is a text field; however, the Customer ID field is a number field.

STEP-BY-STEP 10.3 Continued

7. Click the **Criteria** cell of the *Employee ID* field and key in **1**. (This represents employee number 1.) Your screen should appear similar to Figure 10-9.

FIGURE 10-9
AND query

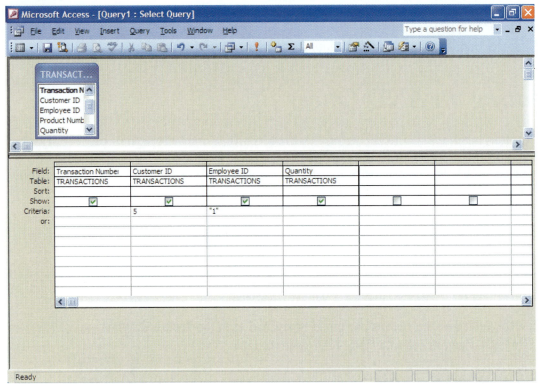

8. Click the **View** button to run the query and view the results. You should see four records. Adjust the column widths if necessary.

9. Save the query as **Qry-Cust 5 and Emp 1**.

10. Print the query results. Close the query and leave the database open for the next Step-by-Step.

Speech Recognition

If your computer has speech recognition capabilites, enable the Voice Command mode and say the appropriate steps to print and close the query.

Creating an OR Query

You can also query a table for records that meet one criteria or another. This is referred to as an OR query. For example, you might want to find records for customers who live in either Ohio or California. To create an OR query, you enter the first set of criteria in the first *Criteria* row in the query grid and the second set of criteria in the criteria cell below the first cell. You can search for additional criteria by clicking in subsequent rows below a criteria cell with previously entered data.

STEP-BY-STEP 10.4

1. If necessary, click **Queries** on the *Objects* bar. Then double-click **Create query in Design view**.

2. Double-click the **TRANSACTIONS** table in the Show Table dialog box, and then close the dialog box.

3. Double-click the **Transaction Number**, **Customer ID**, **Employee ID**, and **Quantity** fields to add them to the grid.

4. Click the **Criteria** cell of the *Customer ID* field and enter **5**.

5. Click the **or** cell of the *Customer ID* field and enter **3**. Your screen should look similar to Figure 10-10.

6. In the query grid, click in the **Sort** cell for the *Customer ID* field, and choose **Ascending**. The sort feature will display the Customer ID numbers in numerical order. In this example, records for Customer 3 appear and then records for Customer 5.

7. Click the **View** button to run the query and view the results. You should see 26 records. Adjust the column widths if necessary, so the complete field names display.

8. Save the query as **Qry-Cust 3 or 5**.

9. Print the query results. Then close the query and leave the database open for the next Step-by-Step.

FIGURE 10-10
OR query

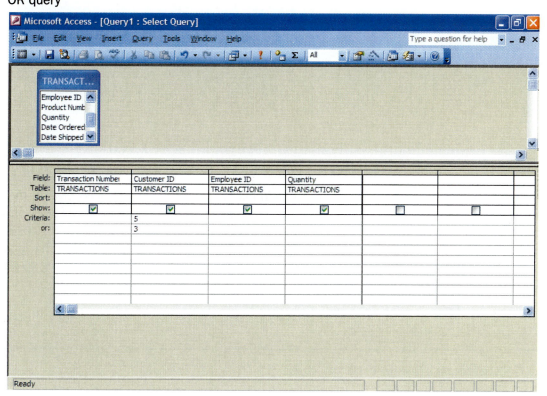

Modifying a Query's Design

You can change a query's design by opening it in Design View. For example, fields can be added or deleted, fields can be reordered, and search criteria can be modified.

To replace one field with another, click the *Field name* box in the query grid, click the drop-down arrow, and then select the new field you want included in the query. To delete a field, click on the thin gray bar above the field name in the query grid as indicated in Figure 10-11. This action selects the entire column. Then press Delete to remove the field from the query grid.

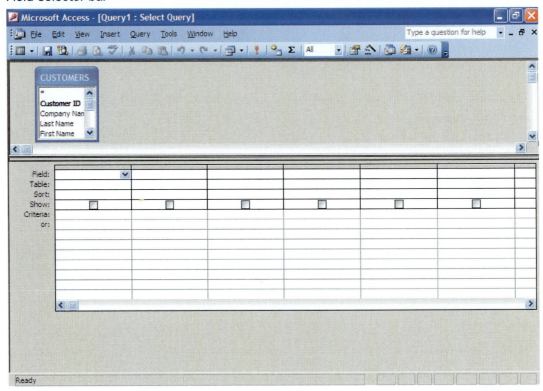

To insert a field, select a field in the table's field list box and drag it to the column in the query grid where you want it to appear. The field(s) to the right of the insertion will shift one column to the right. To move a field to a different spot in the query, click the gray bar above the field in the query grid to select the entire column. Then position the mouse pointer on the gray bar and drag the column to the new location. A dark vertical bar indicates where the field is going to be positioned when you release the mouse button.

STEP-BY-STEP 10.5

1. If necessary, click **Queries** in the *Object* bar.

2. Double-click **Create query in Design view**.

3. Double-click the **Customers** table to add it to the query. Click **Close** to close the Show Table dialog box.

STEP-BY-STEP 10.5 Continued

4. Double-click the **Last Name**, **First Name**, and **State** fields to enter them into the grid.

5. Click the **State** field in the query grid, if necessary. Notice that a down arrow appears on the right side of this cell.

6. Click the down arrow and then click **Postal Code**. This changes the field from State to Postal Code.

7. Place your mouse pointer in the thin gray bar (the Field Selector Bar) above the **First Name** field. Your mouse pointer turns into an arrow pointing downward. Click in this bar to select the field.

8. Press **Delete**. This removes the field from the query grid.

9. Now sort the *Last Name* field in Ascending Order from A to Z. Click the **Sort** box below the *Last Name* field, click the down arrow, and then choose **Ascending**.

10. Place your mouse pointer over the **Phone Number** field in the table's field list.

11. Drag the **Phone Number** field to the first cell in the second column where *Postal Code* is currently located. Release the mouse button. Notice how the Phone Number field is now inserted in the second column, as shown in Figure 10-12.

FIGURE 10-12
Modified query

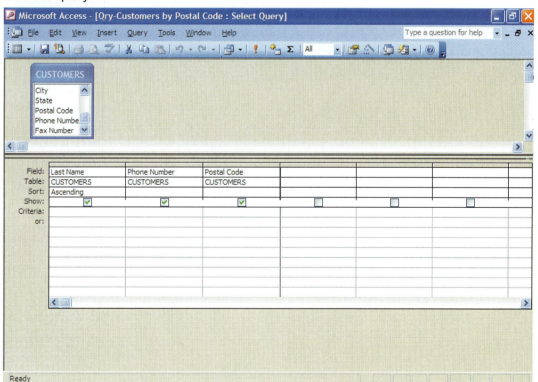

STEP-BY-STEP 10.5 Continued

12. Save the query as **Qry-Customers by Postal Code**.

13. View the query results. Close the query and leave the database open for the next Step-by-Step.

Using Concatenation

When a person's name is part of a record, it is helpful to put first names and last names in separate fields for query, form, and report purposes. However, there may be times when you want the first name and last name combined as one value in a field. To join the

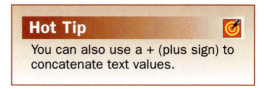

Hot Tip

You can also use a + (plus sign) to concatenate text values.

values of fields together, you may use the concatenation feature. With *concatenation*, Access combines the text from two or more fields into one.

To concatenate fields you first need to switch into Design View. In a *Field* cell of the query grid, first key the field name you want to appear at the top of the column in the query results. Type a colon (:). A colon tells Access that the text before the colon is the field name and the information after the colon is what you want displayed in the field. Then enter the following information to concatenate the First Name and Last Name field. Full Name:[First Name]&" "&[Last Name]

Notice that you enter the exact spelling (including spaces) for the fields. Then entering an ampersand (&) indicates that you want to add something else. In this example, you want to add a space between First Name and Last Name. Because a space is considered text, you will need to place quotation marks around the space. Your screen should appear as shown in Figure 10-13.

FIGURE 10-13
Query with concatenation

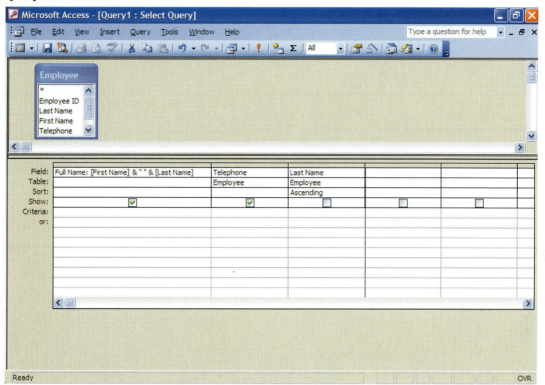

S TEP-BY-STEP 10.6

1. Click **Queries** on the *Objects* bar and then double-click **Create query in Design view**.

2. Double-click the **Employee** table and then close the Show Table dialog box.

3. Click the first *Field* box of the query grid, if necessary.

4. Key **Full Name:[First Name]&" "&[Last Name]**. Press **Enter** when you finish typing the concatenation.

5. Drag the **Telephone** field into the second column of the query grid.

6. Add the **Last Name** field to the third column. You need to add the Last Name field in order to sort the query results alphabetically. However, you do not want this field to display. Therefore, select the **Sort** box for the **Last Name** field and choose the **Ascending** option. Click the **Show** box for the Last Name field to remove the check mark so that this column does not display in the query results.

7. Run the query. Save the query as **Qry-Telephone List**.

8. Adjust the column widths if necessary and then print the query results. Close the query and the database.

Time Saver

To quickly open the Expression Builder dialog box in a query, simply press Ctrl + F2.

STEP-BY-STEP 10.7

1. Open the **Time Savers** database from the data files for this lesson.

2. Create a new query in Design View.

3. Add the **Book Project** table to the query and close the Show Table dialog box.

4. Add the **Book Title** and **Part Number** fields to the query design grid.

5. Click in a blank field cell in an empty column in the query design grid and press **Ctrl+F2**. You can now quickly create an expression such as concatenation.

6. Key **=[book title]+" "+[part number]** into the top box of the Expression Builder.

7. Click **OK**.

8. Click the **View** button, increase the column widths, and view the results.

9. Close the query without saving any changes.

10. Close the database.

SUMMARY

In this lesson, you learned:

■ You can summarize field values by creating a summary query. A summary query lets you summarize groups of records.

■ To concatenate text values in two or more fields, enter the concatenation expression in the query Design View

■ An AND query lets you search for records that meet more than one criteria. An OR query lets you search for records that meet one criteria or another.

■ You can modify the design of a query by adding, inserting, changing, or deleting fields.

VOCABULARY *Review*

Define the following terms:

AND query   Criteria   Query
Concatenation   OR query

REVIEW *Questions*

TRUE/FALSE

Circle T if the statement is true or F if the statement is false.

T   F   **1.** You cannot modify a query after saving it.

T   F   **2.** A concatenated expression can be created by using a plus sign or an ampersand.

T   F   **3.** You click the Query button to add the Total row to the query grid.

T   F   **4.** The MAX function will find the first value in a field.

T   F   **5.** You normally use concatenation to combine text values.

WRITTEN QUESTIONS

Write a brief answer to the following questions.

1.   What is the purpose of a query?

2.   How do you display the Total row in the query grid?

3.   List three of Access's predefined functions.

4. List three ways a query design may be modified.

5. What is the purpose of the text and colon in a concatenation?

PROJECTS

PROJECT 10-1

1. Open the **AA Project10-1** database from the data files.

2. Create a query based on the **CUSTOMERS, TRANSACTIONS,** and **PRODUCTS** tables.

3. If necessary, join the **Customer ID** fields in the **Customers** and **Transaction** tables, and join the **Product Number** and **Product ID** fields in the **Transactions** and **Products** tables.

4. In the query grid, add the **Customer ID** and **Company Name** fields from the **Customers** table, the **Transaction Number** field from **Tranactions** table, and the **Product Description** field from the **Products** table.

5. Sort the **Customer ID** field in Ascending order.

6. Save the query as **Qry-Products Purchased.**

7. Adjust column widths if necessary. Print the results of the query, then close the database file.

PROJECT 10-2

1. Open the **AA Project10-2** database from the data files.

2. Create a query that concatenates the first and last name fields.

3. The query will also need to display the telephone numbers for the students.

4. Save the query as **Qry-Student Telephone List.**

5. Print the results of your query, then close the database file.

 **PROJECT 10-3**

1. Open the **AA Project10-3** database from the data files.

2. Create a query that averages the Grade Point Average for students in each class. (*Hint:* You'll use the Class and Grade Point Average fields. Then, select Avg in the Total row for Grade Point Average.)

3. Save the query as **Qry-Class Averages**.

4. Close the query and then close the database file.

CRITICAL*Thinking*

 ACTIVITY 10-1

You maintain the corporate database for One Star Gas Company. You need to create a number of queries to generate information requested by officers of the company. You want to effectively use the built-in functions in your queries, such as SUM or MIN. Write a brief essay to explain how to use built-in functions. Use Access Help to find the answer.

ACTIVITY 10-2

As the owner of Ben's Wild Animal Feed and Seed Emporium, you would like to find out how certain prices compare to one another. For example, you wish to view prices that are over $20 as well as prices below $2. Use the **AA Activity10-2** data file and save the query as **Qry-Prices above 20 or less than 2**.

ADVANCED QUERIES AND FILTERS

Introducing Queries

Queries locate specific information in your tables. When using a query, if you ask Access a question the query result displays the answer. To ask for specific information, enter criteria that you're searching for in a table. In this lesson, you will explore parameter queries, which asks you to enter the search data each time you run the query. Action queries make changes to tables or create new tables instantly. Finally, you'll discover the advantages of the advanced filtering feature.

Creating a Parameter Query

Parameter queries increase efficiency by providing a single query that you may use many times with various criteria each time the query runs. For example, in a large table of customer numbers, names, and addresses, your sales personnel might need quick customer contact information. Rather than creating a query for each customer, Access provides parameter queries, which allow you to enter new criteria each time you run the query. Therefore, if a salesperson enters a customer number, the customer contact information quickly displays.

Computer Concepts

You can run a parameter query by clicking the **Run** button in the Design View or by switching to Datasheet View.

To create a parameter query, you must enter a "prompt" in the desired field's *Criteria* cell. This prompt indentifies the criteria data that needs to be entered. In the previous example, you may want the parameter query to ask for a customer number. A parameter box should appear as shown in Figure 11-1.

FIGURE 11-1
Parameter dialog box

STEP-BY-STEP 11.1

1. Open the **AA Step11-1** database from the data files.

2. Click **Queries** in the *Objects* bar if necessary.

3. Double-click **Create query in Design view**.

4. Double-click the **Customers** table in the Show Table dialog box and then close the dialog box.

5. Double-click the **Customer ID, Company Name, Last Name, First Name,** and **Phone Number** fields to add them to the query grid.

6. Click in the **Criteria** cell of the *Customer ID* field and key **[Enter Customer ID #]**. Press **Enter**. Your screen should appear as shown in Figure 11-2.

FIGURE 11-2
Parameter query design

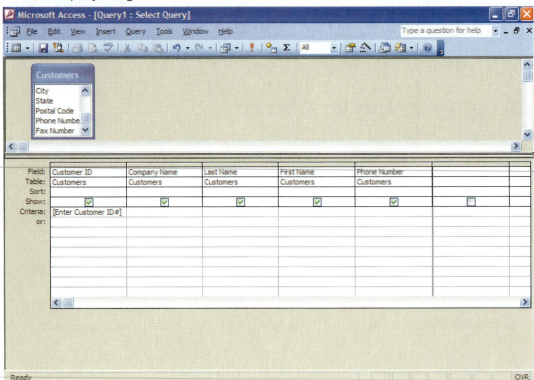

STEP-BY-STEP 11.1 Continued

7. Save the query as **Qry-Customer Contact Info by ID#**.

8. Click the **Run** button to run the query.

9. In the Enter Parameter Value dialog box, key **9**. Click **OK** or press **Enter**. Your screen should look like Figure 11-3.

FIGURE 11-3
Parameter query results

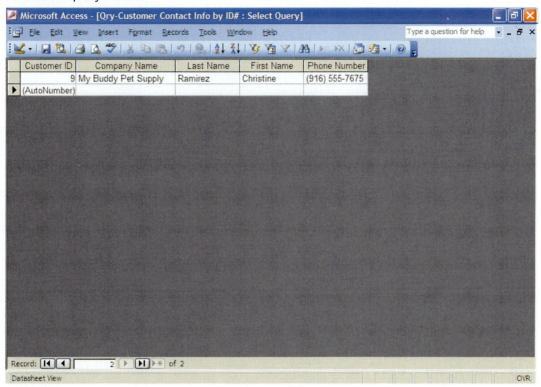

10. Close the query. Double-click on the query in the database window. Enter **5**. Click **OK** and view the results.

11. Close the query and close the database. Leave Access open for the next Step-by-Step.

Understanding Action Queries

A query is considered an *action query* if it makes changes to a table. The types of action queries are append, delete, update, and make-table. An *append* query adds records from one table to another table. The *delete* query deletes records within a table. An *update* query changes the values in a field for a specified group of records. Finally, a *make-table* query creates a new table from existing fields in one or more tables.

To create an action query, click the Query Type button arrow and select the type of action query, as shown in Figure 11-4. After saving an Action query, its associated icon will display with an exclamation mark in the database window.

FIGURE 11-4
Query type list

Query Type Button

Creating an Update Query

Update queries let you change field values in a table. For example, if you want to give sales personnel a 6% raise, you can use an update query to locate sales personnel within the table and increase their salaries by 6%. Table records are permanently changed when the update query is run and confirmed.

STEP-BY-STEP 11.2

1. Open the **AA Step11-2** database file.

2. Open the **Sales Department** table and print the table. You can verify whether the changes made in this Update query are correct. Note that the salary for Rose Navarro, a sales rep, is $129,000. Close the table.

3. Click **Queries** in the *Objects* bar.

4. Double-click **Create query in Design view**.

5. Double-click the **Sales Department** table in the Show Table dialog box, then close the dialog box.

6. Double-click the **Title** and **Salary** fields to add them to the query grid.

7. Click the arrow on the **Query Type** button and then select **Update Query**.

8. Click in the **Criteria** cell of the **Title** field and enter **Sales Rep**.

9. Click in the **Update To** cell of the *Salary* field and enter **[Salary]*1.06**. This expression will calculate a 6% raise for each sales rep. Your query should display as shown in Figure 11-5.

FIGURE 11-5
Update query design

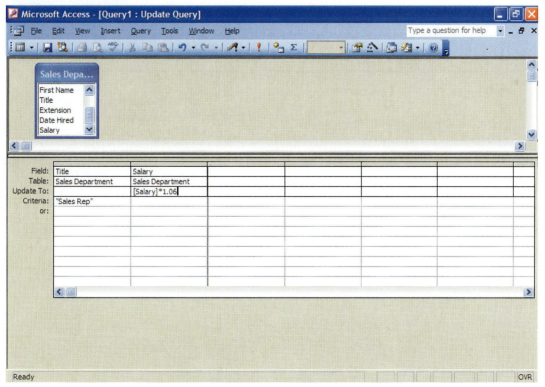

STEP-BY-STEP 11.2 Continued

10. Click the **Run** button. You should see a message box showing that nine rows will be updated. Click **Yes** to confirm the update.

11. Close the query without saving.

12. Open the **Sales Department** table and check the salary amount for Rosa Navarro. Her salary should now be $136,740. Adjust the column widths if necessary. Print the table in landscape orientation and then close it. Leave the database open for the next Step-by-Step.

> **Hot Tip**
>
> Be careful to click the **Run** button only one time. Each time you run the query, it will calculate another 6% raise for the sales reps.

Creating a Make-Table Query

A make-table query is ideal for creating new tables from existing records and fields in other tables. For example, you may want a new table that displays employee names and telephone numbers. However, the existing Employee table also contains social security numbers and addresses, which are not authorized for distribution. You can use the Make-Table query to create a new table with specified fields, such as employee last name, first name, and telephone number.

The new table is not linked to existing tables in the Make-Table query. Therefore, if information in the original table changes, you will need to run the query again to update the information in the new table. You can use the same table name by simply choosing Replace when asked to do so.

STEP-BY-STEP 11.3

1. Click **Queries** in the *Objects* bar.

2. Double-click **Create query in Design view**.

3. Double-click the **Sales Department** table in the Show Table dialog box and then close the dialog box.

4. Double-click the **Last Name**, **First Name**, **Title**, and **Extension** fields to add them to the query grid. Sort the **Last Name** field in **Ascending** order.

5. Click the **Query Type** button and then select **Make-Table Query**.

> **Integration Tip**
>
> You can use an Access table as a data source in a Word mail merge. Selecting **Merge It with Microsoft Office Word** within Access starts this process or you may also select the database table as the data source if you are in a Word document.

STEP-BY-STEP 11.3 Continued

6. The Make Table dialog box appears. Enter **Telephone List** for the new table name and click **OK**. The query window should appear as shown in Figure 11-6.

FIGURE 11-6
Make-table query design

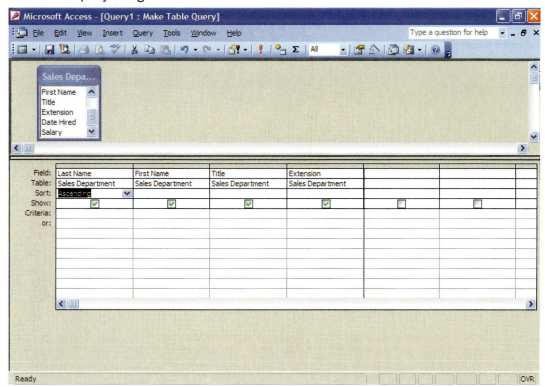

7. Click the **Run** button. A message box similar to that shown in Figure 11-7 opens.

FIGURE 11-7
Message box

8. Click **Yes** to confirm that you want to create a new table.

9. Save the query as **Qry-Make Telephone List Table**.

10. Close the query.

11. Click **Tables** on the *Objects* bar and open the **Telephone List** table and view the results. Print the table, then close it and the database.

Specifying and Applying Advanced Filters

The Advanced Filter feature allows you to filter or display records that meet specific criteria. Advanced Filters are different from the typical Filter feature in that they let you filter for several criteria in one or more fields. Figure 11-8 shows an Advanced Filter window. Notice that it appears similar to a query. A *filter* creates a temporary view and, if saved, it is saved as a query. To apply the filter, simply click the Apply Filter button.

FIGURE 11-8
Advanced Filter window

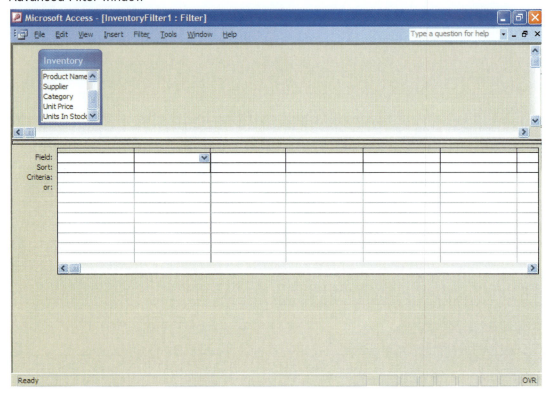

S TEP-BY-STEP 11.4

1. Open the **AA Step11-4** database file.

2. Double-click the **Inventory** table to open it.

3. Select **Filter** from the **Records** menu, and then **Advanced Filter/Sort**.

4. Double-click the **Category** field and the **Units In Stock** field as these are the fields you'll use in the filter. You want a filter to indicate when a Business category item has fewer than 50 units in stock.

5. Click in the **Criteria** cell for *Category* and enter **Business**.

6. Click in the **Criteria** cell for *Units In Stock* and enter **<50**. Your screen will appear as shown in Figure 11-9.

STEP-BY-STEP 11.4 Continued

FIGURE 11-9
Advanced Filter design

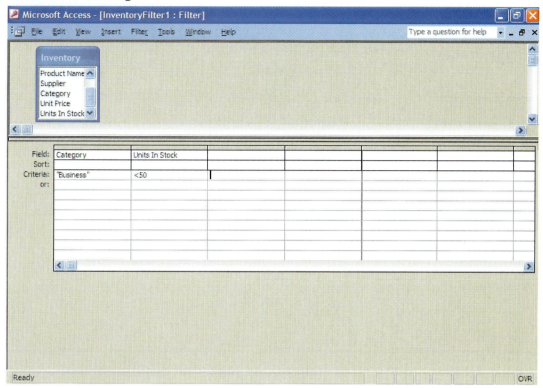

7. Click the **Apply Filter** button on the toolbar. You will see four records as displayed in Figure 11-10.

FIGURE 11-10
Advanced Filter results

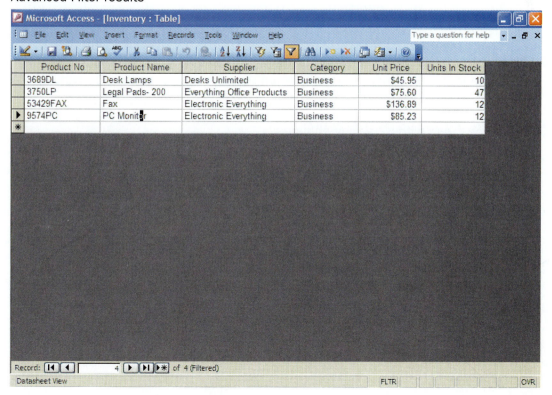

STEP-BY-STEP 11.4 Continued

8. Switch to the Query Design window and click the **Save as Query** button. (*Hint:* You may have to move the table window to see it.)

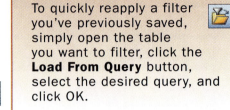

9. Save the filter/query as **Qry-Business Inventory Filter Below 50**.

10. Switch to the Inventory table and remove the filter by clicking the **Remove Filter** button.

11. Close the table without saving any changes. The filter will close automatically. Close the database file.

Time Saver

Access lets you quickly add all fields from a table into the query design grid by double-clicking the title bar of the table in the query.

STEP-BY-STEP 11.4

1. Open the **Time Savers** database from the data files for this lesson.

2. Create a new query in Design View.

3. Add the **Book Sales** table to the query and close the Show Table dialog box.

4. Double-click the **Book Sales** title bar. Notice how all the fields within the table box are highlighted.

5. Place your mouse pointer over the highlighted fields and drag these fields down into the first field location of the query grid. When you release the mouse button, all the fields should now be in the query grid.

6. Close the query without saving changes.

7. Close the database.

SUMMARY

In this lesson, you learned:

■ Parameter queries allow you to enter new criteria each time the query runs.

■ It is simple to make changes to several records in a table at one time by using the Update action query.

■ New tables can be created from existing tables with the Make-Table query option.

■ Advanced Filters let you display records meeting certain criteria in one or more fields.

VOCABULARY *Review*

Define the following terms:

Action Query	Filter	Parameter Query

REVIEW *Questions*

TRUE/FALSE

Circle T if the statement is true or F if the statement is false.

T   F   **1.** Advanced Filters allow you to use a maximum of one criterion.

T   F   **2.** With a parameter query, you add records from one table to another table.

T   F   **3.** The results of an update action query are irreversible after the update is confirmed.

T   F   **4.** Action queries are identified by an asterisk in the Database window.

T   F   **5.** A make-table query creates a new table from information in one or several tables.

WRITTEN QUESTIONS

Write a brief answer to the following questions.

1. What is the purpose of a parameter query?

2. When would you use an update query?

3. What are the similarities and differences between an update query and a make-table query?

4. When would you use an Advanced Filter versus a query?

5. Explain the main difference between an Advanced Filter and a typical filter in Access.

PROJECTS

PROJECT 11-1

1. Open the **AA Project11-1** database from the data files. Print the Inventory table.

2. Create an update query that finds the records in the **Inventory** table whose *Product ID* field begins with **4**. Update the *Reorder Point* field to **0**. (*Hint*: Use the criteria of **4*** in the *Product ID* field.)

3. Save the query as **Qry-Product 400 Reorder Change**. Close the query.

4. Open the **Inventory** table and view the changes. Sort the **Inventory** table by the *Product ID* field. Print the table.

5. Close the query and then close the database file.

PROJECT 11-2

1. Open the **AA Project11-2** database from the data files.

2. Create a parameter query on the **Customers** table. In the Design window, add the **Company Name, Last Name, First Name, City, State,** and **Phone Number** fields to the query grid.

3. Enter a prompt in the *State* that will prompt the user to enter a state.

4. Sort the query in ascending order by the *Last Name* field.

5. Save the query as **Qry-Customers by State**.

6. Run the query using the **TX** parameter. Adjust the column widths if necessary. Print the query results.

7. Run the query using the **OR** and the **CA** parameters. Print the results of each query.

8. Close the query and the database file.

CRITICAL*Thinking*

 ## ACTIVITY 11-1

Access provides two tools for searching database tables: the filter and the query. Use the Help feature in Access to locate information on filters and queries. Write a brief essay that outlines the differences between filters and queries, and provides an example of when you would use each.

ACTIVITY 11-2

As an adjunct professor at Collinsborough Community College, you're going to give a presentation to your Access class on the various types of Action queries. Write a brief summary of the four types of action queries discussed in this lesson and give an example of when you would use each query.

ADVANCED REPORT FEATURES

OBJECTIVES

Upon completion of this lesson, you should be able to:

- Create a title page.
- Add controls to a report.
- Add a subreport to a report.
- Group and sort data.
- Create a report in the Design view.

Estimated time: 1.5 hours

VOCABULARY

Bound control

Calculated control

Footer

Header

Subreport

Unbound control

Introducing Advanced Reporting

A report is a database object used primarily for summarizing and printing information from tables and queries. You've explored creating reports using the Report Wizard. Now, you'll discover the powerful reporting features available in Access. First, you will learn how to create a title page for your report and how to add controls that allow you to add pictures and calculations to your report. Next, you will include a subreport in your report, and the different ways of sorting and grouping information are discussed. Finally, you will create a report from scratch in the Report Design screen.

Creating a Title Page

As you've discovered, several sections make up a report, such as *headers*, *footers*, and the detail section. Anything that appears in the report header section will print only on the first page of the report. And information found in the report footer section will print only on the last page of the report. Page footers can be used to add a variety of items, such as report date, report name, and page numbers. A page footer appears at the bottom of every page in the report. A page header prints at the top of each report page.

You might also decide to include a title page for your report. Access makes creating title pages a simple process by printing information in the report header on its own page.

By selecting *Force New Page* in the report header Properties dialog box, Access will place a page break after the report header. The Properties dialog box for a Report Header is shown in Figure 12-1.

FIGURE 12-1
Report Header properties dialog box

STEP-BY-STEP 12.1

1. Open the database **AA Step12-1** from the data files.

2. Click **Reports** on the *Objects* bar, if necessary.

3. Open the report **Marketing Department ID Report** in Report View to review the report.

4. Maximize the report.

5. Click the **View** button to switch to Design view.

6. Click the gray bar for the *Report Header* section to select it and then click the **Properties** button.

7. In the Properties dialog box, click the **All** tab if necessary, then click in the *Force New Page* text box.

8. Click the arrow and choose **After Section**. Close the **Properties** dialog box.

9. Click **Print Preview** to view your report.

STEP-BY-STEP 12.1 Continued

10. Click the **Two Pages** button. Your screen should appear similar to Figure 12-2.

FIGURE 12-2
Two page report

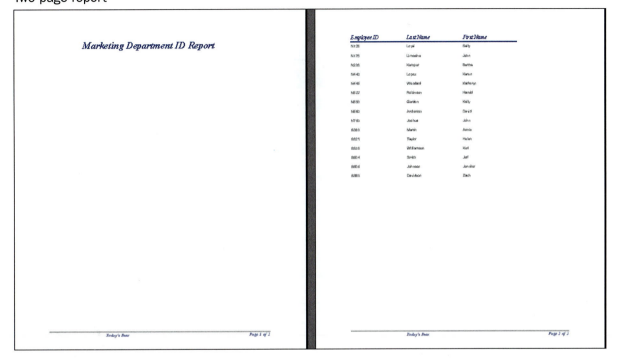

11. Save and print the report.

12. Close the report and leave the database open for the next Step-by-Step.

Adding Controls

Controls offer a wide variety of uses within a report. For example, a report for regional sales may be created using the Report Wizard. After viewing the report, you decide that a total of regional sales is beneficial to the report. By adding a control and entering a calculation into the control, total company sales will appear in the desired location within a report.

Three types of controls are bound, unbound, and calculated controls. A *bound control* is linked to (or bound to) a field in a table or query. This type of control displays information from a field in the report.

An *unbound control*, such as a label, displays information that is not found in a table or query. An example of an unbound control would be the report's title. A report title describes the information found in a report and is created by the person designing the report.

Hot Tip

You can also open a Properties dialog box by right-clicking the control and selecting Properties from the shortcut menu.

A *calculated control* displays the result of a mathematical calculation. Using the above example, you may want a calculated control showing a sales total for a company. Calculated controls are created using the Text Box tool and are also considered unbound.

You'll find the tools necessary for creating controls on the Toolbox toolbar. The Toolbox is shown in Figure 12-3. Your Toolbox may be displayed on the left side of your screen or with the other toolbars.

FIGURE 12-3
Toolbox toolbar

In this Step-by-Step exercise, you will add a report title using an unbound control and then you'll create a calculated control.

STEP-BY-STEP 12.2

1. Click **Reports** on the *Objects* bar, if necessary.

2. Open the report **Transaction Report Totals** in Report view to review the report.

3. Maximize the report if necessary.

4. Click the **View** button to switch to Design View.

5. If the Toolbox is not displayed, click the **Toolbox** button on the toolbar or choose **Toolbox** from the **View** menu. Click the **Control Wizards** tool to turn this feature off for now. The Control Wizard takes you through the steps of creating a report object. However, labels are extremely easy to add and do not typically require the assistance of a Wizard.

6. Click the **Label** button and click at the **1"** mark on the horizontal ruler in the *Report Header* section.

7. Key **Transaction Report** and press **Enter**. Notice how the label takes on the same text formatting as the report. Your screen should look similar to Figure 12-4.

FIGURE 12-4
Report with label

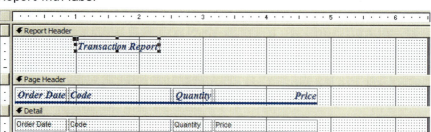

STEP-BY-STEP 12.2 Continued

8. Click the **Text Box** button, place your mouse pointer in the *Detail* section of the report at **5"** on the horizontal ruler and click. A label box and its associated text box should appear (the label box will be overlapping the already existing text *Price* in the detail section).

9. Click the **label box** (left box) of the control and press **Delete**. We only want to show the results of the calculation in the *Detail* section.

10. Click the text box (reads *Unbound*) to select it and then click in the box again to place the insertion point in the box.

11. Key **=[Quantity]*[Price]**. Press **Enter**. (Be sure to use the square brackets around the field names.)

12. Right-click the text box and choose **Properties** on the shortcut menu.

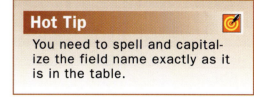

Hot Tip

You need to spell and capitalize the field name exactly as it is in the table.

13. Click the **All** tab if necessary, and then click in the **Format** box. Click the drop-down arrow and choose **Currency**. The Text Box properties box should appear as shown in Figure 12-5.

FIGURE 12-5
Text Box properties

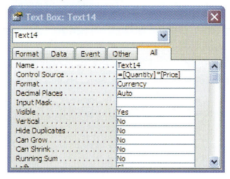

14. Close the Properties dialog box.

15. Click the **View** button to switch to Print Preview. Notice how the calculated control has multiplied quantity by price.

16. Click the **View** button to switch back to Design View then click the **Label** button and click at the **5 ¼"** mark on the horizontal ruler in the *Page Header* section.

Computer Concepts

You can move a control by selecting it and then dragging it to a new location. When you move a control, your mouse pointer will appear as a hand. You can resize a control by selecting it and then dragging a selection handle. To select more than one control at a time, hold down the **Shift** key as you click each control.

STEP-BY-STEP 12.2 Continued

17. Type **Total Price** and press **Enter**. The label should display as shown in Figure 12-6.

FIGURE 12-6
Report with controls

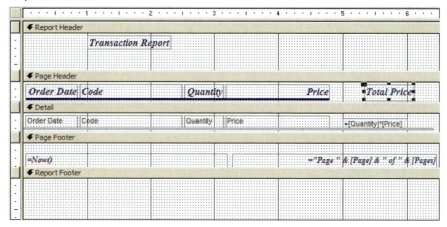

18. Let's add a grand total at the bottom of the report. Click the **Text Box** button, place your mouse pointer in the *Report Footer* section of the report at **5"** on the horizontal ruler and click. A label box and its associated text box should appear.

19. Click the label box (left box) to select it and then click in this box again to place the insertion point inside. Delete the existing text, key **Grand Total:**, and press **Enter**.

20. Click the text box (reads *Unbound*) to select it and then click in the box again to place the insertion point in the box.

21. Type **=SUM([Quantity]*[Price])**. Press **Enter**. (Be sure to use the square brackets around the field names.)

22. Right-click the text box and choose **Properties** on the shortcut menu.

23. Click the **All** tab if necessary, then click in the **Format** box. Click the drop-down arrow and choose **Currency** as displayed in Figure 12-7.

FIGURE 12-7
Text Box properties dialog box

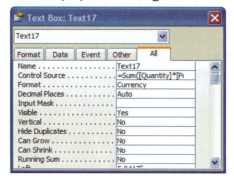

STEP-BY-STEP 12.2 Continued

24. Close the **Properties** dialog box.

25. Click the **View** button to switch to Print Preview. Notice how you now have a grand total on page 2 of the report similar to Figure 12-8.

FIGURE 12-8
Report with calculated controls

Order Date	Code	Quantity	Price	Total Price
28-Mar-03	DP-DP	95	$19.95	$1,895.25
28-Mar-03	TT-BE	50	$15.95	$797.50
28-Mar-03	TT-AE	50	$19.95	$997.50
28-Mar-03	TT-AE	25	$19.95	$498.75
			Grand Total	$47,264.55

26. Save and print the report.

27. Close the report, but leave the database open for the next Step-by-Step.

Adding a Subreport to a Report

A *subreport* is simply a report located within another report, called the main report. Subreports are very useful when you want to show records within the subreport that are related to a specific record in the main report.

For example, let's say you have a table containing data on each of your customers. The fields in this table might include the *customer's name*, *address*, *phone number*, and a *customer ID number*. You have another table in the database that tracks sales. The fields in this table might include the *customer name*, *customer ID number*, and *sales*. As there is a common field between these two tables, the *customer ID number*,

> **Integration Tip**
>
> Objects, such as pictures and clip art, you've created in forms and reports can be used in other Microsoft Office applications. Simply copy the paste the object between the programs.

Access allows you to view records from both tables at one time. Your main report would include fields from the customer's table and the subreport would include records from the sales table. The main report and subreport are displayed together on your screen as shown in Figure 12-9.

FIGURE 12-9
Report with subreport

Employee ID	Last Name	First Name	
N660	Anderson	David	
January Orders			
1024	27-Jan-03 CG-HM		60
S880	Davidson	Zach	
January Orders			
1007	07-Jan-03 TT-BE		62
N550	Gordon	Kelly	
January Orders			
1005	06-Jan-03 TT-TT		65
1022	26-Jan-03 BP-BT		62
1023	26-Jan-03 BP-AT		62
S605	Johnson	Jennifer	
January Orders			
1008	07-Jan-03 TT-AE		62
N750	Joshua	John	
January Orders			
1013	13-Jan-03 TT-BE		34

To add a subreport to a main report, you will first need to open the main report in Design View. Click the Subform/Subreport button in the Toolbox. Then click within the area of the main report where you want the subreport to appear. The Subreport/Subreport Wizard will begin to take you step-by-step through the process of creating a subreport.

S TEP-BY-STEP 12.3

1. Click **Reports** on the *Objects* bar if necessary.

2. Open the **Marketing Department ID Report** in Design View.

STEP-BY-STEP 12.3 Continued

3. Enlarge the *Detail* section so that it's about 1 ½" deep as shown in Figure 12-10. If necessary, display the **Toolbox**.

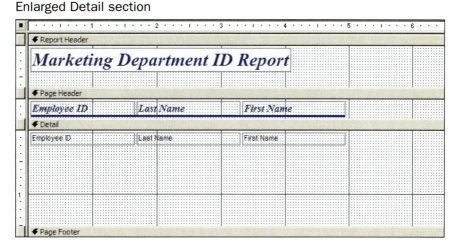

4. Click the **Control Wizards** button to activate this feature. You might activate this feature if you feel you need help creating an object in the report. Click the **Subform/Subreport** button in the Toolbox. Then, position the crosshair at the left margin of the *Detail* section under the Employee ID field and click. The SubReport Wizard should start.

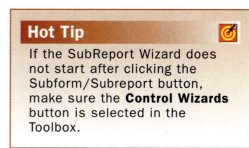

Hot Tip

If the SubReport Wizard does not start after clicking the Subform/Subreport button, make sure the **Control Wizards** button is selected in the Toolbox.

5. Select the **Use an existing report or form** option and then click **January Orders Report**. The SubReport Wizard should appear as shown in Figure 12-11.

STEP-BY-STEP 12.3 Continued

6. Click **Next**. The SubReport Wizard asks you to define the fields that link the main report to the sub-report. See Figure 12-12.

FIGURE 12-12
SubReport Wizard

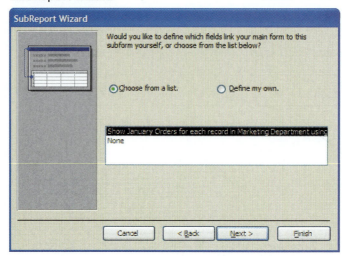

7. The **Choose from a list** option should be selected. From the list, select **Show January Orders for each record in Marketing Department using Employee ID** if necessary.

8. Click **Next**. Enter **January Orders** for the Subreport name. Figure 12-13 shows the dialog box with the new name entered for the subreport.

FIGURE 12-13
SubReport Wizard

STEP-BY-STEP 12.3 Continued

9. Click **Finish**. The main report/subreport should look similar to that shown in Figure 12-14.

FIGURE 12-14
Main Report/SubReport

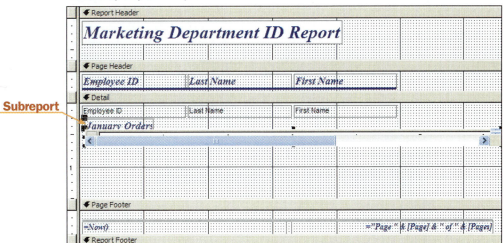

10. Click the **Save** button.

11. Click the **View** button to display the report.

12. Print the report and remain in this screen for the next Step-by-Step.

Sorting and Grouping

The Report Wizard lets you select one or more fields to group together. For example, you may want to keep records for each customer together in a group rather than having all sales records for all customers displayed in a list.

Sorting allows you to display information in ascending order or descending order. Ascending order sorts records from A to Z or from smallest to largest. Descending order arranges records from Z to A or largest to smallest. In this next exercise, you will group and sort customer information.

STEP-BY-STEP 12.4

1. You should be in the Design screen for the **Marketing Department ID Report**. You should see both the main report and subreport.

2. Click the **View** button to view the report. Move to page 3 and notice how the report sorts by Employee ID number. To make the report easier to read, you can sort the report by employee Last Name.

3. Switch back to Design View, right-click the **Page Header** bar, and select **Sorting and Grouping** from the shortcut menu.

STEP-BY-STEP 12.4 Continued

4. Click the down arrow in the **Field/Expression** box and select **Last Name**.

5. Click in the **Keep Together** box, click the down arrow, and then select **Whole Group**. The Whole Group option will keep the orders for each salesperson together rather than splitting this information on two pages. Your Sorting and Grouping dialog box should look like Figure 12-15.

Hot Tip

If your report has blank pages, decrease the size of the report's *Detail* section by placing your mouse pointer over the top of Page Footer bar until a double-headed arrow appears. Then drag the bar upwards to decrease the size of the *Detail* section.

FIGURE 12-15
Sorting and Grouping dialog box

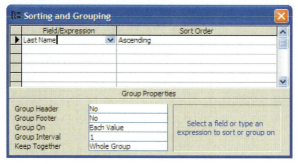

6. Close the **Sorting and Grouping** dialog box. Save the report.

7. Click the **View** button to view the report in Print Preview. Move to page 3 and notice how the report now sorts by Last Name.

8. Close the report but remain in this database for the next Step-by-Step.

Creating a Report in Design View

Although the Report Wizard quickly creates a standard report, you might find that you need additional flexibility with the report's design. For example, your company might want to send invoices to its customers. The information for these invoices is found in a table; however, the desired invoice design is not in the Report Wizard. It's at this point that you create the invoice from scratch in the Report Design screen.

Access provides a number of tools and options for designing reports that are attractive, professional, and easy to read. You can add fields, headers and footers, graphics, text, and even sub-reports.

In this next exercise, you will create a report in the Report Design screen. After adding fields to the *Detail* section, you'll then move the field names into the *Page Header* section so that they appear at the top of the page. Titles and calculated controls will be added.

S TEP-BY-STEP 12.5

1. Click **Reports** on the *Objects* bar if necessary.

2. Double-click **Create report in Design view**.

3. Place your mouse pointer in a blank area (non-dotted area) outside the *Detail* section of the report, but within the Report window, and *right*-click. Choose **Properties** on the shortcut menu.

4. In the Report properties dialog box (for the main report), select the **All** tab if necessary. Click in the **Record Source** text box, click the down arrow, and select **Marketing Department**. You should now see the field list for this table displayed in your work area as shown in Figure 12-16.

Hot Tip

You can also click in the gray report area and then click the **Properties** button.

FIGURE 12-16
Report properties dialog box with field list

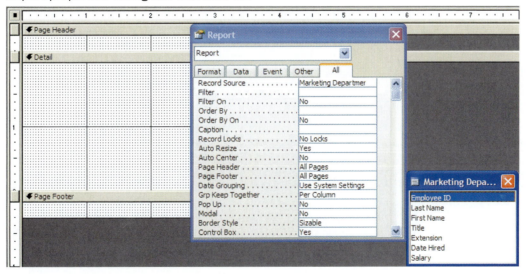

5. Close the Properties box.

6. Place your mouse pointer over the **Employee ID** field and drag it into the *Detail* section at about the **1"** mark on the horizontal ruler. (Don't forget that the indicator used when dragging is actually in the middle of the item to be placed — in between the label and the text.) If your boxes overlap, you can move them after they're placed. Drag the **Last Name** field and position it to the right of Employee ID. Finally, drag the **Salary** and position it to the right of Last Name. (You might need to widen the detail display area.) Close the Marketing Department field list.

7. Move the label boxes (which show the field name) to the *Page Header* section. Right-click on the label for **Employee ID** (left box). Select **Cut** from the shortcut menu.

8. Right-click on the *Page Header* bar and select **Paste** from the shortcut menu. Move the label to the **1"** mark.

STEP-BY-STEP 12.5 Continued

9. Right-click on the label for **Last Name** (left box). Select **Cut** from the shortcut menu.

10. Right-click on the **Page Header** bar and select **Paste** from the shortcut menu. You'll need to drag this label box to the right, to about the **2"** mark, so that it is not on top of the Employee ID label box.

11. Right-click on the label for **Salary** (left box). Select **Cut** from the shortcut menu.

12. Right-click on the *Page Header* bar and select **Paste** from the shortcut menu. You'll need to drag this label box to the right, at about the **3"** mark, so that it is not on top of the Employee ID or Last Name labels.

13. Select the labels in the *Page Header* section and apply the **Bold** format.

14. Drag the labels in the *Page Header* section and their associated text boxes in the *Detail* section until they appear similar to Figure 12-17.

FIGURE 12-17
Location of labels and text boxes

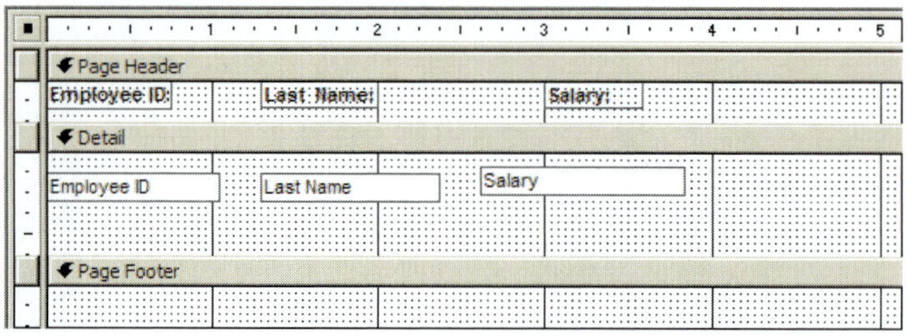

15. Now, let's customize the report's header section. Select the **View** menu and then select **Report Header/Footer**. You should now see these sections in the Design View.

16. Click the **Label** button in the Toolbox and then click in the *Report Header* section at the **2 ½"** mark. (You will move this label later in the exercise.)

17. Key **Sales Report** and press **Enter**. You should see selection handles around this box. If not, click on the label box to select it.

STEP-BY-STEP 12.5 Continued

18. Click the **Bold** button on the Formatting toolbar. Then, click the down arrow on the **Font Size** button and choose **16**. To automatically increase the size of the label box, double-click on the middle right selection handle. Your screen will display as in Figure 12-18.

FIGURE 12-18
Report with label

19. You need only one line for each employee, so you do not need all of the space allocated in the *Detail* section. To decrease the size of the *Detail* section to about ½", place your mouse pointer over the top of the *Page Footer* bar until your mouse pointer becomes a plus sign with arrows. Press and hold the mouse button and drag upwards until the detail section is only about ½" in height.

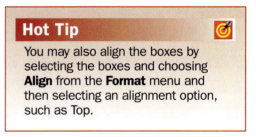

Hot Tip

You may also align the boxes by selecting the boxes and choosing **Align** from the **Format** menu and then selecting an alignment option, such as Top.

20. Select the labels in the *Page Header* section and change the **Font Color** to **Blue**.

21. Select the label in the *Report Header* section and change the **Font Color** to **Blue**.

22. Let's add a calculated control to the *Report Footer* section. Select the **Text Box** tool and click at the **3"** mark on the horizontal ruler in the *Report Footer* section.

23. Click the **label box** (left box) and then click inside the box to place the insertion point inside. Delete the existing text and key **Salary Total** and press **Enter**.

24. Click the **text box** (reads "Unbound") to select it and then click in the box again to place the insertion point in the box.

STEP-BY-STEP 12.5 Continued

25. Type **=SUM([Salary])** and press **Enter**. (Be sure to use the square brackets around the field name.) Change the **Font Color** to **Blue** for the label and text box. Your screen should appear as shown in Figure 12-19.

FIGURE 12-19
Report with calculated control

26. Right-click the **Salary total** text box and choose **Properties** on the shortcut menu.

27. Click the **All** tab, if necessary, and then click in the **Format** box. Click the drop-down arrow and choose **Currency**. Close the Properties dialog box.

28. Drag the *report title* until it is centered above the report.

29. Click the **View** button to switch to **Print Preview**.

30. Save the report as **Sales Report**. Print the report.

31. Close the report and then close the database.

Speech Recognition

If your computer has speech recognition capabilities, enable the Voice Command mode and say the appropriate steps to save and print the report.

Speech Recognition

If your computer has speech recognition capabilities, enable the Voice Command mode and say the appropriate steps to close the report and then close the database file.

Time Saver

Access lets you quickly change the size of controls in a form or report using the Ctrl and Shift keys in conjunction with the arrow keys.

STEP-BY-STEP 12.6

1. Open the **Time Savers** database from the data files.

2. Go to the design view of the **Book Description** form.

3. Click the right box of the *Project Manager Code* field.

STEP-BY-STEP 12.6 Continued

4. Press **Shift +** down arrow several times to increase the height of the selected control.

5. Press **CTRL +** right arrow several times until the right side of the *Project Manager Code* field is even with the right side of the *Book Title* control.

6. Press **Shift +** up arrow several times to decrease the height of the selected control.

7. Close the form without saving any changes.

8. Close the database.

SUMMARY

In this lesson, you learned:

■ Reports are characterized by bound, unbound, and calculated controls. Bound controls are tied to a field in the table or query on which the report is based. Unbound controls are not tied to a field. A calculated control is an unbound control that contains the result of a mathematical calculation.

■ A report header appears once on the first page of the report. You can create a title page for a report by forcing a page break after the *Report Header* section.

■ A report footer appears once on the last page of a report and a page footer appears at the bottom of each page of a report. Page headers appear once at the top of every page.

■ You can easily add a subreport to a main report using the SubForm/SubReport Wizard.

■ Creating a report from scratch in Design View gives you optimum flexibility in the design and appearance of the report.

VOCABULARY *Review*

Define the following terms:

Bound control	Footer	Subreport
Calculated control	Header	Unbound control

REVIEW *Questions*

TRUE/FALSE

Circle T if the statement is true or F if the statement is false.

T   F   **1.** An unbound control displays information that is not tied to a table or query.

T   F   **2.** You click the Label button in the Toolbox to add a field from an underlying table or query to a report.

T   F   **3.** A calculated control is an example of an unbound control.

T   F   **4.** You cannot change the properties of a bound control.

T   F   **5.** A report footer appears at the bottom of every page in a report.

WRITTEN QUESTIONS

Write a brief answer to the following questions.

1. Describe the difference between a report footer and a page footer.

2. How do you create a title page for a report?

3. Explain the purpose of a calculated control and give an example.

4. Explain the difference between a report header and a page header.

5. Discuss the type of information that is displayed in a subreport.

PROJECTS

PROJECT 12-1

1. Open the **AA Project12-1** database from the data files.

2. Create a report with the Report Wizard using **Qry-January Sales**.

3. Include all four fields in the report. **Sort** by **Order No.** in ascending order, use the **Tabular** layout, and the **Corporate** style.

4. Title the report **Total January Sales**.

5. Create a calculated control that multiplies the price by quantity for each order. Place this control into the *Detail* section.

6. Format the calculated control for currency.

7. Enter **Order Total** into the label box of the calculated control and move the label box from the *Detail* section into the page header section and format the label box like the other page headers.

8. Add a calculated control in the *Report Footer* that will display a grand total for calculations in the *Order Totals* column. (Hint: =SUM([Price]*[Quantity]).)

9. Save and print the report.

10. Close the report and then close the database.

CRITICAL *Thinking*

ACTIVITY 12-1

You are the manager for a pet supply company that is undergoing a merger. The new owners of the company ask you to create a report that shows the transactions for each employee. Use the **AA Activity12-1** database in the data files. Create a report with a subreport using Total Employee Transactions as the main report and Transactions subreport as the subreport. Your report should look similar to Figure 12-20.

FIGURE 12-20
Activity report

Total Employee Transactions

Last Name	Employee ID	First Name		
Crawford	1	Katie		
Transactions				

Transactions Subreport

150				
	3		$11.92	$35.77
	5		$11.92	$59.62
162				
	4		$11.03	$44.10
230				
	8		$6.26	$50.05
318				
	5		$7.86	$39.28
326				
	7		$15.63	$109.38

ACTIVITY 12-2

As the vice president of a grocery store chain, you are the expert in analyzing data. You want to create a report that totals sales for each month. With your knowledge of queries and the advanced reporting features you learned in this lesson, explain an easy method for creating this type of report.

IMPORTING AND EXPORTING DATA

Understanding Importing and Exporting

Access lets you easily exchange data with other programs. In this lesson, you'll learn how to import data from and export data to other applications. *Importing* refers to bringing information from another program into Access. You may also bring information from one Access database into another. Once data is imported, it may be treated as any other Access data. *Exporting* refers to placing Access data into another program or another Access database file.

Importing Data

Access can import and read files created in other programs or saved in various formats. Table 13-1 lists the types of files Access can read.

TABLE 13-1

FILE TYPE	FILE EXTENSION
Microsoft Access	*.mbd *.adp *.mda *.mde *.ade
Microsoft Excel	*.xls
Exchange	
Outlook	
Lotus 1-2-3	*.wk*
Lotus 1-2-3/DOS	*.wj*
Paradox	*.db
Text Files	*.txt *.csv *.tab *.asc
HTML Documents	*.html *.htm
dBase III	*.dbf
dBase IV	*.dbf
dBase 5	*.dbf
XML Document	*.xml
ODBC Databases	
Windows SharePoint Services	

You can import a file into a table that already exists in Access, or you can import a file and let Access create the table for you. If you have Access create the table, the file needs to be in a database table format with columns, or fields, of data. If the data you're importing is already set up with column names, Access will automatically transfer this information to the new table as field names. Otherwise Access will assign numbers for the field names, which you may modify in the Table Design view.

To import data into a database file you want to import the data into, open the database file you want to import the data into, and select the Get External Data command on the File menu. From the submenu, choose Import. Access will then take you step-by-step through importing a file. In the following Step-by-Step, you'll import a Microsoft Excel file into Access.

STEP-BY-STEP 13.1

1. Open the **AA Step13-1** database from the data files.

2. Click the **File** menu, choose **Get External Data**, and select **Import**. The Import dialog box opens.

3. In the Import dialog box, click the **Files of type** drop-down arrow and select **Microsoft Excel**.

4. Select the **Mailing List** file from the data files and click the **Import** button.

5. The Import Spreadsheet Wizard appears as shown in Figure 13-1. Notice that the first row of the spreadsheet contains column headings (field names). Select **First Row Contains Column Headings** and click **Next**.

FIGURE 13-1
Import Spreadsheet Wizard

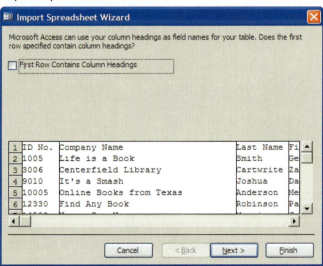

6. The next dialog box of the Import Spreadsheet Wizard appears, as shown in Figure 13-2. If necessary, select the **In a New Table** option and click **Next**.

FIGURE 13-2
Import Spreadsheet Wizard

STEP-BY-STEP 13.1 Continued

7. In the next dialog box, as displayed in Figure 13-3, you can specify information about each field, such as its name and the data type. Typically, Access can correctly determine the data type for each field and no changes are necessary. Click **Next**.

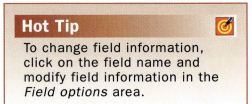

Hot Tip

To change field information, click on the field name and modify field information in the *Field options* area.

FIGURE 13-3
Import Spreadsheet Wizard

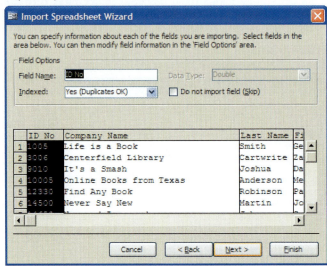

8. A new Wizard dialog box appears. In this dialog box, you select whether you want Access to assign a primary key field. Choose **Choose my own primary key**, click on **ID No**, if necessary, as shown in Figure 13-4, and click **Next**.

FIGURE 13-4
Import Spreadsheet Wizard

STEP-BY-STEP 13.1 Continued

9. The final dialog box appears asking for a table name, as displayed in Figure 13-5. Key **Mailing List** if necessary in the *Import to Table* box.

FIGURE 13-5
Import Spreadsheet Wizard

10. Click **Finish**.

11. You will see a message box letting you know that the import is complete. Click **OK**.

12. Open the **Mailing List** table and view the results. Your screen should look similar to Figure 13-6.

FIGURE 13-6
Imported Mailing List table

ID No	Company Name	Last Name	First Name	Address	City	State	ZIP	Phone N
1005	Life is a Book	Smith	George	2525 West Avenue	Houston	TX	73301	713-555-
3006	Centerfield Library	Cartwrite	Zachary	8767 South Main	Brazos	TX	77822	713-555-
9010	It's a Smash	Joshua	Daniel	1425 East 14th	Irving	TX	76221	214-555-
10005	Online Books from Texas	Anderson	Melissa	2325 Mesa Drive	Austin	TX	75377	512-555-
12330	Find Any Book	Robinson	Pauline	93 North 63rd	El Paso	TX	73445	702-555-
14500	Never Say New	Martin	Jose	14 Hyatt	Houston	TX	73302	713-555-
14650	New and Improved	Johnson	Sally	1900 Oak Street	San Antonio	TX	75443	210-555-
14750	Warehouse Books and Such	Kennedy	Rosa	12 Orchestra Terrace	Riverside	TX	75234	214-555-
15665	Computer Book Sales	Levinson	Victor	7 Main	Lewisville	TX	76055	940-555-
16250	Community College Book Store	Fredrick	Helen	87 Polk Street	Southlake	TX	76056	940-555-
16400	Resale, Resale, and more Resales	Benntly	Lorna	52 Llano Largo	Shreveport	LA	75331	512-555-
17250	Book Sales, Inc.	Davidson	Annabelle	Fifth Avenue	Bossier City	LA	71223	210-555-
17750	Find a Book, Inc.	Burke	Nathan	89 Chiaroscuro Rd	Houston	TX	73303	713-555-
18500	CBS - Computer Books	Taylor	Beverly	12 East St	Grapevine	TX	76055	940-555-
20550	New Book Sales	Jameson	Marty	1924 Norton	Dallas	TX	76099	214-555-

STEP-BY-STEP 13.1 Continued

13. Adjust the column widths in the table if necessary. Save and print the table.

14. Close the table and remain in this database for the next Step-by-Step.

Exporting Data to Other Programs

You can export Access data to other programs. For example, with the *OfficeLinks* feature in Microsoft Office, you can export an Access table, query, form, or report to Word or Excel. The OfficeLink button is located on the Standard toolbar. These OfficeLink selections are shown in Figure 13-7. Exporting may also be accomplished by using the Export selection on the File menu.

FIGURE 13-7
OfficeLinks selections

Selecting Merge It with Microsoft Office Word selection starts a mail merge with Microsoft Word. After starting the mail merge, you need to locate the Word document for the merge and insert the Access fields into the document.

Publish It with Microsoft Office Word creates an instant Word document with the selected Access table information. You may then add any additional text, such as titles, to the document.

A very popular feature you'll want to familiarize yourself with is the Analyze It in Microsoft Office Excel feature. Once the Access data is instantly placed into an Excel worksheet, it may be formatted, have formulas added, and the data manipulated as in any other Excel worksheet.

In the next Step-by-Step, you will first use the Analyze It with Microsoft Office Excel OfficeLink. Then you'll discover how to export using the File, Export option.

STEP-BY-STEP 13.2

1. If necessary, click **Tables** on the *Objects* bar, and then select the **February Orders** table (do not open the table).

2. Click the down arrow on the **OfficeLinks** button and then select **Analyze It with Microsoft** 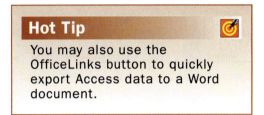 **Office Excel**. The Excel program opens and the records from the March Orders table are automatically inserted in a new worksheet. The Excel file is automatically named **February Orders.xls**.

3. Close the **February Orders.xls** file but leave Excel open.

4. Click the **Microsoft Access** button on the taskbar to return to Access.

> **Hot Tip**
>
> You may also use the OfficeLinks button to quickly export Access data to a Word document.

5. You will now use the File, Export option. If necessary, click **Tables** on the *Objects* bar and then select the **March Orders** table (do not open the table).

6. Open the **File** menu and select **Export**. Click the **Save in** down arrow and select the desired folder.

7. Click the **Save as type** down arrow and select **MicrosoftExcel97-2003**. Your screen should appear as shown in Figure 13-8.

FIGURE 13-8
Export Table dialog box

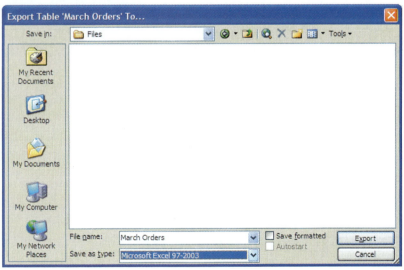

8. Click **Export**. Your file is now ready to view in Excel.

9. Click the **Microsoft Excel** button on the taskbar.

10. Open the **File** menu and select **Open**.   Choose the drive and folder for the exported file.

11. Click **March Orders** and choose **Open**. Your screen should now display the information from the Access March Orders table as shown in Figure 13-9. Notice that Excel recognized the Yes/No Access field as True and False.

FIGURE 13-9
Exported March Orders data

	A	B	C	D	E	F	G	H	I
1	Order No	Order Date	Code	Description	Quantity	Price	Shipping	Employee	Shipped
2	3001	3/4/2003	BP-BT	Beginning Computers	67	$15.95	$5.00	N440	TRUE
3	3002	3/4/2003	BP-AT	Advanced Computers	67	$19.95	$6.00	N440	TRUE
4	3005	3/6/2003	TT-TT	Advanced Spreadsheets	65	$19.95	$2.00	N550	TRUE
5	3006	3/6/2003	BP-BP	Advanced Word Processing	390	$15.95	$1.00	S330	TRUE
6	3007	3/7/2003	TT-BE	Beginning Presentations	62	$15.95	$5.00	S880	TRUE
7	3008	3/7/2003	TT-AE	Advanced Presentations	62	$19.95	$2.00	S605	TRUE
8	3009	3/8/2003	DB-DT	Beginning Database	70	$15.95	$3.00	S535	TRUE
9	3010	3/12/2003	DB-BD	Beginning Publishing	80	$15.95	$4.00	S535	TRUE
10	3011	3/12/2003	DB-AD	Advanced Publishing	80	$19.95	$2.00	S535	TRUE
11	3012	3/12/2003	DP-DP	Desktop Publishing for Beginners	315	$19.95	$1.00	N522	TRUE
12	3013	3/13/2003	TT-BE	Beginning Presentations	67	$15.95	$1.00	N750	TRUE
13	3014	3/13/2003	TT-AE	Advanced Presentations	67	$19.95	$3.00	N205	TRUE
14	3015	3/14/2003	GR-CG	Computer Artist	60	$12.50	$5.00	N175	TRUE
15	3017	3/15/2003	BP-BP	Word Processing for Professional	90	$15.95	$3.00	N522	TRUE
16	3018	3/18/2003	BP-BT	Beginning Databases	62	$15.95	$6.00	N445	TRUE
17	3019	3/18/2003	BP-AT	Advanced Databases	62	$19.95	$7.00	N175	TRUE
18	3020	3/21/2003	DB-BD	Beginning Publishing	55	$15.95	$3.00	N522	TRUE
19	3021	3/21/2003	DB-AD	Advanced Publishing	55	$19.95	$2.00	N522	TRUE
20	3022	3/26/2003	BP-BT	Beginning Computers	62	$15.95	$4.00	N550	TRUE
21	3023	3/26/2003	BP-AT	Advanced Computers	62	$19.95	$4.00	N175	TRUE
22	3024	3/27/2003	CG-HM	History of Microcomputers	60	$9.95	$3.00	N660	TRUE
23	3025	3/28/2003	DP-DP	Desktop Publishing for Beginners	95	$19.95	$3.00	N445	TRUE
24	3026	3/28/2003	TT-BE	Beginning Presentations	50	$15.95	$2.00	S525	TRUE
25	3027	3/28/2003	TT-AE	Advanced Presentations	50	$19.95	$5.00	S525	TRUE
26	3028	3/28/2003	TT-AE	Advanced Presentations	25	$19.95	$3.00	N175	FALSE
27	3029	3/12/2003	DB-AD	Advanced Publishing	80	$19.95	$2.00	S525	TRUE
28	3030	3/12/2003	DP-DP	Desktop Publishing for Beginners	215	$19.95	$1.00	N522	TRUE
29	3031	3/13/2003	TT-BE	Beginning Presentations	67	$15.95	$1.00	N750	TRUE
30	3032	3/13/2003	TT-AE	Advanced Presentations	67	$19.95	$3.00	N205	TRUE
31	3033	3/14/2003	GR-CG	Computer Artist	60	$12.50	$5.00	S535	TRUE

12. Close the workbook and exit Excel.

13. In Access, close the database file but leave Access open.

> **Speech Recognition**
>
> If your computer has speech recognition capabilities, enable the Voice Command mode and say the appropriate steps to close Excel.

Importing and Exporting Using XML

Extensible Markup Language (XML) is now supported by Access. **XML** places structured data, such as table data, in a format that may be read in a variety of applications. It is considered a universal format for data on the Web. You use XML to share Access data, such as a table, query, form, or report, by saving the data in a XML format. And you may bring XML data from the Web directly into Access using the Import feature.

In this Step-by-Step, you will save structured data in a table as an XML file first, then you'll open another Access database and import the XML file.

STEP-BY-STEP 13.3

1. Open the **AA Step13-3a** database from the data files.

2. Select the **Customers** table in the database window (do not open the table).

3. Open the **File** menu and select **Export**. The Export Table To dialog box appears.

4. You will now save this data file in an XML format. Click the **Save as type** arrow and select **XML**. Enter the filename **Customers** if necessary. Your screen should appear similar to Figure 13-10.

FIGURE 13-10
Export Table As dialog box

5. Click **Export**. The Export XML dialog box appears as displayed in Figure 13-11.

FIGURE 13-11
Export XML dialog box

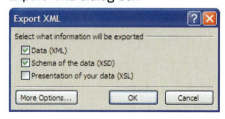

STEP-BY-STEP 13.3 Continued

6. Select **Data (XML)** and **Schema of the Data**, if necessary. These options need to be selected in order to export the data and the schema, which specifies the structure of the data. If you select the **More Options** button, an additional Export XML dialog box displays. The three tabs, Data, Schema, and Presentation offer additional export selections as shown in Figures 13-12, 13-13, and 13-14. The Presentation tab allows the exported data to be viewed on a Client machine or a Server.

FIGURE 13-12
Data tab of the Export XML dialog box

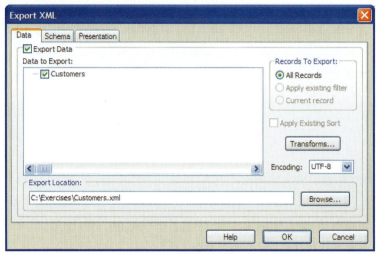

FIGURE 13-13
Schema tab of the Export XML dialog box

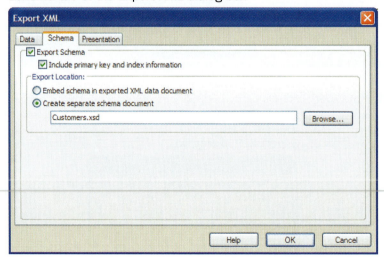

STEP-BY-STEP 13.3 Continued

FIGURE 13-14
Presentation tab of the Export XML dialog box

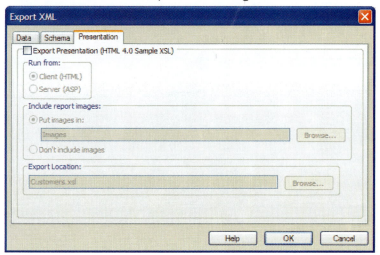

7. Click **OK**. A copy of the Customers table is now an XML document.

8. You will now learn how to import an XML file into an Access database. Close the **AA Step 13-3a** data file.

9. Open the **AA Step13-3b** database from the data files.

10. Click the **File** menu, choose **Get External Data**, and then select **Import**. The Import dialog box appears.

11. In the Import dialog box, click the **Files of type** drop-down arrow and select **XML**.

12. Select the **Customers.xml** file. Click the **Import** button.

13. The **Import XML** dialog box displays as shown in Figure 13-15.

FIGURE 13-15
Import XML dialog box

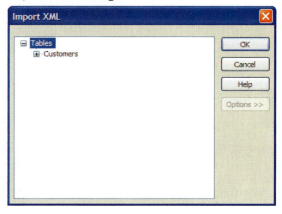

STEP-BY-STEP 13.3 Continued

14. Click **OK**. Click **OK** again to confirm import. Open the **Customers** table. Your screen should appear similar to Figure 13-16.

FIGURE 13-16
Imported table using XML

Customer ID	Company Name	Last Name	First Name	Title	Address	City	State	Postal Code	Phone Number	Fax N
1	Pets Unlimited	Martin	April	Manager	341 Broad Street	Tyler	TX	75024	(972) 555-1234	(972) 55
2	Little Animals	Ho	Randy	Manager	444 8th NE	Waco	TX	75689	(972) 555-1478	(972) 55
3	Pet Palace	Rex	Tyrone	Manager	1805 8th Street	Oakland	CA	94608	(409) 555-4449	(409) 55
4	Anne's Pet Supplies	Hernandez	Anne	Owner	2501 La Jolla Blvd	San Diego	CA	92111	(619) 555-6719	
5	Friendly Groomers	Long	Herbert	Purch Mgr	22 Spruce Way	Eugene	OR	97403	(503) 555-6644	(503) 55
6	Pet Paradise	Hughes	Susan	Admin Asst	2409 Springer Ave	Bellingham	TX	98226	(972) 555-4563	(972) 55
7	Teddy's Pampered Pets	Bayer	Teddy	Owner	1500 Onion Field Way	Grand Prarie	TX	75236	(509) 555-3462	
8	Pets 'n' Such	Marley	Mary	Owner	2500 W. Olympic Blvd	Los Angeles	CA	90028	(213) 555-3333	(213) 55
9	My Buddy Pet Supply	Ramirez	Christine	Purch Mgr	2450 J Street	Sacramento	CA	95831	(916) 555-7675	(916) 55
10	Cats Exclusively	MacDonald	John	Owner	1928 N Yeller	Portland	OR	97101	(503) 555-0487	(503) 55
11	Bow Wow Supplies	Roberts	Dee Dee	Manager	2419 Santa Cruz St	San Jose	CA	95148	(408) 555-7622	
12	Specialty Pets	Walden	Fred	Manager	1720 NW Merchant	Aloha	OR	97035	(503) 555-2938	
13	Anything Goes!!	Martinez	Eunice	Manager	3405 E Puyallup	Lake Texoma	TX	75278	(972) 555-5555	(972) 55
14	Southwest Pet Supply	Watson	Andrea	President	18 Rainier NE	Tualatin	OR	97038	(503) 555-8414	(503) 55
15	Bayview Pet Center	Donahue	Walter	Owner	18 Market St	San Francisco	CA	94116	(415) 555-4098	(415) 55

15. Close the table and close the database file.

Time Saver

You can quickly bring the Database window to the front of your screen using the F11 key.

STEP-BY-STEP 13.4

1. Open the **Time Savers** database from the data files.

2. Open the **Book Description** form and maximize the form window.

3. Press **F11**. Notice how the database window now appears in front of the form window and the form window is reduced.

4. Press **Ctrl + F4** to close the database.

SUMMARY

In this lesson, you learned:

■ Importing refers to bringing data from one Access database or application into another. The Import Wizard takes you step-by-step through the process of importing data.

■ Exporting data from Access is easily done by using the File, Export option.

■ You may also export data using the OfficeLinks button found on the Standard toolbar.

■ XML lets you import data into Access and export Access data as an XML document for shared use on the Web.

VOCABULARY *Review*

Define the following terms:

Exporting   OfficeLinks   XML

Importing

REVIEW *Questions*

TRUE/FALSE

Circle T if the statement is true or F if the statement is false.

T   F   **1.** You can import Excel files into Access.

T   F   **2.** Using the File, Export feature brings Excel data into an Access table.

T   F   **3.** The File, Open option in Access lets you import data.

T   F   **4.** XML refers to Extensible Markup Language.

T   F   **5.** When you import data into an Access table, column headings may be used as field names.

WRITTEN QUESTIONS

Write a brief answer to the following questions.

1. List the steps for importing data into an Excel spreadsheet.

2. Describe the difference between import and export.

3. List two types of file formats that can be imported into Access.

4. Explain the steps for using the Analyze It in Microsoft Office Excel OfficeLink.

5. Describe the steps for exporting data using the File, Export option.

PROJECTS

PROJECT 13-1

1. Open the **AA Project13-1** database file.

2. Import the **Accounting Department** workbook file from the data files into Access as a table.

3. Let Access add the primary key field for you and name the table **AccountingDepartment**.

4. Adjust column widths in the table if necessary. Print the table.

5. Close the database file.

PROJECT 13-2

1. Open the **AAProject13-2** database file.

2. Export the **Marketing Department** table data using the **Microsoft Excel 97-2003** file type. Export the table with the **File, Export** feature. Enter **Marketing Department** for the workbook name. Select the **Save Formatted** check box.

3. Use an **OfficeLink** selection so that you can analyze **January Orders** table information in Excel.

4. Adjust column widths in the January Orders worksheet, if necessary, and then print the table.

5. Close the workbook file and exit Excel.

6. Close the database file and exit Access.

CRITICAL*Thinking*

 ACTIVITY 13-1

You are the database administrator for the Last Resort Sales Company. You want to import a file of employee applicants from Excel into Access. Open the **AA Activity13-1** database from the data files. Import the **Employee Applicants** workbook from the data files. Let Access add the primary key field for you and name the table **Employee Applicants**. Create a report from the new table. Name the report **Employee Applicants Information**. Use the Report Wizard and select a **Columnar** format and the **Corporate** style. Modify the design of the report by decreasing the length of the fields and aligning the field information to the left. Print the report.

 ACTIVITY 13-2

Use the Access Help system to find information on the purpose of schema when using XML. Write a brief explanation of the purpose.

CREATING MACROS AND SWITCHBOARDS

VOCABULARY

Macro

Switchboard

Introducing Macros and Switchboards

A macro is a handy tool you use to automate frequent tasks that you perform in a database. To create a macro, enter a set of commands for the desired task. Then, when you're ready to perform the task, run the macro.

A switchboard is a user-friendly feature that people who understand Access can create to assist people who are not as familiar with Access. A switchboard will appear when the database is opened. It is similar to a main menu. Once the switchboard appears on your screen, you may then select from the available actions, such as open tables and forms, enter and edit records, and print reports. Macro buttons are typically used in a switchboard to assist in performing these tasks.

Creating a Basic Macro

A *macro* contains a set of actions necessary to complete a certain task. For example, you may frequently use a form to enter new records. It can become tedious to open the form and click the New Record button each time you need to enter new records. With a macro, these steps are recorded as a single operation. All you have to do is run the macro to automatically open the form and go to a new record.

You create a macro in the Macro Design window. In the Action column, you determine the actions or steps that you want the macro to perform. If you want to notate an action, such as the purpose of the action, enter the note in the Comment column. In the Action Arguments section, you apply specific directions for each action.

After you create and save a macro, simply click the Run button in the database window. In this next exercise, you will create and run a macro.

S TEP-BY-STEP 14.1

1. Open the **AA Step14-1** database from the data files.

2. Click **Macros** in the *Objects* bar.

3. Click the **New** button.

4. If necessary, click in the first row of the **Action** column, click the down arrow, and then select **OpenForm** from the *Action* list.

5. Click in the **Comment** box for this action and key **Opens the January Orders form**.

6. Click in the **Form Name** box in the *Action Arguments* section, click the down arrow, and then select **January Orders Form** from the list.

7. Click in the **Data Mode** box, click the down arrow, and then select **Edit**. This feature allows you to edit or add new records to the form after it is opened.

8. In the second row of the **Action** column, click the down arrow and select **GoToRecord** from the *Action* list.

9. For the comment, key **Goes to a new record**.

> **Hot Tip**
>
> You may start typing the name of the action in the *Action* column to more quickly locate the item you are searching for, rather than scrolling.

STEP-BY-STEP 14.1 Continued

10. Click the **Object Type** box in the *Action Arguments* section and click the down arrow.

11. Select **Form** from the list.

12. For the **Object Name** action argument, click the down arrow, and select **January Orders Form** from the list.

13. For the **Record** action argument, click the down arrow and select **New** from the list.

14. Click the **Save** button, use **Enter January Orders** for the macro name, and click **OK**. Your screen should look similar to Figure 14-1.

FIGURE 14-1
Macro Design screen

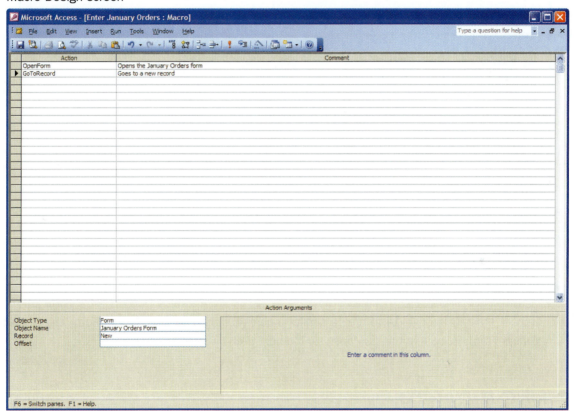

STEP-BY-STEP 14.1 Continued

15. Click the **Run** button. The form should open automatically and a new record should be displayed, as shown in Figure 14-2.

FIGURE 14-2
Executed macro

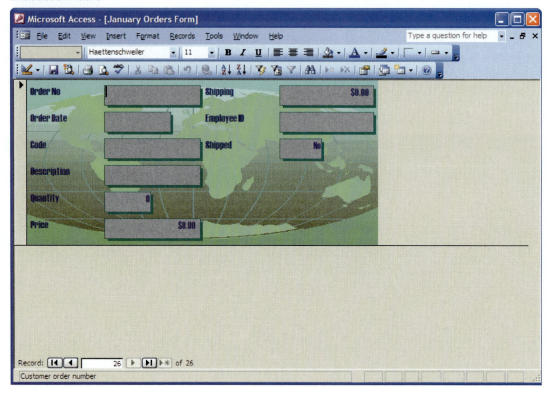

16. Close the form.

17. Repeat steps **3** through **14** to create similar macros for the **February Orders Form** and the **March Orders Form**. Remain in this database for the next Step-by-Step.

Editing a Macro

Macros are easy to modify in the Macro Design window. Simply add or delete actions and change the Action Arguments as necessary. Then make sure you save the changes to the macro.

When you enter the Macro Design window, the Macro Names and Conditions columns may appear. If you want to remove these columns, you can click the Macro Names and Conditions buttons.

STEP-BY-STEP 14.2

1. Display the **Enter January Orders** macro in the Macro Design window. Let's add a third action.

2. Click in the third **Action** row, click the down arrow, and choose **Maximize**. This action will maximize the form when you open it. Your macro design should look similar to Figure 14-3.

FIGURE 14-3
Macro Design window with edited macro

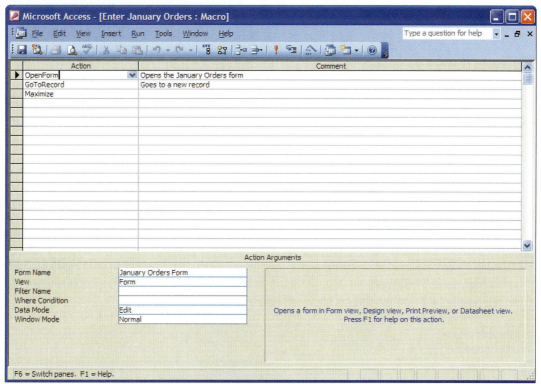

3. Click **Save** and close the Macro Design window.

4. Run the macro from the Database window.

5. Close **January Orders Form**.

6. Repeat steps **1** through **3** to add the **Maximize** action to the **Enter February Orders** and to the **Enter March Orders** macros.

7. Click the **Restore** button of the Database window and remain in this database for the next Step-by-Step.

Creating a Macro Button in a Form

You can represent a macro as a button in a database form or report. For example, you might create a macro that closes a form. This macro can then be placed into the form itself. When you're ready to close the form, just click the macro button.

To create a macro button, drag the macro from the Database window into the object's Design screen. A macro button will appear with its macro name displayed. You can create a macro that can be used in several objects by not specifying the name of the object. In the next exercise, you will create a Close macro that will be used in several forms.

STEP-BY-STEP 14.3

1. You will now create a macro that closes any object where it's placed, such as a form. Click **Macros** in the *Objects* bar if necessary.

2. Click the **New** button.

3. If necessary, click in the first row of the *Action* column, click the down arrow, and then select **Close** from the *Action* list.

4. Click the **Save** button, enter **Close** for the macro name, and click **OK**. Close the Macro Design window.

5. In the database window, select **Forms** in the *Objects* bar. Open the **January Orders Form** in Design View. Select **Macros** in the *Objects* bar and resize the January Orders Form Design window and the Database window so they are side by side, as shown in Figure 14-4.

FIGURE 14-4
Resized windows

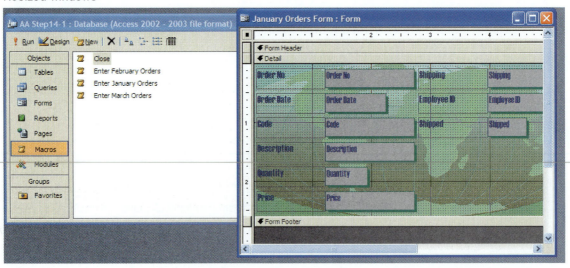

STEP-BY-STEP 14.3 Continued

6. In the Database window, place your mouse pointer over the **Close** macro and drag the **Close** macro to the 4" horizontal ruler and 2" vertical ruler position in the *Detail* section of January Orders Form. See Figure 14-5.

FIGURE 14-5
Design screen with macro button

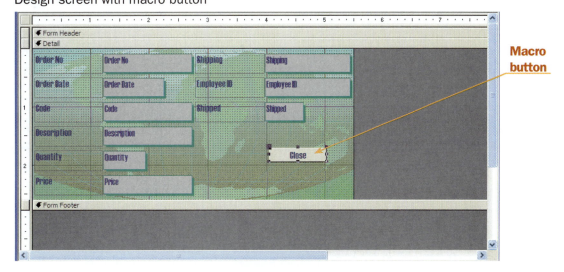

7. Save the form and then click the **View** button. Click the **Close** button to close the form.

8. Repeat steps **5** through **7** to add the **Close** macro in the **February Orders Form** and the **March Orders Form**.

9. Remain in this database for the next Step-by-Step.

You will now create a macro that exits the Access application. This macro will be used in the switchboard form that you'll construct in the next Step-by-Step.

STEP-BY-STEP 14.4

1. Click **Macros** in the *Objects* bar if necessary.

2. Click the **New** button.

3. If necessary, click in the first row of the *Action* column, click the down arrow, and then select **Quit** from the *Action* list.

4. Save the macro as **Exit Access**.

5. Close the Macro Design window and remain in this database for the next Step-by-Step.

Creating a Switchboard

A *switchboard* is a powerful feature in Access. It is typically created by people that understand Access to assist people who are not as familiar with Access. A switchboard is similar to using a "main menu" in that it lets you select from a list of options.

Switchboards contain macro buttons that let you open, close, and perform various actions on database objects simply by clicking a button.

Switchboards are created as forms. To construct a switchboard, you add macros to a new form as macro buttons. You then save and name the form Switchboard or Main Menu (or any name that assists you in recognizing this form as a switchboard). After the switchboard is complete, any user can simply click on a macro button to begin working in the database. As you can imagine, a switchboard is a useful tool for novice users of Access who may not be familiar with various database objects or how to work with them.

If a switchboard form is maximized on your screen and changes need to be made to objects in the database, click the Database Window button to display the database window.

S **TEP-BY-STEP 14.5**

1. Open a new form in Design View.

2. Right-click in the *Detail* section and select **Properties** from the shortcut menu.

3. Select the **Back Color** box and then click the **Ellipses** button. Select a background color of your choice and close the Properties dialog box.

4. Click the **Unbound Object Frame** tool and draw a box in the upper-left corner of the Design screen about 1" by 1". (*Note:* The Control Wizard button should be turned on for this feature.)

5. The Microsoft Access dialog box should appear. Select **Create from File** and click the **Browse** button. Go to the folder where your data files are located and select the **Company Logo** picture. Click **OK** to select the picture and then click **OK** to close the Microsoft Access dialog box.

6. Place your mouse pointer over the icon and right-click. Select **Change To** and then select **Image** from the submenu. A Microsoft Access warning box will appear indicating that you cannot undo this command and that, once completed, you won't be able to edit this object. Click **Yes**.

7. Place your mouse pointer over the icon and right-click again. Select **Properties** from the shortcut menu, click the **All** tab (if necessary), select the **Picture** item and then click on the ellipses. Choose the **Company Logo.tif** file again. Select the **Size Mode** item, and click the down arrow that appears. Choose **Stretch** from the *Size Mode* list box. Close the Properties dialog box. Your screen should look like that in Figure 14-6.

8. You will now add a title to the form with the Label tool. (*Note:* The Control Wizard button should be turned off for this feature.) Click the **Label** tool and draw a box about 2" wide by 1" tall to the right of the picture. Click in the *Label* box and enter **Main Menu**. Select the *Label* box and change the font to **24 point**, **bold**, **White** font color, and **Tahoma** (or a similar Font). See Figure 14-7.

STEP-BY-STEP 14.5 Continued

FIGURE 14-6
Inserted picture in form design

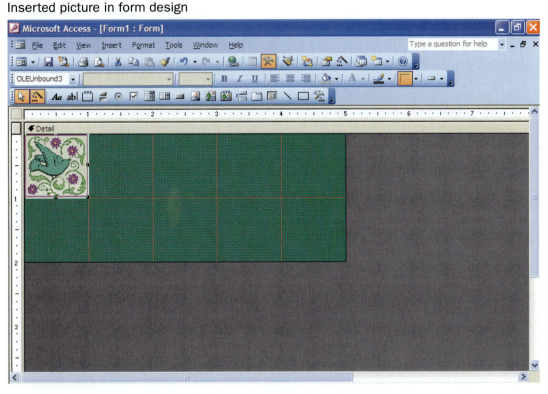

FIGURE 14-7
Label added to form

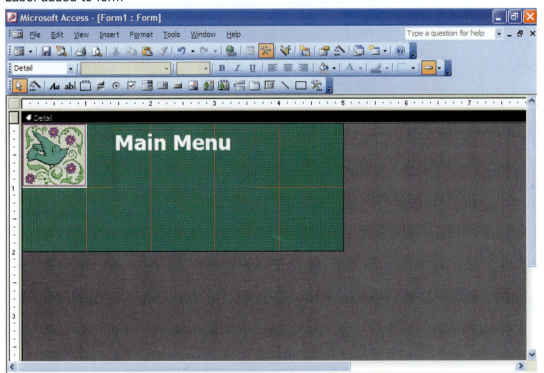

STEP-BY-STEP 14.5 Continued

9. Save the form as **Main Menu**.

10. You'll now create macro buttons in the switchboard form. Display the **Database** window and the **Switchboard** Design window side-by-side.

11. Click **Macros** in the *Objects* bar. Drag the **Enter January Orders, Enter February Orders, Enter March Orders**, and the **Exit Access** macros into the **Main Menu** form centered and below the title as shown in Figure 14-8. (You may need to enlarge the *Detail* area.)

12. Save the form. Click the **View** button and select each of the macro buttons, except Exit Access. Remember to close the forms by choosing the **Close** macro button in each form.

13. Close the Main Menu form but remain in this database for the next Step-by-Step.

> ### Hot Tip
>
> To display the full name of a macro in the macro button, place your mouse pointer over the right-middle selection handle until it turns into a double-headed arrow. Then double-click.

> ### Hot Tip
>
> You can size, align, or create equal vertical spacing for the macro buttons. First, select all the macro buttons. Second, use the Size, Align, and Vertical Spacing options from the Format menu.

FIGURE 14-8
Form with macro buttons

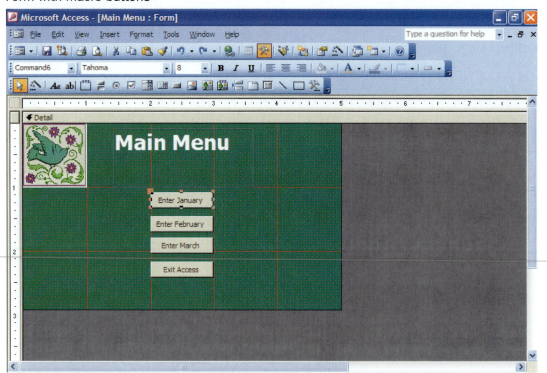

Creating an Autoexec Macro

An autoexec macro runs as soon as a database file opens. Autoexec macros typically open a switchboard form. To create such a macro, save a macro with *autoexec* as the filename.

Hot Tip

Each database file may have only one autoexec macro.

STEP-BY-STEP 14.6

1. In the *Objects* bar, click **Macros** if necessary, and then click **New**.

2. Click in the first *Action* cell and select **OpenForm**.

3. In the *Action Arguments* section, select **Main Menu** from the **Form Name** drop-down list.

4. Click in the second *Action* cell, click the down arrow, and choose **Maximize**.

5. Save the macro as **autoexec**.

6. Close the macro and then close the database file.

7. Open the database file. The Switchboard form should open automatically.

8. Click the **Exit Access** button and click **Yes**, if necessary, to exit Access.

Integration Tip

You can copy the results of an Access query into a Microsoft PowerPoint chart datasheet to create a chart. When copying the results into the datasheet, simply click in one cell of the datasheet and click Paste.

Time Saver

You can quickly view the properties of a macro, such as the date created and the date the macro may have been modified.

STEP-BY-STEP 14.7

1. Open the **Time Savers** database from the data files.

2. Select **Macros** in the *Object* bar and click the **New** button.

3. Click the **Action** arrow in the first Action box and select **Close**.

4. Save the macro as **Close**.

5. Close the Macro Design screen.

6. Right-click on the **Close** macro and select **Properties**. View the properties.

7. Press **Ctrl + F4** twice to close the query and then to close the database.

SUMMARY

In this lesson, you learned:

- A macro lets you automate frequently performed tasks. To create a macro, select the actions you want the macro to perform and then save the macro.

- You can modify the actions in a macro by opening it in the Design window.

- You can display macros as buttons in forms by dragging them from the Database window into the Form Design window.

- A switchboard serves as the command center for a database and resembles a main menu from which you make selections.

- An autoexec macro starts as soon as a database opens and can be used to display the switchboard.

VOCABULARY *Review*

Define the following terms:

Macro   Switchboard

REVIEW *Questions*

TRUE/FALSE

Circle T if the statement is true or F if the statement is false.

T   F   **1.** You create macro buttons by cutting and pasting the macro into a form.

T   F   **2.** You would use an OpenForm macro to open a switchboard automatically when the database opens.

T   F   **3.** You may run a macro directly from the Database window.

T   F   **4.** Macros are commonly created to perform frequent tasks.

T   F   **5.** A database file may have only one *autoexec* macro.

WRITTEN QUESTIONS

Write a brief answer to the following questions.

1. What is the purpose of a macro?

2. Why is it good practice to enter comments for an action in the Macro Design window?

3. List the steps for creating a macro.

4. Discuss the purpose of a switchboard.

5. After a macro is created and saved, can changes be made to the macro? Explain.

PROJECTS

PROJECT 14-1

1. Open the AA **Project14-1** database from the data files.
2. View the **Dairy and Grains** form and the **Discontinued Items** forms to familiarize yourself with them.
3. Create a macro that opens each form in Form view and maximizes the form window.
4. Save the macros as **Open Dairy and Grain Form and Maximize** and **Open Discontinued Items Form and Maximize**.
5. Run the macros.
6. Close the forms and close the database.

PROJECT 14-2

1. Open the **AA Project14-2** database from the data files.

2. Create a macro that closes the object in which it is placed. (*Hint*: Do not select an Object Type or Object Name.)

3. Create another new macro that goes to a new record. Save the macro as **New Record**.

4. Display both of these macros as buttons in the **Dairy and Grains** form and the **Discontinued Items** form.

5. Create a macro to exit the Access program. Save it as **Exit Access**.

6. Create a switchboard that contains macro buttons for the Open Dairy and Grains Form, Open Discontinued Items Form, and Exit Access. Save the form as **Switchboard**.

7. Make any modifications you feel are necessary to the Switchboard form's design.

8. Create an autoexec macro that displays the Switchboard form and maximizes it when the database is opened.

9. Close the database.

CRITICAL *Thinking*

 ## ACTIVITY 14-1

You've been designated as the expert to create a database switchboard for your company, One Star Gas Company. You want to learn more about macros, and in particular, a macro that saves an object. Use the Access Help feature to briefly describe how to create a macro that saves a database object.

ACTIVITY 14-2

Using the Access Help facility, write a brief explanation on when you would use a macro.

WORKING WITH WEB FEATURES

Introducing Data Access Pages, PivotTables, and PivotCharts

Data access pages are Web pages that are linked to a database. These pages let you report and analyze database information online or through e-mail. In addition, multiple users can view and enter data into the database online via data access pages.

A *PivotTable* is an interactive table that lets you summarize and calculate data. It is an interactive table because you can rotate the column and row headings to display data in various views.

PivotCharts are similar to PivotTables except the data displays visually in a chart. Using a visual representation of the data, with the ability to rearrange the data, presents a uniquely powerful method for viewing database information.

Creating Data Access Pages

A *data access page*, or page, makes it easy to distribute, view, enter, and edit Access database information through an Internet browser. Data access pages are Web pages that have a link to a database. These pages display live data and allow for interactive changes to the way data is viewed. Additions, deletions, or changes made to the data using a data access page are made in the database as well. However, changes made to the data access page itself only affect the current view of the page. An example of a data access page displayed in an Internet browser is shown in Figure 15-1.

FIGURE 15-1
Data access page displayed in a browser

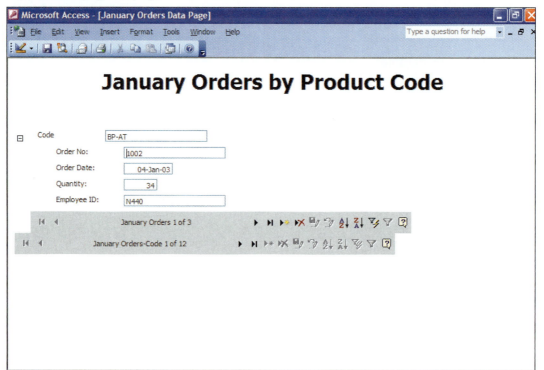

Pages display current data because they are connected to a database. For additional flexibility, you can use the sort and filter features to view specific records. You can also e-mail data access pages.

There are several methods for creating a data access page:

- *Page Wizard.* Takes you step-by-step through the process of creating a data access page.

- *Design View.* Displays the data access page layout screen in which you drag and drop fields into desired locations.

- *Save Forms as Pages.* After creating a form, PivotTable, or PivotChart you may select Save As from the File menu and choose Data Access Page from a list.

In the next two Step-by-Step exercises, you will first create a data access page using a Wizard, then, you will create a data access page in the Design View.

S TEP-BY-STEP 15.1

1. Open the **AA Step15-1** database from the data files.

2. Click **Pages** on the *Objects* bar and double-click **Create data access page by using wizard**. Then, select **Table: January Orders** in the *Tables/Queries* list box.

3. Double-click the **Order No.**, **Order Date**, **Code**, **Quantity**, and **Employee ID** fields to place them into the *Selected Fields* list. The first screen of the wizard should now display as shown in Figure 15-2.

Speech Recognition

If you have speech recognition capabilities, enable the Voice Command mode and say the appropriate series of commands to open the database file.

FIGURE 15-2
Step 1 - Page Wizard

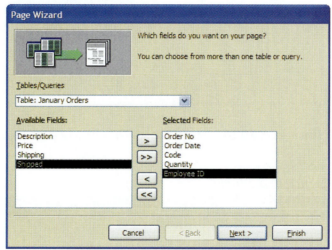

4. Click **Next**. Double-click on **Code** for a grouping level. Your screen should look similar to Figure 15-3.

FIGURE 15-3
Step 2 - Page Wizard

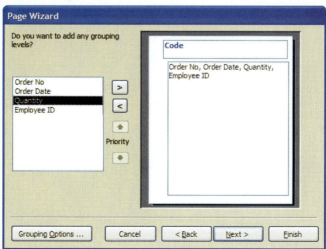

STEP-BY-STEP 15.1 Continued

5. Click **Next**. Click the down arrow of the first sort box and select **Order No.** Choose **Order Date** for the second sort box as shown in Figure 15-4. Select **Ascending** order for the sort order, if necessary.

FIGURE 15-4
Step 3 - Page Wizard

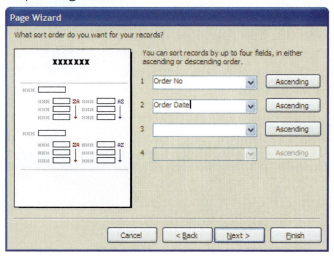

6. Click **Next**. Enter **January Orders Data Page** for the name of your page as displayed in Figure 15-5.

FIGURE 15-5
Step 4 - Page Wizard

STEP-BY-STEP 15.1 Continued

7. Click **Finish**. The data access page should appear on your screen in Design View. Click in the area that reads *Click here and type title text*. Enter **January Orders by Product Code** for the title text as shown in Figure 15-6.

FIGURE 15-6
Data access page in Design view

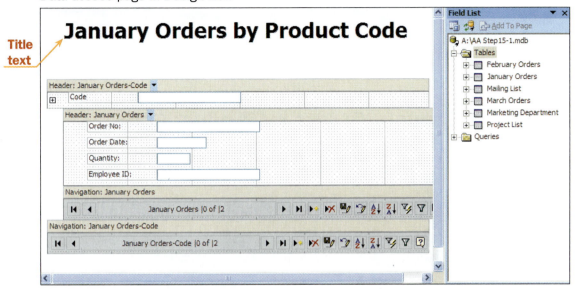

8. Click the **Save** button and save the data page as **January Orders Data Page** in the **Save As Data Access Page** dialog box. If Access displays a message indicating that the path specified when you saved is not a network path, click **OK**.

9. Select the **View** button to display the Data Access Page in Page View. Click the plus sign next to *Code* to display the remaining page fields. Your screen should appear similar to Figure 15-7.

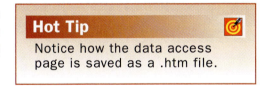
Hot Tip

Notice how the data access page is saved as a .htm file.

FIGURE 15-7
Data access page in Page view

January Orders by Product Code

Code	BP-AT	
Order No:	1002	
Order Date:	04-Jan-03	
Quantity:	34	
Employee ID:	N440	

STEP-BY-STEP 15.1 Continued

10. To see how the **January Orders Data Page** will appear on the Internet, select the **File** menu and then choose **Web Page Preview**. Click the plus sign next to *Code* to display the remaining page fields. Figure 15-8 shows the data access page in Web Page Preview.

FIGURE 15-8
Data access page in Web Page Preview

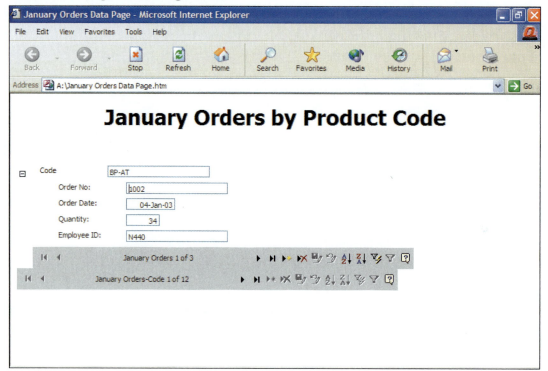

11. Close the browser and close the data page but remain in this database for the next Step-by-Step.

In Step-by-Step 15.1, you created a data access page using the design wizard. Next, you'll create a data access page in Design View.

STEP-BY-STEP 15.2

1. Click **Pages** on the *Objects* bar, if necessary, and then double-click **Create data access page in Design View**. Your screen should appear as shown in Figure 15-9. (*Note*: If the field list does not appear, click the **View** menu and select **Field List**.)

FIGURE 15-9
Data access page in Design View

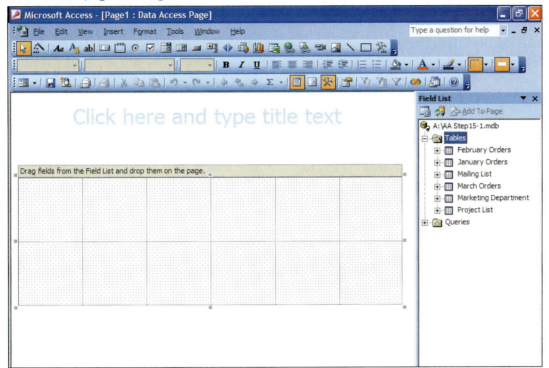

STEP-BY-STEP 15.2 Continued

2. Select the **Click here and type title text** area and enter **March Orders by Salesperson** for the title text. You'll now drag fields from the *Field List* into the Data Access Page layout. First, click the plus sign in front of *March Orders* in the *Field List*. Drag the March Orders fields as described in Table 15-1 into the Page layout. When you finish, the fields should be placed in the layout as displayed in Figure 15-10.

TABLE 15-1
Fields for placement in layout

MARCH ORDERS TABLE FIELD	LAYOUT PLACEMENT
Code	Grid area - at the 1" across by ½" down intersection.
Order Date	Below the *Code* field.
Quantity	Below the *Order Date* field.
Employee ID	Section above *March Orders* header. Note: A new section will appear as you drag the Employee ID field toward the *March Orders* header. This section displays "Create new section above March Orders" as shown in Figure 15-11.

FIGURE 15-10
Data Access Page in Web Page Preview

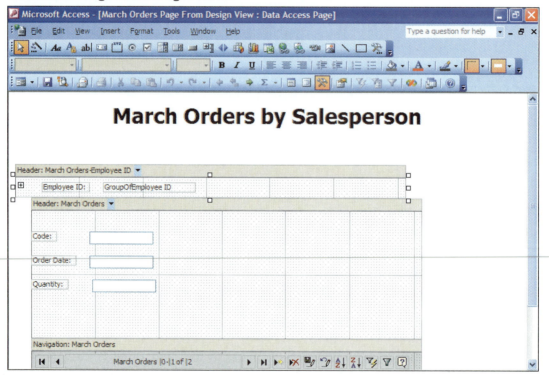

STEP-BY-STEP 15.2 Continued

FIGURE 15-11
New section in Data Access Page layout

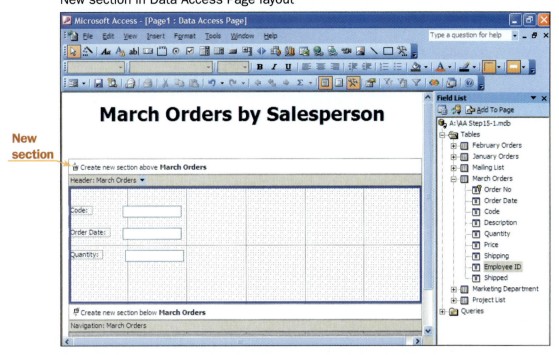

3. Click **Save** and save the data page as **March Orders Page from Design View**.

4. Click the **View** button to display the Data Access Page in viewing mode. Click the plus sign beside any salesperson to view their March sales.

5. Close the page and remain in this database for the next Step-by-Step.

Making Changes to Data Access Page Design

You can change a page's design as easily as you would modify the design of a form. Fields can be added or removed and controls sized, moved, and formatted just as with forms and reports. When you place the mouse pointer over a field in the Page Design view, your mouse pointer appears as a hand. You can then click to select the field and make any necessary changes.

S TEP-BY-STEP 15.3

1. Open the **March Orders Page from Design View** in Design View. If necessary, change *Files of Type* to **All Files**.

2. Select the labels for the field controls (left box) and change the font style to **Bold**. If necessary, increase the size of the *Order Date* label box so that the label completely displays.

STEP-BY-STEP 15.3 Continued

3. Left align the data in the **Order Date** and **Quantity** field controls (right box) by selecting each field and clicking the **Align Left** button.

4. View the changes in Page View by clicking the **View** button.

5. Save and close the page. Remain in this data base for the next Step-by-Step.

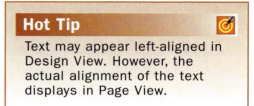

Hot Tip

Text may appear left-aligned in Design View. However, the actual alignment of the text displays in Page View.

Creating a PivotTable Form

A *PivotTable* form is a unique tool that lets you rearrange and summarize data in order to analyze it in a variety of ways. It is an interactive table because you can rotate the column, row, and page headings around to give various views of the data. An example of a PivotTable is shown in Figure 15-12. This feature is a quick method for swapping your rows and columns around.

FIGURE 15-12
PivotTable

		DB-DT	DP-DP	GR-CG	TT-AE	TT-BE	TT-TT	Grand Total
Months	Days/Total	OrderTotal	OrderTotal	OrderTotal	OrderTotal	OrderTotal	OrderTotal	OrderTotal
Jan	76.00	$1,116.50	$2,294.25	$750.00	$1,236.90	$988.90	$1,296.75	$542.30
	77.25		$1,895.25		$678.30	$542.30		$678.30
					$997.50	$797.50		$1,296.75
					$498.75			$1,595.00
								$988.90
								$1,236.90
								$1,116.50
								$1,276.00
								$1,596.00
								$2,294.25
								$542.30
								$678.30
								$750.00
								$1,435.50
								$988.90
	2	1	2	1	4	3	1	25
Grand Total	2	1	2	1	4	3	1	25

The PivotTable Wizard will take you step-by-step through the process of creating a PivotTable form. Or you may select the AutoForm:PivotTable feature that instantly takes you to the PivotTable layout screen. In the next Step-by-Step, you will create a PivotTable using the PivotTable Wizard.

STEP-BY-STEP 15.4

1. Select **Forms** on the *Objects* bar. Click the **New** button on the database window toolbar.

2. Click the down arrow for the table/query list box and choose **Qry-January Orders Totals** and then click **PivotTable Wizard**. Your screen should appear similar to Figure 15-13.

FIGURE 15-13
New Form dialog box

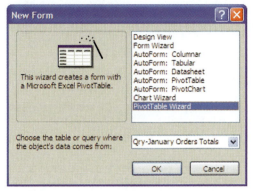

3. Click **OK**. The next dialog box explains the basics of a PivotTable as shown in Figure 15-14.

FIGURE 15-14
Step One - PivotTable wizard

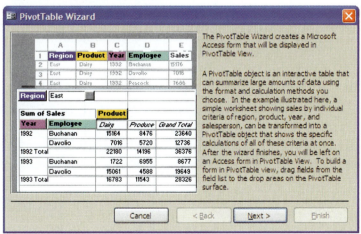

STEP-BY-STEP 15.4 Continued

4. Click **Next**. Double-click the **Order No.**, **Order Date**, **Code**, **Order Total**, and **Employee ID** fields to place them into the Fields Chosen for Pivoting list. The wizard dialog box should look like Figure 15-15.

FIGURE 15-15
Step Two - Form wizard

5. Click **Finish**. The PivotTable layout window appears as shown in Figure 15-16. (*Note:* The *Field List* may appear anywhere on your screen. However, you may move it, resize it, or close it.)

Hot Tip

To remove an unwanted field from a layout location, simply drag the field outside the layout window.

FIGURE 15-16
PivotTable Layout Page

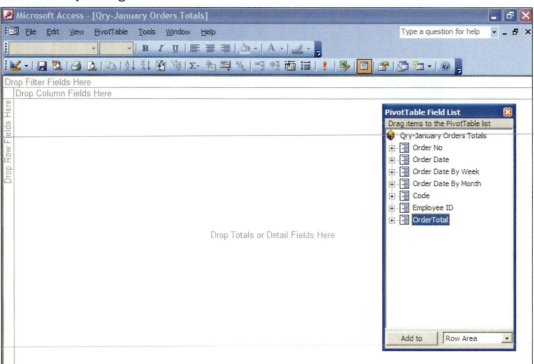

STEP-BY-STEP 15.4 Continued

6. You'll now drag fields from the PivotTable Field List into the PivotTable layout as described in Table 15-2. When you finish, the fields should be placed in the layout as displayed in Figure 15-17. (*Note*: Depending on your monitor size, more or less of the PivotTable will appear on screen.)

> **Hot Tip**
>
> You may also add fields to the PivotTable by selecting a field in the *Field List* box, clicking the down arrow and choosing a PivotTable area, and then clicking the **Add to** button.

TABLE 15-2
Fields for placement in PivotTable layout

JANUARY ORDERS TABLE FIELD	LAYOUT PLACEMENT
Employee ID	Drop Filter Fields Here
Code	Drop Column Fields Here
Order Date	Drop Row Fields Here
Order Total	Drop Totals or Details Fields Here

FIGURE 15-17
Completed PivotTable in Design view

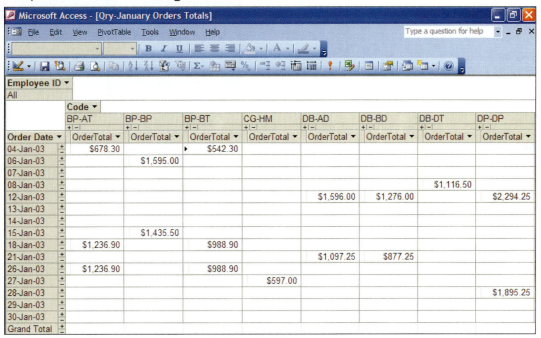

7. Click the plus sign next to the row *Grand Total* and view the sum of products sold for each day. Click the **Save** button and save the PivotTable as **January Orders PivotTable Form.**

8. Let's rearrange the data. Place your mouse pointer over the **Order Date** heading and start dragging this heading off the page. When you see a red X appear over the heading icon, release the mouse button. The heading is removed.

STEP-BY-STEP 15.4 Continued

9. Click the plus sign in front of *Order Date by Month* item in the PivotTable Field List to display the Order Date options. Drag **Months** to the *Drop Row Fields Here* area. Scroll the screen to view the results as shown in Figure 15-18.

FIGURE 15-18
Rearranged PivotTable in Design view

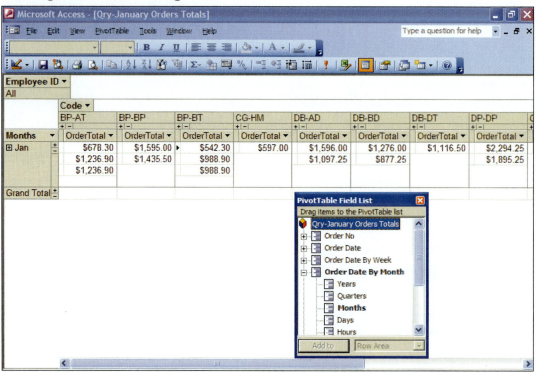

10. Click the plus sign next to the row *Grand Total* and view the sum of products sold.

STEP-BY-STEP 15.4 Continued

11. Place your mouse pointer over any grand total and *right* click. Select **AutoCalc** from the shortcut menu, and choose **Count**. Click the minus sign next to *January* to collapse the display of individual orders. Notice how the number of orders by product code are now displayed along with their totals by day. See Figure 15-19.

FIGURE 15-19
Calculated PivotTable in Design view

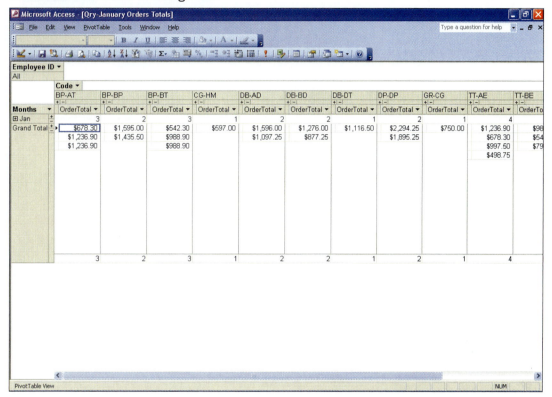

12. Save the PivotTable. Close the Design window and remain in this database for the next Step-by-Step.

Creating a PivotChart Form

PivotCharts allow users to view data in a graph. As with PivotTables, PivotCharts give you the ability to rearrange data in various ways in order to view and analyze the data. In a PivotChart, however, data is viewed in a visual format. Access makes creating PivotCharts a simple process. For example, the AutoForm:PivotChart form feature instantly takes you to the PivotChart layout page so that you may place fields where you want them. An example of a PivotChart is shown in Figure 15-20.

FIGURE 15-20
PivotChart

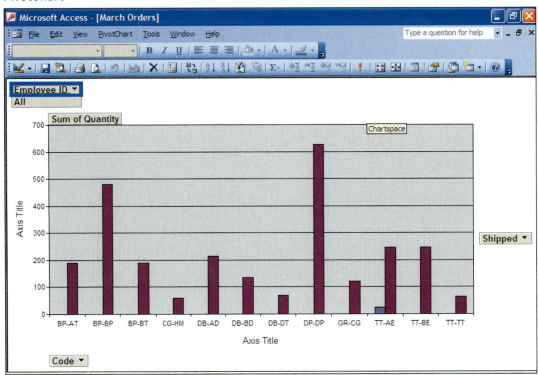

STEP-BY-STEP 15.5

1. Select **Forms** on the *Objects* bar, if necessary. Click the **New** button on the database window toolbar.

2. Click the down arrow for the table/query list box and choose **March Orders** and then click **AutoForm:PivotChart**.

Integration Tip

The easiest method to copy a PivotChart into another Microsoft Office document is to open the PivotChart and use the Print Screen button on your keyboard. You can then Paste the chart picture into another document.

STEP-BY-STEP 15.5 Continued

3. Click **OK**. The PivotChart layout window appears as shown in Figure 15-21. (*Note*: The *Field List* may appear anywhere on your screen. However, you can move the list to any location.)

FIGURE 15-21
PivotChart layout window

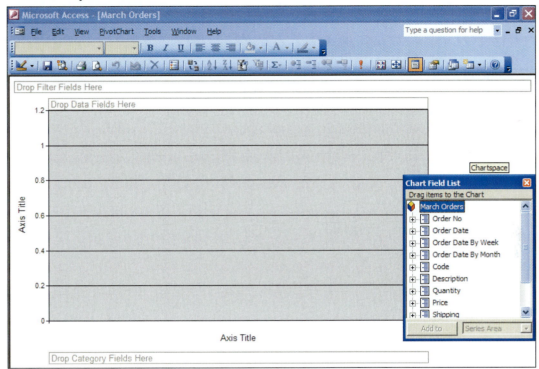

4. You'll now drag fields from the *Field List* into the PivotChart layout as described in Table 15-3.

TABLE 15-3
Fields for placement in PivotChart

MARCH ORDERS TABLE FIELD	LAYOUT PLACEMENT
Employee ID	Drop Filter Fields Here
Quantity	Drop Data Fields Here
Code	Drop Category Fields Here
Shipped	Drop Series Fields Here

5. Save the data page as **March Orders PivotChart**.

6. Click the **Employee ID** arrow and clear all arrows by clicking **All**. Then, display the quantity sold for a specific salesperson by clicking their Employee ID number. When you finish, select **All** from the *Employee ID* list to view all salesperson data.

STEP-BY-STEP 15.5 Continued

7. Practice rearranging the fields by dragging them to new locations. When you finish, arrange the fields as they are in Table 15-3.

8. Close the Design window and remain in this database for the next Step-by-Step.

Saving PivotTable and PivotChart Views to Data Access Pages

To make PivotTables and PivotCharts available for viewing on the Web, you will need to save their form views as data access pages. These data access pages may then be distributed and reviewed in an Internet browser or via e-mail. You may then analyze the data in a variety of ways.

STEP-BY-STEP 15.6

1. Select **Forms** on the *Objects* bar, if necessary. Click the **January Orders PivotTable Form** to select it (but do not open the form).

2. Select the **File** menu and choose **Save As**. Enter **January Orders PivotTable Form Data Page** in the *Save Form* text box and select **Data Access Page** for the *As* text box as shown in Figure 15-22.

FIGURE 15-22
Save As dialog box

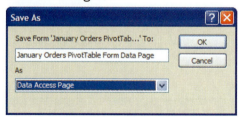

3. Click **OK**. The New Data Access Page dialog box appears.

4. The file name should already be filled in as **January Orders PivotTable Form Data Page.htm**. (*Note*: The file extension .htm may or may not appear on screen depending on your Access View settings.)

5. Click **OK**.

6. Save the **March Orders PivotChart** as a data access page named **March Orders PivotChart Data Page** and view the page.

7. Close the data access page windows if necessary, and close the database file.

Time Saver

Access lets you quickly display grouped records in data access pages by using the Spacebar.

STEP-BY-STEP 15.7

1. Open the **AA Step15-1** database from the data files.

2. Open the **March Orders Page from Design View** (which you created in SBS 15.3).

3. Press the **Tab** key three times until the record indicator for Record 3 is selected.

4. Press the **Spacebar** to quickly display the records for this employee ID.

5. Press **Ctrl + F4** twice to close the query and then to close the database.

SUMMARY

In this lesson, you learned:

■ Data access pages let you report and analyze database information online or through e-mail. You may also make changes to database data using pages.

■ You can dynamically view and anayze data in various ways by changing the layout of a PivotTable. This feature provides a quick method for switching columns and rows of data around.

■ PivotCharts are a visual representation of the data that give you the ability to rearrange the data.

■ PivotTable and PivotChart views may be saved as data access pages and viewed online through an Internet browser.

VOCABULARY *Review*

Define the following terms:

Data access page	PivotChart	PivotTable

REVIEW *Questions*

TRUE/FALSE

Circle T if the statement is true or F if the statement is false.

T   F   **1.** A data access page can be viewed online or through e-mail.

T   F   **2.** PivotTables graphically represent data.

T   F   **3.** Data bases can be pivoted just as you would do in a PivotTable.

T   F   **4.** Modifying the design and format of data access page is similar to modifying forms.

T   F   **5.** You cannot change fields to a PivotChart once it's been saved.

WRITTEN QUESTIONS

Write a brief answer to the following questions.

1. Explain the similarities and differences between a PivotTable and a PivotChart.

2. Briefly discuss how you would remove a field from PivotTable layout.

3. What is the purpose of a data access page?

4. Explain how you could view a data access page in an Internet browser.

5. Name the two methods for creating a PivotTable in the New Form dialog box.

PROJECTS

 PROJECT 15-1

1. Open the **AA Project15-1** database from the data files.

2. Create a data access page for **Qry-January Sales by Rep**.

3. Use all the query fields and group by **Employee ID**. Sort the records by **Order No.** and then by **Order Date**. Enter **January Sales by Rep** for the page title.

4. Save the data access page as **January Sales by Rep**.

5. Close the database.

PROJECT 15-2

1. Open the **AA Project15-2** database from the data files.

2. Create a PivotChart for **Qry-February Orders by Rep**. Use **Employee ID** for the *Filter* field, **Last Name** for the *Series* field, **Code** for the *Category* field, and **Quantity** for the *Data* field. Save the PivotChart as **February Orders by Rep PivotChart**.

3. Create a PivotTable for **Qry-February Orders by Rep**. Use **Employee ID** for the *Filter* field, **Last Name** for the *Row* field, **Order Date** for the *Column* field, and **Quantity** for the *Totals* or *Detail* field. Save the PivotTable as **February Orders by Rep Form**.

4. Save both the PivotTable and PivotChart views as data access pages. Save the PivotTable as **February Orders by Rep PivotTable**. Save the PivotChart as **February Orders by Rep PivotChart**.

5. Close the database.

CRITICAL *Thinking*

ACTIVITY 15-1

You are the Access expert at the Bright New Day Clothes Manufacturing Company. You decide to create data access pages for some of the company's inventory tables so that they can be viewed online. Learning more about data access pages would increase your productivity and efficiency when creating these pages as you would have a greater understanding of how they work. Use the Help feature in Access to find out how to work with data in page view Write a brief explanation of how you would add a new record in a data access page.

ACTIVITY 15-2

Discuss the procedure for adding fields to a PivotTable using the options in the Field List rather than by dragging the fields into the layout area. Use the Access Help system if necessary.

USING MANAGEMENT TOOLS

VOCABULARY

Compacting

Encode

Permissions

Introducing Management Tools

Access offers a variety of management tools to help you maintain and secure your database files. For example, you may compact a fragmented database so that it is stored more efficiently on disk. Since databases often contain sensitive information, such as employee salaries or addresses, you will learn about the various security features that can be applied to a database. And, finally, you will learn about splitting a database, which enables several users to create their own forms, reports, and other objects from one source of data.

Compacting and Repairing a Database

When you use a database over a period of time, it becomes fragmented. Fragmentation occurs when parts of the database file are scattered over an area of the disk where the file is stored. This separation may cause the database to run slower and less efficiently. *Compacting* a database removes wasted space within the database file and decreases the file size. A database should be compacted on a regular basis.

Hot Tip

Compacting is also a great method for making a copy of your database.

Also, serious problems may sometimes occur as you are working in a database file. The repair operation in the compact and repair feature will replace the original file with a compacted version that will often eliminate any problems.

The actual compacting of a database file takes place "behind the scenes." After selecting Compact and Repair Database, your database is compacted within just a few seconds.

STEP-BY-STEP 16.1

1. Open the **AA Step16-1** database from the data files.

2. Open the **Tools** menu and select **Database Utilities**.

3. Click **Compact and Repair Database**. The status bar at the bottom of your screen will quickly display the word Compacting. When the Ready status reappears, your database is compacted. (This will usually take only a few seconds.)

4. Close the database file.

Setting a Password

An easy method for securing a database file is to assign a password to the file. Only people who know the password will then be able to open the file.

Passwords can be changed on a regular basis or removed altogether. When entering a password, you will need to remember exactly how it is entered because passwords are case-sensitive. For example, if you entered Cat as your password, you will need to enter Cat for the password every time. You could not use cat, CAT, cAT, or any other uppercase or lowercase combination.

In the following Step-by-Step, you will first open the database file in an exclusive mode that prevents others from opening the database, and then you will create a password for it. You will also try opening the database using the password.

Speech Recognition

If you have speech recognition capabilities, say the appropriate steps to open the database file.

Hot Tip

To make a copy of a database, you need to leave the database file closed. Then, choose **Database Utilities** from the **Tools** menu and select **Compact and Repair Database**. In the Database To Compact From dialog box, select the database you want to copy and click **Compact**. In the Compact Database Into dialog box, enter a filename for the file copy.

Speech Recognition

If you have speech recognition capabilities, say the appropriate steps to close the database file.

STEP-BY-STEP 16.2

1. Open the **File** menu and choose **Open**. Select **AA Step16-2** database from the data files. Click the down arrow on the **Open** button and select **Open Exclusive** from the list box.

2. Open the **Tools** menu, select **Security**, and then click **Set Database Password**. The dialog box shown in Figure 16-1 will open.

STEP-BY-STEP 16.2 Continued

FIGURE 16-1
Password dialog box

3. In the Password box, key **CAT**.

4. In the Verify box, key **CAT** again.

5. Click **OK**. The password is now set. The next time you or anyone else tries to open the database, a password will be required before it will open. Let's test the password.

6. Close the database file.

7. Open the **AA Step16-2** database file. You should see a message box like that shown in Figure 16-2. Key the password and click **OK**. Close the database.

FIGURE 16-2
Password Required dialog box

8. Open the **AA Step16-2** database using the **Open Exclusive** feature. Key the password. To remove the database password, open the **Tools** menu, select **Security**, and then click **Unset Database Password**.

9. Key **CAT** in the Unset Database Password dialog box, and then click **OK**.

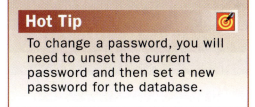

Hot Tip

To change a password, you will need to unset the current password and then set a new password for the database.

10. Close the database and then reopen it. You do not need to enter a password now. Close the database again.

Adding Permissions

*P*ermissions limit the parts of a database that can be viewed or changed by other users of the database. The database administrator assigns security levels for Users and Administrators. Users are allowed to enter, view, or edit data only as designated by the administrator. Each user receives specific access to tables, queries, forms, reports, and macros. Adminstrators, or Admins, typically have all rights to a database file.

When a database is secured with user-level security, each user will need to type an identification code and password after starting the Access program. The code and password provided by the user identify the specific areas of the database to which he or she has permission.

The database administrator establishes the user IDs and passwords. There are no set rules that all administrators must follow to establish ID numbers; however, such numbers are frequently based on employee ID numbers already chosen by the company. The password is typically a random number.

In the following Step-by-Step exercise, the User-Level Security Wizard will quickly take you through the process of securing your database. When your database is secured, you will access the secured database through an icon on your desktop created by Access.

STEP-BY-STEP 16.3

1. Open the **AA Step16-3** database from the data files.

2. Open the **Tools** menu, select **Security**, and choose **User-Level Security Wizard**. The first wizard dialog box appears on your screen as shown in Figure 16-3. (*Note*: If you are asked to install this wizard, click Yes and follow the steps given.)

FIGURE 16-3
Step 1 - Security Wizard dialog box

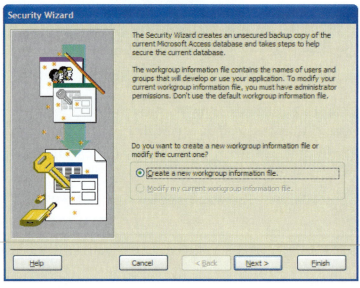

3. Select **Create a new workgroup information file**, if necessary, and then click **Next**.

4. Key **5551212** in the WID (Workgroup ID) text box and remove any name in the Your name (optional) text box. Select **I want to create a shortcut to open my Security-enhanced database** if necessary. The dialog box should display as in Figure 16-4.

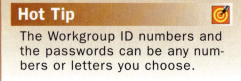

Hot Tip

The Workgroup ID numbers and the passwords can be any numbers or letters you choose.

STEP-BY-STEP 16.3 Continued

FIGURE 16-4
Step 2 - Security Wizard dialog box

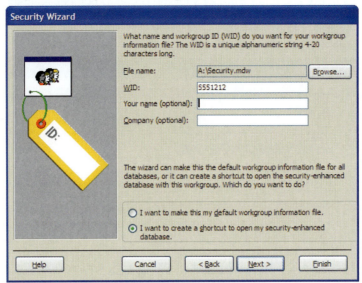

5. Click **Next** and view the wizard dialog box as seen in Figure 16-5. In this dialog box, you select the database objects for security. In this exercise, you will leave all objects selected so that security can be applied to each object.

FIGURE 16-5
Step 3 - Security Wizard dialog box

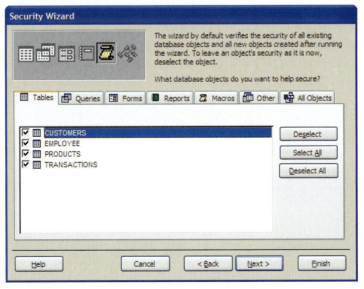

STEP-BY-STEP 16.3 Continued

6. Click **Next**. This dialog box asks you to choose the user groups to which security will be applied. Select **Full Data Users** and enter **5551213** for the *Group ID* number, as displayed in Figure 16-6.

FIGURE 16-6
Step 4 - Security Wizard dialog box

7. Click **Next**. Select the **Yes, I would like to grant some permissions to the Users group** option.

8. You will now choose which permissions you will allow for the User group. On the Database tab, select **Open/Run**.

9. Click the **Tables** tab and select **Update Data**, **Insert Data**, and **Delete Data**. As you select permissions in the Table tab, the Read Design and Read Data permissions will automatically select. These permissions are also necessary for the three permissions you chose. Your screen should appear similar to Figure 16-7.

STEP-BY-STEP 16.3 Continued

FIGURE 16-7
Step 5 - Security Wizard dialog box

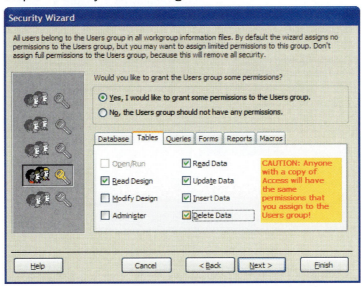

10. Click **Next**. You will now add users to the workgroup. Enter **Student01** in the *User name* text box and **std01** in the *Password* text box as shown in Figure 16-8. Click the **Add This User to the List** button. You should now see this user in the box on the left.

FIGURE 16-8
Step 6 - Security Wizard dialog box

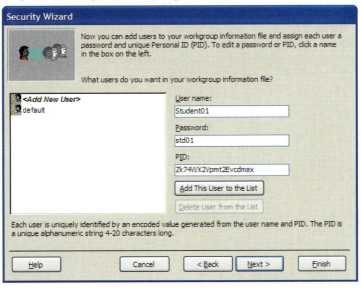

11. Enter **Student02** in the *User name* text box and **std02** in the *Password* text box. Click the **Add This User to the List** button.

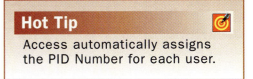

Hot Tip

Access automatically assigns the PID Number for each user.

STEP-BY-STEP 16.3 Continued

12. Enter **Student03** in the *User name* text box and **std03** in the *Password* text box. Click the **Add This User to the List** button. Your dialog box should display as in Figure 16-9.

FIGURE 16-9
Step 6 - Security Wizard dialog box

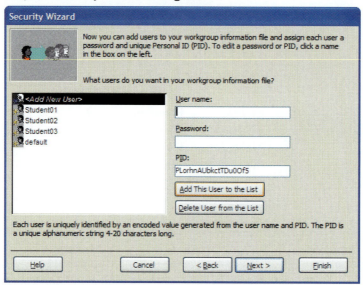

13. Click **Next**. In this dialog box, you will assign Users to Groups. Click the down arrow for *Group or user name* and select **Student01** and choose **Admins** for the group as shown in Figure 16-10. This step will give Student01 full administrative rights to the database.

FIGURE 16-10
Step 7 - Security Wizard dialog box

14. Click the down arrow for *Group or user name* and select **Student02** and choose **Full Data Users** for the group. This step allows Student02 to open the database and update, insert, and delete data.

STEP-BY-STEP 16.3 Continued

15. Click the down arrow for *Group or user name* and select **Student03** and choose **Full Data Users** for the group. Your screen will appear as shown in Figure 16-11.

FIGURE 16-11
Step 7 - Security Wizard dialog box with changes

16. Click **Next**. You'll now choose a database filename for the backup copy of this database. Access creates a backup as a protection in case the permissions are not set correctly. Click **Browse**, select the desired folder, and enter **AA Step16-3 Copy** for the backup filename as displayed in Figure 16-12. Click **Select**.

FIGURE 16-12
Choose a database name dialog box

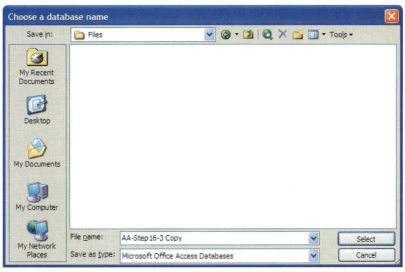

STEP-BY-STEP 16.3 Continued

17. Click **Finish**. The One-step Security Wizard Report should display on your screen as shown in Figure 16-13. Print this document for future reference.

FIGURE 16-13
One-step Security Wizard Report

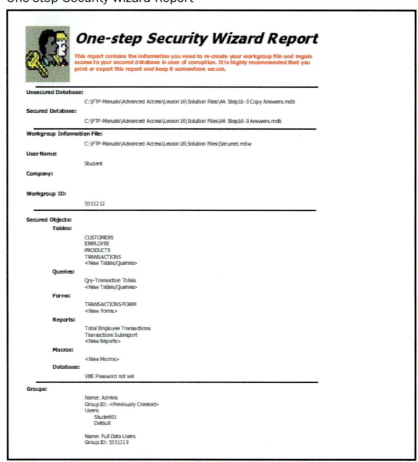

18. Close the Security Wizard window. Access now asks if you want to save this file. Click **Yes**. This report is now saved with the database filename with a .snp file extension. Close the Snapshot Viewer window.

19. A message box will now appear on your screen as shown in Figure 16-14 indicating that the database is now encrypted with the specified permissions. Click **OK**.

FIGURE 16-14
Security Wizard message box

STEP-BY-STEP 16.3 Continued

20. If necessary, close the database file. You will now check the permissions you've created. Go to your desktop and locate the **AA Step16-3** icon for the secured file and double-click it.

21. A logon message box appears as in Figure 16-15. Enter **Student02** for the *Name* and **std02** for the *Password*. Click **OK**.

FIGURE 16-15
Logon dialog box

22. Open the **CUSTOMERS** table. Notice that you can view the table data. Now, click the **View** button to look at the Table's design. A message box will appear, as shown in Figure 16-16, indicating that you do not have permission to modify the table's design. Click **No**. If desired, you can close the database file and reopen it as Student01 and Student03 and test your permissions as these users.

FIGURE 16-16
Microsoft Access message box

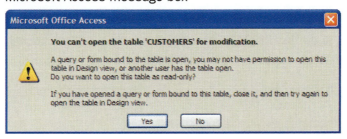

23. Close the database file.

Setting Startup Options

As you've worked through this course, you've become familiar with certain screens each time you start Access and open a database file. For example, you typically see the menu bar and the database window after opening a database file. You can, however, manage what is viewed on-screen when starting Access by setting startup options. For example, you could set a switchboard form to automatically appear when the database opens. These actions allow users to instantly start working in the database by selecting options from the switchboard.

> **Hot Tip**
>
> Recall from Lesson 14 that a switchboard is a form containing buttons from which you can open forms to enter, edit, and view data, print reports, and exit Access. A switchboard is created by persons who know Access very well for users who are not as familiar with Access.

To display the Startup dialog box, you'll select Startup from the Tools menu. The Startup dialog box opens, as shown in Figure 16-17. Notice that you can select the application, menus, toolbars, window, form, and page that will display on-screen when the user opens the file.

FIGURE 16-17
Startup dialog box

STEP-BY-STEP 16.4

1. Open the **AA Step16-4** database from the data files.

2. Open the **Tools** menu and select **Startup**.

3. Click the down arrow for **Display Form/Page** and choose **Switchboard**. This step will set the Switchboard form to open each time the database opens.

4. Deselect **Display Database Window** so that the database window will not display on the screen.

5. Click **OK**. Close the database file. Then re-open it.

6. Notice how the switchboard appears as this database file opens. Close the database file.

Splitting a Database

The Database Splitter divides a database file into two files, a back-end and front-end file. The back-end file contains tables and the front-end file contains queries, forms, reports, data access pages, macros, and modules. By splitting the database into two files, users can access the table data and create their own queries, forms, reports, and macros. This feature is especially helpful in a multi-user environment because it allows for continuous front-end database development without affecting data or interrupting users.

In addition, this feature allows for a single source of data on a network. To separate a database into two files, you will use the Database Splitter Wizard. The wizard moves tables from your current database to a new back-end database.

S TEP-BY-STEP 16.5

1. Open the **AA Step16-5** database from the data files. View each object tab. Notice the forms that are already created.

2. Open the **Tools** menu, select **Database Utilities**, and then choose **Database Splitter**. The first Database Splitter dialog box appears as shown in Figure 16-18.

FIGURE 16-18
Database Splitter dialog box

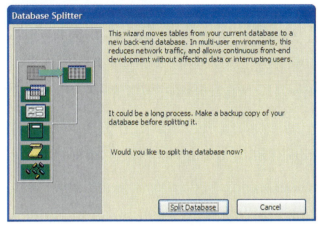

3. Click the **Split Database** button. Access will display a dialog box indicating the filename for the back-end database that will contain only table data. (By default, the name of the file will be the original name followed by "_be".) Select the folder for the student files and click **Split**.

4. You should receive a message indicating that the database split successfully as shown in Figure 16-19. Click **OK**.

FIGURE 16-19
Database Splitter message box

5. Close the database file.

6. Open the backend database file, **AA Step16-5_be**, and view each object tab. Notice that the only objects in this database are the tables. In this database file, other users can create their own forms, reports, and so on.

7. Close the database file.

Encoding a Database

Encoding is a simple method for databses securtiy by preventing the database file from being read in a word processor. This feature provides security if you transmit the file electronically or store the file on a disk. When you encode a database, you must be the owner of the database.

S TEP-BY-STEP 16.6

1. Open the **File** menu, choose **New**, and select **Blank Database**. Enter **AA Step16-6** for the filename and click **Create**.

2. Click the **Tables** tab if necessary and double-click **Create table in Design view**.

3. Enter the following information.

Field Name	Type	Primary Key
ID	Text	Yes
Last Name	Text	
First Name	Text	

4. Save the table as **Addresses**.

5. Click **View** and enter the following records.

ID	Last Name	First Name
001	Smith	William
002	Jones	Ti

6. You will now encode the database. Close the database file. Open the **Tools** menu, select **Security**, and choose **Encode/Decode Database.** The Encode/Decode Database dialog box appears as in Figure 16-20.

STEP-BY-STEP 16.6 Continued

FIGURE 16-20
Encode/Decode Database dialog box

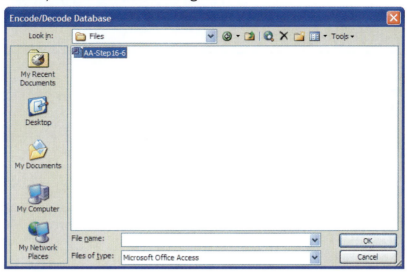

7. Select **AA Step16-6** from the file list in the Encode/Decode Database dialog box and click **OK**.

8. Enter **AA Step16-6 Encode** for the filename in the Encode/Decode Database dialog box and click **Save**. The database file is now encoded and may be sent electronically.

9. To decode the database, click **Tools**, select **Security**, and then select **Encode/Decode Database**.

10. Select **AA Step16-6 Encode** from the file list in the Encode/Decode Database dialog box, and then click **OK**.

11. Select **AA Step16-6 Encode** again in the Decode Database As dialog box. Click **Yes** when asked if you want to replace the existing database.

Time Saver

Microsoft Office lets you view the latest news about Access online.

STEP-BY-STEP 16.7

1. Press **F1** to display Access Help.

2. Select **Get the latest news about using Access**.

3. View the topics you see of interest.

4. Close the browser.

5. Close the Access Help pane.

SUMMARY

In this lesson, you learned:

■ Compacting a database compresses the database and removes any wasted space within the file.

■ A database can be secured by setting a password for the file. Passwords are case-sensitive.

■ User and Admin security can be applied to a database enabling you to set permissions for users.

■ You can control the way your screen looks when you start Access by modifying the startup options.

■ A database can be split into two files. One file contains table data only and allows users to create their own forms, reports, and so on.

■ Encoding scrambles database information so that it is unusable; decoding unscrambles the encryption.

VOCABULARY *Review*

Define the following terms:		
Compacting	Encode	Permissions

REVIEW *Questions*

TRUE/FALSE

Circle T if the statement is true or F if the statement is false.

T F **1.** You would choose the User-Level Security Wizard if you wanted to apply a password to a database file.

T F **2.** A form can be selected to open when Access starts in the Startup dialog box.

T F **3.** In order to encode a database file, you must be the owner of the file.

T F **4.** When going through the User-Level Security Wizard, Access asks you to create a backup copy of the database file in case the user permissions do not work as you thought.

T F **5.** Compacting a database file removes excess space from the file.

FILL IN THE BLANK

Complete the following sentences by writing the correct word or words in the blanks provided.

1. To create two files from one database file, one file having forms, reports, pages, and macros, you would use the _____ _____ feature.

2. Encoding a database _____ the code.

3. When adding User-level security, you need to assign _____ to their respective workgroups.

4. To display a form when Access opens, you would select this form in the _____ dialog box.

5. A(n) _____ can be set for a database file and is case-sensitive.

PROJECTS

PROJECT 16-1

1. Open the **AA Project16-1** database from the data files.

2. Assign a password of **DOG** to the file.

3. Close the file and reopen it to test the password.

4. Close the database file.

PROJECT 16-2

1. Open the **AA Project16-2** database from the data files.

2. Change the startup options so that the Switchboard form opens when Access opens. Also, do not allow the database window or the Full Menu options to appear at startup.

3. Close the file and reopen it to test the startup features.

4. Close the database file.

CRITICAL *Thinking*

 ACTIVITY 16-1

As the new systems manager for a small business, you want information about encoding (or encrypting) a database. Use Access Help to locate information on encoding/encryption and decoding/decryption. Write a brief explanation of decoding and explain who can encode a database file.

ACTIVITY 16-2

Use the Access Help system to find out whether passwords are stored encoded or unencoded.

UTILIZING ADVANCED MANAGEMENT TOOLS

OBJECTIVES

Upon completion of this lesson, you should be able to:

- Use the Linked Table Manager.

- Replicate a database.

- Create Access modules using Visual Basic routines.

Estimated Time: 1 hour

VOCABULARY

Decision structure

Procedures

Replication

Syntax

Introducing Advanced Management Tools

Advanced management tools afford greater flexibility and efficiency for maintaining and protecting database file information. The Linked Table Manager assists with linking Access tables between databases. This feature allows data to be entered into a table and its linked table at the same time.

Replication creates copies of a database so that the copies can exchange updates of data or objects. By replicating a file, many users can work in their own replicated copies at the same time.

In addition, Visual Basic is used to write procedures that create, delete, or modify data and objects. Visual Basic is an important tool for situations in which you are unable to create a desired procedure in a macro. And, as a final safety feature, you may save a file in the MDE format to prevent users from viewing or editing Visual Basic code within a database.

Using the Linked Table Manager

By linking tables, you increase efficiency by entering data into one table and having the same data appear in linked tables as well. To create linked tables, first you need to import the table from another database using the Link Tables option. If a linked table is moved to another drive or folder, you will need to use the Linked Table Manager to re-link tables between Access databases.

It is not necessary for both tables to use the same table name as Access will still recognize the link between these tables. Also, if you link tables between Access databases, the linked tables will use the same property settings. For example, if a table has validation rules in the original database, data entered into the linked table must follow these same rules.

STEP-BY-STEP 17.1

1. Open the **AA Step17-1** database from the data files.

2. Open the **File** menu, choose **Get External Data**, and then select **Link Tables**.

3. Select the **AA Step17-1a** database from the data files and click **Link**. The Link Tables dialog box appears similar to Figure 17-1. *Note:* Depending on your installation selections, you may have additional items appear in the Link Tables dialog box.

FIGURE 17-1
Link Tables dialog box

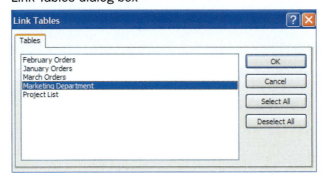

4. Choose the **Marketing Department** table and click **OK**. Notice that an arrow is placed in front of the table icon indicating that the table is linked.

5. Open the **Marketing Department** table and enter the following record.

Field Name	Record Data
Employee ID	S900
Last Name	Ingles
First Name	Joanne
Title	Marketing Manager
Extension	100
Date Hired	6/30/03
Salary	273,500

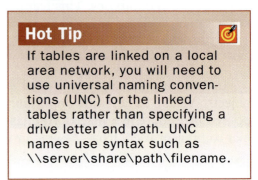

Hot Tip

If tables are linked on a local area network, you will need to use universal naming conventions (UNC) for the linked tables rather than specifying a drive letter and path. UNC names use syntax such as \\server\share\path\filename.

6. Close the **Marketing Department** table and then close the **AA Step17-1** database.

7. Open the **AA Step17-1a** database from the data files.

8. Open the **Marketing Department** table. You will see the record you entered in the AA Step17-1 database.

9. Close the **Marketing Department** table and close the **AA Step17-1a** database.

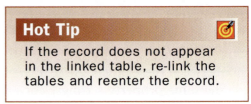

Hot Tip

If the record does not appear in the linked table, re-link the tables and reenter the record.

10. You will now use the Linked Table Manager to re-link these tables. Open the **AA Step17-1** database from the data files.

STEP-BY-STEP 17.1 Continued

11. Open the **Tools** menu, choose **Database Utilities**, and then select **Linked Table Manager**.

12. The Linked Table Manager displays. Select the **Marketing Department** table by placing a check mark in the box in front of it and then click the **Always prompt for new location** check box. *Note:* The file location in parentheses will vary depending on the location of the file.

13. Click **OK**. In the Select New Location of Marketing Department dialog box, select **AA Step17-1a**, and then click **Open**. You should see a message box indicating that all linked tables were successfully refreshed.

14. Click **OK** and then choose **Close**.

15. Close the database file.

> **Hot Tip**
>
> The Linked Table Manager is often used to refresh links or to reestablish links between tables if the link is broken by one of the databases moving to a new location. The Linked Table Manager only works if tables have already been linked.

Replicating a Database

Replication is the process of creating copies of a database so that the copies can exchange updates of data or objects. This exchange of information between replicated databases is called synchronization.

During the replication procedure, Access creates a backup of the original database file for added protection. The original database is then referred to as the Design Master. Changes to the database design may only be made in the Design Master, not in the replicas. However, any data updates in the replicas will appear in the Design Master after synchronization.

In the following Step-by-Step, you will create a replica of a database file and add a new record to a table in the replica. Then you will synchronize these databases and see the new record appear in the Design Master.

STEP-BY-STEP 17.2

1. Open the **AA Step17-2** database from the data files.

2. Open the **Tools** menu, choose **Replication**, and select **Create Replica**.

> **Speech Recognition**
>
> If you have speech recognition capabilities, enable the Voice Command mode and say the appropriate series of steps to open the database file.

STEP-BY-STEP 17.2 Continued

3. A message box appears as shown in Figure 17-2. Choose **Yes**. Access will now close the database file and start the replication process.

FIGURE 17-2
Microsoft Access message box

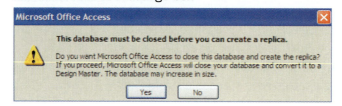

4. After a minute or so, a message box displays as shown in Figure 17-3 indicating the importance of creating a backup file before replicating the database. Click **Yes** to have Access create a backup file.

FIGURE 17-3
Microsoft Access message box

5. In the Location of New Replica dialog box, enter **Replica of AA Step17-2** for the filename if necessary. Click **OK**.

6. A message box appears similar to Figure 17-4 stating that the replica is successfully created and changes to the database design may be made only in the Design Master (original database). Click **OK**. The Design Master of AA Step17-2 opens automatically. Notice the replica icon that now appears in front of the database objects.

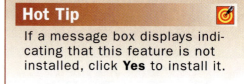

Hot Tip

If a message box displays indicating that this feature is not installed, click **Yes** to install it.

FIGURE 17-4
Message box

STEP-BY-STEP 17.2 Continued

7. Close the **AA Step17-2 Design Master** and open **Replica of AA Step17-2**.

8. Add the following record to the **Employee** table.

Field Name	Record Data
Employee ID	8
Last Name	Savage
First Name	Debi
Telephone Number	608-555-1213
Region	South

Notice how the word (Replicated) displays next to *Table*. Click the *Employee ID* field name at the top of the column and then click the **Sort Ascending** button on the Standard toolbar. After entering the record and sorting the table by the Employee ID field, your screen should appear similar to Figure 17-5.

FIGURE 17-5
Replicated Table with new record

9. Click the **View** button to go into Design View. Notice that a message box indicates that you may not make changes to the table's design, but you may view the design in a read-only mode. Click **No**.

10. Close the table and then close the database.

11. Open the **AA Step17-2** database (Design Master) and open the **Employee** table. Notice that the new record added in the replica does not appear yet. Close the table.

STEP-BY-STEP 17.2 Continued

12. Open the **Tools** menu, choose **Replication**, and then select **Synchronize Now**. The Synchronize Database dialog box displays as shown in Figure 17-6.

FIGURE 17-6
Synchronize Database dialog box

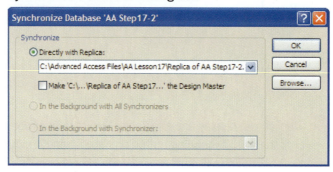

13. In the Synchronize Database dialog box, select **Directly with Replica**, if necessary, and then click the **Browse** button to select the replica file location and the replicated file.

14. Click **OK**. You will be instructed that the database will need to be closed for synchronization, choose **Yes**.

15. A message box displays as shown in Figure 17-7 indicating that the synchronization is successful. Click **OK**.

FIGURE 17-7
Microsoft Access message box

16. In the AA Step17-2 Design Master open the **Employee** table, if necessary. Notice that the new record is now added to the Employee table. Close the table and close the database.

Creating Visual Basic Modules

Visual Basic (VB) is a user-friendly, powerful language that can help you create *procedures*. Procedures perform actions. You may use VB to write procedures that create, delete, calculate, or modify data and objects.

Procedures are entered in a specific *syntax* format. Syntax refers to how language, such as a procedure, is put together. A procedure name typically contains eight characters and is created by the person entering the module. The procedure name may be any random name or letters that the creator chooses. The syntax of a function procedure is as follows:

Function ProcedureName (argument1, argument2, etc.)

 Statement 1

Statement 2

End Function

As you enter a function in the module, Access adds color coding to your text to assist you as you type. For example, comments display in green and function words, such as If, Then, and Else, display in blue. In addition, End Function is automatically added after you enter the function name and press Enter. Each part of the function procedure is described in Table 17-1.

TABLE 17-1
Parts of a function procedure

FUNCTION PART	DESCRIPTION
Function	This word begins each function procedure.
ProcedureName	The name you give a procedure.
Arguments	One or more variables that will be used in the calculation or determination of the function results. Notice that arguments are located inside parentheses.
Statements	The actual commands that you write.
End Function	These words end each function procedure.

The following example displays the parts of an actual function procedure.

```
Function PurchPrc (Price as Single)
   Discount = Price * 0.15
   Price = Price - Discount
End Function
```

The parts of the function procedure example are described in Table 17-2.

TABLE 17-2
Parts of a function procedure example

FUNCTION PART	DESCRIPTION
Function	Begins the funtion procedure.
ProcedureName	PurchPrc.
Arguments	Price as Single. This argument indicates that the price to be entered in the calculation is a single integer.
Statements	Discount = Price * 0.15. Price = Price - Discount. These statements discount a price by 15% and then subtract the 15% discount from the actual price to calculate the discounted price.
End Function	Ends the procedure function.

A group of statements that contain alternate actions is referred to as a ***decision structure***. A decision structure evaluates alternatives and decides which action needs to be carried out. For example, an If-Then-Else statement is one type of decision structure. Access first looks at the If statement. If the condition in the If statement is true, the action in the Then statement will be carried out. If the condition in the If statement is false, the action in the Else statement is carried out.

An example of an If-Then-Else decision structure is shown next.

```
If Price>500 Then
Discount = Price * 0.15
Price = Price - Discount
Else
Discount = Price * 0.05
Price = Price - Discount
End If
```

In this procedure, if the price entered is greater than 500, then a discount of 15% will be given to the customer and the discounted price will be calculated for you as price minus discount. If the price is not greater than 500, then only a discount of 5% is applied and the discounted price is calculated.

Additional terms and comments may be added to a procedure. For example, the following term identifies that the amount to be entered in the PurchPrc function refers to Price in statements.

```
PurchPrc=Price
```

Comments are indicated by an apostrophe (') at the beginning of the text. Comments are simply notes that assist you and others in understanding the procedure. Some examples of comments are displayed next.

```
'Accepts an integer value called Price
'Returns a new price reflecting the
 discount
```

Hot Tip

When entering a VB statement, do not use the lowercase L (l) key for the number 1. Always use number keys for numbers. Indenting a line may assist you when entering or reviewing a line, but it is optional.

A complete procedure statement is shown below.

```
Function PurchPrc(Price as Single)
'Accepts an integer value called Price
'Returns a new price reflecting the discount
If Price>500 Then
Discount = Price * 0.15
Price = Price - Discount
Else
Discount = Price * 0.05
Price = Price - Discount
End If
PurchPrc = Price
End Function
```

STEP-BY-STEP 17.3

1. Open the **AA Step17-3** database from the data files.

2. Click **Modules** in the *Objects* bar and then click the **New** button.

3. Enter the following code:

```
Function PurchPrc(Price As Single)
'Accepts an integer value called Price
'Returns a new price reflecting the discount
If Price>500 Then
Discount = Price * 0.15
Price = Price - Discount
Else
Discount = Price * 0.05
Price = Price - Discount
End If
PurchPrc = Price
End Function
```

4. Your screen should now look like Figure 17-8. Click the **Save** button, save the module as **Module1**, the default name, and click **OK**. Remain in this window for the next exercise.

FIGURE 17-8
Module1 VB code

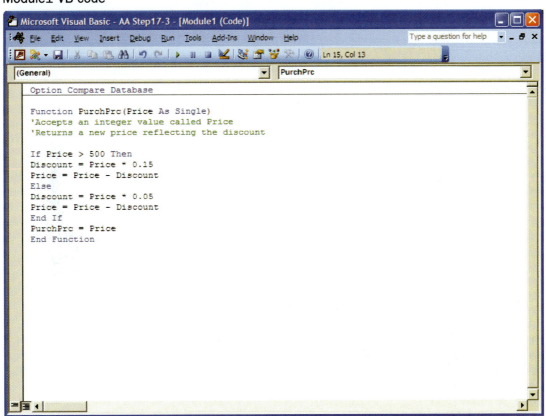

Testing a Visual Basic Statement

You may use the Immediate window, shown in Figure 17-9, to test your VB statement. To display the Immediate window, click the Immediate Window button located on the Debug toolbar. Or you can select the View menu and then choose Immediate Window.

In the next Step-by-Step, you will test the If-Then-Else you've created. You will enter a purchase price and Access will calculate the price less the discount.

Hot Tip

If the function does not work, double-check the spelling of words and be certain that the entire statement is entered.

STEP-BY-STEP 17.4

1. Select the **View** menu and then select **Immediate window** or display the Debug toolbar and click the **Immediate Window** button.

2. Enter the text **Print PurchPrc (675)**.

3. Press **Enter**. You should see a purchase price of 573.75 as shown in Figure 17-9. This price reflects the purchase price of 675 less the 15% discount.

FIGURE 17-9
Immediate window results

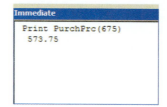

4. Enter the text **Print PurchPrc (400)**.

5. Press **Enter**. You should see a purchase price of 380. This price reflects the purchase price of 400 less the 5% discount.

6. Enter the text **Print PurchPrc (150)**.

7. Press **Enter**. You should see a purchase price of 142.5. This price reflects the purchase price of 150 less the 5% discount.

8. Close the Immediate window and close the Module.

9. Close the database.

Time Saver

You can quickly view the SQL or language of a query by clicking a button.

STEP-BY-STEP 17.6

1. Open the **Time Savers** database from the data files.

2. Open the **Qry-Book Titles** query.

3. Click the down arrow to the right of the **View** button and select **SQL View**. Notice the programming language involved with this query.

4. Press **Ctrl + F4** twice to close the query and then to close the database.

SUMMARY

In this lesson, you learned:

■ Linking tables lets you make changes in one table, such as adding a record, and have the change appear in the linked table as well.

■ Replication creates copies of a database and synchronization updates the replicated database copies.

■ Visual Basic is used to write procedures that can modify, calculate, edit, or add data and objects in a database.

■ Visual Basic procedures can be tested in the Immediate window.

VOCABULARY *Review*

Define the following terms:

Decision structure	Replication	Syntax
Procedures		

REVIEW *Questions*

TRUE/FALSE

Circle T if the statement is true or F if the statement is false.

T   F   **1.** If a linked table is moved, you can use the Linked Table Manager to find and recreate the link between the tables.

T   F   **2.** Visual Basic is a user-friendly, powerful language that can be used to create procedures.

T   F   **3.** Visual Basic Code can be typed and edited within the module window.

T   F   **4.** To update replicated files, you use the synchronization feature.

T   F   **5.** Visual Basic procedures can be tested in the Immediate window.

FILL IN THE BLANK

Complete the following sentences by writing the correct word or words in the blanks provided.

1. _____ refers to how language is put together.

2. The word _____ begins a function procedure and the words _____ _____ are found at the end of a function.

3. Arguments are entered in _____.

4. A group of statements that must choose from alternate actions is referred to as a(n) _____ _____.

5. In a Visual Basic procedure, the _____ _____ appears after the word Function.

PROJECTS

PROJECT 17-1

1. Open the **AA Project17-1** database from the data files.

2. Enter the following Visual Basic code into a module. Save the module as **Module1.**

```
Function Celsius(fDegrees)
    Celsius = (fDegrees - 32) * 5 / 9
End Function
```

3. Test the function in the Immediate window with a celsius of **32** degrees (should return 0) and a celsius of **50** degrees (should return 10).

4. Close the module and then close the database.

CRITICAL*Thinking*

 ACTIVITY 17-1

Use the Access Help feature to find information on changing the display of your Visual Basic Code.

ACTIVITY 17-2

Use the Access Help feature to find information on saving a replicated file as MDE.

ADVANCED MICROSOFT ACCESS

COMMAND SUMMARY

FEATURE	MENU COMMAND	TOOLBAR BUTTON	LESSON
Add Label to Form or Report			9
Apply Filter	Records, Apply Filter/Sort		11
Control Wizard Assistance			14
Create a Textbox			12
Display Object Properties	View, Properties		9
Display Toolbox toolbar	View, Toolbox		12
Display Totals Row in Query	View, Totals		10
Display/Hide Database Window	Window, Hide and Window, Unhide		14
Display/Hide Immediate Window	View, Immediate Window		17
Insert Subform/Subreport			9, 12
Insert Unbound Object			9
Load from Query	File, Load from Query		11
Remove Filter	Records, Remove Filter/Sort		11
Run a Macro	Run, Run		14
Run a Query	Query, Run		11
Save As Query	File, Save As Query		11
Show Conditions in Macros	View, Conditions		14
Show Relationships	Tools, Relationships		8
Show Table List	Relationships, Show Table		8
Use Office Links	Tools, Office Links		13
View Macro Names	View, Macro Names		14

Note: You need to be in Design view for some of these menus and options to appear.

REVIEW *Questions*

TRUE/FALSE

Circle T if the statement is true of F if the statement is false.

T   F   1. A switchboard can be set to open when the database is opened by using an autoexec macro.

T   F   2. Compacting a database removes excess space from the file and typically decreases the file's size.

T   F   3. AND queries are created when criteria is entered for two or more fields on the same *Criteria* row.

T   F   4. Visual Basic code in modules can be protected from viewing or editing by saving the database as an MDE file.

T   F   5. Applying an Advanced Filter to a table is similar to creating a query for a table.

MULTIPLE CHOICE

Select the best response for the following statements.

1. To add a subform to a main form, you need to be in which view?
    A. Tools view
    B. Report design view
    C. Form design view
    D. Print Preview
    E. None of the above.

2. Which of the following is an action query?
    A. Make-Table query
    B. Delete query
    C. Append query
    D. Update query
    E. All of the above are action queries.

3. The primary field in the Field List is _____.
    A. indicated on the status bar
    B. bolded
    C. the field that is not used
    D. all of the above
    E. None of the above.

4. To create a parameter query, you will need to enter a prompt into the field's _____.
   A. *Show* row
   B. *Total* row
   C. *Criteria* row
   D. All of the above.
   E. None of the above.

5. One of the easiest methods for protecting a database from unauthorized access is to _____.
   A. set a password for the database
   B. use one-to-many relationships between tables
   C. create custom input masks
   D. Both A and B are correct.
   E. Both B and C are correct.

PROJECTS

PROJECT 1

1. Open the **AA Project1** database from the data files.

2. Create a query using the **Employees** table that displays only those employees who work in the **Sales Department**.

3. Show the necessary fields in the query and save the query as **Qry-Sales Department**.

4. Print the query results in landscape orientation.

5. Create a query using both the **Employees** and **Personnel Information** tables that displays the last name, first name, department, and telephone number for each employee. Sort the query by **Last Name** in ascending order.

6. Save the query as **Qry-Telephone List**.

7. Print the query results.

8. Create a report from the **Telephone List** query with the employee information grouped by **Department** and sorted by **Last Name** and then **First Name** within the department. Use a layout and style of your choice.

9. Save the report as **Telephone List**. Make any modifications to the design of the report that you feel are necessary. An example of the first portion of the Telephone List report is shown in **Figure UR-1**.

FIGURE UR-1
Example of Telephone List report

10. Print the report.

11. Close the database file.

PROJECT 2

1. Open the **AA Project2** database from the data files.

2. Create a one-to-many relationship between the **Marketing Department** table and the **January Orders** table using the **Employee ID** field as the common field. Enforce Referential Integrity.

3. Create a query for the **Marketing Department** table using the **Employee ID, Last Name,** and **First Name** fields. Sort the query in ascending order by **Last Name** and then by **First Name**. Save the query as **Qry-Marketing Department**.

4. Create a form using the Form Wizard from the **Marketing Department query**. Include the **Employee ID, Last Name,** and **First Name** fields on the form. Choose the **Columnar** layout and select a style of your choice. Name the form **Marketing Department Employee List**.

5. Create a subform in the **Marketing Department Employee List** form using the existing **January Orders** table. Include the **Order No, Order Date, Quantity,** and **Price** fields in the subform. Accept the default name of **January Orders subform** for the subform. (*Note*: If asked to install the subform feature, click **Yes** to install the feature and follow the steps given.)

6. Make any desired changes to the form that you feel makes it attractive and professional. You might need to change the column widths in the subform for the *Price* field to display. *Hint:* Column widths in the subform would not be changed in Design View.

7. Change the title of **January Orders subform** to **January Orders**.

8. Save and print the form for Harold Robinson's record.

9. Close the form and the database.

PROJECT 3

1. Open the **AA Project3** database from the data files.

2. Create a query in Design View based on the **Customers**, **Transactions**, and **Products tables.**

3. If necessary, join the **Customer ID** fields in the **Customers** and **Transaction** tables in the query, and join the **Product Number** and **Product ID** fields in the **Transactions** and **Products** tables respectively. *Hint:* You drag the **related** fields from the primary table **to the** related table within the query itself.

4. In the query Design window, add the **Customer ID** and **Company Name** fields from **the Customers** table, the **Transaction Number** and **Quantity** fields from **Transactions table,** and the **Product Description** field from the **Products** table.

5. Sort the **Transaction Number** field in ascending order.

6. Save the query as **Qry-Products Purchased.**

7. Create a report for **Qry-Products Purchased.** Title the report **TRANSACTIONS. View the** report by **Transaction Number.**

8. Increase the size of the column headings and **align the data appropriately.**

9. Create a data access page from the report and **save the page as Products Purchased. An** example of how your page might **appear is displayed in Figure UR-2.**

FIGURE UR-2
Example of Products Purchased Page

Transaction Number	Customer ID	Company	Quantity	Product Description
100	5	Friendly Groomers	3	Wonder Diet - Dogs
101	7	Teddy's Pampered Pets	5	Nail Trimmer - Small
102	3	Pet Palace	8	Wonder Diet - Cats
103	1	Pets Unlimited	5	Flea Shampoo
104	9	My Buddy Pet Supply	24	Clippers - Hair
105	4	Anne's Pet Supplies	5	Silkie Shampoo
106	9	My Buddy Pet Supply	3	Linatone for Coats
107	15	Bayview Pet Center	18	Dog Vitamins
108	3	Pet Palace	4	Nail Trimmer - Large
109	2	Little Animals	7	Rawhide Bone - Small

Qry-Products Purchased 1-10 of 101

10. Close the data access page and **close the database.**

PROJECT 4

1. Open the **AA Project4** database from the data files.

2. Import the **Finance Department** file into Access as a table. The Finance Department file is a workbook created in Excel.

3. Let Access add the primary key field for you and name the table **Accounting Department**.

4. Adjust column widths in the table, if necessary. Print the table.

5. Close the database file.

SIMULATION

JOB 1

Over the past three months, you've hired several new employees for your expanding company. Although the employees, especially the data entry administrative assistants, are highly qualified, you've noticed an increase in data entry errors with information entered into the incorrect table. Therefore, you decide to create a switchboard that opens automatically as the database file is opened. In addition, you'll create macros and add buttons to forms that clearly identify each form.

1. Open the **AA Job1** database from the data files.

2. Create a macro that closes any object. Add this macro as a button to the **January Orders, February Orders,** and **March Orders** forms.

3. Create a macro that goes to a new record. Add this macro as a button into the **January Orders, February Orders,** and **March Orders** forms.

4. Create a macro that exits Access.

5. Create macros that open and maximize the **January Orders, February Orders,** and **March Orders** forms.

6. Create a form to be used as a switchboard for this database. Add the macros as buttons that open and maximize forms created in the previous step to the switchboard. Also, add the macro that exits Access as a button.

7. Create a macro that opens and maximizes the switchboard form as the database file is opened.

8. Close and reopen the **AA Job1** database. The switchboard form should appear maximized when the database opens.

9. Test the switchboard and macro buttons on each form.

10. Close the database.

JOB 2

You are the new administrative assistant for the Registrar's Office at WUC University. The employees in the Registrar's Office are challenged by the current database and they want you to make it easier for them to use. Open the **AA Job2** database from the data files. In reviewing the objects in the database, you realize that in order to make it more user-friendly, you need to do the following:

1. Create a parameter query that will show each class of student, such as Freshman, Sophomore, and so on, depending on the parameter entered. Name the query **Qry-Students by Class**. Print the query results for each of the four classes.

2. Create a query that shows students with a grade point average less than 2.0. Name the query **Qry-GPA Below 2**. Then, create a form from this query. Name the form **View Scholastic Probations**.

3. Create a query that shows students with a grade point average greater than or equal to 3.5. Name the query **Qry-GPA above 3.5**. Create a form from this query and name the form **Deans List**.

4. To make these forms user-friendly, you decide to include a Close macro button in each form. After you have added the macro button, print both forms.

5. Close any open forms, close the database, and exit Access.

WINDOWS BASICS

VOCABULARY

Mouse

Pointer

Desktop

Channels

Scroll bar

Scroll box

Scroll arrows

Maximize button

Minimize button

Close button

Restore Down button

Menus

Dialog box

Drop-down menu

Mnemonic

Link

Folder

This appendix will familiarize you with the Windows 2000 and Windows XP operating systems. It contains the basic information you need to move around your desktop and manage the files, folders, and other resources you work with every day. It also discusses the Windows Help system.

Starting Windows

If Windows is already installed, it should start automatically when you turn on the computer. If your computer is on a network, you may need some help from your instructor.

STEP-BY-STEP A.1

1. Turn on the computer.

2. After a few moments, Windows 2000 or Windows XP appears.

Navigating in Windows

The Mouse

A *mouse* is a device that rolls on a flat surface and has one or more buttons on it. The mouse allows you to communicate with the computer by pointing to and manipulating graphics and text on the screen. The *pointer*, which appears as an arrow on the screen, indicates the position of the mouse. The four most common mouse operations are point, click, double-click, and drag.

OPERATION	DESCRIPTION
Point	Moving the mouse pointer to a specific item on the screen.
Click	Pressing the mouse button and quickly releasing it while pointing to an item on the screen. (The term *click* comes from the noise you hear when you press and release the button.)
Double-click	Clicking the mouse button twice quickly while keeping the mouse still.
Drag	Pointing to an object on the screen, pressing and holding the left mouse button, and moving the pointer while the button is pressed. Releasing the button ends the drag operation.

The Desktop

When Windows starts up, the desktop displays on the screen. The *desktop* is the space where you access and work with programs and files. Figure A-1 illustrates a typical desktop screen. Your screen may vary slightly from that shown in the figure. For example, your screen may display icons that were installed with Windows or shortcut icons you've created. You can customize and organize your desktop by creating files, folders, and shortcuts.

FIGURE A-1
Typical desktop screen

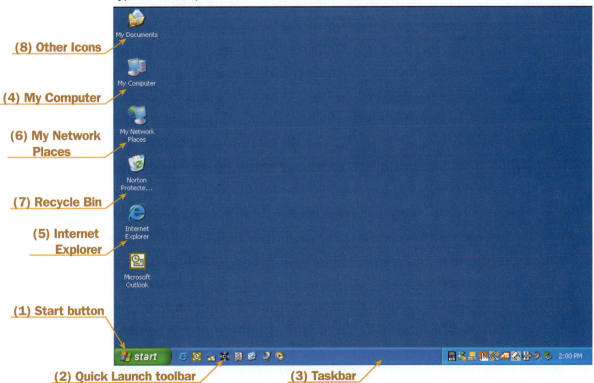

The main features of the desktop screen are labeled and numbered on the figure and discussed below:

1. The Start button brings up menus that give you a variety of options, such as starting a program, opening a document, finding help, or shutting down the computer.

2. The Quick Launch toolbar to the right of the Start button contains icons so you can display the desktop or quickly start frequently used programs.

3. The taskbar, located at the bottom of the screen, tells you the names of all open programs.

4. My Computer is a program that allows you to see what files and folders are located on your computer.

5. Internet Explorer is a Web browser that allows you to surf the Internet, read e-mail, or download your favorite Web sites right to your desktop.

6. My Network Places shows all the folders and printers that are available to you through the network connection, if you have one.

7. The Recycle Bin is a place to get rid of files or folders that are no longer needed.

8. Other icons, or small pictures, represent programs waiting to be opened.

9. Windows makes it easy to connect to the Internet. Just click the Launch Internet Explorer Browser button on the Quick Launch toolbar. The Quick Launch toolbar also has buttons so you can launch Outlook Express, view channels, and show the desktop.

With Windows you can incorporate Web content into your work by using the Active Desktop, an interface that lets you put "active items" from the Internet on your desktop. You can use *channels* to customize the information delivered from the Internet to your computer. By displaying the Channel bar on your desktop you can add, subscribe to, or view channels.

S TEP-BY-STEP A.2

1. Click the **Launch Internet Explorer Browser** button on the Quick Launch toolbar.

2. Click the **Show Desktop** button on the Quick Launch toolbar to display the Windows desktop.

Desktop

3. Click the **Internet Explorer** button on the taskbar to return to the browser window.

4. Choose **Close** on the **File** menu to close Internet Explorer.

5. Point to the **Start** button.

6. Click the left mouse button. A menu of choices appears above the Start button, as shown in Figure A-2.

FIGURE A-2
Start menu in Windows XP

7. If you are using *Windows 2000*, Point to **Settings** and then click **Control Panel** on the submenu. If you are using *Windows XP*, click **Control Panel** on the menu. A new window appears. The title bar at the top tells you that Control Panel is the name of the open window. If necessary, click the button in the Task pane that says **Switch to Classic View**. Leave this window open for the next Task.

Using Windows

Many of the windows you will work with have similar features. You can work more efficiently by familiarizing yourself with some of the common elements, as shown in Figure A-3 and explained below.

FIGURE A-3
Window elements

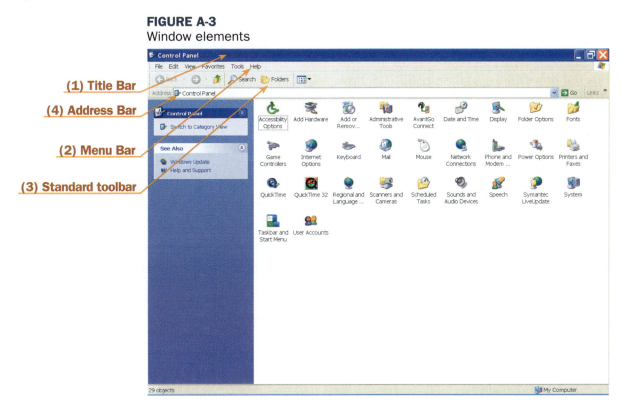

1. A title bar is at the top of every window and contains the name of the open program, window, document, or folder.

2. The menu bar lists available menus from which you can choose a variety of commands. Every option that is available for the current window is accessible through a menu.

3. The standard toolbar, located directly below the menu bar, contains common commands you can use by simply clicking the correct button.

4. The Address bar tells you which folder's contents are being displayed. You can also key a Web address in the Address bar without first opening your browser.

5. At the bottom of the window is the status bar that gives you directions on how to access menus and summarizes the actions of the commands that you choose. If the status bar does not appear on your screen, open the **View** menu and choose **Status Bar**.

Moving and Resizing Windows

Sometimes you will have several windows open on the screen at the same time. To work more effectively, you may need to move or change the size of a window. To move a window, click the title bar and drag the window to another location. You can resize a window by dragging the window borders. When you position the pointer on a horizontal border, it changes to a vertical two-headed arrow. When you position the pointer on a vertical border, it changes to a horizontal two-headed arrow. You can then click and drag the border to change the width or height of the window. It is also possible to resize two sides of a window at the same time. When you move the pointer to a corner of the window's border, it becomes a two-headed arrow pointing diagonally. You can then click and drag to resize the window's height and width at the same time. This maintains the proportions of the existing window.

STEP-BY-STEP A.3

1. Switch to the List view by clicking the **View** button and choosing **List**.

2. Move the Control Panel window by clicking on the title bar and holding the left mouse button down. Continue to hold the left mouse button down and drag the Control Panel until it appears to be centered on the screen. Release the mouse button.

3. Point anywhere on the border at the bottom of the Control Panel window. The pointer turns into a vertical two-headed arrow.

4. While the pointer is a two-headed arrow, click the left mouse button and drag the bottom border of the window down to enlarge the window.

5. Point to the border on the right side of the Control Panel window. The pointer turns into a horizontal two-headed arrow.

6. While the pointer is a two-headed arrow, click and drag the border of the window to the right to enlarge the window.

STEP-BY-STEP A.3 Continued

7. Point to the lower-right corner of the window border, and place your pointer on the sizing handle. The pointer becomes a two-headed arrow pointing diagonally.

8. Drag the border upward and to the left to resize both sides at the same time until the window is about the same size as the one shown in Figure A-4. Leave the window on the screen for the next Task.

FIGURE A-4
Scroll bars, arrows, and boxes

Scroll Bars

A *scroll bar* appears on the edge of a window any time there is more to be displayed than a window can show at its current size (see Figure A-4). A scroll bar can appear along the bottom edge (horizontal) and/or along the right side (vertical) of a window. A scroll bar appeared in the last step of the preceding exercise because the window was too small to show all the icons at once.

Scroll bars are a convenient way to bring another part of the window's contents into view. On the scroll bar is a sliding box called the *scroll box*. The scroll box indicates your position within the window. When the scroll box reaches the bottom of the scroll bar, you have reached the end of the window's contents. *Scroll arrows* are located at the ends of the scroll bar. Clicking on a scroll arrow moves the window in that direction one line at a time.

STEP-BY-STEP A.4

1. On the horizontal scroll bar, click the scroll arrow that points to the right. The contents of the window shift to the left.

2. Press and hold the mouse button on the same scroll arrow. The contents of the window scroll quickly across the window. Notice that the scroll box moves to the right end of the scroll bar.

STEP-BY-STEP A.4 Continued

3. You can also scroll by dragging the scroll box. Drag the scroll box on the horizontal scroll bar to the left.

4. Drag the scroll box on the vertical scroll bar to the middle of the scroll bar.

5. The final way to scroll is to click on the scroll bar. Click the horizontal scroll bar to the right of the scroll box. The contents scroll left.

6. Click the horizontal scroll bar to the left of the scroll box. The contents scroll right.

7. Resize the Control Panel until the scroll bar disappears. Leave the window open for the next Task.

Other Window Controls

Three other important window controls, located on the right side of the title bar, are the *Maximize button*, the *Minimize button*, and the *Close button* (see Figure A-5). The Maximize button enlarges a window to the full size of the screen. The Minimize button shrinks a window to a button on the taskbar. The button on the taskbar is labeled, and you can click it any time to redisplay the window. The Close button is used to close a window.

When a window is maximized, the Maximize button is replaced by the Restore Down button (see Figure A-6). The *Restore Down button* returns the window to the size it was before the Maximize button was clicked.

FIGURE A-5
Maximize, Minimize, and Close buttons

FIGURE A-6
Restore Down button

STEP-BY-STEP A.5

1. Click the **Maximize** button. The window enlarges to fill the screen.

2. Click the **Restore Down** button on the Control Panel window.

3. Click the **Minimize** button on the Control Panel window. The window is reduced to a button on the taskbar.

4. Click the **Control Panel** button on the taskbar to open the window again.

5. Click the **Close** button to close the window.

Menus and Dialog Boxes

To find out what a restaurant has to offer, you look at the menu. You can also look at a menu on the computer's screen to find out what a computer program has to offer. *Menus* in computer programs contain options for executing certain actions or tasks.

When you click the Start button, as you did earlier in this appendix, a menu is displayed with a list of options. If you choose a menu option with an arrow beside it, a submenu opens that lists additional options. A menu item followed by an ellipsis (...) indicates that a dialog box will appear when that item is chosen. A *dialog box*, like the Turn off computer dialog box shown in Figure A-7, appears when more information is required before the command can be performed. You may have to key information, choose from a list of options, or simply confirm that you want the command to be performed. To back out of a dialog box without performing an action, press Esc, click the Close button, or choose Cancel (or No).

FIGURE A-7
Turn off computer dialog box

STEP-BY-STEP A.6

1. Click the **Start** button. A menu appears.

2. If you are using *Windows 2000*, click **Shut Down**. The Shut Down Windows dialog box appears. If you are using *Windows XP*, the button on the Start menu and the title on the dialog box is *Turn Off Computer*, as shown in Figure A-7.

3. Click **Cancel** to back out of the dialog box without shutting down.

In a Windows application, menus are accessed from a menu bar (see Figure A-8). A menu bar appears beneath the title bar in each Windows program and consists of a row of menu names such as File and Edit. Each name in the menu bar represents a separate ***drop-down menu***, containing related options. Drop-down menus are convenient to use because the commands are in front of you on the screen, as shown in Figure A-8. Like a menu in a restaurant, you can view a list of choices and pick the one you want.

FIGURE A-8
Drop-down menu

You can give commands from drop-down menus using either the keyboard or the mouse. Each menu on the menu bar and each option on a menu is characterized by an underlined letter called a ***mnemonic***. To open a menu on the menu bar using the keyboard, press Alt plus the mnemonic letter shown on the menu name. To display a menu using the mouse, simply place the pointer on the menu name and click the left button.

Just as with the Start menu, drop-down menus also have items with right-pointing arrows that open submenus, and ellipses that open dialog boxes. Choosing an item without an ellipsis or a right-pointing arrow executes the command. To close a menu without choosing a command, press Esc or click anywhere outside of the menu.

STEP-BY-STEP A.7

1. If you are using *Windows 2000*, open the Notepad accessory application by clicking **Start**, **Programs**, **Accessories**, and then **Notepad**. (See Figure A-9.) If using *Windows XP*, open the Notepad accessory application by clicking **Start**, **All Programs**, **Accessories**, and then **Notepad**.

FIGURE A-9
Opening menus in an application

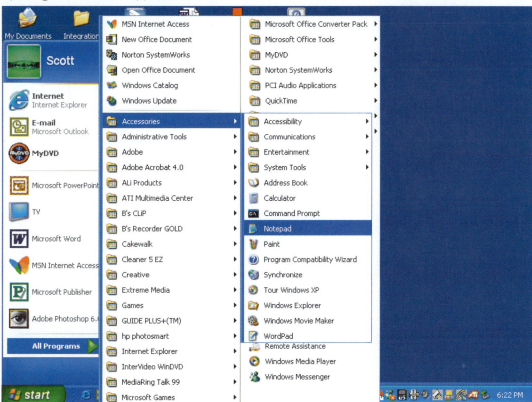

2. Click **Edit** on the menu bar. The Edit menu appears.

3. Click **Time/Date** to display the current time and date.

STEP-BY-STEP A.7 Continued

4. Click **File** on the menu bar. The File menu appears. Point to **Exit**. The Exit option is selected (see Figure A-10).

FIGURE A-10
Exit command on the File menu

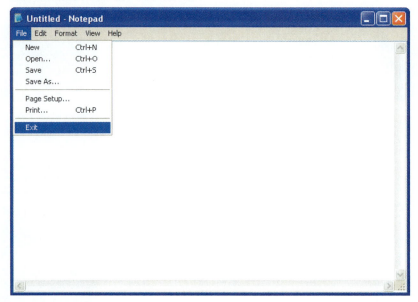

5. Click **Exit**. A save prompt dialog box appears.

6. Click **No**. The Notepad window closes (without saving your document) and you return to the desktop.

Windows Help

This appendix has covered only a few of the many features of Windows. For additional information, Windows has an easy-to-use Help system. Use Help as a quick reference when you are unsure about a function. Windows Help is accessed through the Help option on the Start menu. Then, from the Windows Help dialog box, you can choose to see a table of contents displaying general topics and subtopics, or you can choose to search the Help system using the Index or Search options. If you are working in a Windows program, you can get more specific help about topics relating to that program by accessing help from the Help menu on the menu bar.

Many topics in the Help program are linked. A *link* is represented by colored, underlined text. By clicking a link, the user "jumps" to a linked document that contains additional information.

Using the buttons on the toolbar controls the display of information. In Windows 2000, the Hide button removes the left frame of the Help window from view and the Show button will restore it. In both Windows 2000 and Windows XP, Back and Forward buttons allow you to move back and forth between previously displayed Help entries. The Options button offers navigational choices, as well as options to customize, refresh, and print Help topics.

The Contents tab (or Locate in Contents button in Windows XP) is useful if you want to browse through the topics by category. Click a book icon to see additional Help topics. Click a question mark to display detailed Help information in the right frame of the Help window.

S TEP-BY-STEP A.8

1. If you are using *Windows 2000*, open the Windows Help program by clicking the **Start** button, and then **Help**. If you are using *Windows XP*, click **Start** and then **Help and Support**.

2. If you're using *Windows 2000*, click the **Hide** button on the toolbar to remove the left frame, if necessary. If you are using *Windows XP*, skip to step 5.

3. Click the **Show** button to display the left frame again, if necessary.

4. Click the **Contents** tab if it is not already selected.

5. *Windows 2000* users: Click **Introducing Windows 2000 Professional** and then click **How to Use Help**.

   Windows XP users: Click **What's new in Windows XP**.

6. *Windows 2000* users: Click **Find a Help Topic**.

   Windows XP users: Click **What's new topics** in the left pane and then **What's new for Help and Support** in the right pane.

7. Read the Help window and leave it open for the next Task.

When you want to search for help on a particular topic, use the Index tab (or button) and key in a word. Windows will search alphabetically through the list of Help topics to try to find an appropriate match. Double-click a topic to see it explained in the right frame of the help window. Sometimes a Topics Found dialog box will appear that displays subtopics related to the item. Find a subtopic that you'd like to learn more about and double-click it.

S TEP-BY-STEP A.9

1. *Windows 2000* users: Click the **Index** tab.

   Windows XP users: Click the **Index** button.

2. *Windows 2000* users: Begin keying **printing** until *printing* is highlighted in the list of index entries.

   Windows XP users: Begin keying **help** until *help and support for Windows XP* is highlighted in the list of index entries.

3. *Windows 2000* users: Click **printing Help topics** and then **from a Server** to display information in the right frame.

   Windows XP users: Double-click the **copying and printing Help topics**, then double-click **To print a Help topic or page**.

STEP-BY-STEP A.9 Continued

4. *Windows 2000* users: Read the Help window, and then print the information by following the instructions you read.

   Windows XP users: Read the Help window, and then print the information by clicking the **Print** button on the toolbar.

5. *Windows 2000* users: Click the **Back** button to return to the previous Help screen.

   Windows XP users: Click the **Back arrow** button to return to the previous Help screen.

6. *Windows 2000* users: Click the **Forward** button to advance to the next Help screen.

   Windows XP users: Click the **Forward arrow** button to advance to the next Help screen.

7. Close the Help program by clicking the **Close** button.

The Search function is similar to the Index function, but will perform a more thorough search of the words or phrases that you key. By using the Search option, you can display every occurrence of a particular word or phrase throughout the Windows Help system. Double-click on the topic most similar to what you are looking for and information is displayed in the Help window.

If you need assistance using the Windows Help program in Windows 2000, choose *Introducing Windows, How to Use Help* from the Contents tab; or, if you are using Windows XP, choose *What's new in Windows XP* from the Home page and then *What's new topics*.

If you are using an Microsoft Office application, you can also get help by using the Office Assistant feature.

Other Features

One of Windows' primary features is its file management capabilities. Windows comes with two file management utilities: My Computer and Windows Explorer. The Recycle Bin utility also helps you manage files. When open, these utilities display a standard toolbar similar to the one shown in Figure A-11. Your toolbar may look different from Figure A-11 depending on if it has been customized. To customize your toolbar, choose Toolbars on the View menu, and Customize on the submenu.

FIGURE A-11
Windows XP Standard toolbar

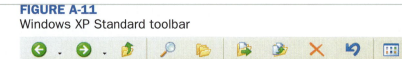

The Back and Forward buttons let you move back and forth between folder contents previously displayed in the window. The Up button moves you up one level in the hierarchy of folders. You can use the Cut, Copy, and Paste buttons to cut or copy an object and then paste it in another location. The Undo button allows you to reverse your most recent action. The Delete button sends the selected object to the Recycle Bin. The View button lists options for displaying the contents of the window.

My Computer

As you learned earlier, there is an icon on your desktop labeled My Computer. Double-clicking this icon opens the My Computer window, which looks similar to the one shown in Figure A-12. The My Computer program is helpful because it allows you to see what is on your computer. Double-click the icon for the drive you want to view. That drive's name appears in the title bar and the window displays all the folders and files on that drive.

FIGURE A-12
Windows XP My Computer window

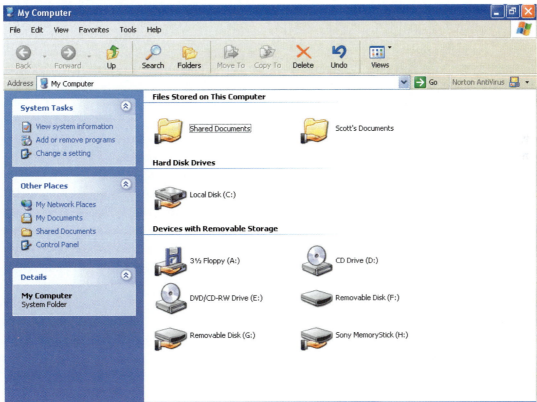

Because computer disks have such a large capacity, it is not unusual for a floppy disk to contain dozens of files, or for a hard disk to contain hundreds or thousands of files. To organize files, a disk can be divided into folders. A *folder* is a place where files and other folders are stored. They help keep documents organized on a disk just the way folders would in a file cabinet. Folders group files that have something in common. You can also have folders within a folder. For example, you could create a folder to group all of the files you are working on in computer class. Within that folder, you could have several other folders that group files for each tool or each chapter.

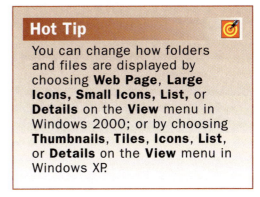

Hot Tip

You can change how folders and files are displayed by choosing **Web Page**, **Large Icons, Small Icons, List,** or **Details** on the **View** menu in Windows 2000; or by choosing **Thumbnails**, **Tiles**, **Icons**, **List**, or **Details** on the **View** menu in Windows XP.

When you double-click a folder in My Computer, the contents of that folder are displayed—including program files and data files. Double-clicking a program file icon will open that program. Double-clicking a data file icon opens that document in the program that created it.

To create a new folder, double-click a drive or folder in the My Computer window. Choose New on the File menu and then choose Folder on the submenu. A folder titled *New Folder* appears, as shown in Figure A-13. You can rename the folder by keying the name you want. Once you have created a folder, you can save or move files into it.

FIGURE A-13
New folder (Tiles view)

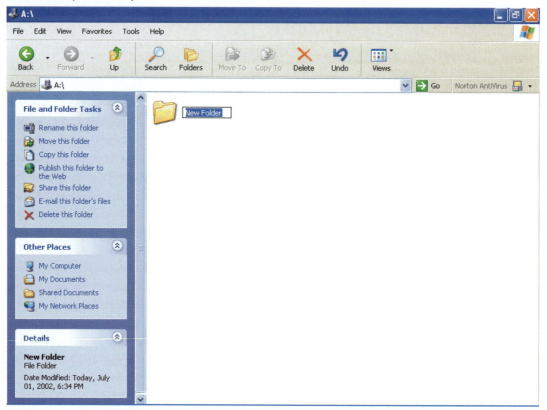

S TEP-BY-STEP A.10

1. Double-click the **My Computer** icon on your desktop.

2. Double-click the drive where you want to create a new folder.

3. Open the **File** menu, choose **New** and then choose **Folder** on the submenu. A folder titled *New Folder* appears.

4. Name the folder **Time Records**. Press **Enter**.

5. Open the **File** menu and choose **Close** to close the window.

Windows Explorer

Another way to view the folders and files on a disk is to use the Windows Explorer program. To open it, click Start, Program (or All Programs), Accessories, and then click Windows Explorer. The Explorer window is split into two panes. The left pane shows a hierarchical or "tree" view of how the folders are organized on a disk; the right side, or Contents pane, shows the files and folders located in the folder that is currently selected in the tree pane. Explorer is a useful tool for organizing and managing the contents of a disk because you can create folders, rename them, and easily delete, move, and copy files.

STEP-BY-STEP A.11

1. *Windows 2000* users: Open Windows Explorer by clicking **Start**, **Programs**, **Accessories**, and then **Windows Explorer**.

   Windows XP users: Open Windows Explorer by clicking **Start**, **All Programs**, **Accessories**, and then **Windows Explorer**.

2. In the tree pane, click the drive where the *Time Records* folder you just created is located.

3. Select the **Time Records** folder in the Contents pane of the Explorer window.

4. Open the **File** menu and choose **Rename**.

5. Key **Finance**. Press **Enter**.

6. Leave Windows Explorer open for the next Task.

Recycle Bin

Another icon on the desktop that you learned about earlier is the Recycle Bin. It looks like a wastebasket and is a place to get rid of files and folders that you no longer need. Items that have been "thrown away" will remain in the Recycle Bin, from which they can be retrieved until you empty the Recycle Bin.

STEP-BY-STEP A.12

1. Windows Explorer should still be open from the previous Task.

2. Right-click the **Finance** folder.

3. Choose **Delete** on the shortcut menu. The Confirm Folder Delete dialog box appears.

4. Click **Yes**. The folder is removed.

5. Open the **File** menu and choose **Close** to close Windows Explorer.

SUMMARY

In this appendix, you learned:

- The desktop organizes your work. Clicking the Start button displays options for opening programs and documents and shutting down the computer.

- You can connect to the Internet using the Internet Explorer browser, and you can use the Active Desktop and channels to incorporate Web content into your work.

- Windows can be moved, resized, opened, and closed. If all the contents of a window cannot be displayed in the window as it is currently sized, scroll bars appear to allow you to move to the part of the window that you want to view. Windows can be maximized to fill the screen or minimized to a button on the taskbar.

- Menus allow you to choose commands to perform different actions. Menus are accessed from the Start button or from a program's menu bar near the top of the window. When you choose a menu command with an ellipsis (...), a dialog box appears that requires more information before performing the command. Choosing a menu option with an arrow opens a submenu.

- The Windows Help program provides additional information about the many features of Windows. You can access the Help program from the Start button and use the Contents, Index, or Search tabs to get information. You can also get help from the Help menu within Windows programs.

- Folders group files that have something in common. To organize a disk, it can be divided into folders where files and other folders are stored. Other useful features of Windows include My Computer and Windows Explorer, which let you see what is on your computer and help you organize and manage your files; as well as the Recycle Bin for deleting unneeded files or folders.

COMPUTER CONCEPTS

What Is a Computer?

A computer is a mechanical device that is used to store, retrieve, and manipulate information (called data) electronically. You enter the data into the computer through a variety of input devices, such as a keyboard, mouse, or joystick; the computer processes it, and then it can be output in a number of ways: such as with a monitor, projector, or printer. Computer software programs run the computer and let you manipulate the data.

Hardware

The physical components, or parts, of the computer are called hardware. The main parts are the central processing unit (CPU), the monitor, the keyboard, and the mouse. Peripherals are additional components, such as printers and scanners.

Input Devices. You enter information into a computer by keying on a keyboard or by using a mouse—a hand-held device—to move a pointer on the computer screen. Tablet PCs allow you to input data by writing directly on the computer screen. They use a technology called handwriting recognition to convert your writing to text. A joystick is an input device similar to the control stick of an airplane that moves a pointer, or character, on the screen. A modem is another input device; it receives information via a telephone line. Other input devices include scanners, track-balls, and digital tracking devices. You can use scanners to "read" text or graphics into a computer from a printed page, or to read bar codes (coded labels) to keep track of merchandise or other inventory in a store. Similar to a mouse, a trackball has a roller ball that turns to control a pointer on the screen. Digital tracking devices are an alternative to the trackball or mouse; situated on the keyboard of a laptop, they allow you to simply press a finger on a small electronic pad to control the pointer on the screen. See Figure B-1.

FIGURE B-1
Keyboard, controller, and mouse

Processing Devices. The central processing unit (CPU) is a silicon chip that processes data and carries out instructions given to the computer. The data bus includes the wiring and pathways by which the CPU communicates with the peripherals and components of the computer.

FIGURE B-2
Motherboard

Storage Devices. The hard drive is a device that reads and writes data to and from a round magnetic platter, or disk. The data is encoded on the disk much the same as sounds are encoded on magnetic tape. The hard drive is called hard because the disk it reads is rigid; unlike a floppy disk drive, which reads and writes data to and from a removable non-rigid disk, similar to a round disk of magnetic tape. The floppy disk is encased in a plastic sleeve to protect its data. The floppy disk's main advantage is portability. You can store data on a floppy disk and transport it for use on another computer. A floppy disk will hold up to 1.4 megabytes (MB) of information. A Zip disk is similar to a floppy disk. A Zip disk is also a portable disk contained in a plastic sleeve, but it will hold 100MB or 250MB of information. A special disk drive called a Zip drive is required to use a Zip disk.

At one time, the largest hard drive was 10MB, or 10,000,000 bytes, of data. A byte stands for a single character of data. At the current time, typical hard drives range from 40 gigabytes (GB) to 120 gigabytes.

Another storage device is the CD, or compact disc, which is a form of optical storage. Compact discs can store 650MB. Information is encoded on the disk by a laser and read by a CD-ROM drive in the computer. These discs have a great advantage over floppies because they can hold vast quantities of information—the entire contents of a small library, for instance. However, most computers cannot write (or save) information to these discs; CD-ROMs are Read-Only Memory (ROM) devices. Drives are now available that write to CDs. Although these drives used to be very expensive and therefore were not used widely, they are becoming more affordable. The great advantage of CDs is their ability to hold graphic information—including moving pictures with the highest quality stereo sound.

Similar to a CD, the digital video disc drive (DVD) can read high-quality cinema-type discs. A DVD is a 5-inch optical disc, and it looks like an audio CD. It is a high-capacity storage device that can contain 4.7GB of data, which is a seven-fold increase over the current CD-ROMs. There are two variations of DVDs that offer even more storage—a 2-layer version with 9.4GB capacity, and double-sided discs with 17GB. These highest-capacity discs are designed to eventually replace the CD-ROM to store large databases. A DVD holds 133 minutes of data on each side, which means that two two-hour movies can be stored on one disc.

Another storage medium is magnetic tape. This medium is most commonly used for backing up a computer system, which means making a copy of files from a hard drive. Although it is relatively rare for a hard drive to crash (that is, for the data or pointers to the data to be partially or totally destroyed), it can and does happen. Therefore, most businesses and some individuals routinely back up files on tape. If you have a small hard drive, you can use floppy disks or CD-ROMs to back up your system.

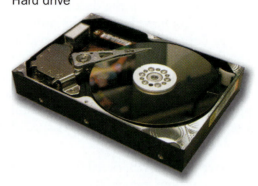

Output Devices. The monitor on which you view your work is an output device. It provides a visual representation of the information stored in or produced by your computer. The typical monitor for today's system is the SVGA (super video graphics array), which uses a Cathode-ray tube (CRT) similar to a television. It provides a very sharp picture because of the large number of tiny dots, called pixels, which make up the display as well as its ability to present the full spectrum of colors. Most laptop computers use a liquid crystal display (LCD) screen that is not as clear a display because it depends on the arrangement of tiny bits of crystal to present an image. However, the latest laptops use new technology that gives quality near or equal to that of a standard monitor.

Printers are another type of output device. They let you produce a paper printout of information contained in the computer. Today, most printers are of the laser type, using a technology similar to a photocopier to produce high-quality print. Like a copy machine, the laser printer uses heat to fuse a powdery substance called toner to the page. Ink-jet printers use a spray of ink to print. Laser printers give the sharpest image. Ink-jet printers provide nearly as sharp an image, but the wet printouts can smear when they first are printed. Most color printers, however, are ink jet. These printers let you print information in its full array of colors just as you see it on your SVGA monitor. Laser color printers are available, but are significantly more costly.

Modems are another type of output device, as well as an input device. They allow computers to communicate with each other by telephone lines. Modems convert information in bytes to sound media in order to send data and then convert it back to bytes after receiving data. Modems operate at various rates or speeds; typically a computer will have a modem that operates at 33.6 Kbps (Kilobytes per second) to 56 Kbps baud (a variable unit of data transmission) or better.

Local telephone companies currently offer residential ISDN services that provide connection speeds up to 128 Kbps and digital subscriber line technologies (DSL), which can provide speeds beyond 1.5 Mbps (Megabytes per second). Other alternatives include fast downstream data connections from direct broadcast satellite (DBS), fixed wireless providers, and high-speed cable.

FIGURE B-4
Monitor

Laptops and Docking Stations. A laptop computer is a small folding computer that literally fits in a person's lap. Within the fold-up case is the CPU, data bus, monitor (built into the lid), hard drive (sometimes removable), a 3.5-inch floppy drive, a CD-ROM drive, and a trackball or digital tracking device. The advantage of the laptop is its portability—you can work anywhere because you can use power either from an outlet or from the computer's internal, rechargeable batteries. The drawbacks are the smaller keyboard, liquid crystal monitor, smaller capacity, and higher price, though newer laptops offer full-sized keyboards and higher quality monitors. As technology allows, storage capacity on smaller devices is making it possible to offer laptops with as much power and storage as a full-sized computer. A docking station is a device into which you slide a closed laptop so that it becomes a desktop computer. Then you can plug in a full-sized monitor, keyboard, mouse, printer, and so on. Such a setup lets you use the laptop like a desktop computer while at your home or office. See Figure B-5.

FIGURE B-5
Laptop and docking station

Personal Digital Assistants (PDA). A Personal Digital Assistant is a pocket-sized electronic organizer that helps you to manage addresses, appointments, expenses, tasks, and memos. This information can be shared with a Windows-based or Macintosh computer through a process called synchronization. By placing your PDA in a cradle that is attached to your computer, you can transfer the data from your PDA's calendar, address, or memo program into your computer's information manager program, such as Outlook. The information is updated on both sides, making your PDA a portable extension of your computer.

FIGURE B-6
Personal Digital Assistant

Functioning

All of the input, processing, storage, and output devices function together to make the manipulation, storage, and distribution of data and information possible.

Data and Information Management. Data is information entered into and manipulated within a computer. Manipulation includes computation, such as adding, subtracting, multiplying, and dividing; analysis planning, such as sorting data; and reporting, such as presenting data for others in a chart. Data and information management is what runs the software on the computer hardware.

Memory. There are two kinds of memory in a computer—RAM and ROM. RAM, or Random Access Memory, consists of a number of silicon chips inside a computer that hold information as long as the computer is turned on. RAM is what keeps the software programs up and running and keeps the visuals on your screen. RAM is where you work with data until you save it to another media such as a hard or floppy disk. Early computers had simple programs and did little with data, so they had very little RAM—possibly 4 or fewer megabytes. Today's computers run very complicated programs that stay resident (remain available to the user at the same time as other programs) and contain graphics. Both of these tasks take a lot of memory; therefore, today's computers have at least 128 or more megabytes of RAM. ROM, or read-only memory, is the small bit of memory that stays in the computer when it is turned off. It is ROM that lets the computer boot up, or get started. ROM holds the instructions that tell the computer how to begin to load its operating system software programs. Figure B-7 shows random access memory.

FIGURE B-7
Random Access Memory

Speed. The speed of a computer is measured by how fast the drives turn to reach information to be retrieved or to save data. The measurement is in megahertz (MHz). Hard drives on early personal computers worked at 4.77 to 10 megahertz; today, machines run at 1000 MHz (or 1GHz) or more. Another factor that affects the speed of a computer is how much RAM is available. Since RAM makes up the work area for all programs and holds all the information that you input until you save, the more RAM available, the quicker the machine will be able to operate.

One other area of speed must be considered, and that is how quickly the modem can send and receive information. As mentioned earlier, modem speed is measured in baud. The usual modem runs at 33,600 or 56,000 baud per second or more; whereas cable modems, DSL lines, ISDN lines, and DSB offer much faster transfers of information.

Communications. Computers have opened up the world of communications, first within offices via LANs (local area networks that link computers within a facility) and, later, via the Internet. Using the Internet, people can communicate across the world instantly with e-mail and attach files that were once sent by mailing a floppy disk. Also, anyone with a modem and an access service can download information from or post information to thousands of bulletin boards. Figure B-8 shows a network diagram.

FIGURE B-8
Diagram of a network

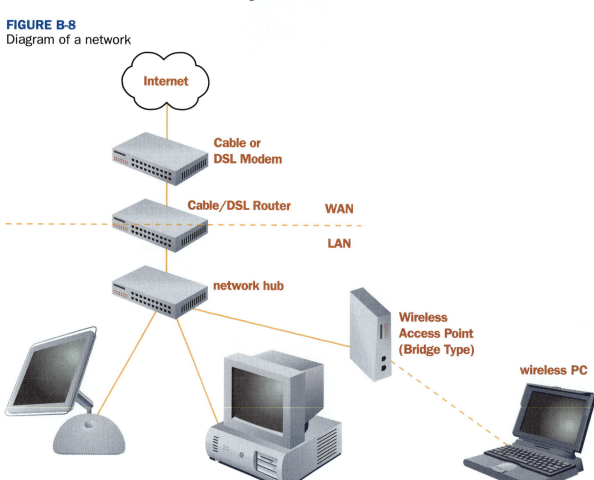

Software

A program is a set of mathematical instructions to the computer. Software is the collection of programs and other data input that tells the computer how to operate its machinery, how to manipulate, store, and output information, and how to accept the input you give it. Software fits into two basic categories: systems software and applications software. A third category, network software, is really a type of application.

Systems Software. Systems software refers to the operating system (OS) of the computer. The OS is a group of programs that is automatically copied in RAM every couple of seconds from the time the computer is turned on until the computer is turned off. Operating systems serve two functions: they control data flow among computer parts, and they provide the platform on which application and network software work—in effect, they allow the "space" for software and translate its commands to the computer. The most popular operating systems in use today are the

Macintosh operating system, and a version of Microsoft Windows, such as Windows 98, Windows NT, Windows 2000, or Windows XP.

Macintosh has its own operating system that has evolved over the years since its introduction. Macintosh has used a graphical user interface (GUI) operating system since its introduction in the mid-1970s. The OS is designed so users "click" with a mouse on pictures, called icons, or on text to give commands to the system. Data is available to you in WYSIWYG (what-you-see-is-what-you-get) form; that is, you can see on-screen what a document will look like when it is printed. Graphics and other kinds of data, such as spreadsheets, can be placed into text documents. However, GUIs take a great deal of RAM to keep all of the graphics and programs operating.

The OS for IBM and IBM-compatible computers (machines made by other companies that operate similarly) originally was DOS (disk operating system). It did not have a graphical interface. The GUI system, Windows™, was developed to make using the IBM/IBM-compatible computer more "friendly." Windows 3.1, however, was a translating system that operated on top of DOS—not on its own. It allowed you to point and click on graphics and words that then translated to DOS commands for the computer. Data was available to you in WYSIWYG form. Graphics and other kinds of data, such as spreadsheets, could be placed into text documents by Object Linking and Embedding (OLE). However, Windows 3.1, because it was still using DOS as its base, was not really a stay-resident program. In other words, it did not keep more than one operation going at a time; it merely switched between operations quickly. Using several high-level programs at the same time, however, could cause problems such as memory failure. Therefore, improvements were necessary and inevitable.

The improvements came with the release of Windows 95 and then Windows 98. These versions of Windows had their own operating system, unlike the original Windows 3.1. Windows 95/98 has DOS built in but does not operate on top of it—if you go to a DOS prompt from Windows, you will still be operating inside a Windows system, not in traditional DOS. Today's Windows applications are the logical evolution of GUI for IBM and IBM-compatible machines. Windows is a stay-resident, point-and-click system that automatically configures hardware to work together. You should note, however, that with all of its ability comes the need for more RAM, or a system running Windows will operate slowly.

Windows 95 and 98 were designed for the consumer. They are easy to use, compatible with most peripheral products, and have features that you would most likely use for personal applications. Windows NT and Windows 2000 were designed for businesses, and include enhanced features for reliability and security. Windows XP brought these two divergent operating systems back together into one product for all users. It combines the versatility of Windows 98 with the stability and security of Windows 2000. Newer versions of Windows continue to be released.

Applications Software. When you use a computer program to perform a data manipulation or processing task, you are using applications software. Word processors, databases, spreadsheets, desktop publishers, fax systems, and online access systems are all applications software.

Network Software. Novell™ and Windows NT are two kinds of network software. A traditional network is a group of computers that are hardwired (hooked together with cables) to communicate and operate together. Today, some computer networks use RF (radio frequency) technology to communicate with each other. This is called a wireless network, because you do not need to hook the network together with cables. In a typical network, one computer acts as the server, which controls the flow of data among the other computers, called nodes, on the network. Network software manages this flow of information. Networks have certain advantages over stand-alone computers: they allow communication among the computers; they allow smaller capacity nodes to access the larger capacity of the server; they allow several computers to share peripherals, such as one printer; and they can make it possible for all computers on the network to have access to the Internet.

History of the Computer

Though various types of calculating machines were developed in the nineteenth century, the history of the modern computer begins about the middle of the last century. The strides made in developing today's personal computer have been truly astounding.

Early Development

The ENIAC, or Electronic Numerical Integrator and Computer, was designed for military use in calculating ballistic trajectories and was the first electronic, digital computer to be developed in the United States. For its day, 1946, it was quite a marvel because it was able to accomplish a task in 20 seconds that took a human three days to do. However, it was an enormous machine that weighed more than 20 tons and contained thousands of vacuum tubes, which often failed. The tasks that it could accomplish were limited, as well.

FIGURE B-9
ENIAC

From this awkward beginning, however, the seeds of an information revolution grew. Significant dates in the history of computer development are listed in Table B-1.

TABLE B-1
History or computer development

YEAR	DEVELOPMENT
1948	First electronically stored program
1951	First junction transistor
1953	Replacement of tubes with magnetic cores
1957	First high-level computer language
1961	First integrated circuit
1965	First minicomputer
1971	Invention of the microprocessor (the silicon chip) and floppy disk
1974	First personal computer (made possible by the microprocessor)

These last two inventions launched the fast-paced information revolution in which we now all live and participate.

The Personal Computer

The PC, or personal computer, was mass marketed by Apple beginning in 1977, and by IBM in 1981. It is this desktop device with which people are so familiar and which, today, contains much more power and ability than did the original computer that took up an entire room. The PC is a small computer (desktop size or less) that uses a microprocessor to manipulate data. PCs may stand alone, be linked together in a network, or be attached to a large mainframe computer.

FIGURE B-10
Early IBM

Computer Utilities and System Maintenance

Computer operating systems let you run certain utilities and perform system maintenance. When you add hardware or software, you might need to make changes in the way the system operates. Beginning with the Windows 95 version, most configuration changes are done automatically; however, other operating systems might not perform these tasks automatically, or you might want to customize the way the new software or hardware will interface (coordinate) with your system. Additionally, you can make alterations such as the speed at which your mouse clicks, how quickly or slowly keys repeat on the keyboard, and what color or pattern appears on the desktop or in GUI programs.

You need to perform certain maintenance regularly on computers. You should scan all new disks and any incoming information from online sources for viruses (a small program that is loaded onto your computer without your knowledge and runs against your wishes). Some systems do this automatically; others require you to install software to do it. From time to time, you should run a program that scans or checks the hard drive to see that there are not bad sectors (areas) and look for corrupted files. Optimizing or defragmenting the hard disk is another way to keep your computer running at its best. You can also check a floppy disk if it is not working properly. Programs for scanning a large hard drive could take up to half an hour to run; checking programs run on a small hard drive or disk might take only seconds or minutes. Scanning and checking programs often offer the option of "fixing" the bad areas or problems, although you should be aware that this could result in data loss.

Society and Computers

The Electronic Information Era has probably impacted society as much or more than the Agricultural and Industrial Eras affected the lives of our ancestors. With the changes of this era have come many new questions and responsibilities. There are issues of ethics, security, safety, and privacy.

Ethics Using Computers

When you access information—whether online, in the workplace, or via purchased software—you have a responsibility to respect the rights of the creator of that information. Treat electronic information in a copyrighted form—the intellectual property of the author—the same way as you would a book, article or patented invention. For instance, you must give credit when you access information from a CD-ROM encyclopedia or a download from an online database. Also, information you transmit must be accurate and fair.

When you use equipment that belongs to your school, a company for which you work, or others, you must not:

1. Damage computer hardware and add or remove equipment without permission.

2. Use an access code or equipment without permission.

3. Read others' electronic mail.

4. Alter data belonging to someone else without permission.

5. Use the computer for play during work hours or use it for personal profit.

6. Access the Internet for nonbusiness use during work hours.

7. Add to or take away from software programs without permission.

8. Make unauthorized copies of data or software.

9. Copy software programs to use at home or at another site in the company without multisite permission.

10. Copy company files or procedures for personal use.

11. Borrow computer hardware for personal use without asking permission.

Security, Safety, and Privacy

The Internet provides us access to improve our economic productivity and offer life-enhancing features, such as distance learning, remote medical diagnostics, and the ability to work from home more effectively. Businesses throughout the world depend on the Internet every day to get work done. Disruptions in the Internet create havoc for people around the world.

The September 11, 2001, terrorist attack on the World Trade Center and the Pentagon raised the awareness of the entire country about the security of our citizens and our country. In response to this attack, President George W. Bush established the Department of Homeland Security and created a division called the National Cyber Security Division (NCSD) to protect our interest in the Internet.

In order to keep the Internet safe for everyone, the National Cyber Security Division encourages all users to use updated antivirus software and keep your operating systems up to date by adding patches designed to enhance your computer's security. They also request that you "report information concerning suspicious or criminal activity to law enforcement or a DHS watch office."

Because electronic communication is the fastest way for terrorists to communicate, we must all raise our level of security awareness when communicating using computers.

Just as you would not open someone else's mail, you must respect the privacy of e-mail sent to others. When interacting with others online, you must keep confidential information confidential. Do not endanger your privacy, safety, or financial security by giving out personal information to someone you do not know. A common scam (trick) is for someone to pretend to work for the online service you are using and ask for the access code or password that controls your service account. Never give this information out to anyone online. The person can use it and charge a great deal of costly time to your account as well as perhaps access other personal information about you. Also, just as you would not give a stranger your home address, telephone number, or credit card number if you were talking on the street, you should take those same precautions online.

Career Opportunities

In one way or another, all of our careers involve the computer. Whether you are a grocery checker using a scanner to read the prices, a busy executive writing a report on a laptop on an airplane, or a programmer creating new software—almost everyone uses computers in their jobs. And, everyone in a business processes information in some way. There are also specific careers available if you want to work primarily with computers.

Schools offer degrees in computer programming, repair, and design. The most popular jobs are systems analysts, computer operators, and programmers. Analysts figure out ways to make computers work (or work better) for a particular business or type of business. Computer operators use the programs and devices to conduct business with computers. Programmers write the software for applications or new systems.

There are courses of study in using CAD (computer-aided design) and CAM (computer-aided manufacturing). Computer engineering and architectural design degrees are also available. Scientific research is done on computers, and specialties are available in that area as well. There are positions available to instruct others in computer software use within companies and schools. Technical writers and editors must be available to write manuals on using computers and software. Computer-assisted instruction (CAI) is a system of teaching any given subject on the computer. The learner is provided with resources, such as an encyclopedia on CD-ROM, in addition to the specific learning program with which he or she interacts on the computer. Individuals are needed to create these instruction systems. Designing video games is another exciting and ever-growing field of computer work. And these are just a few of the possible career opportunities in an ever-changing work environment.

FIGURE B-11
Person in a computer-related job

What Does the Future Hold?

The possibilities for computer development and application are endless. Things that were dreams or science fiction only 10 or 20 years ago are a reality today. New technologies are emerging. Some are replacing old ways of doing things; others are merging with those older methods and devices. We are learning new ways to work and play because of the computer. It is definitely a device that has become part of our offices, our homes, and our lives.

Emerging Technologies

Today the various technologies and systems are coming together to operate more efficiently. For instance, since their beginnings, Macintosh and Windows-based systems could not exchange information well. Today, you can install compatibility cards in the Power Macintosh and run Windows, DOS, and Mac OS on the same computer and switch between them. Macs (except for early models) can read from and write to MS-DOS and Windows disks. And you can easily network Macintosh computers with other types of computers running other operating systems. In addition, you can buy software for a PC to run the Mac OS and to read Macintosh disks.

Telephone communication is also being combined with computer e-mail so users can set a time to meet online and, with the addition of voice technology, actually speak to each other. This form of communication will certainly evolve into an often-used device that will broaden the use of both the spoken and written word.

Another technology is the CUCME (see you, see me) visual system that allows computer users to use a small camera and microphone wired into the computer so, when they communicate, the receiver can see and hear them. For the hearing impaired, this form of communication can be more effective than writing alone since sign language and facial expression can be added to the interaction. CUCME is a logical next step from the image transfer files now so commonly used to transfer static (nonmoving) pictures.

A great deal of research and planning has gone into combining television and computers. The combined device has a CPU, television-as-monitor, keyboard, joystick, mouse, modem, and CUCME/quick-cam. Something like the multiple communications device that science fiction used to envision, this combined medium allows banking, work, entertainment, and communication to happen all through one piece of machinery—and all in the comfort of your home. Another combined technology is a printer that functions as a copier, fax machine, and scanner.

Trends

There are many trends that drive the computer industry. One trend is for larger and faster hard drives. Forty- and 80-gigabyte hard drives have virtually replaced the 540MB drives, and 200GB drives are becoming common. RAM today is increasing exponentially. The trend is to sell RAM in units of 32 or 64 megabytes to meet the needs of 128, 256, and larger blocks of RAM. All of these size increases are due to the expanding memory requirements of GUIs and new peripherals, such as CUCME devices and interfaces with other devices. Although the capacities are increasing, the actual size of the machine is decreasing. Technology is allowing more powerful components to fit into smaller devices—just as the 3½-inch floppy disk is smaller and holds more data than the obsolete 5¼-inch floppy.

Another trend is the increased use of computers for personal use in homes. This trend is likely to continue in the future—especially as the technologies of the PC and standard home electronics such as the television are combined.

Home Offices. More and more frequently, people are working out of their homes—whether they are employees who are linked to a place of business or individuals running their own businesses. Many companies allow workers to have a computer at home that is linked by modem to the office. Work is done at home and transferred to the office. Communication is by e-mail and telephone. Such an arrangement saves companies workspace and, thus, money. Other employees use laptop computers to work both at home and on the road as they travel. A laptop computer, in combination with a modem, allows an employee to work from virtually anywhere and still keep in constant contact with her or his employer and customers.

With downsizing (the reduction of the workforce by companies), many individuals have found themselves unemployed or underemployed (working less or for less money). These people have, in increasing numbers, begun their own businesses out of their homes. With a computer, modem, fax software, printer, and other peripherals, they can contract with many businesses or sell their own products or services. Many make use of the Internet and World Wide Web to advertise their services.

Home Use. As the economy has tightened, many people are trying to make their lives more time- and cost-efficient. The computer is one help in that quest. Maintaining accounting records, managing household accounts and information, and using electronic banking on a computer saves time. Games and other computer interactions also offer a more reasonable way of spending leisure dollars than some outside entertainment. For instance, it might not be feasible to travel to Paris to see paintings in the Louvre Museum; however, it might be affordable to buy a CD-ROM that lets you take a tour of that famous facility from the comfort of the chair in front of your computer. This can be quite an educational experience for children and a more restful one for those who might tire on a trip of that magnitude but who can easily turn off the computer and come back to it later. Young people can benefit enormously from this kind of education as well as using the computer to complete homework, do word processing, create art and graphics, and, of course, play games that sharpen their hand-to-eye coordination and thinking skills.

Concepts for Microsoft Office Programs

Introduction

Microsoft Office is an integrated software package. An ***integrated software package*** combines several computer programs. Office consists of a word-processing program (Word), a spreadsheet program (Excel), a database program (Access), a presentation program (PowerPoint), a schedule/organization program (Outlook), and a desktop-publishing program (Publisher).

The word-processing program (Word) enables you to create documents such as letters and reports. The spreadsheet program (Excel) lets you work with numbers to prepare items such as budgets or to determine loan payments. The database program (Access) organizes information such as addresses or inventory items. The presentation program (PowerPoint) is used to create slides, outlines, speaker's notes, and audience handouts. The schedule/organization program (Outlook) increases your efficiency by keeping track of e-mail, appointments, tasks, contacts, events, and to-do lists. The desktop publishing program (Publisher) helps you design professional-looking documents.

Because Office is an integrated package, the programs can be used together. For example, numbers from a spreadsheet can be included in a letter created in the word processor or in a presentation.

Read below for more information on each Office program.

Word

Word is the word-processing application of the Office programs. In today's busy world, it is necessary to prepare and send many types of documents. Word processing is the use of a computer and software to produce professional-looking documents, such as memos and letters (see Figure C-1). You can also create documents that are more complex, such as newsletters with graphics, and documents that can be published as Web pages.

FIGURE C-1
Business letter in Word

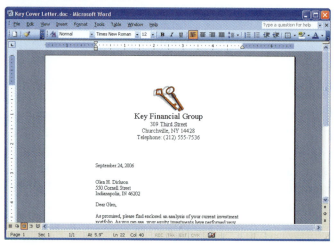

Keying text in Word is easy because it automatically moves, or wraps, text to the next line. After you key your text, you may want to edit it. Use the Spelling and Grammar checker to identify spelling and grammar errors. Correct the errors using the Backspace and Delete keys to delete text, and Overtype to type over text. Cut, Copy, and Paste commands allow you to move and copy data. Word also has an Undo command that reverses your last action.

Word has many automated features that help you create and edit documents. AutoCorrect corrects errors as you enter text; AutoFormat As You Type applies built-in formats as you key; AutoComplete suggests the entire word after you key the first few letters; and AutoText inserts frequently used text.

Word allows you to easily format a document to make it readable and attractive. Formatting includes making decisions about margins, tabs, headings, indents, text alignment, fonts, colors, styles, headers and footers. Word allows you to be creative because you can try new formats and change formats in seconds.

You can also enhance documents by adding graphics or pictures that help illustrate the meaning of the text and make the page more attractive. Word provides pictures called clip art, as well as predefined shapes, diagrams, and charts. Drawing tools permit you to create your own graphics.

Excel

Excel is the spreadsheet application of the Office programs. A *spreadsheet* is a grid of rows and columns containing numbers, text, and formulas. The purpose of a spreadsheet is to solve problems that involve numbers. Without a computer, you might try to solve this type of problem by creating rows and columns on ruled paper and using a calculator to determine results. Computer spreadsheets also contain rows and columns (see Figure C-2), but they perform calculations much faster and more accurately than spreadsheets created with pencil, paper, and calculator.

FIGURE C-2
Spreadsheet in Excel

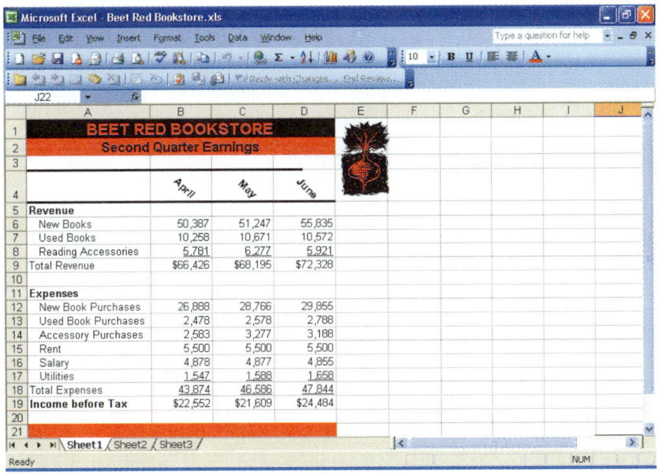

Spreadsheets are used in many ways. For example, a spreadsheet can be used to calculate a grade in a class, to prepare a budget for the next few months, or to determine payments to be made on a loan. The primary advantage of spreadsheets is the ability to complete complex and repetitious calculations accurately, quickly, and easily. For example, you might use a spreadsheet to calculate your monthly income and expenses.

Besides calculating rapidly and accurately, spreadsheets are flexible. Making changes to an existing spreadsheet is usually as easy as pointing and clicking with the mouse. Suppose, for example, you have prepared a budget on a spreadsheet and have overestimated the amount of money you will need to spend on gas and electric and other utilities. You may change a single entry in your spreadsheet and watch the entire spreadsheet recalculate the new budgeted amount. You can imagine the work this change would require if you were calculating the budget with pencil and paper.

Excel uses the term *worksheet* to refer to computerized spreadsheets. Sometimes you may want to use several worksheets that relate to each other. A collection of related worksheets is a *workbook*.

Access

Access is a program known as a *database management system*. A computerized database management system allows you to store, retrieve, analyze, and print information. You do not, however, need a computer to have a database management system. A set of file folders can be a database management system. There are distinct advantages, however, to using a computerized database management system.

A computerized database management system (DBMS) is much faster, more flexible, and more accurate than using file folders. A computerized DBMS is also more efficient and cost-effective. A program such as Access can store thousands of pieces of data in a computer or on a disk. The data can be quickly searched and sorted to save time otherwise spent digging through file folders. For example, a database created in Access could find all the people with a certain ZIP code faster and more accurately than you could by searching through a large list or through folders.

A database is made up of many small sets of data called *records*. For example, in an Employee database, all the information about an employee is a record (see Figure C-3). Information in a record can include the employee's number, name, social security number, address, birth date, department, and title. In a database, these categories of information are called *fields*. In Access, data is organized into a *table*. Tables store data in a format similar to a spreadsheet. In a table, records appear as rows of data and fields appear as columns.

FIGURE C-3
Employee database in Access

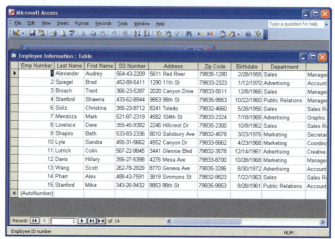

PowerPoint

PowerPoint is a program that is helpful in creating presentations in a variety of ways. Presentations can be created using slides, outlines, speaker's notes, and handouts (see Figure C-4). A PowerPoint presentation can include text, clip art, pictures, video, sound, tables, and charts. PowerPoint allows you to apply design templates, customize animations, and insert hyperlinks into a presentation. Slide transitions can be added to further customize a presentation. Other Office programs can be used in conjunction with PowerPoint. Word outlines, charts, and tables can all be incorporated into PowerPoint presentations. Excel charts can be imported into a presentation, and presentations can be saved as Web pages and published on the Web. After you complete a presentation, you can rehearse your timing and delivery using the rehearsal functions. PowerPoint presentations are usually viewed using a projector on a screen, but you can also use a television monitor or an additional monitor connected to your computer.

FIGURE C-4
Presentation in PowerPoint

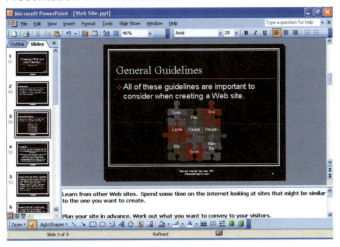

Outlook

Outlook is a desktop information manager that helps you organize information, communicate with people, and manage time. It is easy to use and can quickly summarize your day's activities from Calendar, Tasks, and the Inbox (see Figure C-5). Various features of Outlook allow you to send and receive e-mail messages, schedule events and meetings, record information about business and personal contacts, make to-do lists, record your work, and create reminders. Outlook organizes all this information into categories for viewing and printing. For example, you might group all the information on your important customers into the *Key Customer* category. You can also create a new category for specific groups, such as a *Texas Customers* category, for information on your customers located in Texas.

FIGURE C-5
Outlook Today screen in Outlook

Because Outlook is integrated, you can use it easily with all other Office programs. For example, you can send and receive e-mail messages in Outlook and you can move a name and address from a Word document into your Outlook Contacts List. Outlook has many useful tools and features.

Publisher

Publisher is a desktop publishing program that you can use to create a wide assortment of documents, such as business cards, calendars, personalized stationery, and menus (see Figure C-6). Publisher contains hundreds of predesigned templates you can use as the basis for projects. Personal information sets can be used to store information about your business, organization, or family. Customizations such as logos can be added to an entire series of documents by using the By Design Set option included in the program. All you have to do is add your own custom touches to create professional-looking publications.

FIGURE C-6
Business card in Publisher

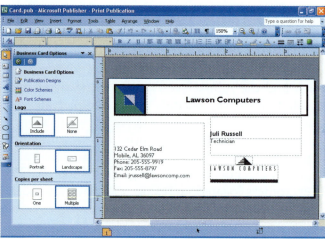

THE MICROSOFT® OFFICE SPECIALIST PROGRAM

What Is Certification?

The logo on the cover of this book indicates that the book is officially certified by Microsoft Corporation at the specialist user skill level for Office 2003 in Word, Excel, Access, and PowerPoint. This certification is part of the Microsoft Office Specialist program that validates your skills in Microsoft Office.

The following grids outline the various skills and where they are covered in this book.

Microsoft Access 2003 Specialist

	SKILL SET AND SKILLS BEING MEASURED	LESSON#	PAGE#(S)	EXERCISE #
AC03S-1	**Structuring Databases**			
AC03S-1-1	Create Access databases	1 1	10	ExtraChallenge (SBS1.4), SBS1.4
AC03S-1-2	Create and modify tables	1	12, 14, 17, 24, 25, 26, 27	Hot Tip (SBS1.5), SBS1.5, SBS1.6, SBS1.8, P1-2, P1-3, P1-4, CT1-1
AC03S-1-3	Define and modify field types	1, 2	14, 39, 43	SBS1.6, SBS2.9, P2-3
AC03S-1-4	Modify field properties	2	39, 42, 43	SBS2.9, P2-1, P2-3
AC03S-1-5	Create and modify one-to-many relationships	4	80	SBS4.10
AC03S-1-6	Enforce referential integrity	4	80	SBS4.10
AC03S-1-7	Create and modify queries	4	70, 72, 89, 90, 91	SBS4.3, SBS4.4, P4-1, P4-4, CT4-3, CT4-4,CT4-5

	SKILL SET AND SKILLS BEING MEASURED	LESSON#	PAGE#(S)	EXERCISE #
AC03S-1-8	Create forms	3	46, 47, 49, 51, 63, 64	SBS3.1, SBS3.2, SBS3.3, SBS3.4, SBS3.5, P3-1, P3-3, CT3-1
AC03S-1-9	Add and modify form controls and properties	3	54, 59, 63	SBS3.7, SBS3.8, P3-2
AC03S-1-10	Create reports	5	94, 95, 99, 97, 98, 101, 112, 113, 114	SBS5.1, SBS5.2, SBS5.3, SBS5.4, SBS5.5, SBS5.6, P5-1, P5-2, CT5-1
AC03S-1-11	Add and modify report control properties	5	103	SBS5.7
AC03S-1-12	Create a data access page	6	126, 134	SBS6.5, P6-4
AC03S-2	**Entering Data**			
AC03S-2-1	Enter, edit, and delete records	1, 2	18, 23, 24, 30, 32,33, 43, 44	SBS1.9, P1-1, P1-2, P1-4, SBS2.1, SBS2.3, SBS2.4, P2-3, CT2-1
AC03S-2-2	Find and move among fields	1, 2	18, 30	SBS1.9, SBS2.1
AC03S-2-3	Import data to Access	6	116	SBS6.1
AC03S-3	**Organizing Data**			
AC03S-3-1	Create and modify calculated fields and aggregate functions	4	70, 84	SBS4.3, SBS4.13
AC03S-3-2	Modify form layout	3	54, 63	SBS3.7, P3-2
AC03S-3-3	Modify report layout and page setup	5	99, 103	SBS5.5, Hot Tip (SBS5.7), SBS5.7
AC03S-3-4	Format datasheets	2	34, 35, 36, 42, 43	SBS2.5, SBS2.6, SBS2.7, SBS2.8, P2-1, P2-2, P2-3
AC03S-3-5	Sort records	3, 4, 5	59, 63, 70, 82, 84, 90, 76, 77, 89, 97	SBS3.8, P3-3, SBS4.3, SBS4.12, SBS4.13, P4-4, SBS4.6, SBS4.7, SBS4.8, P4-2, SBS5.3
AC03S-3-6	Filter records	4	74, 89	SBS4.5, P4-2, P4-3
AC03S-4	**Managing Databases**			
AC03S-4-1	Identify object dependencies	4	86	Did You Know? (SBS4.13)

	SKILL SET AND SKILLS BEING MEASURED	LESSON#	PAGE#(S)	EXERCISE #
AC03S-4-2	View objects and object data in other views	1, 3, 5, 6	20, 53, 101, 18, 114, 129	Hot Tip (SBS1.10), Hot Tip (SBS3.6), SBS5.6, SBS1.9, CT5-3, Did You Know? (SBS6.5)
AC03S-4-3	Print database objects and data	1, 3, 5, 6	21, 53, 101, 126	SBS1.10, SBS3.6, SBS5.6, SBS6.5
AC03S-4-4	Export data from Access	6	120, 123, 124, 132, 133, 135	SBS6.2, SBS6.3, SBS6.4, P6-1, P6-2, P6-3, CT6-1
AC03S-4-5	Back up a database	6	118	Hot Tip (SBS6.1)
AC03S-4-6	Compact and repair databases	2, 3	33, 60	Did You Know? (SBS2.4), SBS3.9

Key: SBS = Step-by-Step   CT = Critical Thinking Activity   P = Project

Microsoft Excel 2003 Specialist

	SKILL SET AND SKILLS BEING MEASURED	LESSON#	PAGE#(S)	EXERCISE #
XL03S-1	**Creating Data and Content**			
XL03S-1-1	Enter and edit cell content	1, 3	9, 11, 18, 19, 47	SBS1.5, SBS1.6, P1-2, P1-3, P1-4, SBS3.3
XL03S-1-2	Navigate to specific cell content	1, 2	13, 19, 36, 8	SBS1.7, P1-4, SBS2.11, SBS1.3
XL03S-1-3	Locate, select, and insert supporting information	6	130	SBS6.10
XL03S-1-4	Insert, position, and size graphics	6	114, 116, 120, 123, 139, 140	SBS6.4, SBS6.5, SBS6.6, SBS6.7, P6-6, CT6-2
XL03S-2	**Analyzing Data**			
XL03S-2-1	Filter lists using AutoFilter	6	113, 137	SBS6.2, P6-3
XL03S-2-2	Sort lists	6	110, 136	SBS6.1, P6-1, P6-2
XL03S-2-3	Insert and modify formulas	4	68, 69, 70, 72, 73, 75, 76, 78, 81, 82, 84, 85	SBS4.1, SBS4.2, SBS4.3, SBS4.4, SBS4.5, SBS4.6, SBS4.7, SBS4.8, P4-2, P4-3, P4-4, P4-5, CT4-1, CT4-2

	SKILL SET AND SKILLS BEING MEASURED	LESSON#	PAGE#(S)	EXERCISE #
XL03S-2-4	Use statistical, date and time, financial, and logical functions	5	90, 92, 94, 97, 99, 102, 103, 105	SBS5.1, SBS5.2, SBS5.3, SBS5.4, SBS5.5, P5-2, P5-3, P5-4, P5-5, P5-6
XL03S-2-5	Create, modify, and position diagrams and charts based on worksheet data	8	161, 164, 165, 166, 168, 169, 173, 174, 176, 177, 178, 180	SBS8.1, SBS8.2, SBS8.3, SBS8.4, SBS8.5, SBS8.6, SBS8.7, SBS8.8, SBS8.9, SBS8.10, P8-1, P8-2, P8-3, P8-4, P8-5, P8-6, P8-8, CT8-1
XL03S-3	**Formatting Data and Content**			
XL03S-3-1	Apply and modify cell formats	2	28, 30, 31, 33, 35, 39, 40, 41	SBS2.6, SBS2.7, SBS2.8, SBS2.9, SBS2.10, P2-2, P2-3, P2-4, P2-5
XL03S-3-2	Apply and modify cell styles	2	33	SBS2.9
XL03S-3-3	Modify row and column formats	2, 3, 6	22, 25, 26, 33, 39, 40, 41, 42, 51, 62, 63, 65, 137, 138, 27, 41	SBS2.1, SBS2.3, SBS2.4, SBS2.9, P2-2, P2-3, P2-5, P2-6, SBS6.3, SBS3.5, P3-2, P3-4, P3-5, P3-7, P6-2, P6-3, P6-4, SBS2.5, P2-4
XL03S-3-4	Format worksheets	7	142, 152, 153, 154	SBS7.1, P7-1, P7-2, P7-3, P 7-4
XL03S-4	**Collaborating**			
XL03S-4-1	Insert, view, and edit comments	6	133, 140	SBS6.11, P6-7
XL03S-5	**Managing Workbooks**			
XL03S-5-1	Create new workbooks from templates	6	126, 138, 140	SBS6.8, P6-5, CT6-1
XL03S-5-2	Insert, delete, and move cells	3	51, 62, 65, 49, 62, 44, 45, 47, 49	SBS3.5, P3-2, P3-5, P3-7, SBS3.4, P3-4, SBS3.1, SBS3.2, SBS3.3, SBS3.4
XL03S-5-3	Create and modify hyperlinks	6	128	SBS6.9
XL03S-5-4	Organize worksheets	7	144, 152, 153, 154	SBS7.2, P7-1, P7-2, P7-3, P7-4
XL03S-5-5	Preview data in other views	3, 6	130, 56, 58	SBS6.10, SBS3.7, SBS3.8

	SKILL SET AND SKILLS BEING MEASURED	LESSON#	PAGE#(S)	EXERCISE #
XL03S-5-6	Customize Window layout	3, 7	53, 62, 144	SBS3.6, P3-3, P3-3, SBS7.2
XL03S-5-7	Set up pages for printing	3, 7	56, 62, 63, 64, 58	SBS3.7, SBS7.4, P3-4, P3-5, P3-6, SBS3.8
XL03S-5-8	Print data	3, 7	58, 148, 152, 153, 154	SBS3.8, SBS7.4, P7-1, P7-2, P7-3, P7-4
XL03S-5-9	Organize workbooks using file folders	1	14	SBS1.8
XL03S-5-10	Save data in appropriate formats for different uses	6	130	SBS6.10

Key: SBS = Step-by-Step   CT = Critical Thinking Activity   P = Project

Microsoft PowerPoint 2003 Specialist

	SKILL SET AND SKILLS BEING MEASURED	LESSON#	PAGE#(S)	EXERCISE #
PP03S-1	**Creating Content**			
PP03S-1-1	Create new presentations from templates	2	23	SBS2.1
PP03S-1-2	Insert and edit text-based content	1, 2, 4	9, 35, 42, 45, 101, 105	SBS1.4, SBS2.7, SBS2.12, SBS2.15, SBS4.1, SBS4.4
PP03S-1-3	Insert tables, charts, and diagrams	3	66, 69, 72	SBS3.3, SBS3.5, SBS3.6
PP03S-1-4	Insert pictures, shapes, and graphics	2, 3	49, 74	SBS2.17, SBS3.7
PP03S-1-5	Insert objects	3, 4	94, 108	SBS3.14, SBS4.5
PP03S-2	**Formatting Content**			
PP03S-2-1	Format text-based content	4	116, 118	SBS4.8, SBS4.9
PP03S-2-2	Format pictures, shapes, and graphics	2, 3	33, 49, 52, 76, 81, 84	SBS2.6, SBS2.17, SBS2.18, SBS3.8, SBS3.10, SBS3.11
PP03S-2-3	Format slides	2, 4	26, 29, 45, 47, 112, 132	SBS2.2, SBS2.4, SBS2.15, SBS2.16, SBS4.7, SBS4.19
PP03S-2-4	Apply animation schemes	2	28	SBS2.3

	SKILL SET AND SKILLS BEING MEASURED	LESSON#	PAGE#(S)	EXERCISE #
PP03S-2-5	Apply slide transitions	2	56	SBS2.21
PP03S-2-6	Customize slide templates	4	112	SBS4.7
PP03S-2-7	Work with masters	2, 3, 4	45, 96, 112	SBS2.15, SBS3.15, SBS4.7
PP03S-3	**Collaborating**			
PP03S-3-1	Track, accept, and reject changes in a presentation	4	131	SBS4.18
PP03S-3-2	Add, edit, and delete comments in a presentation	4	131	SBS4.18
PP03S-3-3	Compare and merge presentations	4	131	SBS4.18
PP03S-4	**Managing and Delivering Presentations**			
PP03S-4-1	Organize a presentation	1, 2, 3, 4	9, 12, 14, 35, 37, 44, 54, 93, 96, 118	SBS1.4, SBS1.7, SBS1.8, SBS2.7, SBS2.8, SBS2.13, SBS2.20 SBS3.13, SBS3.15, SBS4.9
PP03S-4-2	Set up slide shows for delivery	4	120, 122	SBS4.10, SBS4.11
PP03S-4-3	Rehearse timing	4	123	SBS4.12
PP03S-4-4	Deliver presentations	1, 4	7, 120	SBS1.2, SBS4.10
PP03S-4-5	Prepare presentations for remote delivery	4	126, 129	SBS4.14, SBS4.16
PP03S-4-6	Save and publish presentations	4	126, 128	SBS4.14, SBS4.15
PP03S-4-7	Print slides, outlines, handouts, and speaker notes	1, 2	15, 37	SBS1.9, SBS2.8
PP03S-4-8	Export a presentation to another Microsoft Office program	2	56	SBS2.22

Key: SBS = Step-by-Step   CT = Critical Thinking Activity   P = Project

Microsoft Word 2003 Specialist

	SKILL SET AND SKILLS BEING MEASURED	LESSON#	PAGE#(S)	EXERCISE #
WW03S-1	**Creating Content**			
WW03S-1-1	Insert and edit text, symbols, and special characters	1, 2, 3	6, 8, 26, 29, 30, 25, 37, 48, 50, 53, 55, 56, 58, 59	SBS1.2, P1-3, SBS2.2, SBS2.4, SBS2.5, Hot Tip (SBS 2.1), P2-1, P2-2, SBS3.5, SBS3.6, SBS3.7, SBS 3.9, Hot Tip (SBS 3.9), P3-1, P3-2, P3-3, P3-4
WW03S-1-2	Insert frequently used and predefined text	3	43, 46, 54, 58, 59	SBS3.1, SBS3.3, SBS3.8, P3-1, P3-2, P3-4
WW03S-1-3	Navigate to specific content	2	32, 33, 37, 38, 39, 33	SBS2.6, SBS2.7, P2-2, P2-3, P2-5, Hot Tip (SBS2.7),
WW03S-1-4	Insert position and size graphics	6	109, 111, 115, 116, 119, 125, 126, 127, 129	SBS6.3, SBS6.4, SBS6.7, SBS6.8, SBS6.10, P6-1, P6-2, P6-3, P6-4, P6-5
WW03S-1-5	Create and modify diagrams and charts	6	120, 122, 123, 127	SBS6.11, SBS6.12, SBS6.13, P6-4
WW03S-1-6	Locate and insert supporting information	7	139, 150	SBS7.5, P7-1
WW03S-2-1	Insert and modify tables	7	142, 143, 145, 147, 150, 151	SBS7.7, SBS7.8, SBS 7.9, SBS7.10, SBS7.11, P7-2, P7-3, P7-4
WW03S-2-2	Create bulleted lists, numbered lists, and outlines	5	88, 90, 91, 92, 93, 96, 98, 100	SBS5.7, SBS5.8, SBS5.9, SBS5.10, SBS5.11, P5-1, P5-4, P5-6
WW03S-2-3	Insert and modify hyperlinks	8	172, 174, 175, 179	SBS8.14, SBS8.16, Hot Tip (SBS8.16), P8-5
WW03S-3	**Formatting Content**			
WW03S-3-1	Format text	4	64, 65, 66, 68, 69, 71, 74, 75	SBS4.1, SBS4.2, SBS4.3, SBS4.4, SBS4.5, SBS4.7, P4-1, P4-2, P4-3, P4-4, P4-5

	SKILL SET AND SKILLS BEING MEASURED	LESSON#	PAGE#(S)	EXERCISE #
WW03S-3-2	Format paragraphs	5, 6	80, 82, 83, 86, 96, 98, 107,125	SBS5.2, SBS5.3, SBS5.4, SBS5.6, P5-1, P5-2, P5-4, P5-5, SBS6.2, P6-1
WW03S-3-3	Apply and format columns	6	105, 125	SBS6.1, P6-1
WW03S-3-4	Insert and modify content in headersand footers	7	134, 150	SBS7.2, P7-1
WW03S-3-5	Modify document layout and page setup	1, 5, 7	14, 19, 20, 78, 80, 86, 133, 150	SBS1.7, P1-2, P1-4, SBS5.1, P5-2, P5-6, SBS7.1, P7-1
WW03S-4	**Collaborating**			
WW03S-4-1	Circulate documents for review	8	166	SBS8.8, Hot Tip (SBS8.8)
WW03S-4-2	Compare and merge document versions	8	171	SBS8.13
WW03S-4-3	Insert, view, and edit comments	8	167, 168, 178	SBS8.9, SBS8.10, P8-3
WW03S-4-4	Track, accept, and reject proposed changes	8	169, 170 179	SBS8.11, SBS8.12, P8-4
WW03S-5	**Formatting and Managing Documents**			
WW03S-5-1	Create new documents using templates	8	155, 157, 177	SBS8.1, SBS8.2, SBS8.3, P8-1
WW03S-5-2	Review and modify document properties	2, 7	34, 38, 141	SBS2.8, P2-3, SBS7.6
WW03S-5-3	Organize documents using file folders	1	9	SBS1.4
WW03S-5-4	Save documents in appropriate formats for different uses	8	156, 174, 179	Hot Tip (SBS8.2), SBS8.15, P8-5
WW03S-5-5	Print documents, envelopes, and labels	1, 8	15, 19, 164, 165 178	SBS1.8, P1-2, SBS8.6, SBS8.7, P8-2
WW03S-5-6	Preview documents and Web pages	1, 8	14, 19, 20, 174, 179	SBS1.7, P1-2, P1-4, SBS8.15, P8-5
WW03S-5-7	Change and organize document views and windows	1, 2, 7	6, 11, 19, 20, 25, 136	SBS1.2, SBS1.6, P1-3, P1-4, P1-5, SBS2.1, SBS7.3

Key: SBS = Step-by-Step   CT = Critical Thinking Activity   P = Project

APPENDIX E

KEYBOARDING TOUCH SYSTEM IMPROVEMENT

Introduction

Your Goal – Improve your keyboarding skill using the touch system.

Why Improve Your Keyboarding Skills?

- To key faster and more accurately every time you use the computer for the rest of your life.

- To increase your enjoyment while using the computer.

Getting Ready to Build Skills

Get ready by:

1. a. Clearing your desk of everything except your book and a pencil or pen.

    b. Positioning your keyboard and book so that you are comfortable and able to move your hands and fingers freely.

    c. Keeping your feet flat on the floor, sitting with your back erect.

2. Taking a two-minute timed writing, page 14, now according to your teacher's directions.

3. Calculating your Words A Minute (WAM) and Errors A Minute (EAM) using the instructions on the timed writing progress chart, page 15. This will be your base score to compare to future timed writings.

4. On the Base Score line (page 15), recording the Date, WAM, and EAM.

5. Repeating the timed writing as many times as you can.

6. Recording each attempt on the Introduction line of the chart.

> **Hot Tip**
>
> You will key faster and more accurately when using the touch system instead of looking from the copy and then to the keyboard and striking keys with one or two fingers—the "hunt and peck" system.

Skill Builder 1

Your Goal – Use the touch system to key j u y h n m spacebar.

What To Do

1. Place your fingers on the home row as shown in Figure E-1.

FIGURE E-1
Place your fingers on the home row

2. Look at Figure E-2. Notice how later (in step 3) you will strike the letters j u y h n m in a counterclockwise (↺) direction. You will strike the spacebar with your right thumb.

FIGURE E-2
Strike all of these keys with your right index finger—the home finger j

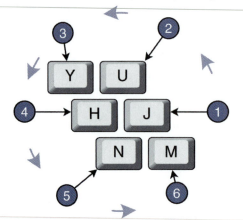

3. Look at your keyboard. Softly say the letters as you strike each key three times (3X), counterclockwise from 1 to 6 with a blank space in between. After striking each letter in the circle, strike j, called the home key, 3X as shown. Don't worry about errors. Start keying:

jjj uuu jjj yyy jjj **hhh** jjj nnn jjj mmm

jjj uuu jjj yyy jjj **hhh** jjj nnn jjj mmm jjj

4. Repeat the same drill as many times as it takes to reach your comfort level.

jjj uuu jjj yyy jjj **hhh** jjj nnn jjj mmm

jjj uuu jjj yyy jjj **hhh** jjj nnn jjj mmm jjj

5. Close your eyes and visualize each key under each finger as you repeat the drill in step 4.

6. Look at the following two lines and key:

jjj jjj jjj juj juj juj jyj jyj jyj jhj jhj jhj jnj jnj jnj jmj jmj jmj

jjj jjj jjj juj juj juj jyj jyj jyj jhj jhj jhj jnj jnj jnj jmj jmj jmj

7. Repeat step 4, this time concentrating on a rhythmic, bouncy stroking of the keys.

8. Close your eyes and visualize the keys under your fingers as you key the drill in step 4 from memory.

9. Look at the following two lines and key these groups of letters:

j ju juj j jy jyj j jh jhj j jn jnj j jm jmj j ju juj j jy jyj j jh jhj j jn jnj j jm jmj

jjj ju jhj jn jm ju jm jh jnj jm ju jmj jy ju jh j u ju juj jy jh jnj ju jm jmj jy

10. You may want to repeat Skill Builder 1, striving to improve keying letters that are most difficult for you.

Hot Tip

- Ignore errors. You will always key text that is bold and is not italicized.
- If you have difficulty reaching for any key, for example the y key, practice by looking at the reach your fingers make from the j key to the y key until the reach is visualized in your mind. The reach will become natural with very little practice.
- You may want to start on a clean line by striking the Enter key.

Skill Builder 2

Your Goal - Use the touch system to key f r t g b v .

What To Do

1. Place your fingers on the home row as you did in Skill Builder 1, Figure E-1.

2. Look at Figure E-3. Notice how (later in step 3) you will strike the letters f r t g b v in a clockwise (◯) direction. Strike the spacebar with your right thumb.

Computer Concepts

Always return your f finger to the home row after striking keys with a quick, sharp stroke.

Teamwork

If possible, ask a student next to you to call out the letters, so low that only you can hear, as you key them with your eyes closed (for example, f g t b v r). You can then call out the letters to your partner. Make suggestions for each other on how to improve using the Keyboarding Technique Checklist on page 16.

FIGURE E-3
Strike all of these keys with your left index finger—the home finger f

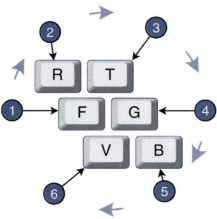

3. Look at your keyboard. Softly say the letters as you strike the keys 3X each, clockwise from 1 to 6, with a blank space in between. After striking each letter in the circle, strike the home key f 3X as shown. Don't worry about errors. Ignore them.

   fff rrr fff ttt fff ggg fff bbb fff vvv

   fff rrr fff ttt fff ggg fff bbb fff vvv fff

4. Repeat the same drill two more times using a quicker, sharper stroke.

   fff rrr fff ttt fff ggg fff bbb fff vvv

   fff rrr fff ttt fff ggg fff bbb fff vvv fff

5. Close your eyes and visualize each key under each finger as you repeat the drill in step 4.

6. Look at the following two lines and key these groups of letters:

   fff fff fff frf frf frf ftf ftf ftf fgf fgf fgf fbf fbf fbf fvf fvf fvf

   fff fff fff frf frf frf ftf ftf ftf fgf fgf fgf fbf fbf fbf fvf fvf fvf

7. Repeat step 6, this time concentrating on a rhythmic, "bouncy" stroking of the keys.

8. Close your eyes and visualize the keys under your fingers as you key the drill in step 4 from memory.

9. Look at the following two lines and key these groups of letters:

   fr frf ft ftf fg fgf fb fbf fv fvf

   ft fgf fv frf ft fbf fv frf ft fgf

10. You are about to key your first words. Look at the following lines and key these groups of letters:

    jjj juj jug jug jug rrr rur rug rug rug

    ttt tut tug tug tug rrr rur rub rub rub

    ggg gug gum gum gum mmm mum

    mug mug mug hhh huh hum hum hum

11. Complete the Keyboarding Technique Checklist, page 16.

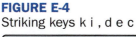

Skill Builder 3

Your Goal – Use the touch system to key k i , d e c.

Keys k i ,

What To Do

<table>
<tr><td>

Teamwork

- Ask your classmate to call out the letters in random order as you key them with your eyes closed. For example: k i , d e c. Do the same for your classmate.
- Ask your classmate or your teacher to complete the Keyboarding Technique Checklist.

</td></tr>
</table>

1. Place your fingers on the home row, as shown in Figure E-4.

FIGURE E-4
Striking keys k i , d e c

2. Look at your keyboard and locate these keys: k i ,

3. Look at your keyboard as much as you need to. Softly say the letters as you strike each key 3X as shown, with a space between each set of letters.

    kkk iii kkk ,,, kkk iii kkk ,,, kkk iii kkk ,,, kkk iii kkk ,,, kkk iii kkk ,,, kkk

4. Look at the line in step 3 and repeat the drill two more times using a quicker, sharper stroke.

5. Close your eyes and repeat the drill in step 3 as you visualize each key under each finger.

6. Repeat step 5, concentrating on a rhythmic, bouncy stroking of the keys.

Keys d e c

1. Place your fingers on the home row.

2. Look at your keyboard and locate these keys: d e c

3. Look at your keyboard. Softly say the letters as you strike each key 3X as shown, with a space between each set of letters.

   ddd eee ddd ccc ddd eee ddd ccc ddd eee ddd ccc ddd eee ddd ccc ddd

4. Look at the line in step 3 and repeat the drill two more times using a quicker, sharper stroke.

5. Close your eyes and repeat the drill in step 3 as you visualize each key under each finger.

6. Repeat step 5, concentrating on a rhythmic, bouncy stroking of the keys.

7. Look at the following lines and key these groups of letters and words:

   fff fuf fun fun fun ddd ded den den den

   ccc cuc cub cub cub vvv vev vet

   fff fuf fun fun fun ddd ded den den den

   ccc cuc cub cub cub vvv vev vet

8. Complete the Keyboarding Technique Checklist, page 16.

Skill Builder 4

Your Goal – Use the touch system to key l o . s w x and the left Shift key.

Keys l o .

What To Do

1. Place your fingers on the home row as shown in Figure E-5.

FIGURE E-5
Striking keys l o . s w x

2. Look at your keyboard and locate the following keys: l o . (period key)

3. Look at your keyboard. Softly say the letters as you strike each key 3X with a space between each set of letters.

   lll ooo lll ... lll ooo lll ... lll ooo lll ... lll ooo lll ... lll ooo lll ... lll ooo lll ... lll

4. Look at the line in step 3 and repeat the drill two more times using a quicker, sharper stroke.

5. Close your eyes and repeat the drill in step 3 as you visualize each key under each finger.

6. Repeat step 5, concentrating on a rhythmic, bouncy stroking of the keys.

Keys s w x

1. Place your fingers on the home row.

2. Look at your keyboard and locate the following keys: s w x

3. Look at your keyboard. Softly say the letters as you strike each key 3X with a space between each set of letters.

   sss www sss xxx sss www sss xxx sss www sss xxx sss www sss xxx sss

4. Look at the line in step 3 and repeat the same drill two more times using a quicker, sharper stroke.

5. Close your eyes and repeat the drill in step 3 as you visualize each key under each finger.

6. Repeat step 5, concentrating on a rhythmic, bouncy stroking of the keys.

Left Shift Key

1. Look at the following two lines and key the line, and then the sentence. Hold down the left Shift key with the little finger of your left hand to make capitals of letters struck by your right hand.

    jjj JJJ jjj JJJ yyy YYY yyy YYY nnn NNN nnn NNN mmm MMM

    Just look in the book. You can key well.

2. Complete the Keyboarding Technique Checklist, page 16.

Skill Builder 5

Your Goal - Use the touch system to key ; p / a q z and the right Shift key.

Keys ; p /

What To Do

1. Place your fingers on the home row as shown in Figure E-6.

FIGURE E-6
Striking keys ; p / a q z

2. Look at your keyboard and locate the following keys: ; p /

3. Look at your keyboard. Softly say the following letters as you strike each key 3X with a space in between:

    ;;; ppp ;;; /// ;;; ppp ;;; /// ;;; ppp ;;; ///

    ;;; ppp ;;; /// ;;; ppp ;;; /// ;;; ppp ;;; /// ;;;

4. Look at the lines in step 3 and repeat the drill two more times using a quicker, sharper stroke.

5. Close your eyes and repeat the drill in step 3 as you visualize each key under each finger.

6. Repeat step 5, concentrating on a rhythmic, bouncy stroking of the keys.

Keys a q z

1. Place your fingers on the home row.

2. Look at your keyboard and locate the following keys: a q z

3. Look at your keyboard. Softly say the following letters as you strike each key 3X with a space in between:

   aaa qqq aaa zzz aaa qqq aaa zzz aaa qqq aaa zzz aaa qqq aaa zzz aaa

4. Look at the line in step 3 and repeat the same drill two more times using a quicker, sharper stroke.

5. Close your eyes and repeat the drill in step 3 as you visualize each key under each finger.

6. Repeat step 5, concentrating on a rhythmic, bouncy stroking of the keys.

Right Shift Key

1. Look at the following lines and key them. Hold down the right Shift key with the little finger of your right hand to make capitals of letters struck by your left hand.

   sss SSS rrr RRR

   Strike the key quickly. Relax when you key.

2. Complete the Keyboarding Technique Checklist, page 16.

Skill Builder 6

Your Goal - Use the touch system to key all letters of the alphabet.

What To Do

1. Close your eyes. Do not look at the keyboard and key all letters of the alphabet as shown:

   aaa bbb ccc ddd eee fff ggg hhh iii jjj

   kkk lll mmm nnn ooo ppp qqq rrr sss

   ttt uuu vvv www xxx yyy zzz

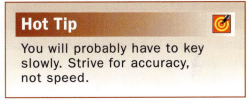

Hot Tip

You will probably have to key slowly. Strive for accuracy, not speed.

2. Repeat step 1, striking keys with a rhythmic, bouncy touch.

3. Repeat step 1, but faster than you did for step 2.

4. Key the following:

   aa bb cc dd ee ff gg hh ii jj kk ll mm nn oo pp qq rr ss tt uu vv ww xx yy zz

   a b c d e f g h i j k l m n o p q r s t u v w x y z

5. Keep your eyes on the following copy. Do not look at the keyboard and key all letters of the alphabet three times each backwards:

   zzz yyy xxx www vvv uuu ttt sss rrr

   qqq ppp ooo nnn mmm lll kkk jjj iii

   hhh ggg fff eee ddd ccc bbb aaa

6. Repeat step 5, but faster than the last time.

7. Key each letter of the alphabet once backwards:

   z y x w v u t s r q p o n m l k j i h g f e d c b a

8. Think about the letters that took you the most amount of time to locate. Go back to the Skill Builder for those letters, and repeat those drills until you are confident about their locations. For example, if you have difficulty with the c key, practice Skill Builder 3 again.

Timed Writing

Prepare to take the timed writing, page 14, according to your teacher's directions.

1. Get ready by:

   a. Clearing your desk of everything except your book and a pencil or pen.

   b. Positioning your keyboard and book so that you are comfortable and able to move your hands and fingers freely.

   c. Keeping your feet flat on the floor, sitting with your back erect.

2. Take a two-minute timed writing, page 14, now according to your teacher's directions.

3. Calculate your Words A Minute (WAM) and Errors A Minute (EAM) scores using the instructions on the timed writing progress chart, page 15.

4. Record the date, WAM, and EAM on the Skill Builder 6 line.

5. Repeat the timed writing as many times as you can and record each attempt.

Skill Builder 7

Your Goal – Improve your keying techniques—which is the secret for improving your speed and accuracy.

What To Do

1. Rate yourself for each item on the Keyboarding Technique Checklist, page 16.

2. Do not time yourself as you concentrate on a single technique you marked with a "0." Key only the first paragraph of the timed writing.

> **Teamwork**
>
> You may want to ask a classmate or your teacher to record your scores.

3. Repeat step 2 as many times as possible for each of the items marked with an "0" that need improvement.

4. Take a two-minute timed writing. Record your WAM and EAM on the timed writing progress chart as 1st Attempt on the Skill Builder 7 line. Compare this score with your base score.

5. Look only at the book and using your best techniques, key the following technique sentence for one minute:

       .   2   .   4   .   6   .   8   .   10   .   2   .   14   .   16

    Now is the time for all loyal men and women to come to the aid of their country.

6. Record your WAM and EAM on the 7 Technique Sentence line.

7. Repeat steps 5 and 6 as many times as you can and record your scores.

Skill Builder 8

Your Goal – Increase your words a minute.

What To Do

1. Take a two-minute timed writing.

2. Record your WAM and EAM scores as the 1st Attempt on page 16.

3. Key only the first paragraph only one time as fast as you can. Ignore errors.

4. Key only the first and second paragraphs only one time as fast as you can. Ignore errors.

> **Hot Tip**
>
> You can now key letters in the speed line very well and with confidence. Practicing all of the other letters of the alphabet will further increase your skill and confidence in keyboarding.

5. Take a two-minute timed writing again. Ignore errors.

6. Record only your WAM score as the 2nd Attempt on page 15. Compare only this WAM with your 1st Attempt WAM and your base score WAM.

Get Your Best WAM

1. To get your best WAM on easy text for 15 seconds, key the following speed line as fast as you can, as many times as you can. Ignore errors.

       .   2   .   4   .   6   .   8   .   10

    Now is the time, now is the time, now is the time,

2. Multiply the number of words keyed by four to get your WAM (15 seconds × 4 = 1 minute). For example, if you keyed 12 words for 15 seconds, 12 × 4 = 48 WAM.

3. Record only your WAM in the 8 Speed Line box.

4. Repeat steps 1-3 as many times as you can to get your very best WAM. Ignore errors.

5. Record only your WAM for each attempt.

Skill Builder 9

Your Goal – Decrease errors a minute.

What To Do

1. Take a two-minute timed writing.

2. Record your WAM and EAM as the 1st Attempt on page 15.

3. Key only the first paragraph only one time at a controlled rate of speed so you reduce errors. Ignore speed.

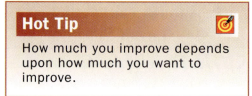

Hot Tip

How much you improve depends upon how much you want to improve.

4. Key only the first and second paragraphs only one time at a controlled rate of speed so you reduce errors. Ignore speed.

5. Take a two-minute timed writing again. Ignore speed.

6. Record only your EAM score as the 2nd Attempt on page 15. Compare only the EAM with your 1st Attempt EAM and your base score EAM.

Get Your Best EAM

1. To get your best EAM, key the following accuracy sentence (same as the technique sentence) for one minute. Ignore speed.

   Now is the time for all loyal men and women to come to the aid of their country.

2. Record only your EAM score on the Accuracy Sentence 9 line.

3. Repeat step 1 as many times as you can to get your best EAM. Ignore speed.

4. Record only your EAM score for each attempt.

Skill Builder 10

Your Goal – Use the touch system and your best techniques to key faster and more accurately than you have ever keyed before.

What To Do

1. Take a one-minute timed writing.

2. Record your WAM and EAM as the 1st Attempt on the Skill Builder 10 line.

3. Repeat the timed writing for two minutes as many times as necessary to get your best ever WAM with no more than one EAM. Record your scores as 2nd, 3rd, and 4th Attempts.

> **Hot Tip**
>
> You may want to get advice regarding which techniques you need to improve from a class-mate or your teacher.

Assessing Your Improvement

1. Circle your best timed writing for Skill Builders 6-10 on the timed writing progress chart.

2. Record your best score and your base score. Compare the two scores. Did you improve?

	WAM	EAM
Best Score	____	____
Base Score	____	____

3. Use the Keyboarding Technique Checklist on page 16 to identify techniques you still need to improve. You may want to practice these techniques now to increase your WAM or decrease your EAM.

Timed Writing

Every five strokes in a timed writing is a word, including punctuation marks and spaces. Use the scale above each line to tell you how many words you keyed.

```
      .       2   .       4   .       6    .
If you learn how to key well now, it
   8    .      10   .      12   .      14   .      16
is a skill that will help you for the rest
      .      18   .      20   .      22   .      24    .
of your life.  How you sit will help you key
 26    .      28   .      30   .      32   .      34    .
with more speed and less errors.  Sit with your
 36    .      38   .      40   .      42   .      44
feet flat on the floor and your back erect.
      .      46   .      48   .      50   .      52
To key fast by touch, try to keep your
      .      54   .      56   .      58   .      60
eyes on the copy and not on your hands or
      .      62   .      64   .      66   .      68   .      70
the screen.  Curve your fingers and make sharp,
      .      72   .
quick strokes.
      74   .      76   .      78   .      80   .
Work for speed first. If you make more
      82   .      84   .      86   .      88   .      90
than two errors a minute, you are keying too
      92   .      94   .      96   .      98   .     100
fast. Slow down to get fewer errors. If you
      .     102   .     104   .     106   .     108
get fewer than two errors a minute, go for
      .     110
speed.
```

Timed Writing Progress Chart

Last Name: _____   *First Name:* _____

Instructions

Calculate your scores as shown in the following sample and footnotes (a) and (b). Repeat timed writings as many times as you can and record your scores for each attempt.

Base Score: Date ____   WAM ____   EAM ____   Time ____

		1st Attempt		2nd Attempt		3rd Attempt		4th Attempt	
Skill Builder	**Date**	**(a) WAM**	**(b) EAM**	**WAM**	**EAM**	**WAM**	**EAM**	**WAM**	**EAM**
Sample	9/2	22	3.5	23	2.0	25	1.0	29	2.0
Introduction									
6									
7									
8					-----				
9				-----					
10									
7 Technique Sentence									
8 Speed Line			-----		-----		-----		-----
9 Accuracy Sentence		-----		-----		-----		-----	

(a) Divide words keyed (44) by 2 (minutes) to get WAM (22)

(b) Divide errors (7) by 2 (minutes) to get EAM (3.5)

Keyboarding Technique Checklist

Last Name: _____   *First Name:* _____

Instructions

1. Write the Skill Builder number, the date, and the initials of the evaluator in the proper spaces.

2. Place a check mark (✓) after a technique that is performed satisfactorily. Place a large zero (0) after a technique that needs improvement.

Technique	Sample										
Skill Builder Number:	Sample										
Date:	9/1										
Evaluator:	SL										
Attitude											
1. Enthusiastic about learning	✓										
2. Optimistic about improving	✓										
3. Alert but relaxed	✓										
4. Sticks to the task; not distracted	✓										
Getting Ready											
1. Desk uncluttered	✓										
2. Properly positions keyboard and book	✓										
3. Feet flat on the floor	✓										
4. Body erect, but relaxed	0										
Keyboarding											
1. Curves fingers	0										
2. Keeps eyes on the book	✓										
3. Taps the keys lightly; does not "pound" them	0										
4. Makes quick, "bouncy," strokes	0										
5. Smooth rhythm	0										
6. Minimum pauses between strokes	✓										

GLOSSARY

A

Action query A query that adds, changes, deletes records in a table or creates a new table from existing table information.

And operator Used to find records that meet more than one criteria.

AND query Lets you find records in a query that meet more than one criteria.

Ascending sort A sort that arranges records from A to Z or smallest to largest.

B

Bound control Control on a database form or report that is connected to a field in a table. Can be used to display, enter, and update data.

C

Calculated control Control on a database form or report that uses an expression to generate the data value for a field.

Channels Means of customizing the information delivered from the Internet to your computer.

Clipboard A temporary storage place in the computer's memory.

Close Removing a document or window from the screen.

Close button "X" on the right side of the title bar that you click to close a window.

Copy A copy of the selected text is placed on the clipboard while the original text remains in the document.

Compacting Removes unwanted excess space from a database file, allowing the database to run efficiently.

Concatenation To combine text from two or more database table fields into one field.

Criteria In Access, information for which you are searching in a table or query. In Excel, information for which you are searching in a data list.

Customize To build according to individual specifications.

Cut Removes selected text from the document and places it on the Clipboard.

D

Data access page An object created in a database that lets you publish to the Web other objects, such as tables, forms, and reports.

Data source A file that contains information that will vary in a form letter.

Database management system Any system for managing data.

Database report A report that allows you to organize, summarize, and print all or a portion of the data in a database.

Datasheet view In a database, a form similar to a spreadsheet that allows records to be entered directly into a table.

Decision structure In Access, a group of statements that must choose from alternate actions.

Default Setting used unless another option is chosen.

Descending sort Sort that arranges records from Z to A or largest to smallest.

Design view Where you design and modify tables in a database.

Desktop Space where you access and work with programs and files.

Detail   Section in a database form or report that displays the records.

Dialog box   A message box that "asks" for further instructions before a command can be performed.

Drop-down menu   A list of commands that appears below each menu name on the menu bar.

E

Encrypt   Scrambles database file codes.

Entry   The data entered into a field.

Exporting (Export)   Placing data from one program into another.

Extensible Markup Language   See *XML*.

F

Field   A category of data that make up records.

Field name   Name that identifies a field in a database table.

Field properties   Specifications that allow you to customize a database table field beyond choosing a data type.

Field selectors   Located at the top of a database table, they contain the field name.

Filter   A method of screening out all database records except those that match your selection criteria. This is a simpler form of a database query that cannot be saved and that displays all fields.

Folder   A place where files and other folders are stored on a disk.

Font size   Determined by measuring the height of characters in units called points.

Font style   Formatting feature that changes the appearance of text such as bold, italic, and underline.

Fonts   Designs of type.

Footer   Text that is printed at the bottom of the page.

Form   A database object that is used primarily to make entering or viewing data in a database more convenient.

Form footer   Section of a database form that displays information that remains the same for every record. Appears once at the end of the form.

Form header   Section that displays information that remains the same for every record. Appears once at the beginning of the form.

Form letter   A word processor document that uses information from a database in specified areas to personalize a document.

Formatting   Arranging the shape, size, type, and general make-up of a document.

G

Grouping   Allows you to work with several objects as though they were one object. In Access, organizing records into parts or groups based on the contents of a field.

H

Header   Text that is printed at the top of the page.

Home page   First page that appears when you start your Web browser.

Hyperlink   Allows you to jump to another location.

I

Icon   Small pictures that represent an item or object.

Importing (Import)   Brining information from one program into another.

Indexing   Feature of databases that allows a field to be more quickly searched.

Input mask   Predetermined formats for data.

Integrated software package   Computer program that combines common tools into one package.

Internet   Vast network of computers linked to one another.

Internet Explorer   Office XP's browser for navigating the Web.

Intranet   A company's private network.

J

Junction Table Refers to the third table with two primary key fields in a many-to-many relationship.

L

Link See **Hyperlink**.

Lookup field Field that pulls data from a field in another table or query in the database.

M

Macro Collection of one or more actions that automate certain routine tasks. Commands and instructions grouped together as a single command to complete a task automatically.

Mail merge Combining a document with information that personalizes it.

Main document The document with information that does not change in a form letter.

Margins Blank spaces around the top, bottom, and sides of a page.

Maximize button Button at the right side of the title bar that you click to enlarge a window to fill the screen.

Menu List of options from which to choose.

Menu bar A bar normally at the top of the screen that lists the names of menus, each of which contains a set of commands.

Merge fields Fields in a main document where you want to print the information from a data source.

Minimize button Button at the right side of the title bar that you click to reduce a window to a button on the taskbar.

Mnemonic An underlined letter that is pressed in combination with the Alt key to access items on the menu bar, pull-down menus, and dialog boxes.

Mouse A device that rolls on a flat surface and has one or more buttons on it. It allows you to communicate with the computer by pointing to and manipulating graphics and text on the screen.

Multitable query Database query that searches related tables.

My Computer Program to help you organize and manage your files.

O

OfficeLinks A feature in Microsoft Office, you can export an Access table, query form, or report to Word or Excel.

One-to-many relationship A database relationship in which a table whose common field is a primary key field is linked to a table that does not have the common field as a primary key field. In Access, a relationship in which a record in table A can have a number of matching records in table B, but a record in table B has only one matching record in table A.

One-to-one relationship A database relationship in which each record in Table A can have only one matching record in Table B and each record in Table B can have only one matching record in Table A.

Open Process of loading a file from a disk onto the screen.

Or operator Used to find data that meet one criteria or another.

OR query Lets you find records in a database query that meet one criteria or another.

P

Parameter query Database query in which you are prompted to enter the criteria each time you run the query.

Paste Text is copied from the Clipboard to the location of the insertion point in the document.

Paste Special Command that allows you to link data among files created in different Office programs.

Permissions Authorization given to specific users in a database, which determines what they can and cannot do in the database.

PivotChart　Refers to a visual representation of table or query data. A PivotChart allows you to interactively rearrange the field in a chart.

PivotTable　An interactive table that lets you view and calculate data from a table or query. It's called a PivotTable because you can rotate the column, row and page headings.

Pointer　An arrow on the screen which indicates the position of the mouse.

Primary key　Field in a database table that contains a value which uniquely identifies each record.

Primary table　A database table with a primary key field that contains the same data as that stored in the common field of another table.

Procedures　Procedures perform actions and, in Access, they are written in Visual Basic code.

Properties　Qualities or traits belonging to a particular item.

Q

Query　A search method that allows complex searches of a database.

R

Record　Complete set of database fields.

Record pointer　The pointer that Access uses internally to keep track of the current record.

Record selectors　Located to the left of a database table record's first field.

Recycle Bin　Place to get rid of files or folders that are no longer needed.

Referential integrity　Rules that ensure valid relationships between database tables and prevent invalid data from being entered.

Relationship　Link between database tables that have a common field, allowing you to create forms, queries, and reports using fields from all tables in the relationship.

Replication　The process of creating a copy of a database so two or more copies can exchange updates of data or replicated objects. The exchange is called synchronization.

Restore Down button　Button at the right side of the title bar that you click to resize a maximized window to its previous size.

S

Save　Process of storing a file on disk.

Scroll arrows　Drag to move the window in the corresponding direction one line at a time.

Scroll bar　Appears at the bottom and/or right side of a window to allow user to view another part of the window's contents.

Scroll box　Box in the scroll bar that indicates your position within the contents of the window.

Search criteria　In a query, it's the information for which you are searching.

Sorting　Arranges a list of words or numbers in ascending order (A to Z; smallest to largest) or in descending order (Z to A; largest to smallest).

Standard toolbar　Toolbar that is normally near the top of the screen and which contains buttons used to perform common tasks.

Start　Button on the taskbar that you click to display menus with a variety of options.

Status bar　Bar normally at the bottom of a screen that contains information summarizing the actions of the commands that you choose.

Subdatasheet　In database tables that are related, you can show records from one table in the related record in the primary table.

Subform　A database form that is entered into another form. The primary form is referred to as the main form and the form within the form is called a subform. When a record displays on the main form, corresponding records display in the subform.

Subreport A database report within a report. Subreports appear with the main report.

Switchboard Serves as the "command center" for working with your database objects. It contains macro buttons that let you open, close, and perform various other actions on database objects by clicking a single button.

Syntax Refers to the structure of language or how language is put together.

T

Task pane Separate window on the right hand side of the opening screen that contains commonly used commands.

Taskbar Bar normally at the bottom of a screen that displays the Start button and the names of all open programs.

Title bar Bar at the top of a window that contains the name of the open program, document, or folder.

Toolbar Bar at the top or bottom of the screen that displays buttons you can click to quickly choose a command.

U

Unbound control Control on a database form or report that is not connected to a field in a table.

Uniform Resource Locators (URLs) Internet addresses that identify hypertext documents.

V

Validation rule A rule ensuring that data conforms to guidelines.

W

Web browser Software used to display Web pages on your computer monitor.

Web site A collection of related Web pages connected with hyperlinks.

World Wide Web System of computers that share information by means of hypertext links.

X

XML (Extensible Markup Language) A universal format that allows for data transfer, especially for data on the web.

INDEX